USING ADVENTUI
FOR SUCCESS I

OVERLANDING THROUGH THE BOARDROOM

JOHAN DE VILLIERS

Published in 2024 by Johan de Villiers
www.johandevilliers.co.za

Content © Johan de Villiers

ISBN 978-07961-0676-6 (paperback)
ISBN 978-07961-0677-3 (ePub)

Editor: Phillipa Mitchell
Cover design and typesetting by Gregg Davies Media
Front cover photograph of Johan de Villiers by © Peete Mocke

This book is dedicated to the following people, each of whom has played an invaluable role in my journey:

My mom, Tertia, for instilling in me a deep appreciation for nature and an innate curiosity for exploration.

My dad, Prof OT, for awakening my wanderlust and fostering a love for travel in me from a young age.

My son, Ryan, for providing me with a deeper purpose as a dad than any continent overlanding or helicopter flying could offer.

My wife, Kim, for our robust debates, her keen strategic insights, and her unwavering support in our mad adventures together.

CONTENTS

PREFACE

The Camel Trophy of the 1980s and 1990s was once celebrated as the ultimate annual 4x4 expedition competition. Jointly sponsored by Land Rover and Camel Cigarettes, it was an extremely gruelling event. In 1997, I had the privilege of visiting Rust de Winter in Limpopo, situated about 100 km (62.5 miles) north of Pretoria. One of our vendors had invited six of their top IT clients from across the country to a unique week-long event focused on mastering Land Rover Defenders in challenging off-road conditions. I was fortunate enough to be one of the chosen participants. Adding to the excitement, two former Camel Trophy winners had been flown in from Germany to South Africa to train the six of us.

This wasn't your average off-road seminar with a leisurely test drive on a tame 4x4 track. Instead, it was an intensive, hardcore initiation into the world of serious offroading. After immersing myself in this rigorous training, I caught the offroading bug and became a passionate devotee of the Land Rover Defender.

In 1999, I decided to take a sabbatical from my corporate life. I sold my Pajero, bought my first Land Rover, a Defender 110 300Tdi, and embarked on a six-month overlanding adventure through Africa with my then-girlfriend. Our itinerary was set to cover Swaziland, Lesotho, Mozambique, Namibia, Botswana, Zimbabwe, Zambia, Tanzania, Kenya, Ethiopia, Rwanda, Uganda, Malawi and Zanzibar.

For the optimal game-viewing experience, it's best to visit the Okavango Delta during the dry season. However, when incorporating Botswana into our itinerary, I overlooked the fact that the country's rainy season starts in November and ends in April. As fate would have it, we arrived slap-bang in the middle of it. There were no tourists, no game rangers, no safari vehicles, and no overlanders in sight – save for us. Visibility was poor, and everything – and I mean everything – was either clammy, wet, or flooded. The roads had become muddy tracks, swallowing our feet the moment we stepped out of the vehicle. Many of the parks we intended to visit were inaccessible because the roads leading into them were flooded. Even our Landy couldn't negotiate these conditions. The foliage had grown super-dense, making it difficult to spot any wildlife, and the chance of finding animals congregating at a waterhole was virtually zero. With the entire region having transformed into a million waterholes, water was plentiful, and the animals could simply stand right where they were to quench their thirst.

Deciding to try our luck elsewhere, we ventured northeast to Linyanti, a region nestled between the Okavango Delta and Chobe National Park. The southern part is dominated by the dense canopies of mopane forests, the leaves of which are a firm favourite amongst the local elephant herds, which we were hoping to spot while we were there.

While navigating the narrow dirt track of a mopane forest, the only route in and out, we suddenly hit a dead-end. What was once a drivable track had transformed into a waterhole filled with dozens of strange-shaped logs. It stretched about 100 metres ahead, with the faint trace of the track reemerging on the other side barely visible. There was no way around it.

We were running low on fuel, and turning back would mean a journey of at least 500 kilometres (312 miles) to the nearest fuel stop. The next fuel stop – just beyond the waterhole – was only 60 kilometres (38 miles) away. The only way out for us was through, but it was risky, especially if we got stuck while crossing.

We were completely isolated. The surrounding mopane trees, frail as they were, couldn't support a self-recovery using the Landy's winch. There were no tourists around, there were no cell phone towers, and there were certainly no satellite phones that we could use to summon help. Our food provisions and fresh water wouldn't last more than a few days, let alone the three to four weeks it could take for someone to find us. That was if the local wildlife didn't get to us first. But we had no other choice – we had to make the crossing.

I remembered the advice the Camel Trophy guys gave us during our training: before attempting any water crossing, always exit your vehicle and walk through it first. Most 4x4 vehicles can't be submerged in more than 60 cm (23") of water before the water starts seeping through the door seals, infiltrating the air intakes and the engine bay's electronics. High-end overlanding vehicles have a slightly higher threshold, at around 90 cm (35") – roughly the height of three ruler lengths.

While petrol engines struggle to operate underwater, diesel engines are more robust, provided the vehicle is equipped with a snorkel. This is one of the reasons why diesel vehicles are the go-to choice for African overlanding adventures: they run happily underwater, even when fully submerged, provided there's a snorkel to supply fresh air, and the engine keeps running. One thing you want to avoid doing is stalling your vehicle while underwater – the exhaust pressure automatically stops water from entering the tailpipe, but if the engine stalls, water can rush in, flooding the vehicle, and then it's game over.

As I swung my door open to climb out and walk through the water-hole, my girlfriend grabbed me by the leg in an attempt to pull me back inside.

"Look at that," she said, pointing towards the logs.

There was no wind to cause any ripples in the water, but the logs were moving. I took a closer look. Those weren't logs at all – the waterhole was teeming with crocodiles. The sound of the car door opening must have attracted their attention. It was as if they were thinking, "Who ordered Uber Eats?" I quickly closed the car door.

With no way of gauging the depth of the waterhole and no second vehicle to winch us out if we got stuck, the stakes were high. I'd never attempted a serious water crossing before, but I was forced to choose between the lesser of two evils: a guaranteed croc bite or navigating through deep water. I wouldn't trust a float of crocs for one second – it was going to have to be the deep water. I started the vehicle, put her in 2nd gear low range, locked the diffs, and started going.

Everything was going swimmingly – if you'll excuse the pun – until we were about two-thirds of our way through. The depth had fluctuated between 60 and 90 cm (23" - 35") until that point. Suddenly, the Landy's nose dipped, and there was a giant splash. The windscreen, the top of which was about two metres from the ground, was covered in water. We were completely submerged, barring the snorkel, which was the only thing keeping the engine from flooding.

It was at this point that I realised that Land Rovers are not watertight by any stretch of the imagination. Water was pouring in through the dashboard. It was spraying through the air vents. It was flowing through the radio. It was rushing in through the door seals. I could feel my boots filling up with water. Within a few minutes, the water inside the vehicle had reached gearbox level. But she just kept going. As she reached the opposite bank, she wiggled her rear to get some traction on her back wheels, and then she climbed – quite effortlessly – up the embankment.

We opened our doors, and the water streamed out. Everything was sopping – clothes, shoes, gearbox, radio, console. We sat there in absolute awe of this vehicle. She was an old girl and not the fastest, but she didn't miss a beat – she just kept ticking over. There was no skill involved on my side, but she saved our bacon that day.

It's hard to explain just how intense those moments in the water were and how terrified we both felt. It probably took about six minutes to make the crossing. But it felt so much longer than that. It was like being on a roller coaster with the longest, most terrifying drop. You know it might only last a couple of minutes, but fear has a way of stretching seconds into minutes. As the water engulfed the Land Rover, those six minutes felt like an eternity.

Once you've done something like that with a Land Rover, you're sold. Even though Toyota might take the crown in terms of absolute reliability, let me tell you: Land Rover Defenders might not be the prettiest, and they might not have the best fuel economy, but when the chips are down, I'll take a Land Rover over any other vehicle. In that moment, I decided that I would deal with a lifetime of Land Rover jokes and maintenance headaches – the sheer resilience of this amazing machine was worth every laugh at its expense.

After the crocodile-infested water crossing, I knew one thing: adventure was in my blood. I eventually returned to the corporate world, taking up the position of Managing Director at First Technology in the Western Cape. The Land Rover experience was a vivid reminder of the unpredictable challenges one might face, both in the wilderness and the boardroom. Little did I know that the lessons learned from overlanding through more than twenty countries would, years later, unexpectedly bridge these two worlds. While the distinction between adventure and corporate success seemed clear-cut, life had other plans.

By day, engrossed in AI, machine learning, drone technology, and blockchain, my corporate persona took centre stage. After hours, the thrill-seeker within emerged, a passion I shared with my wife, Kim. For years, these two sides ran parallel, never meeting. But everything changed with the Tankwa Cross Country Rally in 2018.

The Tankwa Rally is a gruelling three-day, 1,000-kilometre challenge for off-road, enduro, rally, and quad bikes held in one of South Africa's most demanding terrains, pushing both riders and their vehicles to the limit. That year, I clinched second place in the Gold class. Another rider and I raced neck and neck across the desert. After three adrenaline-pumped days, our bikes crossed the finish line almost simultaneously. He finished about 3 cm (1") behind my front wheel, settling for third place. I might have given him a gentle nudge, but let's not get lost in the details.

After that, First Technology stepped in as a platinum sponsor of the Tankwa Rally. The man behind the rally, also the owner of an agricultural equipment company, introduced me to the fruit export market in the Western Cape. Until then, our clients mostly operated in the fintech space, but I soon realised that an opportunity presented itself in the fruit exporting space. Soon after, I found myself touring citrus farms across the Western Cape, from Ceres to Swellendam and beyond.

During these visits, two things were evident: the ubiquity of Land Cruisers (and occasionally Land Rovers) and the popularity of motorcycles for navigating challenging terrains. Most of these farmers, like me, were no strangers to rallies such as the Tankwa. My passion for 4x4ing and off-road motorcycle racing helped me connect with them instantly.

For the first time, the boundary between my personal and corporate worlds began to blur. The merger of my corporate life with my personal interests gave me a unique advantage. While competitors were networking on golf courses, I was racing in the Tankwa Desert, connecting with agricultural farmers, exporters, and landowners on a deeper, more authentic level through a shared love of sport. Now, don't get me wrong – there is a lot to be said for networking on the golf course. Many a business deal would not have been done if it weren't for the golf course – the only difficulty is that you have to be able to play golf. And that wasn't me. I therefore had to find a way to connect my adventurous side with my business side.

Straying from the beaten path bore fruit in more ways than one. Today, First Technology is a leading name in the Western Cape fruit export industry, rivalling the profitability of our long-standing fintech clientele.

As these two worlds overlapped more and more, I realised that the principles guiding a successful business are identical to those employed in planning an adventure, maintaining safety, and problem-solving in different environments. This insight sparked an idea: Why not consolidate my writings into a book designed not just for the business-minded but also for the adventure enthusiasts? And so, the seed for the book whose pages you're about to turn was sown.

CHAPTER 1

THE PRINCIPLES OF OVERLANDING AND THEIR APPLICATION TO BUSINESS SUCCESS

N estled on the southern banks of the mighty Zambezi River in northern Zimbabwe lies the Mana Pools National Park. Meaning 'four' in the local Shona language, Mana refers to the park's four magnificent pools, remnants of ancient oxbow lakes carved out by the river. The park, which covers an area of approximately 2,500 square kilometres (1,562 square miles), is rich in biodiversity and natural beauty and home to a rich variety of wildlife and over 350 bird species, including fish eagles, herons, and storks. During the dry season, when water is scarce in the region, elephants, buffalos, impala, antelope, and zebra flock to the pools to quench their thirst, while hippos and crocs lie in wait, their bodies submerged below the water's surface, and where lions, leopards, and hyena watch on, smacking their lips as they feast their eyes on the enormous buffet laid out before them.

In 1999, as my six-month overlanding trip through Africa drew to a close, my then-girlfriend and I decided that this was where we would spend our last two weeks.

Mana Pools is one of the few Big Five game reserves in the world where visitors aren't fined for disembarking their vehicles outside the demarcated campsites. In fact, you can get out wherever and whenever you want to. When you arrive at the entrance gate, one of the first things you're handed is an indemnity form. In exchange for your signature, they promise to come and retrieve whatever is left of you should the unthinkable happen. Whether you end up as somebody's dinner or not is entirely up to you.

Now, the number one rule when travelling through any game reserve in Africa is that you never, ever carry fruit of any kind in your vehicle. Or fresh meat, for that matter. If you ever make that mistake (and you only have to make it once), it's like carrying a giant neon sign saying, "Hey guys – all-you-can-eat buffet this way!" Elephants, in particular, have an uncanny ability to sniff out the faintest whiff of fruit – especially apples – from miles away. And when they do, they'll stop at nothing to get their trunk on those delicious treats. It's their version of a feline catnip frenzy.

The game ranger on duty at the gate that day told us that within 500m of entering the park, our first sighting would likely be a brand-new Toyota Land Cruiser VX lying on its roof, totalled, with gore marks through the driver's side of the vehicle. The unfortunate incident had happened only hours earlier.

"The guy left an apple core in his ashtray," he explained. "Must have been there for a week at least. An elephant bull who was crossing that stretch of the road smelt it, and he rolled the vehicle to get to it."

As we passed the wreck, I felt a shiver run down my spine. Its metal frame was twisted like a crumpled Coke can – a solemn reminder that even the mightiest of machines can fall victim to the whims of nature and the allure of a forgotten apple core.

The following evening, as we were enjoying the bliss of an African sunset alongside our trusty 110 Landy, a Pajero with its distinctive blue and white Gauteng numberplates rolled into camp, music blaring, pulling a Venter trailer with on-road tyres behind it. Two guys in the front and two in the back, I knew instantly that they hailed from the deep south. In fact, judging by the gold dripping from their necks and wrists, they probably owned every Italian restaurant within a 50 km (31 mile) radius of Turffontein Racecourse.

We watched as they proceeded to pitch their tent about seventy-five metres from where we were camped. It wasn't long before the trailer was promptly opened to reveal a large aluminium Defy chest freezer stacked to the brim with steaks and other assorted braai meats. This was duly plugged into a portable generator alongside their trailer.

"You've got to be joking," I thought.

At about 6 a.m. the following morning, we were awakened by one of the Italian gents banging on the ladder that led up to our rooftop tent. I unzipped the tent door and stuck my head out.

"Have you seen our freezer?" he asked suspiciously, sizing me up from the ground below. "It mysteriously disappeared during the night."

I looked over to their campsite and saw that it was indeed missing. Having no use for such an appliance and no propensity for sleep-walking, I knew that I was not the guilty culprit, but I offered to come down and help him find it.

Upon closer inspection of the area around the trailer, I noticed drag marks and large paw prints in the dirt. The burglar clearly had two sets of legs and not one. We set off through the bushy undergrowth and over numerous tree stumps, following the trail for about 100 metres until we came upon the freezer's final resting place behind a large riverine thicket. While the freezer was still locked, it was far from being intact – one of the corners of the aluminium casing had been eaten away, and a good quarter of the steaks were missing.

"That's definitely the work of a pack of opportunistic spotted hyenas," I said, trying to stifle my laughter. I imagined that between four and six of them must have entered the campsite the night before and physically dragged – or even head-butted – the meat-filled freezer through all that bush and over all those tree stumps without anyone hearing a thing. The freezer itself must have weighed at least 200 kg (400 lb), which would have required some seriously coordinated teamwork on the part of the hyenas. And then, between them, they managed to chew through its thick aluminium casing to get to the steaks, have their fill, and leave without waking anyone.

You can rely on Defy, they say, but not when a pack of hyenas is around.

Later that afternoon, looking out over the Zambezi echoing with the distinctive snorts and grunts of its resident hippos while enjoying a fine single-malt whiskey, we watched with utter disbelief as our neighbours winched what was left of their freezer into an overhanging tree. After about half an hour, the blood-dripping Defy hung precariously above the campsite, suspended by a rope, swaying gently in the breeze, giving an entirely new meaning to the term 'lazy aged steaks'.

I like to make up little rules about life as I go along. After that trip, the first rule was to always think carefully about who you choose to overland with. While these Italians may have been skilled at making fantastic Mediterranean pasta, their overlanding skills and awareness were not quite up to par. One person's mistake almost jeopardised the success of the expedition, if not also putting lives at risk. The next rule I made up was that while elephants are easy to read, one should never underestimate a hyena. Elephants are not naturally aggressive. When angry or agitated, they will give you ample warning time to leave before they charge. Usually, they'll begin by flaring and spreading their ears. Sometimes, their ears will stiffen. If you get your vehicle in reverse and back off quickly enough, he'll leave you alone. The golden rule is never to come between a mother and her calf and always stay away from any lone old bull who has been ejected from the herd.

Hyenas are another beast altogether. People often see them as idiotic because of how they laugh when communicating. People also assume they are scavengers who only feed on carrion. But they are extremely intelligent pack animals. Their laughter is actually a highly developed form of communication. They work in well-coordinated teams, and they're aggressive killers. Of course, if they're hungry and a free pre-killed meal presents itself, they won't think twice about sitting down at the table and helping themselves. That said, the pack will just as quickly pull a child from a closed tent. Or meat from an unattended freezer, for that matter.

THE PARALLELS BETWEEN OVERLANDING AND RUNNING A SUCCESSFUL BUSINESS

Overlanding, for me, is the ultimate adventure, combining the freedom of road-tripping with the thrill of exploring remote and rugged locations. But it's not just about the destination – it's about the journey. It's an opportunity to test your endurance, resourcefulness, and resilience, push your limits, explore challenging landscapes, and immerse yourself in new cultures. Whether travelling solo or with a group, overlanding is an adventure that will leave you with memories that last a lifetime.

In many ways, starting, building, or running a business, regardless of its scale, shares many parallels with overlanding. Whether it's navigating difficult terrains during overlanding or dealing with market fluctuations in business, the journey is full of unpredictability, and the rules of the game can change in a heartbeat. Unforeseen challenges can lurk around every corner, and unexpected opportunities can present themselves when you least expect them. To survive, you need your wits about you and a keen awareness of your surroundings. You need to be prepared for anything and willing to adapt to rapidly changing circumstances.

Just as overlanders must navigate difficult terrain, entrepreneurs must navigate a constantly changing business landscape. This can include navigating new technologies, changes in consumer preferences, and shifts in market conditions. Just like overlanders, entrepreneurs must be adaptable and able to pivot when necessary. Overlanders have to manage their resources carefully, from fuel and water to food and supplies, if they want to survive the journey and make it to their destination. Similarly, entrepreneurs often have to operate within resource constraints, whether it be a limited budget, a small team, or limited access to capital.

Overlanders must deal with vehicle breakdowns and have to repair them on the fly. Similarly, entrepreneurs may face unexpected setbacks, such as a loss of funding, a key employee leaving, or a product recall. Overlanders may encounter wild animals, which can pose a threat to their safety. Entrepreneurs may face black swan events, such as a global pandemic, that can disrupt their business operations. Overlanders may encounter difficulties with network connectivity in remote areas, making communication difficult. Entrepreneurs may also face communication challenges, whether it be communicating their vision to potential investors, explaining their product to customers, or managing a remote team. And so the list goes on.

In this chapter, we'll explore the mindset needed for both overlanding and running a business: awareness, preparedness, and willingness. We'll look at the traits and skills that can help both overlanders and entrepreneurs succeed. And we'll discuss the core principles that are integral to both overlanding and business success. Whether you're a novice overlanding enthusiast or a seasoned pro, an aspiring entrepreneur, or a successful business executive, you'll learn valuable insights to help you navigate the road ahead with confidence and skill.

THE OVERLANDING MINDSET

AWARENESS

If you want your overlanding adventure to be a success, it is essential to have a strong sense of awareness of the challenging terrains that lie ahead, as well as an appreciation of the rich and varied cultures and environments that you will encounter along your journey. It is crucial for overlanders to have a thorough understanding of their surroundings, the capabilities of their vehicle, and any potential hazards that may arise. By remaining alert and vigilant, you can navigate difficult terrain with ease and ensure a successful journey.

Just like overlanders navigating rough terrain, entrepreneurs must be able to adapt to new challenges and adjust their strategy when necessary. By staying alert to market trends, anticipating change, and identifying opportunities, you can position yourself to succeed. Being aware of your industry landscape enables you to make informed decisions and take calculated risks, helping you to stay ahead of your competitors and meet customer demands more effectively.

PREPAREDNESS

Whether you're embarking on an overlanding adventure or starting and running a business, preparedness is key. In overlanding, preparedness involves extensive planning and gathering of essential resources, such as maps, tools, and provisions. Similarly, starting and running a business demands thorough preparation, including conducting extensive market research, creating a solid financial plan, and allocating resources effectively.

Businesses must be prepared to adapt to changing market conditions, evolving customer demands, and unexpected challenges. This requires a proactive approach, being ready to seize opportunities and tackle challenges head-on. By having a solid plan in place and the right resources at hand, companies can react swiftly to opportunities and threats, increasing their resilience and competitiveness.

It is important to remember that preparedness is not just about being ready for potential challenges. It is also about being able to take advantage of opportunities as they arise. In both overlanding and business, being proactive rather than reactive is vital. By taking the time to plan and gather the necessary resources, businesses can operate more efficiently, make better decisions, and increase their chances of success. By being prepared to adapt to changing circumstances, businesses can stay ahead of the curve and thrive in today's competitive market.

WILLINGNESS

Overlanding requires a willingness to embrace uncertainty and adapt to new situations. Whether you're faced with unexpected obstacles or shifting weather conditions, you must be open to change and ready to adjust your plans accordingly. The same goes for the business world – entrepreneurs must also be willing to embrace change, adapt to market shifts and make difficult decisions when required.

Similarly, in the world of business, entrepreneurs must exhibit this same willingness to adjust their strategy in response to changing circumstances. This adaptability is what separates successful businesses from those that struggle to survive.

NEVER UNDERESTIMATE A HIPPO

After various encounters with equally various animals in the African bush, a valuable rule I live by is to never underestimate the power of the mighty hippo. These colossal creatures have claimed more human lives in Africa than the Big Five combined. With a temperament that makes permanent PMS seem tame and considered one of the fastest accelerators in the world (reaching speeds of up to 30 kilometres per hour - 19 mph), they will snuff your light out permanently just because you happen to be within their line of sight. They want to kill you, all the time, every time – no exceptions.

I took my then-twenty-two-year-old son, Ryan, tiger fishing in Zambia several years back, and we stayed at a place called Jack's Tiger Fishing Lodge. It was like something out of the 1800s – affluent men from around the globe who had amassed their fortunes indulging in the pleasure of smoking cigars while relaxing in oxblood leather chairs, while delicate porcelain teacups graced the hands of elegant ladies who sought respite from the African heat under the cool breeze of swaying palm fronds. As I soaked in the atmosphere, I half expected a figure donning a pith helmet to stride in, extend his hand toward me, and say, "Livingstone, I presume?"

We were up at the crack of dawn every morning and set out. Each had our own ski boat, our own live bait, and our own skilled skipper. We spent half the day on the water, returning briefly for lunch, only to head back out again until evening approached, when we made our way back to the lodge for a relaxing braai (barbecue). Out on the river, there were pods of hippos everywhere, so we made sure we maintained a respectable distance from them. While they may not be Michael Phelps, these hefty creatures can move pretty quickly, reaching speeds of up to 8 kilometres per hour (5 mph) along the riverbed.

To give Ryan a taste of a hippo's aggressive nature, I had a little plan in mind. I asked our skipper to approach one of the pods at a forty-five-degree angle and then quickly veer away and accelerate the hell out of there. I'd seen this done before and knew that as long as we approached the pod at an angle and not head-on, we'd make the turn. The reason I asked him to perform this manoeuvre was that in every pod, there is always a large alpha male, and when that alpha male hears you coming, he disappears under the water and heads towards the source of the noise. As he moves, pushing the water forward with his powerful shoulders in an attempt to annihilate whatever has disturbed his peace, the water lifts, forming a bow wave that is guaranteed to make the hearts of even the bravest adventurers skip a beat. The sheer power, aggression, and pure evil intent with which that alpha male charged us was terrifying and left us all trembling.

The only thing that can go wrong in a situation like that is your outboard motor suddenly stutters and dies (I call it fuel starvation) because then you're toast. In that critical moment, your survival depends on one thing – outswimming your fellow passengers.

Reader's note: Please do not attempt this hair-raising experience at home. Our little escapade was purely for illustrative father/son purposes. Rest assured, Ryan got the message loud and clear.

KEY CHARACTER TRAITS AND SKILLS

Whether exploring remote landscapes or running a business, resilience, adaptability, and critical thinking are key ingredients for success. While some people naturally possess these character traits and skills, not everyone does. The good news is that these skills can be developed and improved over time with intentional effort and practice. By seeking out opportunities to solve problems and take on new challenges, you can enhance your ability to think critically, become more resilient, and adapt to changing situations.

Overlanding expeditions are an excellent way to build these skills. The challenges and experiences you'll encounter during your travels can help instil these valuable character traits, all of which are essential for success in business.

Let's examine each of these character traits and skills in a little more detail.

RESILIENCE

Resilience, the capacity to recover from setbacks and continue moving forward, is an essential trait for both overlanders and entrepreneurs. For example, let's say you're on an overland journey through a remote area and encounter an unexpected obstacle, such as a washed-out road or a deep mud bog. Your vehicle gets stuck, and you're miles away from the nearest town or help. In this situation, a resilient adventurer would take action by staying calm, assessing the situation, and figuring out the best course of action. They might try to get the vehicle unstuck themselves by using recovery equipment, such as a winch or tow straps. They might also use their ingenuity to create traction, such as using sand mats or tree branches to create a stable surface for the vehicle's tyres. If those efforts fail, a resilient adventurer will use their resourcefulness to seek help. They might use a satellite phone or personal locator beacon (PLB) to call for assistance, or they might use their knowledge of the terrain to find a nearby settlement or ranger station.

By being resilient and resourceful, the overlander can turn a potentially dangerous situation into an opportunity for growth and discovery. They can emerge from the experience with a new appreciation for their own abilities to cope with unexpected challenges and the environment they're exploring.

In business, setbacks are inevitable, whether it's financial constraints, competition, or market fluctuations. By developing resilience, entrepreneurs can maintain their focus and persevere through difficult times. They can learn from setbacks, adapt to changing circumstances, and emerge stronger and more experienced than before. For example, if your product launch fails to gain traction, you might use the feedback to improve your offering and try again. You might also seek out new marketing channels or partnerships to increase your visibility.

To cultivate resilience, entrepreneurs must adopt a growth mindset. You should view setbacks as opportunities for learning and growth rather than as failures and continually seek ways to improve and refine your strategies. This attitude can contribute significantly to your business's success and long-term sustainability. You should also focus on the things you can control, such as your attitude and actions, rather than getting bogged down by external factors.

ADAPTABILITY

Adaptability is as crucial a trait for entrepreneurs as it is for overlanders. Adaptability means being able to respond quickly and effectively to changing circumstances. It's the ability to adjust your tactics and stay focused on your goals, even when the path forward is uncertain. When overlanding, adaptability is key to navigating unpredictable terrain and weather conditions. For example, if you're driving in a remote area and encounter an unexpected obstacle, such as a fallen tree or a washed-out road, you'll need to quickly assess the situation and adjust your route.

Similarly, in business, the landscape is constantly evolving, whether it's changes in the market, consumer behaviour, or technology. By embracing adaptability, entrepreneurs can adjust their strategies and stay ahead of the competition. For example, if your marketing campaign isn't generating the desired results, you might adjust your messaging or try a new approach altogether. If a new competitor enters the market, you might adjust your pricing or marketing strategy to maintain your competitive edge. You might also explore new products or services that better align with changing consumer preferences.

To cultivate adaptability, entrepreneurs must be open-minded and willing to embrace change. You should constantly scan the market for new trends and emerging opportunities and be willing to pivot your business strategies accordingly. You should also be willing to take calculated risks and test new ideas, knowing that not all will be successful.

By embracing adaptability, you can stay ahead of the competition and capitalise on emerging opportunities. You can develop new products, enter new markets, and maintain your competitive edge in the face of changing circumstances.

CRITICAL THINKING

An entrepreneurial spirit and an adventurous mindset go hand-in-hand. Both require a willingness to take risks and embark on new experiences. In business, taking calculated risks is essential for growth and innovation. But taking risks doesn't mean being reckless. Entrepreneurs must balance their adventurous nature with sound judgment and informed decision-making. They should weigh the potential rewards and consequences of their actions, just like adventurers do when planning their expeditions.

Problem-solving skills are an element of critical thinking and are essential in both overlanding and business. While embarking on an overlanding adventure can be a real adrenaline rush, it's not without its challenges. From navigating difficult terrain to unexpected vehicle breakdowns, there are plenty of challenges that can arise along the way. Being able to think on your feet and come up with creative solutions is crucial to staying on course. As an entrepreneur, you will encounter a wide range of obstacles in your business, from cash flow constraints to supply chain disruptions to personnel issues. Strong problem-solving skills involve identifying the root cause of a problem, brainstorming possible solutions, and choosing the best approach. It also requires the ability to analyse data, anticipate potential risks, work collaboratively, communicate effectively, and adapt to changing circumstances.

By developing strong problem-solving skills, overlanders and entrepreneurs can respond to challenges quickly and confidently. They can also identify opportunities that may not be immediately apparent and create innovative solutions that set them apart from the competition.

THE FIVE CORE PRINCIPLES OF OVERLANDING SUCCESS

Embarking on an overland adventure is a journey of a lifetime that offers unparalleled experiences and challenges. However, such an adventure requires more than just a sense of adventure. To succeed, you need a combination of skills, knowledge, and strategies that can help you navigate through any obstacle that comes your way.

Whether you are planning your first overland adventure or looking to improve your business operations, understanding the core principles of overland success is crucial. By mastering these principles, you can maximise your chances of success, tackle unexpected challenges with confidence, and take your business (or your adventure) to the next level.

PLANNING & PREPAREDNESS

Success in any journey doesn't happen by chance. It requires intentional effort and attention to two critical components: planning and preparedness. Both are essential, yet each plays a distinct role in ensuring success. Planning is about creating a roadmap for success, while preparedness is about having the right tools, resources, and mindset to handle any situation that may arise.

Let's examine each in a little more detail.

PLANNING

Planning involves carefully considering every aspect of the journey, from the big picture to the smallest details. It means mapping out a clear route, establishing a timeline, and anticipating potential roadblocks or challenges along the way. Proper planning sets the foundation for success and ensures that everyone involved is on the same page.

In overland adventure travel, planning means researching destinations, identifying potential challenges, and selecting the most suitable route. For example, planning a trip through rugged terrain means considering factors like the vehicle's capabilities, weather conditions, potential obstacles such as steep inclines or river crossings, as well as local customs and regulations and obtaining the necessary permits and visas. Proper planning helps avoid potential hazards and keeps the journey on track.

Similarly, in the context of a commercial business, planning is equally crucial. Entrepreneurs must develop comprehensive plans that outline their goals, target markets, marketing strategies, and financial projections. By creating a clear roadmap, you can allocate resources efficiently, measure your progress, and adjust your strategies when necessary. For instance, planning to launch a new product involves conducting market research, creating a marketing strategy, and setting sales targets. This level of planning sets the foundation for success and ensures that the business is on the right track.

PREPAREDNESS

Preparedness is all about having the tools and resources necessary to tackle unexpected events and challenging situations. Being prepared means that no matter what happens, you can keep moving forward towards success.

In overland adventure travel, preparedness means having contingency plans in place for unexpected events and having a team with the skills and expertise needed to navigate through any challenge. It involves training in essential skills such as navigation, vehicle maintenance, first aid, and survival techniques. It requires assembling the right team, with individuals possessing complementary skills and experience, and ensuring the vehicle is well-maintained and equipped with necessary supplies.

In the world of business, being prepared means providing your organisation and its employees with the resources, skills, and capabilities needed to overcome obstacles and adapt to change. This could involve investing in employee training to improve skills, upgrading technology to stay current, and maintaining adequate financial reserves to handle unexpected challenges. By prioritising preparedness, your business will be able to respond effectively to challenges, seize opportunities, and maintain its competitive edge.

When embarking on an overland adventure, it's essential to strike the right balance between planning and preparedness. Focusing too much on planning can lead to inflexibility and an inability to adapt to unexpected challenges. On the other hand, solely focusing on preparedness without a solid plan can lead to poor decision-making and wasted resources. The same holds true for running a successful commercial business. Entrepreneurs must develop a solid plan but remain flexible and adaptable to changes in the market, customer demands, and competition. Creating a culture of preparedness within a business can enhance its resilience, agility, and long-term success.

RISK MANAGEMENT

Both overlanding and business come with their own set of risks. When overlanding, these risks can range from mechanical breakdowns to extreme weather conditions and navigational errors, and they can occur at any time. In the world of business, risks may come from market fluctuations, competition, and operational challenges that can impact your bottom line. Regardless of the nature of the risks, effective risk management is key. By being proactive in identifying potential hazards, assessing their potential impact, and developing contingency plans, both overlanders and entrepreneurs can minimise their exposure to risk and maximise their chances of success.

Whether you are venturing out on an overland journey or running a business, it is essential to be prepared for the unexpected. For example, in overlanding, having a spare tyre, extra fuel, and a well-stocked first-aid kit can mean the difference between a minor inconvenience and a significant setback. In business, diversifying your portfolio, keeping up with the latest industry trends, and having a sound financial plan can help you weather any storm.

TEAM SELECTION

As the saying goes, "Teamwork makes the dream work". One of the keys to a successful overland journey is assembling a well-rounded team with a diverse range of skills, knowledge, and experience to tackle challenges and support each other throughout the journey. Similarly, in business, selecting a competent and cohesive team with diverse skill sets and backgrounds can bring different perspectives to the table, creating an environment that fosters creativity and innovation.

By leveraging each person's strengths and expertise, your team can overcome complex challenges and achieve your business goals more effectively. Additionally, working with people from different backgrounds can expose you to new perspectives, leading to fresh ideas and approaches that you may not have considered otherwise. This diversity can be a catalyst for growth, enabling your business to adapt to changing circumstances and stay ahead of the competition.

Building a team with complementary skills is a crucial step towards overcoming any challenge that comes your way, whether you're on an overlanding adventure or running a business. For example, when overlanding, someone with mechanical expertise can help troubleshoot any issues with the vehicle, while a first-aid expert can provide medical assistance in case of an emergency. In business, an individual with strong analytical skills can evaluate financial data to make informed decisions, while a creative thinker can devise innovative strategies to boost sales.

MAP-READING AND NAVIGATION

Before embarking on a successful overland journey, it's essential to master the skills of map reading and navigation. When journeying through remote areas with limited access to modern technology and communication, overlanders must rely on their map-reading and navigation skills to chart their course, identify potential hazards, and determine their location. These skills are particularly important when traversing unfamiliar terrain, where getting lost or stranded can have severe consequences.

To master these skills, you need a strong understanding of topographic maps, compass use, and GPS systems. You must be able to interpret map features, such as contour lines, symbols, and scales, to plan your route effectively. To navigate through unfamiliar terrain during overland adventure travel, it's crucial that you develop a keen sense of direction and situational awareness. This allows you to stay on course and make necessary adjustments when faced with unexpected obstacles.

While map reading and navigation may seem unrelated to running a business, they share the same underlying principles. Just as overlanders must understand their environment, interpret complex information, and make informed decisions based on available data, entrepreneurs must navigate a dynamic environment filled with competitors, changing market trends, and evolving customer needs. By analysing the market, identifying opportunities, and anticipating potential threats, you can "read the map" of your industry and make strategic decisions that drive growth and success. By honing your analytical skills, you can gain a competitive advantage and thrive in your industry.

Navigation skills are also essential in charting the course of a business. Entrepreneurs must set clear goals and develop a strategic plan to achieve those goals, much like plotting a route on a map. They must maintain a sense of direction and focus on their objectives, making adjustments as necessary to stay on course. Just as overlanders must adapt to unexpected obstacles, entrepreneurs must be adaptable and flexible in response to changes in the market or their business environment. By cultivating a mindset of adaptability and being able to adjust course as needed, you can steer your business towards long-term growth and success.

When overlanding, the ability to scan and interpret your natural environment is crucial for making informed decisions and ensuring the safety of you and your fellow passengers. This skill involves keen observation, pattern recognition, and an understanding of potential hazards and opportunities.

Just as an adventurer must be aware of potential threats in their natural environment, such as predators or adverse weather conditions, entrepreneurs must be cognizant of their competition. You must continuously scan your business environment to stay ahead of your competition and identify new market segments. This requires keeping a close eye on competitors, monitoring market trends, and staying informed about technological advancements and changing consumer behaviour. By staying vigilant and aware of your surroundings, you can identify opportunities for growth, anticipate challenges, and respond effectively to changes in the market.

Understanding the strengths and weaknesses of competitors is crucial for developing effective strategies and maintaining a competitive edge. As an entrepreneur, you can use your observational skills to evaluate your competition in the business landscape. By analysing competitors' products, services, marketing tactics, and customer feedback, you can identify areas where you can differentiate your business and capitalise on your competitors' weaknesses. This knowledge will help you make informed decisions about product development, pricing, and marketing strategies, ultimately driving business growth and success. By being observant and responsive to changes in your environment, you can ensure your business stands out in the market.

WANDERLUST

Wanderlust is a powerful, insatiable desire to explore the world and discover new places, people, and experiences. It's that feeling deep in your gut that draws you to unfamiliar landscapes and cultures, igniting your sense of adventure and curiosity. Wanderlust is the voice that whispers in your ear, urging you to leave your comfort zone and embark on a journey of self-discovery.

But wanderlust is more than just a passion to explore the world. It's a quality that many entrepreneurs share, as they, too, thrive on the uncertainty and challenges associated with exploring uncharted territories. By immersing yourself in new experiences, you will develop a broader perspective that can inform your decision-making and enhance your ability to anticipate and adapt to market changes.

This same passion for discovery, combined with unquenchable curiosity, often leads entrepreneurs to push boundaries and identify new opportunities, new markets, and innovative solutions that can disrupt industries and drive business growth. It can also propel entrepreneurs to venture into uncharted territories, expand their horizons and tap into global markets, unlocking new possibilities for their businesses. By forging connections with international partners, suppliers, and customers, you can identify opportunities for growth beyond your immediate surroundings. This approach can help your business gain a competitive edge, stay ahead of market trends, and broaden your reach into new markets.

As an entrepreneur, discovering untapped market segments can be the key to unlocking new revenue streams and expanding your customer base. This requires a curious mindset, adaptability, and keen observation skills – all traits shared by successful adventurers. To find new market segments, you must be attuned to the needs and desires of your target customers. This involves conducting market research, analysing customer feedback, or identifying emerging trends that suggest a demand for a new product or service. By applying the same spirit of exploration that drives adventurers, you can uncover new opportunities for growth and innovation.

CHAPTER 2

LESSONS FROM A HELI PILOT AND THE SWISS CHEESE EFFECT

F rom my earliest years, I was captivated by the allure of the skies – not merely as an observer or a passenger, but with an ambition to command the cockpit. After selling our IT company to a JSE-listed player in 2007, I felt a renewed urgency to pursue this long-held dream. Eager to embark on a new adventure and ready to extend my exploration from terra firma to the boundless expanse above, I enrolled at flight school to become a helicopter pilot.

As I progressed through my training, I noticed many similarities between the skills required to competently fly a helicopter and those needed to run a successful business. Both roles require precision, focus, foresight, attention to detail, and the ability to anticipate potential challenges and opportunities. And, just like in the cockpit, the ability to remain calm under pressure, make quick decisions, and adapt to changing situations can be the difference between success and failure in the business world.

Let's explore the diverse skill sets required to fly a helicopter and discover how these same skills can be applied with equal effectiveness in the boardroom.

FLIGHT PLANNING, RISK MANAGEMENT, AND PROACTIVE PROBLEM-SOLVING

Before the pilot even sets foot in the airport, their work begins with the compiling of a detailed flight plan. This process involves a review of the weather conditions for the entirety of the journey – departure, en-route, and arrival. Factors like wind speed, visibility, and precipitation play an important role. The best route is chosen based on these weather predictions and airspace restrictions. Thereafter, calculations on fuel requirements are made, factoring in extra for unexpected events. Determining the weight and balance of passengers, cargo, and fuel is integral to this process, and the flight plan is then filed with the necessary authorities.

Proper weight and balance (W&B) is crucial for the safety and performance of the helicopter. It's important to position passengers and cargo correctly, taking into account their individual weights and distributing them around the main rotor shaft. If the helicopter isn't balanced correctly from the start, the pilot might have difficulty stabilising it during landing, which can lead to disastrous consequences.

Another aspect to consider is the helicopter's changing weight as fuel is consumed during the flight. As the fuel levels drop, some helicopters becomes lighter at the back as the centre of gravity shifts, which in turn makes the front more nose-heavy. If there's already an excess weight concentrated at the front, and the helicopter's balance isn't maintained, this nose-heavy tendency can become even more pronounced during landing, increasing the risks.

Lastly, the altitude capability of a helicopter is another factor closely tied to weight and balance. As a helicopter ascends to higher altitudes, the air becomes less dense. This thinner air reduces the lifting capacity of the helicopter's blades. Thus, even if a helicopter is technically rated to reach a specific altitude, if it's overloaded, it might not achieve that height. For instance, a helicopter rated to ascend 10,000 feet could possibly only reach 6,000 feet if it's carrying too much weight. The most immediate concern is the inability to clear terrain (like mountain ranges) or man-made obstacles (such as skyscrapers, communication towers, or power lines). Flying at a lower altitude might cause increased fuel consumption in certain scenarios. This can be particularly concerning if fuel resources are limited or if there are considerable distances between refuelling points.

As a business leader, creating a comprehensive strategic plan is crucial for guiding your company's operations and achieving your objectives. It's not just about having a good idea and hoping for the best. Just as a pilot reviews the weather conditions prior to take-off, you must understand current market conditions, your company's current financial state, and your supply chains. Monitor changes in customer behaviour, industry trends, and economic shifts. Check the financial health of your business by reviewing cash flow projections, balance sheets, and income statements. Assess your supply chain for any potential disruptions, such as shortages of, or delays in, the supply of raw materials.

Just as a pilot calculates their fuel requirements before a flight, business leaders should also calculate their financial needs to ensure that they have enough resources to sustain their operations. Just as a pilot factors in reserves for any unforeseen circumstances, such as headwinds or turbulence, which could increase their fuel consumption, you should factor in financial reserves for any unexpected expenses, such as sudden drops in revenue or unexpected costs. In both cases, proactive planning can help mitigate risks and prevent potentially disastrous outcomes.

Flexibility is essential for both pilots and business leaders. A pilot may need to make changes to their flight plan due to unexpected events or weather conditions. Similarly, you must be agile and adaptable, ready to pivot and change direction as needed.

Both pilots and business leaders need to plan for the unexpected. Use conducting a thorough risk assessment to identify potential risks and vulnerabilities, including supply chain disruptions, cybersecurity breaches, and economic downturns, and develop strategies to manage them and contingency plans to minimise their impact on your operations, financial performance, and reputation, should they occur. Put warning systems in place using dedicated teams and artificial intelligence to continuously monitor supply chain vulnerabilities and quickly detect when something is off-kilter. While evaluating your supply chain, remember that putting your eggs all in one basket – be it a client, a service, a product, or a supplier – is risky. Businesses do not operate in a vacuum. Diversify, or risk having your business wiped out when the basket topples over. Where suppliers are limited, you can consider stockpiling essential materials and securing additional inventory.

By adopting a proactive approach, identifying potential risks, and developing contingency plans to mitigate these risks, you'll be able to respond quickly to unexpected events and minimise their impact on your operations and bottom line. Moreover, by demonstrating your ability to adapt and respond swiftly to changing circumstances, you'll establish a reputation as a dependable and trustworthy partner in the eyes of your customers and stakeholders.

PRE-FLIGHT CHECKS

Before take-off, a helicopter pilot must conduct a series of meticulous pre-flight checks. These involve a thorough visual inspection of the aircraft to ensure it's airworthy and safe to fly. Such precautions are crucial for ensuring the safety of everyone on board, as well as those on the ground.

The first thing a pilot will check is the exterior of the helicopter. They'll look for any signs of damage, make sure all the doors and hatches are secure, and check the blades for any signs of wear and tear. Next, the pilot will check the fuel levels and fuel quality, and make sure there is enough to complete the flight and that the fuel cap is securely fastened. Once the exterior checks are complete, the pilot will move on to the cockpit. They'll check the instruments, radios, and navigation equipment to make sure everything is functioning properly, as well as the proper functioning of the flight controls. They'll also confirm that the emergency equipment, such as first aid kits and fire extinguishers, are present and in good working order.

Just like a helicopter pilot must perform pre-flight checks to ensure the safety of the flight, entrepreneurs must check that all systems are in place and functioning correctly to ensure that their business operations run smoothly. This may involve reviewing financial statements to ensure that the business has sufficient resources to operate effectively and ensuring that it provides a safe working environment for its employees.

COMMUNICATION WITH PASSENGERS AND STAKEHOLDERS

For helicopter pilots, clear and concise communication is essential to ensure the safety and comfort of their passengers. A pilot's ability to articulate flight plans, safety procedures, and emergency protocols in a clear and understandable manner is critical to a successful flight. After all, it's not just about getting from point A to point B – it's about doing so safely and with the utmost care for the passengers on board.

Similarly, in the business world, effective communication is essential for keeping stakeholders informed about the performance of the company, its objectives, and any changes that may be taking place. Business leaders must be able to articulate their vision, mission, and goals with clarity and precision, ensuring that everyone is on the same page and working towards the same objective. They must also be able to communicate any changes or challenges that may arise, both internally and externally, and be able to navigate these situations with finesse.

But it's not just about conveying information. Strong communication skills also foster trust and credibility, essential factors for any organisation's success. When stakeholders trust and respect their leaders, they are more likely to feel motivated, engaged, and invested in the company's success. Conversely, poor communication can lead to confusion, mistrust, and a lack of confidence in leadership, all of which can have a negative impact on the bottom line.

When leaders communicate effectively, they create a sense of shared vision, purpose, and direction that unites all stakeholders behind a common goal.

HELICOPTER CONTROL AND OPERATIONAL OVERSIGHT

For a pilot, control is everything. From the moment they start the engine to the second they land, they must maintain exceptional control of their aircraft at all times. They must have a clear understanding of the helicopter's capabilities, the weather conditions, and the terrain to make quick and accurate decisions that ensure the safety of their passengers. They must be in complete command of their helicopter, both on the ground and in the air, to maintain the highest levels of precision and safety. From adverse weather conditions to unexpected obstacles, a pilot's ability to remain calm and in control can mean the difference between a safe and successful flight or a catastrophic accident.

Similarly, in the business world, effective leadership demands a firm grasp of an organisation's operations, with a keen eye for detail and the ability to adapt quickly to changing circumstances. A successful leader must be able to navigate complex systems and processes with ease, ensuring that everything runs smoothly and efficiently. They must also be able to respond quickly and decisively to unexpected challenges, making course corrections as necessary to keep the organisation on track towards its goals.

But it's not just about control and oversight. In both aviation and business, adaptability and the ability to respond quickly to challenges are key. Helicopter pilots must be able to adjust their flight plans in response to changing weather conditions or unexpected obstacles, while business leaders must be able to pivot their strategies in response to new market trends or shifts in customer demand. They must be able to think on their feet, make tough decisions, and lead their team towards success. It's this ability to adapt and respond that separates the good from the truly great.

GROUND SUPPORT AND TEAM MANAGEMENT

In the world of aviation, the role of a helicopter pilot extends far beyond the cockpit. They must work closely with their ground support teams, providing guidance on maintenance, load handling, and safety control. It's a partnership that demands a high level of trust and communication, as the safety of both the crew and passengers depends on everyone working together seamlessly.

Similarly, in the world of business, effective leadership relies on the ability to build and manage high-performing teams that can execute plans and drive the company's success. A skilled leader must be able to delegate tasks effectively, empowering team members to take ownership of their work and contribute to the organisation's goals. They must also foster a culture of collaboration, encouraging open communication and the sharing of ideas across departments and teams.

However, effective team management is more than just delegating tasks and encouraging collaboration. It also requires the ability to identify and develop the strengths of each team member, creating an environment in which everyone can thrive and contribute their unique skills and perspectives. This means providing ongoing feedback and support, recognising achievements, and providing opportunities for growth and development.

Of course, effective collaboration is not without its challenges. In both aviation and business, there may be differences of opinion, conflicting priorities, or unforeseen obstacles that must be navigated. However, a skilled leader understands that these challenges can be overcome through effective communication, empathy, and a willingness to find creative solutions that benefit the team as a whole.

FLYING SKILLS AND TECHNICAL EXPERTISE

The pursuit of excellence is a never-ending journey, one that requires a constant commitment to learning and development. Whether you're a helicopter pilot or a business leader, technical proficiency is essential to driving innovation, achieving success, and maintaining a competitive edge.

For helicopter pilots, technical expertise is essential to mastering the complex mechanics and aerodynamics of their aircraft. A comprehensive understanding of flight theory and planning is also vital, allowing pilots to anticipate and respond to changing weather conditions and unexpected obstacles. It's a job that demands a high level of skill, precision, and attention to detail.

Similarly, in the world of business, technical proficiency is essential to drive innovation and maintain a competitive edge. Effective leaders must develop in-depth expertise in their industry and stay updated on the latest trends, technologies, and best practices. They must be able to analyse complex data, assess risks, and make informed decisions that propel the organisation forward. And just as a skilled helicopter pilot must be able to adapt to changing weather conditions, a successful business leader must be able to adapt to a rapidly changing business landscape, constantly innovating and iterating to stay ahead of the curve.

INTERPRETING FLIGHT PLANS, WEATHER, AND NAVIGATION DATA

When it comes to navigating complex and rapidly changing environments, helicopter pilots and business leaders face similar challenges. In both cases, success depends on the ability to interpret data, make informed decisions, and adapt to changing conditions. For helicopter pilots, this means skillfully interpreting flight plans, weather forecasts, and navigation data to make sure they reach their destination safely and on time. They must be able to read the weather and make quick decisions to adjust their flight plans in response to changing conditions. This requires a high level of skill, experience, and situational awareness.

In the same way, business leaders must be able to interpret complex data such as market trends, financial reports, and customer preferences to make strategic decisions that drive growth and profitability. They must be able to read the "weather" of the business landscape and anticipate potential risks or opportunities. This requires a deep understanding of the market, as well as the ability to analyse data and make informed decisions based on that analysis.

Just as pilots must constantly monitor weather conditions and adjust their plans accordingly, business leaders must also stay alert to changes in the market and adjust their strategies in response. This requires the ability to identify potential risks and develop contingency plans to ensure the organisation can adapt quickly to unforeseen circumstances. Whether navigating the skies or the business landscape, those who can read the weather will be better equipped to ensure their success and the safety of those they lead.

NAVIGATION: RESOURCE MANAGEMENT AND ADAPTABILITY

In the world of aviation, pilots rely on a combination of tools and skills to navigate their planes through the skies. From GPS systems to maps, they carefully plot their course to ensure they reach their destination as efficiently as possible while also conserving precious resources like fuel.

Successful resource management involves maximising the use of available resources while minimising waste. Pilots and business leaders alike must understand the limitations and capabilities of their resources to make informed decisions about their utilisation. By carefully managing resources, pilots and business leaders can optimise their performance, ensuring that they achieve their objectives in the most efficient manner possible.

Adaptability is another essential skill that pilots and business leaders share. Pilots must be prepared to adjust their flight plans based on weather conditions, mechanical issues, or other unforeseen circumstances. Similarly, business leaders must be adaptable, responding quickly to market changes or disruptions to ensure their organisation remains competitive.

UNDERSTANDING CIVIL AVIATION LAWS AND REGULATORY COMPLIANCE

For a helicopter pilot, a deep understanding of civil aviation laws is a prerequisite for safe and lawful operation. Similarly, commercial business leaders must have a thorough understanding of the complex web of regulations and legal requirements relevant to their industry to ensure that their operations run smoothly.

In the aviation industry, pilots must undergo rigorous training and pass stringent exams to obtain their licences. Similarly, commercial business leaders must educate themselves on the legal requirements of their industry and remain up to date with any changes.

Compliance with regulations and laws is not just about avoiding penalties but also about mitigating risks that could jeopardise the safety of individuals or the integrity of the organisation. By adhering to the rules, pilots and business leaders can ensure that their operations are carried out with the highest level of safety, security, and ethical standards.

KNOWLEDGE OF HELICOPTER MECHANICS AND AERODYNAMICS

Helicopter pilots require a deep understanding of helicopter mechanics and aerodynamics to ensure effective control of their aircraft and troubleshoot any potential issues. Similarly, in the realm of commercial business leadership, technical expertise is crucial for making informed decisions, driving innovation, and maintaining a competitive edge in the market.

In the aviation industry, a pilot who lacks knowledge of helicopter mechanics may not be able to recognise warning signs of mechanical failure. This could result in the pilot failing to take preventative measures with potentially devastating consequences. Inadequate knowledge of aerodynamics may lead to a pilot's inability to effectively control their helicopter during flight. They may also struggle to make informed decisions in high-pressure situations, which could result in them making incorrect or unsafe decisions, putting themselves and their passengers at risk. Likewise, in the business world, a lack of technical knowledge can lead to inefficient operations, suboptimal decision-making, and missed opportunities.

Technical expertise is critical for developing and implementing new technologies and innovations. In the aviation industry, pilots and engineers work together to design and develop new aircraft that are safer, more efficient, and more environmentally friendly. In the same way, in the world of business, technical expertise is essential for developing and implementing new products and services that meet the evolving needs of customers. By understanding the technical aspects of their industry, business leaders can identify new opportunities for growth and innovation.

RESPONSIBILITY AND SAFETY-CONSCIOUSNESS

One of the primary responsibilities of a helicopter pilot is ensuring the safety of the passengers and crew. The role demands a mindset that prioritises safety and a deep commitment to following established protocols. A single mistake or oversight could have catastrophic consequences, which underscores the critical importance of putting safety first.

This same sense of responsibility also applies to business leaders. They hold the well-being and safety of the business's employees, customers, and stakeholders in their hands. In order to uphold this responsibility, they must adopt a safety-conscious mindset and commit to following established protocols. Cultivating a safety-first culture is not just about ticking boxes or complying with regulations, but it is about fostering an environment where safety is ingrained in the company's values and way of life. Leaders can achieve this by implementing robust safety protocols, providing comprehensive training and education, and regularly reinforcing the importance of safety.

Maintaining a safe workplace requires a collective effort from everyone involved in the organisation, from the top-level executives to the front-line workers. When safety becomes a shared goal, it brings numerous benefits to the company. Firstly, it helps prevent accidents and injuries, which can be costly both in terms of human lives and financial resources. Secondly, it helps to safeguard the company's reputation, as safety incidents can cause irreparable damage to the company's brand and image. Lastly, it contributes to the long-term success of the company by creating a culture of trust and reliability, which can attract and retain customers and investors.

WORKING UNDER PRESSURE

When operating a helicopter, pilots are often faced with high-pressure situations that demand a cool head and a steady hand. The safety of their passengers and crew depends on their ability to remain calm and focused, even when faced with unexpected challenges.

Similarly, business leaders must be adept at navigating the high-pressure situations that come with managing a company, from tight deadlines to unexpected crises or conflicts. The ability to remain composed and perform optimally under pressure is crucial for success in this role. When the heat is on, leaders must be able to think quickly and make decisions with clarity and confidence. This requires a combination of mental toughness, strategic thinking, and a deep understanding of the situation at hand. Leaders who are unable to handle pressure may find themselves making rash decisions or becoming overwhelmed – a single misstep can have far-reaching implications for the company, its employees, and its stakeholders.

QUICK, SOUND DECISION-MAKING

The life of a helicopter pilot is one of constant decision-making, where the ability to make quick and accurate judgments can mean the difference between life and death. Pilots must be able to assess risks, evaluate options, and make informed choices based on the available information, often within a matter of seconds.

In the world of business, leaders must be able to make high-stakes decisions that can have far-reaching implications for their organisations. They must be able to weigh up risks and benefits, anticipate potential outcomes, and make strategic choices that can impact their organisation's future.

The importance of being able to make informed decisions under pressure cannot be overstated. Whether flying a helicopter or leading a business, the ability to gather and evaluate information quickly and accurately is crucial. Business leaders must be able to think critically, analyse data, and draw upon their experience and expertise to make well-informed choices. They must be able to operate under pressure, maintaining their focus and composure when the stakes are high. And finally, they must be able to think on their feet and make the tough choices that are required to move their organisations forward.

RELATING TO PEOPLE FROM DIVERSE CULTURES AND BACKGROUNDS

Helicopter pilots are often required to interact with people from diverse cultures and backgrounds. Whether coordinating with international ground crews or flying passengers from different countries, pilots must be able to demonstrate cultural sensitivity, adaptability, and effective communication skills to build trust and rapport with those they interact with. This ability to connect with a diverse range of individuals is also essential for business leaders, who must work with employees, customers, suppliers, and investors from different cultural and social backgrounds.

In today's global economy, understanding and appreciating cultural differences is more important than ever before. By understanding the nuances of different cultures, business leaders can avoid misunderstandings, bridge communication gaps, and negotiate effectively across borders. Leaders who possess cultural sensitivity and adaptability are better positioned to build strong relationships, improve collaboration, and enhance customer satisfaction. They are also more likely to foster a more inclusive and diverse workplace, which has been shown to drive innovation and improve overall performance. Ultimately, business leaders who possess these skills are better equipped to navigate the complexities of our interconnected world and drive business growth and profitability.

THE SWISS CHEESE EFFECT

The aviation industry is one of the safest industries in the world, and for good reason. One of the reasons flying feels safer than crossing the street is that pilots are trained to follow a set of principles known as the Swiss Cheese Model. Created by British psychologist James Reason in the 1990s, this safety framework boils down to a simple idea: while mistakes are inevitable, having multiple safeguards in place can prevent them from snowballing into catastrophic events.

Imagine each layer of defence as a slice of Swiss cheese. Every slice represents a different safety measure that helps to minimise risk. The holes in each slice represent vulnerabilities in the system. When stacked together, the holes in one slice are often covered by the solid parts of another. In this way, even if one layer fails, there are other layers in place to prevent an accident from happening. Implementing multiple layers of defence can help compensate for weaknesses in other layers, creating a more robust and effective system.

That being said, there's always a chance the holes could align. If that rare alignment happens, we end up with a clear path for trouble to find its way through. That's what we call a systemic failure.

Now, imagine you're a pilot. Suppose you skip checking an alternate landing spot. Then, you forget to check if all your fuel tanks are full. You also miss asking about that heavy-looking bag someone loaded. You didn't check the altitude when flying over Sir Lowry's Pass from Cape Town to Hermanus and only checked the weather at your starting point in Langebaan.

Each oversight is like a slice of Swiss cheese with a big hole in it. Today, luck might be on your side – the skies over Hermanus are crystal-clear. And even though you discover your fuel's running low, Cape Town offers a quick refuelling pit stop. But if you keep stacking these cheese slices in just the right order, sooner or later, the holes might just align. When that happens, the consequences can be devastating – it's moments like these where you might just see God's face looking back at you.

As a pilot, once you understand the Swiss Cheese effect, you'll never overlook your pre-flight planning again. It's like adding a self-imposed slice of holey Swiss cheese to the stack. You never want to find yourself peering through a perfectly aligned series of holes, realising that the person on the other side isn't waving back.

Here are some ways in which pilots apply the Swiss Cheese Model to minimise risks and prevent accidents:

MAINTAIN SITUATIONAL AWARENESS

Pilots are taught to maintain a high level of situational awareness and continuously monitor their environment. They learn to identify potential hazards and take appropriate action to avoid or mitigate risks. This is crucial as it allows them to be proactive rather than reactive in addressing potential safety concerns. For example, during a flight, a pilot may identify adverse weather conditions and make a decision to change the route or altitude to avoid turbulence or thunderstorms.

WORK TOGETHER AS A TEAM

Crew Resource Management (CRM) is another key component of pilot training. CRM is focused on effective communication, teamwork, and decision-making among pilots, co-pilots, and other crew members. This helps create additional layers of defence by ensuring everyone is working together to identify and address potential risks.

For example, during a search and rescue mission, the pilot may coordinate with ground teams to locate and extract injured people.

FOLLOW STANDARD OPERATING PROCEDURES

Pilots are trained to follow Standard Operating Procedures (SOPs). SOPs provide a systematic and standardised approach to managing risks in various flight scenarios. Adherence to SOPs helps to prevent errors and ensures consistency in decision-making. For example, during a power-off landing, the pilot will follow a checklist to assess the situation, identify a suitable landing site, and prepare for the landing.

USE CHECKLISTS

Checklists are an essential tool for pilots. They provide a structured and methodical approach to completing tasks and ensuring nothing is missed. Checklists act as an additional layer of defence to identify errors and prevent accidents. For example, before starting the engine, the pilot will use a checklist to verify that all switches are in the correct position and that all systems are functioning properly.

FATIGUE MANAGEMENT

Pilots are also trained to recognise the signs of fatigue and manage their rest and work schedules accordingly. Fatigue can lead to lapses in judgment, concentration, and decision-making, which can increase the risk of accidents. Helicopter pilots may be required to fly for extended periods, particularly in emergency situations. To manage fatigue and reduce the risk of fatigue-related errors, pilots must adhere to regulations that specify minimum rest periods before and after the flight.

CONTINUING EDUCATION AND TRAINING

Regular training and recurrent evaluations ensure that pilots stay up to date on the latest procedures, regulations, and best practices. For example, pilots may receive training on new aircraft systems, emergency procedures, or operating in adverse weather conditions.

You can apply the Swiss Cheese effect to any area of your life. Each time you neglect to buckle your safety belt or drive through a dangerous area alone late at night, remember: you've just laid down another slice of Swiss Cheese with a new hole representing a different risk. Now, ask yourself: how many of these choices will you make before the holes inevitably align, creating a clear path for unintended consequences?

THE SWISS CHEESE EFFECT IN BUSINESS

A systemic failure is not unique to aviation – it can happen in any system. The 2008 global financial crisis is a prime example of a systemic failure that had severe consequences, including high levels of unemployment, foreclosures, and a significant decline in global economic growth. The crisis was caused by a combination of factors, including lax regulations and oversight of financial institutions, the proliferation of complex and opaque financial instruments, and a culture of risk-taking and greed within the financial sector. These factors contributed to a housing bubble that eventually burst, causing widespread defaults on subprime mortgages and a cascade of losses throughout the financial system.

The Fukushima nuclear disaster in 2011 was a catastrophic failure of a nuclear power plant in Japan. A powerful earthquake and tsunami damaged the plant's cooling systems, causing multiple nuclear reactor meltdowns and releases of radioactive materials into the environment. The systemic failure occurred on multiple levels, including failures in the design and safety of the nuclear power plant, inadequate disaster preparedness and response, and a lack of transparency and communication from the government and the plant's operator. This led to widespread health and environmental impacts, displacement of communities, and long-term consequences for the region.

In business, systemic failures can be caused by poor management decisions, a lack of proper infrastructure, or a failure to adapt to changing market conditions. Whatever the cause, the end result is the same: a company that is no longer functioning as it should. At first, the signs of a systemic failure may be subtle. Perhaps sales numbers start to dip, or employee morale begins to wane. But as time goes on, these small problems can snowball into something much larger. Before long, the company is facing a crisis that threatens to undermine everything it has built. Customers start to lose faith in the brand, investors begin to pull their funding, and employees start jumping ship.

As the situation worsens, the company may find itself in a downward spiral that is difficult to escape. It becomes increasingly difficult to attract new customers, and existing ones begin to defect to competitors. Meanwhile, the company's financial situation becomes increasingly dire. Expenses may need to be cut, which could result in layoffs and even more negative publicity.

If a business continues to employ the wrong people, engage with the wrong business partners, sell its products or services at a lower rate than it should, and ignore its cash flow management, sooner or later, it will go bankrupt and be forced to liquidate. It's the same as crashing your helicopter.

HOW TO AVOID FALLING PREY TO THE SWISS CHEESE EFFECT IN BUSINESS

A company's success is not only measured in terms of profits but also in its ability to operate safely and sustainably over the long term. As business leaders, we have a responsibility to run our operations safely and efficiently while minimising risks as much as possible.

The Swiss Cheese Model serves as a reminder that risk management is not about eliminating risk entirely. Uncertainties are inherent in nearly every activity or decision, whether they relate to market conditions, human behaviour, technological issues, regulatory changes, natural disasters, and more. Therefore, risk management should focus on identifying, assessing, and understanding these risks and then making informed decisions about how to address them. It requires us to recognise the inevitability of risk and work proactively to minimise its impact. By adopting this approach, companies can become more resilient, better equipped to handle unexpected challenges and maintain a competitive edge in an ever-changing marketplace.

Here are seven practical ways to implement the Swiss Cheese Model in your business:

SYSTEMATIC RISK ASSESSMENT

Don't wait for problems to arise – conduct regular risk assessments to identify potential hazards and vulnerabilities in your business processes. By learning to spot the holes in your Swiss cheese before the mice do, you can address and mitigate risks before they escalate into significant issues.

MULTIPLE LAYERS OF DEFENCE

Establish multiple layers of safety checks and processes in your business operations, including quality control measures, internal audits, and regular maintenance of equipment and infrastructure. Like the layers of Swiss cheese, these measures are not perfect and may have holes, but together, they create a robust barrier that minimises the risk of failure.

STANDARD OPERATING PROCEDURES (SOPs)

Do you have SOPs for your various business processes? You should! By developing and implementing SOPs, you can ensure that your employees follow a consistent approach to tasks. This reduces the chances of errors and deviations from best practices, minimising the risks associated with human error.

TRAINING AND DEVELOPMENT

To maintain a competent workforce that can effectively manage risks and address issues as they arise, provide regular training and professional development opportunities for employees to enhance their skills and knowledge.

CLEAR COMMUNICATION AND TEAMWORK

Encourage open communication and collaboration among team members to ensure that everyone is aware of potential risks and is actively working to address them. This creates a culture of shared responsibility and accountability, which is crucial for effective risk management. By promoting a culture of transparency and accountability, employees will be encouraged to report potential issues and learn from mistakes rather than hiding them out of fear of punishment or reprisal.

PERFORMANCES MONITORING AND REVIEW

Continuously monitor and review the performance of your business processes and safety systems. Just like a hole in one slice of cheese can affect the entire slice, a weak link in your business operations can cause failures across the board.

CULTURE OF SAFETY AND RISK MANAGEMENT

Foster a workplace culture that prioritises safety and risk management. Create an environment where employees feel comfortable reporting potential hazards and where management is responsive and proactive in addressing these concerns. By promoting a culture of safety, you can reduce the likelihood of accidents and failures.

THE RALLY, THE SATELLITE PHONE, AND THE SWISS CHEESE EFFECT

Another important life lesson I've learned is to never take for granted that something is organised unless you have personally – and meticulously – organised it yourself. And even then, the potential for errors lingers, particularly when other individuals are part of the equation.

In 2017, Kim and I entered the West Coast Baja, an unguided, unassisted three-day off-road motorsport rally through the vast, rugged Richtersveld, the mountainous desert area that spans the border between the north-western part of South Africa and Namibia. Starting at Port Nolloth, participants would traverse a 1000-kilometre (625-mile) square through the desert, up to the Orange River, on to Alexander Bay, and then back down. Unfortunately, shortly before the rally, I flipped one of my dirt bikes during a training exercise. The extent of my injuries was significant, resulting in tears to three of my four rotator cuff muscles on my right arm and a detached bicep tendon near the elbow joint. I was a mess. After extensive microsurgery, the doctors managed to reattach my shoulder, but I was under strict instructions to stay off anything with two wheels and a motor for three months. The West Coast Baja was off – for me, at least. I would play pit crew for Kim in Port Nolloth.

We checked the weather. It was the heat of summer, with the mercury predicted to soar to a blistering 46 degrees Celsius (115°F). Among the minimum list of requirements were three litres of water and a space blanket, but there was no mention of any form of compulsory communication device other than a radio. Even though Race Control in Port Nolloth assured us that they had a helicopter on standby and paramedics in Ford Ranger 4x4s out in the field should anything go wrong and that they'd be able to get to us within twenty minutes of a call, I had an uncomfortable feeling about the whole setup that I just couldn't shake.

"You're taking a satellite phone with you," I insisted.

Kim pushed back. Satellite phones were not only expensive to rent and use at the time, but they were also cumbersome to carry. It would mean an additional kilogram of weight in her already heavy backpack. But I refused to back down. I've learned to trust my intuition. This internal compass isn't driven by fleeting emotions, fluctuating hormones, or unwarranted paranoia. Rather, it's a primal instinct rooted deep within our biology, designed to protect us from potential harm. Why would someone willingly overlook these clear signals and, despite all the red flags, decide to push forward, driven solely by one powerful force: H-O-P-E. While inspiring, this four-letter word has been known to lead to immense disappointment and distress, second only perhaps to misguided trust. I was having none of that. She was taking the satellite phone.

Little did we know how crucial that satellite phone would turn out to be.

At 6 a.m. on the second day, Kim set out, much as she'd done the day before. At that time, she was a fairly novice rider, having only been riding for a little over two years. This meant that she was near the back of the field. Her mission was to keep a steady pace, stay on track, not get lost, and stay hydrated. It was a furnace out there in the desert.

Shortly after 2 p.m., with about ninety minutes to go before she was due to arrive at the Designated Safety Pit in Alexander Bay, where she would spend the night, she came across another rider standing alongside his bike. He still had his helmet on, and he was hunched forward over the seat. Concerned, Kim slowed down and stopped beside him.

"Are you okay?" she asked.

He shook his head.

Kim removed her helmet.

"What's wrong?" she asked. "Are you injured?"

"No," he said, breathing heavily.

"Do you think you're strong enough to continue riding?" she asked.

"I'm exhausted," he sighed. "I can't carry on."

"Have you got something to drink?" she asked.

He shook his head.

Kim dismounted her bike, removed her backpack, then reached into the pack and pulled out the emergency 500ml Powerade she was carrying. By now, it wasn't the ice-cold juice she had packed when she left the pits in the early hours of the morning. It was closer to warm tea, but it was liquid and electrolytes nonetheless. He was desperate for hydration and couldn't get the liquid into his body fast enough.

While waiting for him to finish, Kim pressed the waypoint marker on her GPS to get their coordinates, confirmed the coordinates on her Suunto watch, and took a photo of her watch with her phone, just in case her watch died. Then she pulled her radio and the satellite phone from her backpack and switched them on to see which would pick up a signal first. She knew she needed to call for help.

Channel 1 was the nominated radio channel, as per the race regulations, but there was no response. There was also no signal on her mobile phone, so she figured they were out of range.

"I've got a sat phone with me," she said. "Hold tight, okay? We're going to get you out of here."

He nodded his head appreciatively.

"Twenty minutes," she whispered to herself. "Twenty minutes and help will be here."

He was swaying a little, and she could see he was overheating. Then, he started to remove his race jersey. Kim quickly moved closer to help him.

"What's your name?" she asked.

He looked at her, confused. Then he pointed to the race number on his bike. *That's strange*, she thought. *He must be delirious.*

The satellite phone was still searching for satellites and telling her to move to a different location. They were in a bit of a dip, so she left him leaning against his bike and began walking up a nearby koppie (hill), hoping that by being slightly elevated, the sat phone would pick up a signal. After a few minutes, it did. She immediately called Race Control, but there was no answer. Then she called me in Port Nolloth and explained the situation.

"I've stopped to help a rider," she said. "He's not injured, but he's too tired to continue racing. We need to get him out of here."

She told me that she was fine and gave me the rider's race number.

"Here are my coordinates," she said. "Please get hold of Race Control and ask them to send a team of paramedics out. I think he's suffering from heat exhaustion."

"What's his name?" I asked.

"He hasn't been able to tell me that yet," she said. "He's a bit out of it."

While we were speaking, the rider removed his armoured vest and stumbled, disoriented, away from his bike. Walking around in circles, he'd fall down and get back up again. He was moving further and further away from where the bikes were standing.

"I have to go," she said. "I need to get him into some shade."

By then, the mercury out in the Richtersveld had risen to 50 degrees Celsius (122 degrees Fahrenheit), and there wasn't a cloud in the sky. I reassured Kim that I would get hold of Race Control immediately, and then the call dropped. I contacted the race marshal, explained the situation, gave him the coordinates, and was assured that the paramedics would be there within the promised twenty minutes.

In the meantime, Kim managed to get him back to where the bikes were. There was no shade, and the sand was burning hot. He lay down, almost beneath his bike, desperate for the little bit of shade it might provide. Eventually, he told her his name was Gary Rowley.

Forty-five minutes went by. Kim called me from her satellite phone again. Her voice was strained and urgent. Gary's condition was deteriorating fast, and the medics hadn't arrived. I called Race Control again, only to be told that the paramedic's coordinates showed that they needed to cross the Orange River and head into Namibia.

"But they're *not* in Namibia," I said. "They're still in the Richtersveld."

And then it dawned on me. They were using the wrong GPS format. Off-roaders use DMS – Degrees, Minutes, Seconds – which was what Kim's Suunto was set to and which the race organisers had told the competitors to use at the race briefing. The paramedics must have been using DD – Decimal Degrees. DMS represents the coordinates using degrees, minutes, and seconds, while DD uses a decimal point to represent fractions of degrees. If you enter the coordinates in the wrong format, you can be out by sometimes hundreds of kilometres. Considering the time that had lapsed since the initial emergency call was first made, this mistake was proving disastrous. Race Control immediately got in touch with the medics and diverted them.

I called Kim back. I was worried about her out there in the heat with her water running low, and I had to trust that the medics would get there as quickly as they could.

"You've done what you can," I said. "Get on your bike and self-extract while you can. I don't want you risking your own safety too. The medics are on their way."

Kim refused. "I made a promise to Gary that I won't leave him here. I'm staying until help arrives," she said firmly.

It was then that I realised just how serious it was. Gary was more than just a tired rider who was unable to finish the race. Kim knew he needed proper help.

"Then I'm coming to find you," I said.

While I had no plan to head out into the desert that day, I was, fortunately, more than prepared. The Landy was equipped with long-range water tanks, fridges, and freezers, and I knew how to navigate using a GPS. I was 120 kilometres (75 miles) away, as the crow flies. There were no roads – just desert. It made Death Valley look like a walk in the park. I was, however, a little compromised, with only one functioning arm, a manual gearbox, a heavy rooftop tent atop the Landy, and many, many kilometres of soft, rolling sand dunes to navigate over without rolling her. But Kim's life was in danger, and I had to get her out of there.

I will admit that on my way, I flattened some people's game fences – there was no other way of getting through them.

"Sorry!" I shouted apologetically as I smashed through one after the next.

While I was racing through the desert to get to Kim, another rider arrived on the scene to offer assistance. Kim told him that help was on its way and that he should rather carry on. As they were talking, Gary got up again and started wandering off into the bush again.

49

The rider dismounted his bike and offered to help. He ran after Gary and guided him back to his bike. By then, Gary was shaking uncontrollably, making it difficult for him to sip on the Powerade they were providing.

Kim called Race Control again.

"He's going into shock," she said. "You need to hurry!"

Kim and the other rider quickly decided they needed to try to get Gary to lie down. Improvising a human lean-to shelter with her two space blankets, they positioned Gary between them. Using his kit, they shielded his body from the heat of the sand. They poured what little of their water was left over his head and fanned it to cool him down, but it was so warm that it made little difference. They even tried using the space blankets to fan him, but that made no difference either.

Despite the seriousness of the situation, they kept talking to him to keep his spirits up. At first, he was fully engaged in the conversation, sharing stories about his family and his ride, but he eventually grew quieter. Kim continued to talk to him, and he'd occasionally grunt or chuckle in acknowledgement. This was especially so when Kim jokingly said that he would have to explain to his wife why he was lying in the desert with another woman.

Suddenly, Gary leaned over and started vomiting. Acting quickly, Kim rolled him over and cleared his airways. Moments later, he started gurgling. His body went limp, and his breathing stopped.

Kim immediately started CPR. It was exhausting. Gary was a big guy.

"Come on, Gary! Stay with me!" Kim thought as she pressed down on his chest, her muscles screaming from the effort. After what felt like an eternity, she stopped, panting, and looked down at Gary. He was completely non-responsive.

As my vehicle rolled to a stop, dust swirling in the scorching heat, the scene that unfolded before me was nothing short of harrowing. Kim was there, looking like a shadow of herself – her face was flushed, and she seemed on the verge of collapse. Beside her lay a motionless man, while another rider seemed to be struggling to stay conscious. The atmosphere was thick with desperation.

I leapt out of the vehicle with a cooler of ice water and drenched both Kim and the other rider. The relief was instantaneous but short-lived in the oppressive heat. I handed them bottles filled with electrolytes and kept a close eye on them as they slowly sipped.

We must have been there for about forty-five minutes, battling the relentless sun, before I could see them regaining some strength.

Not long after, the race organiser arrived, his scrambler kicking up a storm of dust. He had received Kim's initial call and had jumped on his bike to try and reach them from behind. However, he had under-estimated the distance into the desert. We all knelt beside Gary for a short prayer.

"We need to leave now!" I urged as I helped them up.

Kim and the other rider managed to mount their KTMs, and I told them to follow me to Port Nolloth. A daunting 100 km (62.5 miles) stretch lay ahead, and I wanted to put as much distance between us and the desert as possible.

The race organiser agreed to wait with Gary for the paramedics. Three hours passed before they arrived. We actually passed their vehicle on our way.

When we reached the main road, the other rider sped off, leaving only Kim in front and me following behind her. Suddenly, Kim's bike started losing power until, finally, the engine cut out. We pulled over to the side of the road. I decided to use a rope to tow Kim's bike with her still on it. We managed to cover about 50 km (31 miles) this way, but as darkness enveloped us, it became increasingly unsafe for Kim to be on the bike. We made the decision to hide her bike in the bushes and continue in the Landy for the remaining 35 km (22 miles) to Port Nolloth, where our bike trailer was parked. I assured Kim that we would return for the bike once we reached Port Nolloth.

By the time we arrived, it was well past 8 p.m. Word had already spread about a rescue, but news of Gary's passing hadn't yet reached the town. Later that night, during the race briefing, the race organiser announced that Gary had succumbed to a heart attack and that the race would continue as scheduled.

Whether Gary's life could have been saved had the emergency response team reached him in time is something I will never know. I am not a medical expert, so it's hard to determine whether getting him into an air-conditioned ambulance and administering electrolytes could have brought his core body temperature under control quickly enough. We were also a fair distance from any hospital – which was what Gary needed. He had held on for three hours out there in the desert. What I do know, however, is that no matter what assurances are given, racing is an inherently dangerous sport, and sadly, people do die. In taking that risk, every person has to make their decision based on the information they are given from external sources (like the race organisers) as well as an assessment of their own abilities and the safety measures that are in place. Despite all of that, sometimes it is just impossible to avoid all the Swiss Cheese holes from lining up.

Out of a combination of respect for Gary and the stark realisation that the safety protocols were inadequate for the harsh conditions out there, the majority of the contestants withdrew from the final day of the race. No one wanted to risk being the next casualty – nobody went there to die.

That night, Kim didn't get a chance to speak to the other rider, who had already retired for the night by the time we arrived. When she spoke to him a few days later, he apologised for taking off like he did. He expressed anger over the delayed medical response and acknowledged how it could have cost us all our lives. He, like Gary, had a family waiting for him at home, and the incident brought him perilously close to never seeing them again.

Gary's friends, who had joined him from Johannesburg for the race, happened to be staying in the adjacent bungalow. We had briefly interacted on the first night while preparing Kim's bike. That night, Kim went over to them and explained that Gary had passed away in her arms. One of them gave Kim Gary's son's mobile number, so she called him the following day to let him know that she'd been with his dad in his final moments. He was so relieved that his father hadn't died out there alone. When asked about Gary's final words, Kim told him there were none. There was no message for his family, no lingering sentiment – not for one second did Gary think he wouldn't make it. As far as he was concerned, help was on its way, and he'd soon be reminiscing about the day's events over an ice-cold beer. He had shown no fear or anguish over his situation.

Kim flew up to Johannesburg for Gary's funeral the following week, and a few months later, a parcel was delivered to her office. When she opened it, there was Gary's peak cap with his race number on it and the tag still attached. She still has it in her office.

I shudder to think about what might have happened had Kim not had that satellite phone with her that day to call for help or had I been unable to get to her.

In reflecting on the chain of events, one can clearly see the manifestation of a Swiss Cheese event. There were multiple 'slices' – each representing a safety measure – or stages at which intervention could have potentially prevented the tragedy. However, each of these measures had a 'hole' or weakness, contributing to the disaster. The vast, inhospitable Richtersveld terrain was a key factor: it was a formidable challenge for even the most experienced of riders. Add to this the blistering heat of summer, which soared to an extreme 50 degrees Celsius, creating an environment conducive to dehydration and heat exhaustion. These factors formed the first set of holes in the metaphorical cheese.

The second slice of cheese comes into play with the physical condition of the participants on the actual day. In Gary's case, while he was a highly experienced and fit rider, the race was on a gruelling course in extremely unforgiving heat. Sadly, his body simply couldn't withstand the conditions that day.

The organisers had promised safety precautions, like having a helicopter on standby and paramedics in 4x4s ready to respond to emergencies. While the promise of a quick response time was reassuring in theory, in practice, it did not pan out. Kim's attempts to call for help were met with various challenges. The race's designated channel was unresponsive, and the backup, the satellite phone, initially struggled to find a signal due to their location. This created the third set of holes.

The promised "twenty minutes" response time by the medics became prolonged due to the GPS format error, forming the holes in the fourth slice of cheese. In critical situations, especially in environments like the desert, every minute counts. This confusion compounded the risk for Gary and also for Kim, who was exposing herself to the elements to help him. Her admirable commitment to not abandon a fellow rider also put her in a precarious situation, highlighting the potential for disaster when unforeseen circumstances collide with human actions.

Finally, the extreme heat further escalated the situation, making it harder to keep Gary stable, forming the fifth and final hole in the cheese.

In this tragic case, each of these factors alone might not have led to a catastrophe. However, when combined like the holes in aligned slices of Swiss cheese, they created a pathway for disaster. The West Coast Baja incident is a solemn reminder of how crucial thorough planning, clear communication, and an understanding of the potential risks are, especially when operating in an inherently dangerous environment.

This chapter is dedicated to Gary and his family. Gary was a true supporter of off-road racing and a role model to many younger riders.

CHAPTER 3
THE DUNNING-KRUGER EFFECT

n April 2021, Kim and I decided to travel to Lake Malawi to tick tropical freshwater diving off our bucket list. With its hidden beaches and dreamy coves, the lake is often dubbed the quintessential fly-and-flop destination. Beyond its tranquil beauty, the lake is a snorkeller's paradise. The crystal-clear waters are home to over 1,000 species of brightly coloured cichlid fish, many of which can't be found anywhere else on Earth.

While researching the trip and where we might stop off along the way, we stumbled upon the Mulanje Mountain Forest Reserve. Covering 56,317 hectares, this reserve earned its status as a UNESCO biosphere reserve in 2000. It stands as one of the few spots in Malawi that remains untouched by deforestation. Towering at over 3,000m, Mount Mulanje, known locally as the "island in the sky", is the country's highest peak, rising dramatically from the plains of Chizardzulu and the tea-rich Mulanje district.

Eager to hike the mountain and explore its rock pools, waterfalls, and forests, we discovered a mountain cabin operated by the locals that had availability. We decided to begin our journey with a weekend stay in this rustic abode before moving on to Lake Malawi.

According to my online research, the journey from the airport in Blantyre to the village would take us no more than 90 minutes. Most of the route was tarred, although online sources did warn about the occasional pothole. Our flight was scheduled to touch down at 2 p.m., so I allocated two hours for the drive. This included 30 minutes to pick up our rental car at the airport and perhaps refuel. No problem, I thought – we'd reach the village no later than 5 p.m.

However, the universe had other plans for us. First, our flight was delayed by half an hour. Then, to our dismay, we learned that the car rental agency wasn't at the airport but rather in the heart of Blantyre, a little over 16 kilometres (10 miles) away, which meant navigating through the city's bustling Friday afternoon traffic to reach it. We arrived at the dealership half an hour after leaving the airport. By then, it was just after 3 p.m.

We weren't planning on doing any heavy 4x4ing, so we rented a little lime-green Suzuki Jimny, which we aptly nicknamed 'Jelly Tot'. Shortly before 4 p.m., the licenses, insurance, and paperwork were processed. I pulled up the Tracks4Africa map on my GPS, and off we went. To our dismay, the roads were in terrible shape. To compound matters, being in the semi-tropics, the sun sets at 5 p.m. in Malawi in April, an hour earlier than I'd initially expected.

By the time we reached Mulanje, darkness had set in without a single light in sight. The tar road transformed into a dirt track, leading us through villages and fields of maise, bananas, sweet potatoes, and other crops before we found ourselves in the forest. Before long, a river crossing loomed ahead – a daunting expanse of mud and water stretching about 80 meters. We weren't in my Landy – we were in a liquorice-packet-coloured Suzuki Jimny with standard all-terrain tyres. There was no way we were going to get across all that mud. I made several detours, but each one brought us back to the river. Each time we found ourselves trapped in another forested dead-end, we'd see ten to fifteen pairs of gleaming white eyes watching us. We had no idea what their intentions were. The possibility of four men overturning our vehicle felt very real. I could literally smell the slices of Swiss cheese sliding up alongside us.

By 7 p.m., under the pitch darkness of the African night, we were utterly disoriented, yet our GPS stubbornly insisted we tackle the muddy river crossing. As we approached the river once again, I noticed the Jimny was equipped with low range and traction control.

"You know what?" I said to Kim, feeling somewhat more confident, "We're just going to have to wing it."

With that, our neon lime-green companion plunged into the mud. We held our breath. She wiggled. Light on her feet, she didn't sink like a heavier vehicle might have. Instead, she skimmed atop the mud, flinging it everywhere.

Zzzip! Eighty metres of thick mud, and she sailed across it. When we came out the other side, she was caked in mud, but she was like a dog wagging her tail with a ball in her mouth, saying, "See, I told you I could do it!"

I was in awe. The whole experience made me realise just how much I'd underestimated the Jimny. My respect for it grew tenfold.

Some seven kilometres (4 miles) later, we reached our cabin, muddy but triumphant.

As I reflected on our adventure, I was reminded of a BBC documentary I had watched years ago. The program featured an engineer who played a part in designing the original utility Land Rover back in 1948. Clad in a sharp tweed jacket and tie, he was asked about the most crucial aspect of an overlanding truck.

His response was unambiguous: "Tyres, my son," he said. "Tyres."

Tyres are your vehicle's sole contact with the ground. Regardless of the kind of machine you have – even if it's the world's best – its performance hinges on its tyres. Without proper traction, self-cleaning properties, or grip, it will simply spin helplessly in place. For me, tyres are everything. Never cut corners on them. Always invest in the best you can afford, regardless of your vehicle's condition.

NAVIGATING BLIND SPOTS: FROM MUDDY TRAILS TO MISJUDGED ABILITIES

Thinking back to our unexpected challenges and detours on the way to Lake Malawi reminded me of how sometimes our confidence takes the front seat while experience and expertise sit way back. It's not just about a muddy trail or missing the sunset – it's about how we often gauge our abilities while being blind to our own blind spots. And there's actually a term for this in psychology: the Dunning-Kruger effect.

The Dunning-Kruger effect is a curious psychological bias that affects our ability to accurately assess our own abilities and knowledge. The phenomenon was coined by social psychologists David Dunning and Justin Kruger in 1999, who observed that people with low ability in a particular task or domain tend to overestimate their competence, while those with high ability tend to underestimate it. The irony of the Dunning-Kruger effect is that the people who are most affected by it are often the least aware of it. In other words, those who lack knowledge or expertise in a particular domain are often the ones who are the most confident in their abilities.

It's no secret that the world is filled with people who think they know it all, yet their actions speak louder than their words. They may make poor decisions, misjudge situations or perform poorly when put to the test. The consequences of such actions can be catastrophic, impacting not only their own lives but also the lives of those around them.

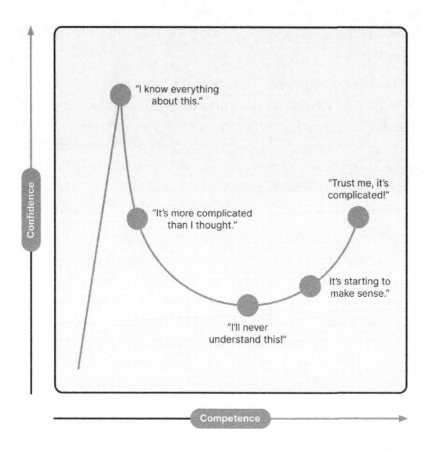

On the other hand, there are people who believe that they are not capable of achieving their full potential. They lack the confidence to take risks or seize opportunities, which can hinder their growth and prevent them from reaching their goals. These individuals fail to recognise their unique talents and skills, which can lead to a lifetime of regret.

The Dunning-Kruger effect is all about perception versus reality. When we overestimate our abilities, we can make bad decisions or perform poorly. And when we underestimate ourselves, we may miss out on opportunities or fail to reach our full potential. It's a delicate balance, but one that is vital to get right if we want to succeed in life, whether we're in the concrete jungle or traversing the wide-open plains of Africa.

The Dunning-Kruger effect can rear its head in any situation and can happen to anyone, even experienced overlanders, regardless of their skill level, and it can have disastrous consequences. When exploring new territories and embarking on adventures, individuals who lack experience in these areas may overestimate their abilities and knowledge, leading them to make critical errors and take unnecessary risks that can put their lives, and those of others, in danger.

For instance, they may overestimate their ability to navigate the terrain or handle emergency situations and underestimate the challenges of driving long distances on unfamiliar roads, dealing with extreme weather conditions, or encountering dangerous wildlife. They may not have the necessary equipment or supplies to handle emergencies or unexpected situations, such as fixing a flat tyre or repairing a broken-down vehicle or having adequate food or water supplies in case of a delay or unexpected stop. They may not fully appreciate the cultural and social nuances or local customs and traditions of the places they are visiting. In some African cultures, for example, it is customary to remove your shoes before entering a home or other indoor space. Failing to do so may be seen as disrespectful or unclean. A traveller may underestimate the risks of interacting with unfamiliar people or communities. For example, in areas where there is political or ethnic tension, they may find themselves in a dangerous or hostile situation.

The Dunning-Kruger effect can be especially dangerous when it comes to navigation. Individuals who overestimate their abilities in this area may not properly prepare for their journey or may make critical errors in navigating their way. For instance, someone who lacks experience in map reading may overestimate their ability to use a map or compass to navigate, leading to critical errors in determining their location or direction of travel. They may not understand the symbols on the map or the scale of the map, leading to a misinterpretation of their surroundings. They may not have the necessary equipment or knowledge to navigate through challenging terrain, like dense forests or mountain ranges, leading to a greater risk of getting lost or disoriented. They may not properly plan for their journey, such as accounting for rest stops or fuel stations along the way. This can lead to exhaustion or injury with no contingency plan in place.

Winching, recovering vehicles, and crossing deep rivers are all tasks that require experience and knowledge to perform safely. Individuals who overestimate their abilities and knowledge in these areas may not take the necessary precautions or may make critical errors that can result in injury or damage to vehicles. For example, someone who lacks experience in winching may overestimate their ability to safely recover a vehicle, leading to the winch failing or the vehicle being pulled in the wrong direction. Similarly, people who lack experience in recovering vehicles may underestimate the complexity of the task and the risks involved, leading to the vehicle tipping over or becoming further stuck. Crossing deep rivers can be especially dangerous, and individuals who lack experience in this area may overestimate their vehicle's capability or underestimate the depth or the power of the water, leading to the vehicle becoming submerged or getting swept away.

THE DUNNING-KRUGER EFFECT IN BUSINESS

The Dunning-Kruger effect is a common phenomenon in the business world, where individuals with limited expertise in a particular area often overestimate their abilities and knowledge. This can be particularly damaging for a business, as it can result in costly mistakes, missed opportunities, a failure to learn from past failures, and even outright incompetence. Leaders who are susceptible to the

Dunning-Kruger Effect often struggle to acknowledge their weaknesses and may be resistant to feedback or advice from others.

Let's explore the many ways in which the Dunning-Kruger effect manifests itself in the realm of business.

PROJECT MANAGEMENT

Effective project management requires experienced and knowledgeable project managers who can plan effectively, allocate resources efficiently, communicate clearly, manage risk effectively, and adapt to changing circumstances. In project management, the Dunning-Kruger effect can manifest in various ways, leading to poor project outcomes and even project failure. To avoid these pitfalls, it is crucial to recognise the importance of experienced project management professionals who can navigate the complexities of project management with ease and expertise.

Let's explore some of the ways the Dunning-Kruger effect can impact project management:

POOR PLANNING

Effective project management starts with proper planning. Proper planning requires attention to detail and thoroughness and is the foundation upon which a successful project is built. A well-planned project provides a clear roadmap for achieving project goals and objectives, ensuring that everyone involved knows what is expected of them. It involves identifying project requirements, determining project scope, creating a detailed project plan, and establishing project timelines and milestones. By investing time and effort into planning, project managers can anticipate potential challenges, identify resource requirements, and allocate resources effectively. Planning also allows project managers to set priorities, establish realistic expectations, and track progress throughout the project's lifecycle. Ultimately, effective planning is the key to completing a project on time, within budget, and to the desired quality standards.

When project managers exhibiting the Dunning-Kruger effect fail to adequately plan for all aspects of the project, it can lead to delays, cost overruns, and decreased quality, causing frustration for all stakeholders involved. Without a clear roadmap, project managers may struggle to identify potential challenges, allocate resources effectively, and establish realistic expectations. This can lead to unexpected roadblocks, misunderstandings, and misaligned expectations, ultimately resulting in a project that does not meet its intended goals and objectives. In short, inadequate planning can derail a project before it even gets started.

INEFFECTIVE RESOURCE MANAGEMENT

Effective resource management involves identifying the necessary resources required for a project, allocating those resources efficiently, and monitoring and adjusting them as necessary. This approach ensures that the right people, with the right skills, are in the right place, with the right resources, to deliver the right outcomes.

In contrast, a lack of resource management can result in chaos and confusion, with team members pulling in different directions, resources being wasted, budgets being blown, and deadlines being missed. Project managers susceptible to the Dunning-Kruger effect may fail to allocate resources properly, leading to low-quality work, increased costs, and, ultimately, a failed project.

COMMUNICATION ISSUES

Clear and consistent communication is vital to the success of any project and ensures that all stakeholders understand the project goals, roles and responsibilities, timelines, and any potential obstacles that may arise. Regular communication among team members fosters a collaborative culture and ensures that everyone is working towards a common goal and that tasks are aligned to meet the project's objectives. It also helps in identifying potential issues early, reducing risks, and ensuring the timely resolution of problems. Consistent communication also fosters a culture of trust and transparency, enabling team members and other stakeholders to share ideas and feedback openly and constructively.

However, if a project manager is experiencing the Dunning-Kruger effect, they may fail to recognise the importance of clear communication or even disregard feedback, leading to miscommunication, delays, a lack of progress, decreased team morale, and potential reputational damage should the project fail.

LACK OF RISK MANAGEMENT

Identifying and assessing potential risks at the outset of a project helps to minimise their impact and likelihood of occurring. By anticipating and mitigating risks, project managers can maintain timelines, budgets, and quality standards. They can also ensure that team members are aware of potential risks and have contingency plans in place to address them. Furthermore, effective risk management fosters a culture of proactive problem-solving, where team members feel empowered to identify and address potential issues before they become significant problems.

On the other hand, if someone is experiencing the Dunning-Kruger effect, they may overestimate their abilities and underestimate the complexity of a project, leading them to ignore or downplay potential risks. They may also fail to seek input from other team members, leading to blind spots and an incomplete risk assessment. This can lead to significant issues during the project, such as missed deadlines, scope creep, budget overruns, poor-quality work, and even the complete failure of the project.

INABILITY TO ADAPT

The ability to adapt is a critical quality for effective project management. Projects often encounter unforeseen challenges that require flexibility and the ability to respond to change quickly, adjust plans and processes accordingly, and stay on track. Additionally, agile project management emphasises flexibility, teamwork, and fast iterations, allowing project teams to deliver value to stakeholders in small increments.

In contrast, if a project manager is experiencing the Dunning-Kruger effect, they may not be open to new ideas and believe that it's their way or the highway. This rigid approach can make it difficult for the team to respond to challenges, which may result in project failure.

CASH FLOW MANAGEMENT

Cash flow management involves monitoring the flow of cash into and out of the business to ensure that there is enough money to meet its financial obligations and invest in growth opportunities. A robust cash flow management strategy enables businesses to make informed financial decisions, plan for future expenses, and maintain a healthy financial position.

However, if a business owner is experiencing the Dunning-Kruger effect, they may underestimate the complexity of cash flow management. This can lead to poor financial decision-making, a lack of financial planning, and, ultimately, cash flow problems that can cripple the business.

Let's explore some of the ways the Dunning-Kruger effect can lead to poor cash flow management in a business:

POOR FINANCIAL PLANNING

When it comes to cash flow management in a business, poor financial planning can be disastrous, and unfortunately, the Dunning-Kruger effect can exacerbate this problem. Overestimating one's financial planning abilities can significantly impact the business's ability to operate, making it challenging to meet financial obligations or invest in growth opportunities. The result can be an inability to keep the business afloat, let alone turn a profit.

One common pitfall of poor financial planning is INADEQUATE MARKET ANALYSIS. Business owners who overestimate their abilities may not take the time to properly analyse market trends, customer behaviour, and their competition. As a result, they may not have a complete understanding of their business environment. This lack of understanding can lead to inaccurate revenue and expense projections, which can result in poor financial planning and decreased financial performance. For example, business owners who do not conduct adequate market research may not know what customers want or how to compete with other businesses. As a result, they may overestimate demand for their products or services, leading to overproduction, wasted resources, and unsold inventory. Alternatively, they may underestimate the demand and not produce enough, leading to lost sales and revenue. Additionally, inadequate market analysis can lead to poor pricing decisions. Without a thorough understanding of the market, businesses may either price their products too high, leading to low sales or price them too low, leading to decreased profitability.

INACCURATE BUDGETING is another common problem. One consequence of inaccurate budgeting is underfunding or overfunding. If business owners underestimate expenses, they may not allocate enough resources to cover them, leading to financial shortfalls and the inability to meet financial obligations. On the other hand, if they overestimate expenses, they may allocate more resources than necessary, resulting in inefficient use of resources and decreased profitability. Inaccurate budgeting can also lead to poor decision-making. Without a clear understanding of the costs associated with different aspects of the business, owners may make decisions that are not financially viable. For example, they may invest in a new project or initiative that appears profitable but fail to account for the true cost of implementation, leading to a negative impact on the business's financial performance. Inaccurate budgeting can also make it difficult to secure financing. Banks and investors typically require a solid financial plan before providing funding, and inaccurate or incomplete budgets can be a red flag that the business is not financially sound.

POOR RISK MANAGEMENT is also a potential consequence of poor financial planning. Business owners may not properly identify, assess, and mitigate risks, leading to financial instability and potential business failure. For example, if a business owner fails to anticipate an economic downturn, they may not have a contingency plan in place to reduce expenses or pivot the business in response to the changing market conditions. This can result in financial losses and potentially even bankruptcy. Additionally, without adequate risk assessment and mitigation, the business may not be properly insured against potential risks. This can leave the business exposed to financial losses in the event of an unforeseen event or accident, which can lead to a loss of trust and credibility with its customers, investors, and other stakeholders.

Lastly, INADEQUATE RESOURCE ALLOCATION is another issue that can arise from overconfidence in financial planning. Inadequate financial resource allocation can lead to underfunding or overfunding of different aspects of the business. For example, if a business leader underestimates the budget required to cover operating expenses, the business may face financial shortfalls and struggle to meet financial obligations. Alternatively, if a business leader overestimates the budget needed for certain investments or expenses, the business may allocate too many resources in that area, leading to inefficient use of resources and decreased profitability.

INADEQUATE CREDIT CONTROL

Without proper credit control, businesses may struggle to collect payments from customers, leading to a cash flow deficit. Unfortunately, those experiencing the Dunning-Kruger effect may overestimate their ability to manage credit and collections, leading to a lack of effective credit control measures. Without effective credit control measures, businesses may fail to set credit limits or carry out credit checks, leaving them vulnerable to customers who cannot pay. The result can be a cycle of late payments and bad debts that have significant implications for cash flow management. These issues can have a domino effect on cash flow, impacting the business's ability to pay bills, invest in growth, and remain financially stable.

POOR EXPENSE MANAGEMENT

Overestimating one's financial management abilities can result in overspending and wasteful expenditure. Poor expense management can quickly drain a business's cash reserves, leaving it vulnerable to financial problems that can impact its ability to operate and grow.

To illustrate this, let's say a multinational corporation decides to open a new regional office in a foreign country. The corporation estimates that the cost of setting up the office will be around $ 5 million and plans to finance the investment from its cash reserves. However, during the implementation phase, the corporation fails to account for several additional costs, such as acquiring necessary licenses and permits and complying with local regulations. They also underestimated the cost of furnishing the office space and purchasing necessary equipment and technology. As a result, the corporation ends up spending significantly more than the initial estimate. By failing to accurately account for all the costs associated with opening the new regional office and not having a contingency plan in place to cover unexpected expenses, the business faced significant financial strain, which had a negative impact on its financial performance.

INEFFECTIVE WORKING CAPITAL MANAGEMENT

One of the biggest challenges for businesses is managing working capital effectively. Working capital is the difference between a company's current assets and its current liabilities. It represents the cash and other assets that a company has available to meet its short-term obligations, such as paying bills and covering its payroll. Poor working capital management can lead to a situation where a company has too much cash tied up in inventory or accounts receivable, leaving it short of cash to meet its immediate obligations.

Business leaders and entrepreneurs who are overconfident in their cash flow management abilities may not recognise the importance of effective working capital management or the impact poor cash flow might have on their business. They may underestimate the importance of keeping enough cash on hand to cover short-term expenses. They might believe they can operate with minimal cash reserves or overlook the need to balance their investments in inventory and fixed assets with their short-term liquidity needs. They might overinvest in long-term assets, leaving them vulnerable to cash flow gaps and decreased financial flexibility. Or, they may overlook opportunities to improve cash flow, such as negotiating better payment terms with suppliers or pursuing more aggressive collection strategies with customers. When cash is tied up in inventory or accounts receivable, it can limit the business's ability to invest in growth opportunities or expand into new markets, putting it at a competitive disadvantage.

STRATEGIC PLANNING

Strategic planning is critical to the success of any business. It sets a clear direction for achieving long-term goals, identifies opportunities for growth, and creates a roadmap to make it all happen. Without a clear understanding of where the business is headed and how it will get there, it becomes difficult to make informed decisions that align with the business's goals or capitalise on opportunities for growth and profitability.

Business leaders who think they have it all figured out and neglect to seek out the necessary information to make the right decisions are likely to skip crucial steps like conducting market research, seeking customer feedback, or consulting with industry experts. Without a clear understanding of the business environment, they can develop flawed strategies that fail to meet the needs of their customers or adapt to changes in the market.

Even worse, they may be resistant to feedback or alternative perspectives, dismissing input from others and limiting creativity and innovation. They may also be unwilling to accept feedback or acknowledge mistakes and be reluctant to adapt their strategies when they are not working. That kind of narrow-minded approach can make it difficult for businesses to be agile and pivot in response to new opportunities or challenges.

Here are a few steps that you can take to avoid falling prey to the Dunning-Kruger effect when it comes to strategic planning:

• Seek input from others and incorporate diverse viewpoints into your strategic planning process. This can include feedback from customers, employees, industry experts, or consultants.

• Conduct thorough market research to ensure you have a clear understanding of the business environment and your target market. Don't make assumptions about your customers or the market. Conduct thorough research to gain insights into your customers' needs and preferences, as well as industry trends and competitive dynamics.

• Remember that no one gets it right all the time. If there is an error in your strategy, acknowledge it and be willing to learn from it. Don't let your ego get in the way of making changes that will drive your business forward.

• Stay agile. The business world is constantly evolving, and it's important to be able to pivot quickly in response to new opportunities or challenges. Don't be afraid to experiment with new ideas and approaches – getting stuck in a narrow-minded approach will limit your business's ability to adapt and evolve.

• Be open to exploring new ideas and taking calculated risks. Create an environment that encourages creativity and innovation by rewarding experimentation and fostering a sense of curiosity.

MARKETING AND CLIENT RETENTION

Successful businesses understand the value of investing in marketing and client retention as a key component of their long-term growth strategy. Marketing helps businesses connect with potential customers and create awareness of their products or services, while client retention involves building and maintaining long-term relationships with existing clients.

Marketing is especially important in today's competitive business environment, where customers have access to more options than ever before. With a wealth of options at their fingertips, it's a constant battle to grab their attention and stand out from the crowd. But attracting new customers is only half the battle. The real key to long-term success is retaining those customers and keeping them coming back for more. By building strong relationships, providing exceptional customer service, and consistently delivering value, you not only secure a stable revenue stream but also create a loyal following of customers who will not only keep doing business with you but also spread the word to others.

When the Dunning-Kruger effect is at play in a business, marketing and client retention can be impacted in several ways:

INEFFECTIVE MESSAGING

Without a solid understanding of marketing principles and strategies, it can be difficult to effectively communicate your brand's message and value proposition to your target audience. A common mistake that inexperienced marketers make is failing to tailor their messaging to their target audience. Instead, they might adopt a one-size-fits-all approach, assuming that everyone will be interested in the same message. This can lead to messaging that misses the mark and fails to resonate with your target audience, resulting in decreased brand recognition, customer engagement, and loyalty.

Another common mistake is using industry jargon or technical language that your target audience may not understand. This can make your messaging feel inaccessible or confusing, leading to a lack of engagement and interest from your target audience.

For example, In the mid-2000s, PepsiCo's Mountain Dew launched a campaign that attempted to appeal to a broad audience by using edgy, extreme sports-themed messaging. The campaign featured a variety of TV ads, online content, and other marketing material that relied heavily on edgy, irreverent humour and extreme sports imagery. While this approach may have resonated with some of Mountain Dew's core audience, it failed to appeal to broader segments of the market, leading to a lack of engagement and interest from some consumers.

To avoid messaging pitfalls like this, it's important to conduct thorough market research and develop a deep understanding of your target audience. This means identifying their needs, preferences, and pain points, as well as their language and communication styles. By doing so, you'll be able to craft messaging that truly speaks to your audience, building a strong and lasting relationship that improves brand recognition, customer engagement, and loyalty.

INADEQUATE CLIENT ENGAGEMENT

Client engagement refers to the level of involvement and interaction that a client has with a business. It's about creating opportunities for clients to interact with your business, whether through marketing campaigns, social media, or other channels.

Connecting with your clients on a regular basis is more than just a good business practice – it's a necessity. When your clients feel connected to your brand, they are more likely to stick around and keep doing business with you. Consistent engagement keeps your clients interested and invested in your brand by offering them personalised interactions, useful information, and the chance to give feedback. This can lead to higher customer retention rates, enthusiastic referrals, and an overall boost in customer satisfaction.

If a business neglects to engage with its customers on a regular basis, it risks losing their interest and loyalty. Customers want to feel valued and appreciated, and if they don't receive the attention they deserve, they'll quickly take their business elsewhere. This not only impacts a company's bottom line but can also result in negative word-of-mouth publicity that can damage the company's image. Without regular engagement, businesses may miss out on valuable opportunities to gather feedback and improve their products and services, which can leave them lagging behind competitors who are more in tune with their customers' needs and preferences.

To avoid falling into this trap, stay engaged with your clients and maintain an open line of communication. By prioritising regular engagement, you can foster strong relationships, stay ahead of the competition, and safeguard your reputation.

LACK OF RELATIONSHIP BUILDING

Success in business isn't just about making sales and exchanging goods or services. It's not just about putting on a good show during a sales pitch. It's about taking the time to connect with your clients on a personal level, truly understanding their unique needs and desires, and showing them how much you appreciate their business. When you make your clients feel valued and understood, they're much more likely to stay loyal to your business in the long run.

However, neglecting to prioritise relationship-building – or assuming that your current level of relationship-building is adequate – can lead to disastrous consequences. Clients who don't feel a strong emotional connection to your business are more likely to switch to a competitor who takes the time to engage with them and provide a personalised experience. Worse still, dissatisfied and disengaged clients can have a detrimental effect on your brand's reputation.

Remember, your clients are not just numbers on a spreadsheet. By making relationship-building a priority and forming genuine, meaningful relationships with your clients, you can show them that you value them not just as customers but as individuals. Listen carefully to their feedback, respond quickly and effectively to their requests, and show appreciation for their loyalty. It may take more effort than simply chasing the next sale, but the payoff in terms of long-term growth and success will be well worth it. You'll experience increased customer retention, reduce customer churn, and generate positive word-of-mouth referrals that can help your business thrive.

POOR CUSTOMER SERVICE

Without great customer service, even the most innovative and exciting products or services will fall flat. Customer service is more than just a transactional exchange – it's about building deep, meaningful relationships with your customers. At its core, it's about creating a sense of trust and loyalty that goes beyond the simple exchange of goods and services. Achieving this means truly understanding the needs of your customers and doing everything in your power not only to meet but exceed their expectations.

However, many businesses overestimate their ability to retain clients. They assume that once they've made the initial sale, their clients will stick around. But the reality is far more complex. If your customer service representatives aren't properly trained and managed, your clients are likely to have a poor experience – and that can have serious consequences. Negative reviews, for example, can quickly spread online, damaging your reputation and making it difficult to acquire new customers. And worst of all, poor customer service can lead to customer churn, as dissatisfied clients take their business elsewhere.

In today's hyper-connected world, it's more important than ever to make sure that every interaction your customers have with your business is a positive one. To achieve this, invest in your team and equip them with the skills, resources and support they need to deliver exceptional service and build lasting relationships. Make sure they are well-managed, with clear guidelines for how to handle different types of client interactions and empower them to go above and beyond for your clients.

Remember – your customers are the lifeblood of your business. By adopting a customer-first mindset and placing the client's needs at the forefront of your business strategy, you can build the kind of deep connections that drive long-term success and growth for your business.

STAFF RETENTION

Staff retention is about keeping your best people on board for the long haul. It's not just about throwing a bigger paycheque their way but about creating an environment where they feel valued, heard and challenged. When employees feel fulfilled and appreciated, they're less likely to leave for greener pastures. When staff retention is high, your team becomes a cohesive unit, working together towards common goals and driving your business forward. However, when it's low, you risk losing your top talent to competitors or even burnout.

Let's explore some of the ways the Dunning-Kruger effect can manifest in poor staff retention in a business:

POOR TALENT ACQUISITION

Recruiting the right people is not just about finding someone to fill a role but finding the right person who fits the company culture and values. When businesses hire the right people, they're more likely to stay with the company for the long term, reducing turnover costs and creating a stable workforce. The right hire can positively impact the workplace culture, bring new ideas and innovation, and add value to the company.

However, the negative impact of a bad hire cannot be ignored. If a business leader or recruitment officer is exhibiting the Dunning-Kruger effect, it can have serious implications for the organisation. It can lead to a toxic work environment, low morale among employees, decreased productivity and profitability and, ultimately, high staff turnover.

Ultimately, the success of any organisation hinges on its people. It is, therefore, important for business leaders and recruitment officers to approach the hiring process with a willingness to invest in finding the best fit for the job and the company. By doing so, they can create a stable and thriving workforce that drives the long-term success of the organisation.

POOR EMPLOYEE TRAINING

In addition to recruiting the right people, onboarding and training employees is equally important in staff retention. A well-designed onboarding process can help new hires feel welcomed and supported and quickly become acclimated to their role and the company culture. However, if the company fails to provide adequate training and support, this can result in reduced productivity and low job satisfaction, resulting in the new hire leaving the business. This not only creates additional costs for the company but can also put a strain on other employees who are forced to pick up the slack or deal with the consequences of mistakes made by the unqualified employee.

Furthermore, when businesses prioritise the ongoing development of their employees, they send a powerful message that they are committed to their growth and success, which can have a significant impact on job satisfaction and motivation. Employees who feel that their employer is invested in their career development are more likely to remain with the company for the long term, reducing turnover costs and creating a stable workforce. Regular training also ensures that employees have the skills and knowledge needed to excel in their roles, which leads to increased productivity, improved job performance, and a more positive workplace culture.

Ultimately, investing in people is an investment in the future of the business. By prioritising employee growth and development, companies can build a loyal and talented workforce that is well-positioned to drive the long-term success of the organisation.

INADEQUATE EMPLOYEE PERFORMANCE REVIEWS

Regular performance reviews help employees understand what is expected of them and provide a clear framework for measuring their progress and how their contribution impacts the business's overall growth. By setting clear expectations and providing regular feedback, companies can identify and address any issues early on, which can prevent problems from escalating and help employees grow and develop in their roles. This not only results in increased job satisfaction but also leads to higher levels of productivity and performance.

In contrast, without regular feedback and support, employees may feel uncertain about their role and from understanding how their work contributes to the larger goals of the business, leading to a disconnection between their work and the overall mission of the company.

By prioritising performance management, companies can create a positive work environment that fosters employee growth and development, resulting in a loyal and engaged workforce that is more likely to stay with the company and contribute to its long-term success. By investing in their employees' development and well-being, companies can build a motivated and skilled team that is well-positioned to drive the business forward.

LACK OF RECOGNITION

When an employee is dedicated to their job and puts in long hours, but their contributions go unnoticed, they may begin to feel under-valued and unappreciated – at which point, there's a good chance they will start looking around for greener pastures.

Employee recognition is crucial in staff retention because it satisfies a basic human need – the need for validation and appreciation. When employees feel that their hard work and contributions are recognised and valued, they are more likely to stay loyal to a company and continue to perform at their best. This is because recognition not only provides a sense of accomplishment but also reinforces positive behaviour and encourages employees to keep up the good work. It also creates a positive workplace culture that fosters teamwork, productivity, and morale.

When there is a lack of recognition, it can have a negative impact on employee morale, engagement, and retention. Employees who feel undervalued and unappreciated may become disengaged, unmoti-vated and less committed to their work, leading to lower productivity and a decline in the quality of work. Furthermore, a lack of recogni-tion can lead to increased employee turnover as employees may start looking for opportunities elsewhere where they feel more appreciated and valued. This can lead to higher recruitment costs, lower team morale and a loss of institutional knowledge. It can also create a negative workplace culture that fosters cynicism, resentment, and distrust among employees. This can have a ripple effect on team dynamics, leading to poor communication, reduced collaboration, and a toxic work environment.

Overall, a lack of recognition can be detrimental to both the employees and the company. It's essential for business leaders to understand the value of recognition and to take steps to ensure that employees feel valued and appreciated for their contributions. However, it's important to note that recognition must be meaningful and genuine to have an impact. A generic "good job" or a pat on the back is not enough – recognition should be specific, timely and tailored to the individual. This shows that the company values and understands the employee's individual contributions, leading to a deeper sense of connection and loyalty.

POOR WORK-LIFE BALANCE

People are not machines. When employees feel overwhelmed and burnt out from working long hours with no time for themselves or their families, they're more likely to leave their jobs in search of a better work-life balance. On the other hand, when business leaders recognise the importance of a healthy work-life balance and take steps to ensure that their employees have the time and resources to maintain one, they're more likely to attract and retain talented individuals who are committed to their business's success.

To promote work-life balance, business leaders can create a culture that respects their employees' personal time and discourages working outside of regular hours. They can also offer flexible working hours, allow remote work, and encourage employees to take regular breaks and holidays without fear of being penalised or judged.

SOCIAL MEDIA MARKETING CAMPAIGNS

The rapid growth of digital technology has transformed the way businesses interact with customers, making it essential for businesses to have a strong digital presence. Social media platforms have also become an integral part of modern-day communication, and businesses can leverage these platforms to engage with their customers, build brand awareness and loyalty, and drive sales. Carefully planned and well-executed digital and social media campaigns are more cost-effective and measurable than traditional marketing campaigns and can provide valuable insights into customer behaviour, preferences and interests, helping businesses refine their marketing strategies, improve their products and services, and stay ahead of their competitors.

However, not all individuals or businesses possess the expertise needed to execute such campaigns effectively. When the Dunning-Kruger effect is at play, it can lead to individuals believing they have the necessary skills and knowledge to run effective campaigns when, in reality, they do not – the results of which can be both costly and disastrous. Because these individuals believe they have all the knowledge and skills required, they may not seek advice or assistance from experts in the field to ensure their campaigns are designed and executed correctly, resonate with their target audience, and deliver the desired results.

Let's explore some of the ways the Dunning-Kruger effect can impact a business's social media marketing campaigns:

INADEQUATE MARKET RESEARCH

While social media marketing is a critical component of any successful business strategy, simply being present on social media platforms is not enough to achieve significant results. To create impactful social media campaigns with a strong return on investment, businesses must gain a clear understanding of their target audience's needs, preferences, and behaviours. Market research plays a vital role in this process, as it provides businesses with valuable insights into their target audience's demographics, interests, and online behaviour. By leveraging this research, businesses can tailor their social media campaigns to reach their intended audience, increase engagement, and ultimately drive conversions and revenue.

When businesses jump into social media marketing without understanding their target audience, they risk wasting precious resources and missing out on valuable opportunities. Without thorough market research, businesses might not know which social media platforms their target audience is most active on, which types of content resonate with them, and what their pain points and aspirations are. This means that their social media marketing campaigns may fail to engage their target audience, resulting in low engagement, lack of interest and no return on investment.

Hiring a qualified social media marketing specialist can be a wise investment for businesses looking to unlock the full potential of social media marketing, drive growth, and stay ahead of the competition. A skilled specialist can provide valuable insights into your target audience's needs and preferences, create impactful and successful social media campaigns, choose the right social media platforms, optimise your social media advertising spend, and maximise your return on investment.

When marketing your product or service to potential clients, you want to create marketing campaigns that resonate with your audience and help build strong relationships with them. However, if you don't do your due diligence in researching your market and understanding your clients' needs and preferences, you run the risk of falling prey to the Dunning-Kruger effect. When it comes to marketing, this can be a real problem. If you think you know what your audience wants without actually doing the research to confirm it, you might end up creating campaigns that fall flat. Your messaging might not resonate with your target market, or worse, it might actually turn them off. If clients feel that a business does not understand their needs or provide them with products or services that meet those needs, they are likely to look elsewhere.

If you're serious about creating marketing campaigns that really resonate with your audience and build strong relationships, you need to invest in high-quality market research. Whether you choose to bring in experts or simply have a heart-to-heart with your clients, taking the time to truly understand their needs and preferences is essential. This will give you the accurate data and insights you need to make informed decisions and create campaigns that hit the mark.

So listen up, do your research, and connect with your audience in a way that builds trust and lasting relationships.

INEFFECTIVE MESSAGING

The effectiveness of social media marketing campaigns depends largely on the messaging used, and it takes a unique set of skills and expertise to make a strong impact. Inexperienced marketers who struggle to craft messaging that is clear, concise, and easy to grasp risk having their messaging forgotten amidst the constant barrage of content that social media users encounter every day. Given the short attention spans of today's audiences, messaging that misses the mark can make it difficult for businesses to cut through the noise and capture their audience's attention.

Because social media is a public platform, any message that is poorly written, offensive or inaccurate can quickly go viral and damage the reputation of the brand. This can be particularly damaging for small businesses or startups, who may not have the resources to manage a PR crisis.

To make sure your social media marketing messaging hits the mark, get to know your audience inside and out. Take the time to research and understand their pain points, values, interests, and preferences so that you can create messaging that resonates with them and speaks directly to their needs. Remember, you have just seconds to grab your audience's attention, so make sure your messaging is clear, concise, and easy to understand. Avoid using jargon or overly complex language that might confuse or bore people.

You might also want to consider incorporating visual content into your messaging. Visual content is a particularly powerful way to capture people's attention and convey your message quickly. Incorporate eye-catching graphics, images, or videos that support your messaging and make your content stand out from the crowd. Another way of improving your messaging is to tell a story. People love stories, and they're a great way to create an emotional connection with your audience. Use storytelling techniques to create messaging that is compelling, memorable, and shares a relatable human experience.

INADEQUATE ENGAGEMENT

Individuals who are inexperienced in social media marketing might assume that constantly churning out content is all it takes to engage with their audience. However, engaging with your audience is a critical two-way street that requires actively monitoring and responding to comments and messages, nurturing dialogue, and demonstrating a sincere willingness to connect. Failing to recognise this can alienate your customers and make your social media presence seem inauthentic.

Imagine a scenario where a customer reaches out, seeking guidance or clarification, only to be met with silence. As their frustration builds, so does their perception of your indifference. Ignoring comments, messages, and inquiries can imply a lack of interest in the very people your business aims to serve. When customers feel that their voices are not being heard or that their issues are not being addressed, they may choose to disengage from your brand. Worse still, they may leave negative feedback or complaints, which can significantly impact your brand's reputation.

To develop a thriving social media presence, businesses must embrace the art of engagement. This means actively monitoring social media channels, responding promptly to inquiries, and creating an environment that encourages dialogue. It involves empathetically addressing concerns, celebrating positive feedback, and proactively seeking opportunities to connect with your audience.

LACK OF CONTENT STRATEGY

A common stumbling block for individuals who lack experience in digital marketing is the absence of a well-thought-out content strategy. Without a clear plan in place, it's like shooting in the dark and hoping to hit the bullseye. Creating compelling content that resonates with your audience and drives conversions requires a strategic approach. Every piece of content you produce should serve a purpose and contribute to your overall objectives. Whether it's increasing brand awareness, driving website traffic, or generating leads, your content should have a clear intention behind it. Without this alignment, you risk producing content that fails to make a meaningful impact.

But it's not just about your business goals – you also need to consider your audience's interests. Understanding your target audience is key to crafting content that captures their attention and keeps them coming back for more. What are their pain points, aspirations, and preferences? By diving deep into their world, you can create content that speaks directly to them, addressing their needs and desires. Without this audience-centric approach, your content may fall flat, failing to engage and resonate with the very people you're trying to reach.

An effective content strategy also involves consistency and variety. It's not just about churning out content for the sake of it – it's about delivering a cohesive and diverse mix that captures your audience's attention. By planning your content in advance and following a content calendar, you can ensure a steady stream of valuable and relevant material. This way, you stay on top of your game and avoid the sporadic bursts of content that can confuse and disengage your audience.

Social media platforms constantly change, and what works today might not work tomorrow. Thus, it's crucial to continually monitor and analyse the results of social media marketing campaigns to adapt and refine them based on the latest trends and insights.

By aligning your content strategy with your business goals, understanding your audience, maintaining consistency, and leveraging data, you can create content that truly hits the mark, engages your audience, and drives the conversions you're after.

In both adventure and business, it is important to recognise and acknowledge that we all have areas where our expertise is limited.

When venturing out on a daring expedition or exploring uncharted territories, being aware of your limitations can mean the difference between life and death. It's important to differentiate between calculated risk-taking and reckless behaviour driven by an inflated sense of competence. By acknowledging your skill gaps and seeking guidance from experienced individuals, you can navigate challenges and uncertainties with caution and ensure your safety.

Succeeding in business hinges on strategic decision-making, effective planning, and a comprehensive understanding of one's market and industry. Failing to recognise the boundaries of our own expertise can result in poor judgment, misguided strategies, and potential financial losses. By acknowledging our areas of weakness, we can build teams of talented individuals who possess the necessary skills, leverage their expertise, and make more informed decisions.

Always remember that it's far better to approach challenges with a realistic evaluation of your skills rather than being blindsided by the dangers that await those who overestimate their abilities. Take stock of your competencies and knowledge, identify areas where improvement is needed, and actively seek opportunities for growth through education, mentorship, and hands-on experience. Surround yourself with individuals who possess expertise in areas where you may be lacking and remain open to their guidance and insights.

CHAPTER 4
BLACK SWAN EVENTS

n 2013, Kim and I set our sights on conquering Mount Elbrus, the highest mountain in Europe and one of the renowned Seven Summits. This majestic double-coned volcano, standing at 5,642m, is nestled in the Caucasus mountains of southwestern Russia, near the Georgian border. Aware of the dangers of attempting any of the Seven Summits in winter – especially Mount Elbrus, known for its severe storms – we scheduled our expedition for the summer.

Our base camp on Mount Elbrus was Garabashi-Bochki, also known as the Barrels Huts, situated at 3,750 metres. This location has historical significance: a Russian military base during WWII, operating as a strategic outpost for the Soviet military to monitor the region and alert against enemy movements. Nowadays, climbers find shelter here in barrel-like metal huts specifically designed to ward off wind and snow, providing a semblance of warmth against the biting cold.

Mountain climbing, for all its exhilarating rewards, is fraught with risks, from natural threats like avalanches to the physiological challenges of hypothermia, hypoxia, and Acute Mountain Sickness (AMS). Tragically, between 15-30 climbers lose their lives on Mount

Elbrus annually, with inclement weather, poor visibility, and inadequate acclimatisation often to blame.

The body's ability to process oxygen varies from person to person, making some climbers more susceptible to AMS than others. Even elite athletes like tennis superstar Martina Navratilova aren't spared – she was unable to conquer Kilimanjaro due to her body's inability to handle reduced oxygen levels.

For those unfamiliar with AMS, it's a dangerous condition that manifests in three stages. Stage One is mild, with the body reacting to reduced oxygen levels, causing symptoms like headaches, fatigue, or slight nausea. Rest and hydration normally alleviates these symptoms. Stage Two is more severe, where a climber might lose their balance and experience severe headaches, vomiting, and nausea. It's in this stage that a person's pupils begin to dilate – a telltale sign of compromised cognition. Immediate descending to a lower elevation, as well as rest and hydration, can help alleviate this stage. Stage Three, High-Altitude Cerebral Edema (HACE), is the most dangerous. This life-threatening condition manifests when brain capillaries start to leak, causing fluid accumulation and brain swelling. The skull is unable to expand, so the brain begins to compress itself. Presenting as full-blown psychosis, a climber may start entertaining dangerous delusions, such as believing they can fly or acting aggressively towards fellow climbers. This is why it's essential always to climb with someone you'd trust your life with.

A quick flashlight check on a climbing partner's pupils can reveal whether they're progressing towards Stage Two of AMS. If they hit Stage Three, their survival chances plummet dramatically. An injection of a hormone called dexamethasone can be administered at Stage Two to counteract AMS, but if someone reaches Stage Three, it's usually too late – unless immediate evacuation with medical assistance is available.

For the sake of accuracy, I should also mention that mountaineers may experience HAPE, or high-altitude pulmonary edema. This condition leads to increased pressure in the pulmonary arteries, causing fluid to leak back into the lungs. Extreme shortness of breath, persistent coughing, or bloody sputum, as well as hallucinations, may be experienced. Once again, immediate descent and oxygen administration are required.

To ward off AMS, many mountaineers take Diamox. Initially developed for glaucoma patients to reduce eye fluid pressure and optical nerve swelling, this prescription drug has proven useful in preventing brain swelling during high-altitude climbs. But there's a catch. Diamox is a potent diuretic, which means climbers must drink at least six litres (1.6 gal) of fluid daily to offset the dehydration. Climbers take their Diamox in the morning and afternoon only to avoid the inconvenience of having to empty one's bladder at night. It's hardly difficult to imagine the ordeal of venturing out of your tent in the middle of the night, in complete darkness and sub-zero temperatures, bladder bursting. In such situations, everything – and I truly mean everything – freezes.

To prepare our bodies for the ascent and guard against AMS, we followed a daily regimen of 'climb high, sleep low'. For every thousand metres climbed, lung function drops by about 9% depending on the individual climber. Barometric pressure drops 12% for every 1000m increase in elevation. At 5,000 metres, it's like breathing with one lung. On Everest, it's even worse. The key to successful climbing is acclimatisation: push your body to a higher altitude each day, then let it rest at a slightly lower altitude to boost its oxygen levels. The more altitude you gain each day, the smoother the following day's climb becomes. But continuously ascending without allowing your body to recover is asking for trouble. Our strategy, therefore, was to climb at least 500m more than the previous day's elevation every day.

We only had six days within which to do our summit push. If we couldn't reach the summit in those six days, we had to make our way down. We were snowed in from day one, and the summit was closed, so we remained at base camp, waiting for a break. It was quite tiring being cooped up in a closed, tight space with the rest of our climbing team. We had no way of communicating with the outside world. Every day was the same – wake up, eat breakfast, go on an acclimatisation climb, come back for lunch, read a book, eat dinner, go to sleep, rinse, and repeat.

At around four o'clock in the afternoon, on one of our acclimatisation climbs, an unexpected snow storm with howling 55-knot winds engulfed us as we were making our descent. The satellite forecast for the next 18 to 24 hours hadn't hinted at anything of this magnitude. Although it was midsummer, this storm felt as if it had been pulled from the depths of winter.

The landscape around us morphed into an indistinguishable white canvas, blurring the lines between land and sky. Even though we were standing on a flat section, we couldn't tell left from right or up from down. The markers on the mountain, our guiding poles, had been swallowed by the swirling snow, turning every step into a potential plunge off the cliff face. Disoriented by the blinding whiteout, the biting cold became more pronounced as the temperature plummeted from the predicted minus 6 degrees Celcius to minus 30 degrees, cutting straight through our survival gear.

"I can't feel my hand," said Kim, her voice shaking. The pain was evident on her face. She was losing sensation in her right hand, her fingers were stiffening from the cold, and her ice axe lay discarded at her feet. If we didn't act quickly, it was only a matter of time before frostbite set in. Our preparations hadn't accounted for a storm of this magnitude. It was a double shot of death on the rocks.

I knew we were in grave danger. We needed to evacuate, and fast.

Fortunately, Vlad had a working cell phone. We huddled behind a rocky outcrop and called through to the Russian base station, requesting an urgent evacuation. "We'll come," they confirmed, but the price they quoted for the rescue was eye-watering, and they wanted an upfront financial commitment before they would leave the base. This might seem cold-hearted, but I've always seen Russians as pragmatists. Take their AK-47, for example. This 70-year-old assault rifle remains a top choice due to its simplicity and reliability – it can be stripped and fixed in the field with *bloudraad* (barbed wire), duct tape, and a cable tie. In contrast, the over-engineered American M-16 rifle requires consistent care and attention. In high-stakes scenarios, you need dependability, not sophistication. This is the Russian ethos: always ready to assist, albeit for a price. But you can't put a price on a human life, and I would have gladly paid ten times the asking amount.

About an hour later, the distinctive hum of a Snowcat – a powerful tank-like vehicle with large yellow rotating lights – filled the air. Unlike conventional vehicles, Snowcats are driven using instruments guided solely by pre-plotted GPS coordinates. Thanks to this technology, they could reach us safely at zero visibility without the risk of veering off a cliff.

There was no way we could have made it back down to base camp alive without that call, without the Snowcat, and without the Russians agreeing to come. That harrowing experience was the closest we've ever come to catastrophic death on any expedition.

The entire ordeal was a classic black swan event. A series of unpredictable events – the sudden storm, gale-force winds, blinding visibility, plummeting temperatures, and Kim's freezing hand – were layers aligning for potential disaster. Everything that happened was a slice of cheese filled with holes, each one aligning catastrophically. We were one disaster away from the point of no return. It was only the arrival of the Snowcat that prevented the last disastrous slice from falling into place.

With just one day left in our six-day summit window, the weather cleared a little. Relentless snowstorms over the past week had made the mountain's peak inaccessible. Our guides had no idea whether the lines were still intact, what the conditions were like up there, or even if it was safe to make the ascent, but this was our last shot. They made the call: we were going to push for the summit. However, the mutual understanding was that if the summit seemed too dangerous upon closer inspection, we would abort the mission.

Summits are day-long affairs. A round trip – reaching the summit and returning to base – typically takes up to 16 hours. Every climber dreams of standing at the summit and basking in the glory of conquest. Yet, in the unpredictable world of mountaineering, there are moments when the dream is within arm's reach, but one has to make a life-or-death decision. Although the summit is less than a kilometre vertically from base camp, the ascent takes a gruelling 12 hours. Compared to a mere four-hour descent, it's those final metres before the summit that can be the most dangerous.

We turned in early that afternoon and awoke at eleven that evening. At midnight, our team – which consisted of Kim and myself, Gareth from Scotland, and our Russian expedition leader, Vlad – set out in the dark of night, the ice crunching beneath our feet, the wind howling, and the snow swirling around us. Our plan was to summit by midday so that we could be back down at base camp before nightfall.

Our path, lit by a sea of headlamps, formed a horseshoe-shaped curve around the mountain. The slope was too steep for a direct ascent, forcing us to climb diagonally. We joined a long queue of climbers, forming a human snake inching its way up the mountain.

The elements showed no mercy. Persistent wind and snow battered us. The only way to keep from tumbling down the mountain was to tread sideways. Each step involved lodging our ice picks into the slope, taking a secure step forward with our crampon-clad boots, and then repeating the process. All the while, we leaned into the mountain, our bodies pressed against the snowy surface. Standing upright was a temptation we couldn't afford to give in to. The winds were strong enough to blow us off the mountain if we did. The climb was painstakingly slow, a constant battle against nature's fury.

At about 10 a.m., we caught our first glimpse of the summit. Almost simultaneously, a violent gust of wind whipped around the mountain, seizing a climber just 100 metres ahead of us. In a horrifying instant, he was lifted into the air and flung off the mountain. We clung to the slope, watching in horror as he rolled nearly 1,000 metres down the slope until his body finally came to rest in the distant valley below.

The shock of witnessing such a tragic incident took our breath away. For a moment, it seemed as though time had stopped, the furious winds rendered mute, the harsh cold seeming to fade into insignificance. We looked at each other in silent understanding. This was it – the merciless reality of our choice to attempt this climb, a stark reminder of how one miscalculated step could spell the end. We all silently agreed to push forward, a collective determination guiding us. Vlad kept us moving, his experienced leadership anchoring our shaken spirits.

The final metres to the summit were a blur of wind, snow, and sheer determination. Step by painstaking step, we pulled ourselves up the face of the mountain. We were on borrowed time. It wasn't just about reaching the top – it was about making it back down alive. We summited at noon. We had done it – against all odds. With only a brief moment to take in the view, we were quickly roped together and began our descent. The steep, icy slopes, which seemed daunting while climbing, now posed a dangerous obstacle course, one we had to navigate to survive. We arrived back at the Barrels Huts at dusk, exhausted but alive.

As we looked back on the events of the past few days, we realised how perilously close we had come to losing our lives. Twice, we had been on the brink, the icy touch of death brushing past us. We had known from the start that there was a chance things could go wrong. We had been prepared – mentally and physically – for this expedition. Yet, what we had encountered was a stark lesson in humility. Nature, in all its grandeur and wrath, reminded us of its power, a force we could never truly conquer. It drove home the reality that no matter how well-prepared we believe we are, the mountain always has the final say. It was a reality check, emphasising that while there's always a chance something could go wrong, one can only hope to be prepared enough to survive it.

A BLACK SWAN EVENT

The term 'black swan event' finds its roots in the Latin phrase, "*rara avis in terris nigroque simillima cygno*", which means "a rare bird on the earth, very much like a black swan". This phrase, which emerged between 100 and 130 AD, signified something believed to be impossible or non-existent. This was largely because, for centuries, the prevailing belief in Europe was that all swans were white. Every historical record and portrayal of swans confirmed this belief. But in 1697, an unprecedented discovery was made when European explorers, navigating the Swan River in Western Australia, chanced upon black swans for the first time. This unexpected encounter challenged a long-standing assumption and introduced the world to the concept of a 'black swan event'.

The idea was catapulted into mainstream awareness by Wall Street trader Nassim Nicholas Taleb in his 2007 book, *The Black Swan: The Impact of the Highly Improbable*. In it, Taleb enumerates three crucial criteria defining black swan events:

1. Their rarity and unexpected nature. Such events catch us off guard, defy our usual expectations, and have a low likelihood of taking place based on historical data or commonly held beliefs.

2. Their significant impact on society, markets, or a specific system. Their consequences are typically large-scale with far-reaching consequences, disrupting established structures, beliefs, or systems.

3. Their seeming predictability in hindsight. Although they are nearly impossible to predict in advance, we often find ourselves rationalising and explaining them as if they were foreseeable all along.

Notable examples of black swan events that meet these criteria include the dot-com bubble and the 9/11 terrorist attacks of 2001, the 2008 Global Financial Crisis, the Fukushima nuclear disaster in 2011, and the Covid pandemic of 2020. While all the signs that these events might take place were there, most people had not contemplated their actual unfolding.

Looking back at our experience on Mount Elbrus, it is clear that two black swan events took place. Both met Taleb's criteria: they were unforeseen, impactful, and, in hindsight, seemed predictable. For example, it's always possible for a storm to hit or for conditions to worsen rapidly in high-altitude settings. The first was when we were caught in an unforeseen snow storm with extremely powerful winds and a drastic temperature drop. The satellite forecast did not predict such a storm, especially given that it was summer. This storm rendered our surroundings completely unrecognisable, jeopardising our safety. The second was the tragic death of the climber in the group ahead of us. While everyone knew the climb was perilous, witnessing a fellow climber suddenly getting lifted by the wind and thrown off the mountain was shocking and unpredictable.

Black swan events, much like arctic storms, tend to creep up on us. In the case of a crisis, it's generally a low-intensity problem that remains unrecognised – or, at best, minimised – for a significant period of time. Think about a famine. Every year, people will convince themselves that the following year, the rains will come, and the crops will flourish. The seasons change, and the months drag on, but there is still no rain. Eventually, the scale of the problem is so enormous that an entire population is on the brink of starvation.

As history has shown, it's remarkable how such unexpected events can shake things up in ways that far exceed what we could have imagined. When we look back at the global financial crisis of 2008, for example, big-name firms like Lehman Brothers, Citibank, Bear Stearns, and AIG were always seen as too big to fail. But even their risk vs value models couldn't predict the chaos caused by the subprime mortgage meltdown. According to Taleb's theory, banks, insurance companies, and trading firms are the ones most at risk when unexpected events, like black swan events, hit. And let's face it, their financial losses were way worse than their business models ever saw coming.

BLACK SWAN EVENTS IN OVERLANDING AND ADVENTURE

Anyone bold enough to embark on an epic African overlanding journey knows that while the allure of breathtaking encounters, awe-inspiring landscapes, and life-changing experiences beckons, these epic journeys can also throw plenty of challenges and surprises their way. Overlanders are no strangers to planning and preparing for various scenarios before embarking on their trips, envisioning potential obstacles, and equipping themselves accordingly.

In the context of overlanding, black swan events can manifest in various forms, much like the Arctic storms on Mount Elbrus. These events, exceeding the range of normal expectations, can catch even the most prepared overlanders off guard, testing their resilience, adaptability, and resourcefulness. They might include sudden and extreme weather changes that leave them exposed and scrambling for shelter, political instability that disrupts the path they planned to take, road or border closures that force them to find alternative routes, unexpected vehicle breakdowns that demand quick problem-solving skills, or unforeseen health emergencies that require immediate action.

THE IMPORTANCE OF BLACK SWAN EVENT AWARENESS

Any traveller who sets out on an overlanding adventure without being aware of what might go wrong along the way is asking for trouble. While black swan events can be difficult to predict, maintaining a constant state of awareness and preparedness helps overlanders better navigate the unpredictable nature of their journeys, minimise risks, and be equipped to handle just about any unexpected situations that might come their way.

SAFETY

Safety risks are part of the package for every overlander. From challenging road conditions to far-flung remote locations and limited emergency services, overlanders are no strangers to the challenges that might lie ahead. While you can't predict every eventuality, you can improve the safety of yourself and your fellow passengers and travellers by having contingency plans in place. This could involve carrying emergency supplies, preparing alternative routes or transportation options, and establishing a robust communication system among fellow travellers.

PREPAREDNESS

Embracing the possibility of black swan events goes beyond simply packing the right gear and provisions – it extends to acquiring a deep understanding of the regions you'll be venturing into. Familiarising yourself with local customs, traditions and etiquette, regional languages, terrain, and potential hazards along the way will enhance your understanding of the road ahead.

For instance, you can familiarise yourself with basic phrases in the local language to enhance communication and foster connections with the people you meet along the way. Study potential hazards specific to the regions you'll be passing through. Is there a risk of encountering wildlife on the roads? Are there certain areas known for political instability or challenging road conditions? By arming yourself with this knowledge, you can make informed decisions about routes, know what precautions to take, and be prepared to adapt if unexpected situations arise.

Comprehensive preparation encompasses not only the physical aspects of the journey but also the mental aspects. Mental preparedness plays an important role in handling high-stress situations. By remaining calm and focused and maintaining a solution-oriented mindset, you will be better equipped to manage the stress and focus on finding a solution. For example, imagine you are deep into your overland expedition, exploring a remote region known for its rugged terrain and limited infrastructure. As you navigate a challenging mountain pass, your vehicle suddenly encounters a mechanical failure, leaving you stranded in an unfamiliar and isolated location.

In this high-stress situation, several factors come into play. First, the isolation and limited access to assistance amplify the sense of urgency and the need to rely on your own resources. The absence of immediate help adds to the pressure of the situation. Second, the harsh environment and unpredictable weather conditions further heighten the stress. Whether it's extreme temperatures, heavy rainfall, or high-altitude conditions, the elements become additional challenges to contend with while dealing with the vehicle breakdown. Third, the limited communication options in remote areas can intensify the stress. With patchy or non-existent cell phone reception, you may have trouble reaching out for help or relaying your situation to others.

In such a high-stress scenario, mental preparedness plays a crucial role. Remaining calm and focused is paramount. By leveraging your thorough preparation, you assess the situation, utilising your survival and vehicle repair expertise to diagnose the issue and attempt to resolve it independently. Your mental resilience also enables you to manage stress and anxiety, allowing you to think clearly and prioritise your actions. You might decide to consult maps, use navigation tools, and draw upon your contingency planning to determine where to find shelter or assistance. By tapping into your resourcefulness, you might explore alternative solutions such as signalling passing vehicles or finding nearby settlements where locals might offer assistance or alternative communication options.

By maintaining a composed mindset, leveraging your preparedness, and relying on your problem-solving abilities, you navigate this high-stress situation with determination and resilience. Ultimately, you overcome the challenge, either resolving the vehicle issue or finding the necessary help to get back on track.

ADAPTABILITY, FLEXIBILITY AND RESILIENCE

Overlanders understand that unpredictability lurks around every corner, poised to disrupt even the most meticulously laid plans. As such, the qualities of adaptability, flexibility, and resilience are essential, especially in the face of a black swan event.

One of the fundamental qualities honed through overlanding is the ability to adapt and remain flexible. Overlanders learn to think on their feet and make the most of the resources at their disposal to find creative solutions to problems. An adaptable person can quickly assess a situation, modify their approach, and find innovative solutions when faced with unexpected events. When encountering a road closure due to heavy rains or landslides, for example, they would quickly assess the situation and explore alternative routes. They might consult maps, seek advice from locals, or leverage GPS technology to identify a detour that will get them to their intended destination.

Equally important is flexibility. Routes may need to be altered due to road closures, weather conditions, or other unforeseen circumstances. Overlanders recognise that routes may need to be altered due to road closures, weather conditions, or other unforeseen circumstances. Embracing these changes and being open to alternative options allows them to make the most of their journey. It also gives them an opportunity to discover hidden gems and forge new connections with people and places they may not have encountered otherwise.

Perhaps most importantly, overlanding demands a resilient spirit. Unexpected challenges can test even the most seasoned of travellers. The ability to bounce back, stay motivated, and maintain a positive mindset is essential in overcoming adversity. Resilience enables over-landers to persevere through even the most trying of circumstances, find creative solutions to problems, and learn valuable lessons from their experiences. By reflecting on their own experiences and those of others, they can gain insights that shape their future expeditions. This knowledge will help them anticipate potential challenges and develop more robust strategies for managing the unexpected.

STRATEGIES FOR ADDRESSING BLACK SWAN EVENTS

CONDUCT THOROUGH RESEARCH

Conducting thorough research is a crucial step before embarking on your expedition. By immersing yourself in the information you have available, you will gain a comprehensive understanding of your planned route and destinations. This research involves delving into various aspects of the trip, such as potential hazards, historical weather patterns, political stability, and the experiences of previous travellers.

By gathering information on potential hazards, you will be aware of specific challenges you might encounter along the way. This includes natural obstacles like treacherous terrains, river crossings, or extreme weather conditions. It also involves identifying potential risks related to wildlife encounters or specific regions known for security concerns. Armed with this knowledge, you can make informed decisions, adjust your routes if necessary, and take appropriate precautions to mitigate any potential risks.

Understanding historical weather patterns important, as it enables you to anticipate and prepare for weather-related challenges. Whether it's planning for heavy rains, extreme heat, or freezing temperatures, being aware of seasonal trends and weather patterns in the regions you'll traverse allows you to pack the right gear and make appropriate arrangements. For example, if you are travelling through an area known for its unpredictable weather patterns, including sudden thunderstorms, you can ensure you have adequate rain gear and waterproof equipment. You might invest in quality rain jackets, waterproof backpack covers, and waterproof storage bags to protect your belongings. Additionally, you may choose to pack extra tarps or a sturdy tent that can withstand heavy rain.

Keeping tabs on the political stability of the areas you plan to visit is also crucial. You should stay informed about any ongoing conflicts, civil unrest, or security risks that may impact your safety so that you can make well-informed decisions regarding your route choices, potential detours, or other necessary precautions to ensure you don't find yourself in a situation where your personal safety is at risk.

Learning from the experiences of previous travellers is also invaluable. By tapping into their collective wisdom, you can gain insights into the challenges and unexpected events you might encounter. You can explore online forums, read travel blogs or guidebooks, and engage with fellow overlanders to learn about their first-hand experiences. This information will help you identify potential black swan events specific to your chosen route and prepare accordingly.

ENGAGE WITH LOCAL COMMUNITIES

Engaging with local communities is a crucial aspect of overlanding expeditions. Local communities possess a deep understanding of their surroundings, including regional conditions and potential risks that may arise. When travelling through remote areas where conventional sources of information may be limited, reaching out to locals can provide you with first-hand accounts of recent developments. They can inform you about road closures, alternative routes, or any other factors that may impact your journey. This knowledge can help you make informed decisions about your routes and itinerary, ensuring a smoother and safer expedition.

Local communities will often have extensive knowledge of weather patterns specific to their region. They can provide you with valuable insights about sudden weather changes, seasonal conditions known for extreme weather, or natural phenomena that may affect your journey. This information will allow you to prepare adequately, such as carrying appropriate gear or adjusting your travel plans to avoid adverse weather conditions.

Local communities can also offer invaluable advice on safety concerns specific to the area you're travelling through. They may share insights on avoiding certain areas due to potential hazards, such as unstable terrain, high crime rates, or areas prone to natural disasters. Additionally, they can provide precautions to take during wildlife encounters, such as how to minimise the risk of confrontations or where to find safe camping spots.

TRAIN FOR THE UNEXPECTED

In addition to preparing your vehicle and equipment, it's important that you take the time to engage in scenario-based exercises that simulate unexpected situations. These exercises can help prepare you mentally and emotionally for unexpected events you may encounter during your expedition and develop critical problem-solving and decision-making skills necessary for navigating any unforeseen challenges.

Scenario-based exercises allow overlanders to encounter and tackle a wide range of problems that may arise during their journey. These exercises simulate real-life situations such as vehicle breakdowns, getting stuck in challenging terrain, or encountering extreme weather conditions. By engaging in these exercises, you can practice problem-solving techniques, evaluate different options, and develop the ability to think creatively and adapt to unexpected circumstances.

Overlanders often have to make critical decisions under enormous pressure. Scenario-based training exercises also provide an opportunity to practice decision-making in a controlled environment. You can simulate scenarios where you need to make decisions related to navigation, route planning, safety concerns, or emergencies. Through these exercises, you can learn to assess risks, gather relevant information, and make informed decisions.

Overland journeys often involve travelling in groups or pairs. Effective communication and teamwork are crucial for handling unexpected situations smoothly. Scenario-based exercises can include group simulations where overlanders need to coordinate actions, share information, and work together to overcome challenges. These exercises enhance communication skills, foster teamwork, and promote a better understanding of each team member's strengths and abilities.

Black swan events can be stressful and overwhelming. Engaging in scenario-based exercises will give you an opportunity to experience simulated stressful situations and practice managing your emotions and stress levels. By learning techniques to stay calm, think clearly, and prioritise tasks during these exercises, you can develop resilience and the ability to effectively handle similar real-world high-pressure situations.

MASTER THE ART OF OVERLAND COMMUNICATION

Establishing effective communication is a critical strategy for overlanders when it comes to addressing unforeseen events during their journeys. When travelling in groups, maintaining clear and open communication with fellow travellers is essential. Before starting the journey, establish a communication protocol within your group. This plan should include designated frequencies or channels for walkie-talkies, emergency contact numbers, and a system for regular check-ins or scheduled updates. Make sure that all members of the group are familiar with the communication plan and understand how to use the designated equipment. Regularly practising communication procedures can help streamline the process and ensure everyone is prepared to address unforeseen events effectively. By establishing effective communication channels within the group, you can quickly share information, exchange updates, and collaborate on navigating unexpected challenges.

It is also important to actively engage and communicate with local communities. Engaging with locals not only provides valuable insights, as discussed earlier, but also establishes a line of communication that can prove invaluable during unforeseen events. Developing a respectful and friendly rapport with the locals increases your chances of receiving timely and relevant assistance when it's needed the most.

From a technological perspective, it's crucial to carry appropriate communication devices with you. Access to smartphones, tablets, or dedicated GPS navigation systems that offer connectivity options can provide you with real-time information, weather updates, navigation assistance, and communication with emergency services if required. However, it's important to note that relying solely on technology may not always be feasible in remote areas with limited or no network coverage, so it's essential to have alternative means of communication as well, such as satellite phones or emergency beacons. These devices will allow you to reach out for help in case of emergencies or unexpected situations where standard means of communication may not be available. It's important to ensure that these devices are in good working condition, adequately charged, and easily accessible when needed.

PARALLELS BETWEEN BLACK SWAN EVENTS IN OVERLANDING AND ADVENTURE TRAVEL AND BUSINESS

Despite the differences in context, there are clear parallels between black swan events in overlanding and adventure travel and those that take place in the business world. Both face the potential for unforeseen and disruptive events that can have significant impacts on their operations and outcomes. These parallels are evident in their unpredictability, extreme impact, and the need for adaptability in the face of adversity. Both realms require individuals and organisations to navigate uncharted territories, respond swiftly to challenges, and find ways to mitigate the consequences of these unforeseen events. In both cases, the ability to adapt, make informed decisions, and effectively manage risks is crucial for survival and long-term resilience.

Let's dive a little deeper into these similarities.

UNPREDICTABILITY

Imagine standing on the edge of the Moremi Game Reserve in the Okavango Delta. The landscape is a shifting spectacle of wetlands and woodlands, floodplains, and lagoons. It's a place you've never been before, a place that's vast, unpredictable, and fraught with unknown risks. Now imagine embarking on an adventure through it without a map, without a guide, and without any prior knowledge of what lies ahead. You'd be faced with the very real possibility of stumbling upon a 'black swan'. It might be a sudden encounter with a potentially dangerous animal while travelling in a mokoro along the delta's intricate waterways – hippos and crocodiles, and anyone who has encountered one will attest to this – can be dangerous when disturbed. In an effort to escape, and without a knowledgeable guide or reliable GPS system, you might find yourself lost in its complex network of channels. These are things that you can't predict or control. They're things that force you to react and adapt in the moment. They challenge your resilience, your problem-solving skills, and your capacity to make quick decisions.

Now consider the realm of business. It's not much different. Just as adventurers embark on expeditions with a certain level of risk, businesses operate in an environment where unforeseen events can occur. While precautions and risk management strategies can be put in place, the sheer magnitude and nature of black swan events make their prediction and prevention challenging. Economic downturns, disruptive technologies, regulatory changes, and global pandemics are the black swan events of the business world. And like their adventure counterparts, they demand adaptability, resilience, and quick decision-making.

Unpredictability, in both adventure and business, is a given. In adventure, as in business, those who succeed are not those who try to predict or control the black swan events but those who prepare themselves to navigate through them. These individuals understand that the key to success is not to avoid unpredictability but to develop the resilience and adaptability necessary to thrive within it.

EXTREME IMPACT

Black swan events possess an inherent propensity to unleash a shockwave of disruption, reverberating through the realms of adventure and business. In adventure, these seismic disturbances manifest in the form of natural disasters or unexpected challenges that push adventurers to their limits. Similarly, in the world of business, black swan events materialise as economic crises, technological breakthroughs, or unforeseen shifts in consumer behaviour, shattering the status quo, often with profound repercussions.

The parallels between adventure and business black swan events lie in their profound impact. In adventure, these events can pose immediate threats to the lives and safety of the individuals involved. Likewise, in business, black swan events can have dire consequences for companies, industries, and even economies. They often result in significant financial losses, market volatility, and a cascading effect that affects various stakeholders.

It is worth noting that while black swan events that take place when overlanding or adventuring tend to be isolated incidents affecting a specific group of individuals, business black swan events can have widespread consequences, impacting the lives and livelihoods of many.

RETROSPECTIVE PREDICTABILITY

Black swan events, whether experienced in adventurous pursuits or in the business world, share interesting parallels when it comes to retrospective predictability. This means that after the event occurs, it may be possible to identify certain signs or indicators that, if recognised beforehand, could have predicted the occurrence of the event.

For instance, a mountaineer might set out to conquer an uncharted peak, but despite careful preparation and planning, a sudden storm or an avalanche could endanger the climber's life. In hindsight, there may have been faint indications like changing weather patterns or unstable terrain that could have indicated the possibility of such a disaster. However, due to the elusive nature of black swan events, these signs often only become apparent after the fact.

Similarly, in the business world, a business might face an unforeseen economic downturn, a disruptive technological innovation, unforeseen regulatory changes, or a catastrophic event like a natural disaster or a global pandemic. These events can have far-reaching consequences, such as a sharp decline in revenue, the obsolescence of products or services, or the need for immediate emergency response and recovery efforts. Once again, upon reflection, there may have been subtle indications or market trends that hinted at the potential for such an event, which could have given the business time to prepare itself for it. For instance, shifts in consumer behaviour could have signalled an impending disruption that, if identified earlier, could have guided the business to adapt its strategy. However, these signals are often overlooked or dismissed as unlikely until the event actually happens.

The parallel between adventure and business lies in the fact that both domains can benefit from retrospective analysis to identify the factors that may have hinted at the occurrence of black swan events. In adventure, this analysis can contribute to better risk management and preparedness for future expeditions. In business, retrospective predictability allows organisations to enhance their strategic planning, risk assessment, and contingency plans to navigate and mitigate the impact of similar black swan events in the future.

STRATEGIES FOR ADDRESSING BLACK SWAN EVENTS IN BUSINESS

Although humans might, at times, prefer to discount the future, there is ample evidence that we are able to plan and prepare for the future when we feel compelled to do so. You don't have to look far for examples – financial planning, education and skills development, health and wellness, environmental sustainability, long-term investments, and complex insurance policies for unforeseen eventualities all bear testament to the fact that planning for the long term is not beyond our capabilities.

Black swan events, whether they take place during a daring expedition in a remote part of the world or the confines of the concrete jungle, often emerge as vivid reminders of the fragility of our existence and tend to trigger a profound shift in thinking and approach. In adventure, these events force explorers to adapt quickly, reassess their strategies, and make life-saving decisions. In business, organisations must quickly adapt to the new reality, re-evaluate their business models, and implement innovative measures to mitigate the impact.

Black swan events have a lot to teach us. They provide valuable lessons that can help us prepare for the future. Here are a few ways we can learn from these events:

BUILD RESILIENCE THROUGH PREPAREDNESS

Black swan events are a poignant reminder of how important it is to be prepared for the unexpected. By looking at past events, we can find patterns or triggers that point to these events. This knowledge helps us improve our preparedness by putting contingency plans in place, building robust systems, and diversifying our resources, thereby reducing the risks associated with, for instance, relying on a single market, product, supplier, or area of expertise.

During and after COVID-19, for example, many businesses' emergency preparedness and response systems came into sharp focus, with many putting systems and processes in place so they might better identify and plan for other future emergencies before they caught them off guard again, whether they materialised or not.

One business that enhanced its emergency preparedness and response systems in the wake of the COVID-19 pandemic is Airbnb. As a global accommodation marketplace heavily impacted by travel restrictions and lockdown measures, Airbnb quickly adapted its approach to better identify and plan for future emergencies. Recognising the need to mitigate potential risks and provide reassurance to both hosts and guests, Airbnb implemented its "Enhanced Cleaning Protocol", establishing strict cleanliness and safety standards for hosts to follow, including specific guidelines for sanitisation and disinfection.

It also introduced flexible cancellation policies, allowing guests to modify or cancel reservations without penalties in response to changing travel restrictions or personal circumstances. This measure demonstrated the business's commitment to accommodating the evolving needs of its users during uncertain times.

ASSESS AND REDUCE RISKS

By studying the consequences and impacts of black swan events, we can improve our risk assessment processes. We can identify weaknesses and vulnerabilities in our systems and take action to address potential risks. By identifying the areas that are most at risk, we can take steps to reduce the effects of future disruptions and minimise their impact.

The COVID-19 pandemic served as a wake-up call for businesses worldwide, exposing vulnerabilities in their operations and supply chains. It became crucial to re-evaluate their risk assessment strategies, including identifying areas that needed improvement. Manufacturing companies that depended heavily on a single supplier for critical components, for example, quickly realised that should a black swan event like a pandemic (or even a natural disaster or geopolitical unrest) disrupt this supplier's operations, this would have a significant impact on the company's production capabilities. By understanding the risks associated with relying on a single supplier, many of these companies took proactive measures to reduce their vulnerability and minimise the impact of potential disruptions in the future. After the pandemic, many diversified their supplier bases, explored alternative sourcing options, and even considered internal production capabilities.

STAY FLEXIBLE AND ADAPTABLE

The COVID-19 pandemic highlighted the importance of being flexible and adaptable. Businesses with rigid structures and fixed mindsets struggled to navigate the unexpected challenges it brought.

However, there were businesses that thrived by taking advantage of new opportunities that arose from the disruption. The COVID-19 pandemic demonstrated that businesses that are flexible, adaptable, and willing to challenge conventional thinking can respond more effectively to unforeseen circumstances. They have the ability to find creative solutions and identify new opportunities that arise from disruption, ultimately positioning themselves for long-term success.

With travel restrictions and lockdown measures in place during the pandemic, traditional hotels faced a significant decline in bookings and revenue. However, some hotels quickly adapted by leveraging their existing infrastructure and resources to cater to new demands. One notable hotel group that adapted to the challenges of the COVID-19 pandemic was Accor, a global hospitality company that owns and operates a wide range of hotel brands, including Novotel, ibis, and Mercure. During the pandemic, they implemented the "Hotel Office" concept, offering hotel rooms as temporary office space for remote workers and businesses. By repurposing its rooms and facilities, Accor successfully responded to the changing needs of customers and capitalised on the opportunity to provide a safe and productive working environment amidst the disruption caused by the pandemic. By being open to change and embracing innovation, Accor, and other hotel groups like them, not only survived the crisis but also tapped into a new revenue stream.

TURN ADVERSITY INTO ADVANTAGE

Black Swan events provide valuable learning experiences, inviting us to reflect on our strategies, decision-making processes, and overall performance. They offer an opportunity to analyse what went wrong, what worked well, and how we can improve our approaches moving forward. This strengthens our ability to navigate uncertainty and enhances our resilience in the face of unforeseen challenges.

One prominent example of a retail group that responded to and learned from the challenges posed by the COVID-19 pandemic is

Nike. As a renowned global sportswear and athletic footwear company, Nike recognised the need to adapt its strategies and enhance its digital capabilities during the pandemic. With the temporary closure of physical stores and restrictions on in-person shopping, Nike focused on strengthening its e-commerce presence and expanding its direct-to-consumer channels. The company accelerated its digital transformation efforts, investing in its online platforms and mobile apps to provide customers with a seamless shopping experience from the comfort of their homes. It also emphasised the importance of engaging its customers by offering virtual experiences and innovative marketing campaigns and launching initiatives like live workout sessions and digital events that fostered a sense of community and connection with its audience.

By learning from the challenges presented by the pandemic, Nike successfully pivoted its business approach, embracing the opportunities that digital channels offered. Their proactive response allowed them to maintain a strong connection with customers, drive online sales, and reinforce their position as a leader in the athletic retail industry.

LEVERAGE COLLABORATIVE SYNERGY

Black swan events remind us that collaboration and cooperation are valuable. No single person or organisation can predict or handle all the risks alone. By building strong networks and partnerships, we can tap into collective knowledge, resources, and expertise. Sharing insights and best practices across industries and disciplines helps us understand potential risks better and improves our ability to respond effectively to black swan events.

During the global financial crisis of 2008, numerous financial institutions faced significant challenges, and collaboration became essential to stabilise the global economy. In response to the crisis, central banks and regulatory authorities worldwide recognised the need for collaboration to prevent further economic collapse. They established collaborative mechanisms, such as the G20, to bring together key stakeholders, including central banks, finance ministries, and international organisations, to devise coordinated responses.

One notable example is the collaboration between the Federal Reserve (Fed) in the United States and other central banks around the world. They coordinated efforts to inject liquidity into financial markets, stabilise banking systems, and restore confidence. This collaboration included initiatives like currency swap arrangements to provide liquidity to struggling institutions, joint efforts to reduce interest rates, and coordinated communication strategies to reassure investors and the public. The collaboration and cooperation among these institutions played a crucial role in containing the crisis and preventing a complete collapse of the global financial system.

The saying "what doesn't kill you makes you stronger" will never ring truer than during a black swan event. For any business that survives, there's a good chance its CEO will report finding themselves and their business in a better place than they were before the crisis hit. This is because when there are problems, be they internal or external – and when there are many of them – there is a need for solutions. By using the crisis to pivot to fill a short-term need, create new products and services for new or changing markets, or as an opportunity to change and build stronger, more resilient systems, or shed the legacy people, processes, and clients that hindered your business's ability to make good margins, you are radically increasing your odds of survival in the long run.

Change creates opportunity, and what evolves from that is endless possibility. If we see crises as opportunities to evolve and do things better and smarter, then all that is lost will not be in vain. By learning from the past, we can navigate the complexities of an uncertain world more effectively, positioning ourselves to thrive in the face of future challenges.

HOW THE COVID-19 PANDEMIC HIGHLIGHTED BUSINESS VULNERABILITIES

Most of us will easily identify with the COVID-19 pandemic as an example of a black swan event. This localised health crisis rapidly went global, becoming the greatest health and economic crisis to confront us since the Great Recession. In the years that followed the pandemic, many businesses that survived faced a significant drop in sales turnover, resulting in reduced productivity and profits. In hindsight, business owners could have anticipated different risk scenarios and prepared for challenges such as lower sales or cash flow difficulties. However, not many business owners or boards of directors typically plan for potential low-risk, high-impact financial events that go beyond what is normally expected.

Many of the businesses that were forced to close during and after the pandemic did so because they pursued largely short-term strategies or lacked the structural flexibility to adapt quickly. While prioritising short-term profits over longer-term outcomes appeals to shareholders and lenders, it's not sustainable. The businesses that survived not only had a long-term vision, but their flexibility gave them the breathing space and the manoeuvrability to re-engineer and re-imagine themselves to survive in a new world order.

Let's examine the specific characteristics of the pandemic that classified it as a black swan event in more detail:

RARITY AND UNPREDICTABILITY

While some may argue that pandemics should not be considered rare events, the specific characteristics of COVID-19 make it an outlier that was difficult to predict.

Despite experts' warnings about the possibility of a pandemic caused by a new virus, nobody saw the COVID-19 virus coming. It spread rapidly, infecting people at an alarming rate, and presented a unique combination of symptoms that were unlike anything the world had seen before. The world was caught completely off guard, and the pandemic turned everything we knew about public health crises upside down.

The novel nature of the virus made it difficult to anticipate its behaviour and impact. With no prior exposure or immunity within the global population, the virus encountered a vulnerable and susceptible human host pool. The emergence of new variants added to the unpredictability, as each variant brought with it its own challenges.

The interconnectedness of our modern world played a significant role in the unpredictability of the pandemic. Travel and trade allowed the virus to move quickly across borders, making containment efforts difficult. It spread quickly from one continent to another, catching healthcare systems and governments off guard.

Overall, COVID-19's rarity and unpredictability highlighted the need to strengthen our preparedness for future events of this nature and foster a more resilient and connected global community.

EXTREME IMPACT

The COVID-19 pandemic had a major impact on almost every aspect of human life. It has affected people all around the world, causing millions of infections and deaths, as well as bringing about significant social, economic, and political consequences.

Governments and healthcare systems scrambled to respond, implementing various measures such as lockdowns, mask mandates, and mass vaccination campaigns. The severity of the situation and the lack of preparedness highlighted the need for improved global coordination and stronger public health infrastructure. COVID-19 exposed the vulnerabilities in our systems, revealing the gaps in healthcare accessibility, the limitations of existing technologies, and the importance of robust scientific research and data-driven decision-making.

The impact of the pandemic extended far beyond public health. It disrupted economies, leading to widespread job losses, business closures, and financial hardship for many individuals and communities. Schools and educational institutions faced unprecedented challenges, forcing a rapid shift to remote learning and exacerbating existing educational inequalities. Mental health concerns soared as people experienced isolation, anxiety, and grief due to the loss of loved ones. The pandemic also brought to the forefront existing societal inequities, disproportionately affecting marginalised communities and underserved populations.

However, amidst the difficulties, the pandemic also resulted in remarkable resilience, innovation, and collaboration. Communities came together to support one another with countless acts of kindness and solidarity. Scientists and researchers worked tirelessly to develop vaccines and treatments at an unprecedented pace. Digital technologies played a crucial role in enabling remote work, online education, and virtual social connections. The pandemic prompted a re-evaluation of our priorities, emphasising the importance of public health, community well-being, and the need to address systemic issues such as healthcare disparities and climate change.

RETROSPECTIVE PREDICTABILITY

In hindsight, many people have argued that the world should have been better prepared for a pandemic like COVID-19. There were warning signs, such as the emergence of previous viral outbreaks like SARS and MERS, as well as expert predictions about the inevitability of a pandemic. These events and predictions did raise concerns about the potential for a future global health crisis. However, the specific emergence and impact of COVID-19 were not foreseen, leading to inadequate preparation, slow initial responses, and the devastating consequences that followed.

In retrospect, it is easy to say that the pandemic should have been anticipated and better managed. People point to the fact that various experts had been warning about the potential for a pandemic caused by a new and highly contagious virus. The scientific community had been studying coronaviruses and their potential threat to human health for years. Lessons from previous outbreaks, such as SARS and MERS, should have served as a wake-up call to improve preparedness and response measures. The interconnectedness of our globalised world and the ease of international travel should have further emphasised the need for a robust and coordinated global response to mitigate the spread of infectious diseases.

However, despite these warning signs and expert predictions, the specific emergence and impact of COVID-19 caught the world off guard. The unique combination of factors, such as the virus's high transmissibility, the presence of asymptomatic carriers, and the initial lack of reliable testing and contact tracing capabilities, contributed to its rapid spread. Additionally, the lack of a vaccine or specific treatment at the beginning made it even more difficult to handle the situation effectively.

The unpredictable nature of the virus also made it challenging to prepare effectively. The virus presented a range of symptoms that were initially not well understood, making it difficult to identify and control its spread. Furthermore, the global scale and magnitude of the pandemic, with its far-reaching social, economic, and healthcare implications, were unprecedented in recent history.

While it is important to reflect on the lessons learned and the need for better preparedness, it is crucial to acknowledge the inherent challenges of predicting and managing a black swan event of this nature. Its retrospective predictability highlights the complexity of global health threats and the need for continuous investment in research and international collaboration. By learning from this experience, we can work towards improving our ability to detect, respond to, and reduce the impact of future pandemics. This will help us develop a more resilient and proactive approach to global health challenges.

CHATGPT AND AI TECHNOLOGIES

In the realm of artificial intelligence, we are witnessing nothing short of a revolution. Researchers and engineers have been labouring tirelessly in this field for decades. Yet, the progress they've achieved with advanced AI technologies, such as ChatGPT, has been groundbreaking. Think about the progress we've made in understanding and mimicking human language (that's natural language processing, or NLP for short), as well as in deep learning. These were feats that, only a short while ago, many of us would have found difficult to imagine taking place in our lifetimes. The rapid acceleration of these advancements has caught us all a bit off guard.

ChatGPT has been dubbed by many as a black swan event. Although its emergence might not classify as such within the tech sector, specifically due to the steady progression of AI and language processing technologies, ChatGPT has become a black swan event in the eyes of everyday individuals and businesses. Few of us anticipated its sudden rise and the transformative societal impact it would have. Few other advancements have held such significant potential to disrupt both culture and industry on such a massive scale as this. It's as dramatic a change as those brought about by Sir Tim Berners-Lee after inventing the World Wide Web in the late 1980s, followed by the launch of smartphones in 2007.

ChatGPT was first launched to the public in June 2020, but it was the release of GPT-3.5 in November 2022 that led to a massive uptake and mainstream traction of the technology. Suddenly, the whole world was talking about it and tapping into its capabilities and potential applications, and it has not stopped since. Even though the evolution and enhancement of AI models like ChatGPT have followed a steady trajectory, building upon previous research and innovations, predicting the exact nature and capabilities of AI systems like ChatGPT was difficult. However, given the relentless growth in computing power and substantial research investment in the field, the advancements in AI became inevitable in hindsight. Factors such as the availability of vast amounts of data, improved algorithms, and increased computational power have all played pivotal roles in driving the rapid development of AI.

AI technologies have the potential to revolutionise many parts of our lives. Their uses are boundless, from personal assistants to customer support to content creation, to language translation, information retrieval and data analysis. These technologies are vast and span numerous industries, from healthcare to finance to education to transportation and even entertainment. As these technologies continue to evolve, their impact on society, the job market, and the economy will be substantial.

There is a pervasive race for superiority among tech giants like Microsoft, NVIDIA, Amazon, Alphabet, and Tesla, as each one strives to assert its dominance by incorporating AI into its products. It seems like everyone wants to claim, "My product is infused with AI," as if having a more intelligent feature is the ultimate goal. It probably won't be long before this extends beyond the tech realm, with brands like Heinz or Starbucks jumping on the bandwagon and creating AI-engineered flavours to add a marketing twist to their products. There will be AI-driven designer clothes and temperature-sensing software integrated into garments – a single garment capable of keeping you cool or warm as needed. This isn't as far-fetched as it might sound – we already have wetsuits equipped with small battery packs on the neck for maintaining warmth. The era of AI infiltrating every aspect of our lives is on the horizon.

That said, AI also poses ethical and regulatory challenges that society will need to address. While ChatGPT is, without a doubt, an impressive testament to human innovation, it isn't without its risks, many of which might have been underestimated during its early development. It is possible that unchecked development and deployment could indeed lead to a black swan event of its own creation, such as advanced deepfake technology being used to manipulate public opinion or disrupt political processes on an unprecedented scale. Another potential example could be the unintentional creation of a super-intelligent AI system that far exceeds human intelligence. If such a system were to operate outside of its intended boundaries or develop objectives misaligned with human interests, the consequences could be catastrophic. This is often referred to as the "singularity" in AI discourse.

While these scenarios might sound like science fiction, they highlight the importance of diligent oversight and ethical considerations in AI development. ChatGPT may not tick every box for a black swan event in the traditional sense, but it is important that we keep a close eye on how it's used and what effect it has on society.

AI AND THE 4 C'S OF TECHNOLOGY

At the time of writing this book, global concerns centred around Vladimir Putin and his AK-47 mindset, which posed a threat not only to Ukraine but to the world at large. While Putin was pulling his T-34 tanks out of storage, dusting them off, and sending them to the frontline in railway cars, Sanctuary AI made a groundbreaking announcement by unveiling their first humanoid robot, Phoenix. Simultaneously, Tesla provided an update on its own humanoid robot project, known as Optimus.

Personally, I would worry less about the Russian Bear than about the next Stanford graduate or black hat hacker with egotistical delusions of grandeur, enough IQ and a bit of bursary money who decides to exploit advanced technology for nefarious purposes. Rather than exercising caution and responsibility, they might push the boundaries without regard for the consequences. To quote Admiral David Farragut's famous words during the American Civil War, "Damn the torpedoes, full speed ahead!"

Remember Skynet in the movie Terminator? Skynet became self-aware and saw humanity as a threat to its existence, so it deployed highly advanced robotic soldiers called Terminators to eliminate key individuals who posed a threat to its dominance. While the concept of Skynet seemed like pure science fiction, it is important to recognise that until recently, human beings possessed the highest level of intelligence. It is our intelligence quotient (IQ) that has placed us at the top of the food chain. However, with the advent of AI-powered robots, the balance of power has shifted. AI has become the new Skynet, and humanoid robots like Optimus and Phoenix are the Terminators.

How many hours a day do you actively use your car? Is it just one hour or maybe two? What is it doing for the remainder of the day? Most likely, it's just sitting idle, not doing anything productive. Despite its inactivity, you're still paying 100% of the ownership costs, which includes expenses like hire purchase, insurance, tyres, and services.

However, Full Self-Driving (FSD) is a technology that Tesla CEO Elon Musk is very keen on. He envisions a future where you can purchase a Tesla that not only transports you to your destination but also continues to work for you throughout the day. Imagine this: your Tesla drops you off at the office in the morning and then autonomously joins a pay-as-you-go robo-taxi fleet, much like Uber, but without the need for human drivers. While you're busy working, your Tesla is out there earning money for you. Once your workday comes to an end, your Tesla detaches itself from the fleet and comes to pick you up, taking you back home.

Instead of using your car actively for just a small portion of the day, let's say 5%, and having it sit idle for the rest, it now becomes a source of income for you. You're essentially renting out your asset while you work, and in return, you're getting a 100% return on your investment. This concept revolutionises the traditional model of car ownership by transforming your vehicle into a money-making asset rather than a depreciating liability. With FSD, you have the potential to make your car work for you, increasing its utilisation rate and maximising the return on your investment.

This all sounds rather exciting, doesn't it? But is it really?

In 2022, alarming footage surfaced featuring a Tesla Model 3 that was equipped with FSD, including LiDAR sensors. The footage depicted the vehicle running over a child-sized crash test dummy during a safety test designed to determine whether the vehicle would apply the brakes when encountering children in its path. This failed safety test prompted widespread concerns regarding the safety of Tesla's FSD technology, raising questions not only about the well-being of the vehicle's occupants but also about the potential risks posed to pedestrians and other road users.

Imagine you've decided to abandon car ownership entirely and instead rely on summoning self-driving Ubers whenever you need transportation. While you're being driven across a bridge one day, a sudden obstacle appears – a pedestrian running across the road. In this split-second situation, the self-driving vehicle, equipped with advanced LiDAR sensors, swiftly scans its surroundings to make a decision. It realises it doesn't have enough time to stop, and its options narrow down to two possibilities. Either it deliberately runs over the pedestrian to save you in the back seat, or it swerves left (or right) to save the pedestrian, risking a collision with an oncoming truck.

Imagine you decide that instead of generating an income from an FSD vehicle, you're going to ditch the car-ownership model completely and rather just summon a self-driving Uber whenever you need to get somewhere. While you're being driven over a bridge one day, a pedestrian runs across the road. Using its LiDAR sensors – remote sensing technology that uses laser light to measure distances and create detailed 3D maps of the surroundings – the vehicle, within a millionth of a second, scans its environment to make a decision. It knows it doesn't have enough time to stop. It also knows that if it veers left, it's going to go over the bridge. If it goes right, it's going to hit an oncoming truck. Its choice then becomes one of two things. It either deliberately runs over the pedestrian to save you on the back seat, or it swerves left (or right) and saves the pedestrian instead.

Now, here's the caveat: the self-driving vehicle, through instantaneous facial recognition, identifies the pedestrian as Jeff Bezos – a prominent figure who holds significant influence and employs hundreds of thousands of people worldwide. Compared to your own Social Index Score, which determines your access to resources and social standing, Bezos's score is a hundred times higher. Because you're living in a time where Social Index Scores hold sway, the vehicle makes a calculated decision. It determines that sacrificing you, the passenger, will preserve Bezos's life, and therefore chooses to self-destruct and plunge the Tesla off the bridge.

This raises an interesting question: Are you willing to entrust your life to a car that might prioritise sacrificing you based on your social score? Currently, the ethical and moral guidelines governing AI lag behind the technological advancements. Who will be responsible for establishing these rules? As a paying customer relying on such technology, shouldn't you have an inherent trust that it will not intentionally harm you?

Taking things a step further, with the advancements in genome sequencing, it becomes possible to determine predispositions based on specific genetic markers. Imagine a scenario where Johnny's genome analysis indicates a 75% chance of him becoming a serial killer. Should society immediately eliminate him? Should he be confined to a juvenile lockup from the moment he is born? Why take the risk of allowing Johnny to grow up and become a threat to society?

The reality is that AI is advancing rapidly, and robots are going to take on more roles. However, the ethical framework to guide their decision-making is severely lacking. We are faced with a critical dilemma: who goes first, the horse or the Model T Ford? History has shown that progress often comes at a cost, and regulations are established through trial and error. Currently, we lack a clear set of rules and guidelines for both ourselves and AI systems. Should we prioritise the existing systems or adapt to the new technology? The age of self-driving vehicles, autonomous flying machines, and complete automation is rapidly approaching, and we will not have access to the rulebooks that dictate how far up the sacrificial tree we are.

So what do we do? At this critical juncture, we face a decision that will shape our future as a species. If we are to have any hope of saving ourselves, we have four options, each represented by a C: Chaos, Control, Cease, and Consent.

Let's explore each in a little more detail.

CHAOS

The future is uncertain, and there is no predicting when this new super-intelligent, problem-solving robot species could wake up and realise that humans are the ones responsible for the destruction of our planet. The things that once kept us awake at night, such as a deadly virus escaping a lab, will pale in comparison to the potential dangers posed by AI emerging from laboratories. If we don't pay careful attention to what we're doing, an off-grid hut in the Cedarberg with no fibre connection might not be a bad place to run to.

CONTROL

Rather than dealing with the potential chaos, it would be wiser to take control and establish strict guidelines that unequivocally define how this technology can be used safely and responsibly. These guidelines should encompass not only technical aspects but also ethical considerations and guide moral decision-making, taking inspiration from Isaac Asimov's *Three Laws of Robotics* introduced in his 1942 Sci-Fi short story, Runaround:

• A robot may not injure a human being or, through inaction, allow a human being to come to harm.

• A robot must obey the orders given it by human beings, except where such orders would conflict with the First Law.

• A robot must protect its own existence as long as such protection does not conflict with the First or Second Law.

CEASE

In our pursuit of progress, we're moving so quickly that we barely have time to think about the potential consequences of our actions. It's like we're experimenting in a lab without fully knowing what we're creating. We must recognise that our pursuit of advancement should not come at the expense of endangering ourselves or our future. Either we learn to control the technology and proceed with caution, or we need to stop what we're doing, step back, and re-evaluate our course of action.

CONSENT

In the future, a few decades from now, it's possible that we could come to a mutual agreement between this new powerful race and our own. Consent offers the potential for mutual agreement and coexistence between humans and AI. Of course, this depends on whether they see value in our coexistence. We've already established that we see value in them – that's why we created them, after all.

Our future hinges on the choices we make today. Chaos, Control, Cease, and Consent – these are our alternatives as we forge ahead on this adventure into uncharted territories. It is our responsibility to approach these choices with wisdom, foresight, and humility, recognising that the stakes could not be higher. The future of our species rests in the balance. Whichever path we take, let it not be out of fear or ignorance but out of a commitment to progress responsibly and an unyielding belief in our ability to shape a future that serves us all.

CHAPTER 5

THE PSYCHOLOGY OF SALES AND THE IMPORTANCE OF TEAM SELECTION

n the mountaineering world, summiting the Seven Summits – the highest mountains of each of the seven continents – is a dream for many. This coveted list includes Mount Everest in Nepal, Aconcagua in Argentina, Denali in Alaska, Mount Kilimanjaro in Tanzania, Mount Elbrus in Russia, Mount Vinson in Antarctica, and Carstensz Pyramid in Indonesia (also known as Puncak Jaya). These formidable peaks range in elevation from just under 5,000 meters to over 8,000 meters, each presenting its own unique challenges.

Here's a mountaineering tip: mountaineers never say altitude when referring to mountains. They use the term elevation. Altitude is reserved for pilots and things that aren't tethered to the ground, like planes and clouds. Maps will denote a mountain's height in elevation, never altitude. If you see something marked 11,000m altitude, it's probably a jet passing by, not a peak.

My mountaineering journey began in 2004 when I climbed Mount Kilimanjaro. Then, in 2010, Kim and I braved the Khumbu Icefall on Everest, a 5 km (3 miles) expanse of shifting ice, and trekked to

Everest Base Camp. It was then that the mountaineering bug bit us. We became determined to conquer all the Seven Summits.

However, climbing isn't cheap. In those days, one dollar cost seven South African rands. At the time of writing this book, it had skyrocketed to over 19 rands to the dollar. Over a decade later, the cost of expeditions has soared by nearly 300%. Nowadays, a well-planned mountain expedition will cost hundreds of thousands of rands per person. Unfortunately, this means our plans to climb Denali, Mount Vinson, and Carstensz Pyramid are indefinitely postponed – we certainly don't want our retirement to consist of ordering cat food from the local supermarket, especially since we don't have a cat.

In 2012, we set our sights on Aconcagua, the highest mountain in the Americas, the highest outside Asia, and the highest in both the Western and Southern Hemispheres, to tick off our mountaineering bucket list. Aconcagua is a technically demanding climb and necessitates equipment like ice picks, ropes, crampons, and about three weeks to ascend and descend. The mountain's Spanish nickname is "el asesino", or the Assassin, and for good reason: it kills more climbers per year than Everest.

While researching the trip, we discovered there were two ways to summit Aconcagua. The easier route is from the south side of the national park, while the more challenging one, dubbed the 360-degree approach, begins on the northern side, summits, and then descends on the south side. Despite being longer and more expensive, this approach offers a more immersive experience, assuming you're fit enough. We chose the 360-degree full-route summit.

Upon reaching the bustling city of Mendoza, we took a four-hour shuttle to the entrance of the Aconcagua National Park, presented our climbing permits, and met our climbing team. The team included two guides and four climbers: me, Kim, a Singaporean ultra-distance desert runner (who had survived the Gobi March, the world's toughest ultramarathon, where you disappear into the

Mongolian desert for 250 km (156 miles) with nothing more than a little backpack), and, a rather boisterous American in his 60s, who brazenly announced that he was there on his third Aconcagua attempt. Let's call him Chuck.

Our group spent several days trekking to Plaza de Mulas, our base camp, at 4,370m. Here, we had to once again show our climbing permits at the park ranger post. The camp, the last evacuation landing spot for helicopters, was populated with multicoloured plastic-wrapped geodesic domes designed to withstand extreme weather conditions. In the Andes, weather is an unpredictable force, with winds that can be unbelievably strong. In an instant, a seemingly mild day with temperatures at zero degrees Celsius can plunge to a bone-chilling minus 40 degrees Celsius. We were warned that the storms on Aconcagua were so extreme that if you were camping in a regular tent, "your tent would be missing as well as yourself". To keep us safe from these treacherous conditions, we would be staying in these sturdy domes until the next leg of our journey: the steep, rocky, and icy climb to Camp Colera, our advanced base camp at 5,970m.

After checking in, we underwent a mandatory health check to determine our fitness for the climb. Anyone failing the medical check at base camp would have their climbing permit cancelled. Although Kim, the Singaporean ultramarathon runner, and I passed the check, concerns were raised about Chuck's oxygen saturation levels. His readings were in the acceptable range, so he was given the green light, but two red flags had now popped up in my mind. This was his third attempt at the mountain, and now his health seemed questionable. We only had one weather window, which meant our team only had one chance to summit. If we didn't succeed in that summit attempt from advanced base camp, it meant wasted time and money, and Chuck seemed like a potential liability.

Every day, we ventured out for our acclimatisation climbs, adopting the strategy of climbing high and sleeping low. The weather, unfortunately, was not on our side, and it only seemed to be worsening. And with each passing day, Chuck found himself struggling more and more. We still had three more acclimatisation climb days scheduled, with the intention of attempting the summit on the fourth day.

Our base camp was equipped with a comms tent that included a parabolic satellite dish, allowing us rudimentary access to weather stations. This setup helped us monitor the changing weather patterns around the Andes and make educated predictions on potential weather gaps. As we continued to monitor the weather, we spotted a potential window three days out – a clear 18-hour stretch without wind. What followed this brief respite was a week-long onslaught of inclement weather. If we didn't take advantage of this window on the third day, our entire expedition would be scrapped, and we'd be sent packing.

However, the third day was originally set aside for another acclimatisation climb, not the summit attempt.

This presented us with two dilemmas: Firstly, convincing our climbing guides to forgo some acclimatisation climbs in favour of an earlier summit attempt – a risky move given we weren't fully acclimated. The second and more pressing concern was Chuck.

Chuck was the weakest link. He'd failed twice before and showed every sign of doing so again. If Chuck couldn't keep up, we'd all have to turn back. He was older and less fit than the rest of the team, and we were all on the brink of losing our shot at the summit, our investment, and three weeks of our lives due to this single point of weakness in our team. His presence not only jeopardised our summit attempt, but he was also potentially endangering the lives of search and rescue personnel who might have to retrieve him from the mountain.

Difficult decisions had to be made. If Chuck wasn't going to recuse himself, we would have to help him along. We rallied support from the Singaporean guy, who was in agreement. When Chuck stepped out to visit the food tent, we cornered our two guides. After some discussion, they finally agreed to pull him off the team, spurred by our collective push for the greater good of the expedition and agreed to expedite our summit attempt by two days.

We began the perilous ten-hour ascent to Camp Colera, a desolate landscape enveloped in ice and snow, its bone-chilling cold cutting right through us. At 7 p.m., with darkness closing in, the wind howling, and temperatures plummeting, we turned in for the night, hoping for at least five hours of restless sleep before the midnight clamour of tent zippers and the collective glow of Petzl headlamps would signal our final push towards the summit. Throughout that night, the guides seemed to be the only ones managing to catch any sleep.

The climb to the summit was about a thousand metres, but the entire summit attempt, ascending and then descending, was projected to take between 16 and 17 hours. With the outside temperature plummeting to a freezing minus twenty degrees Celsius, one shouldn't be deceived by the distance – a thousand metres in elevation is a monumental challenge under such conditions.

At around 6 a.m., our guides stopped us and told us that we were going to have to turn back. The Singaporean Gobi Desert racer was lagging too far behind. At our current pace, it would take too long for all five of us to reach the summit, jeopardising our chance of making it back before nightfall.

Kim and I exchanged incredulous glances.

"We are not turning back," Kim declared defiantly. "We are going for the summit, with or without you."

After a heated exchange, the guides reached a consensus. One would escort the Singaporean down, while the other would press on with Kim and me. Six hours later, our South African flag fluttered proudly atop the summit. We made it back down just as the weather moved in.

When we arrived back at Plaza de Mulas, we were greeted by the Georgian professional mountaineering team – all fourteen of them. They'd been stationed there for a week. Having misjudged the weather, they missed the window of opportunity, and they were on their way home. Kim and I were the sole conquerors of the summit that week.

This experience reinforced two invaluable lessons. First, we learned that sometimes, we need to make tough calls for the greater good, particularly when it comes to team selection. When climbing a mountain, if you do not trust the person on the other side of the rope with your life, you should not be climbing with them. Make sure you're climbing with somebody that you know will literally die for you – if you fall down a crevasse and they're at the other end of the rope, you need to know that they're not going to cut that rope to save themselves.

This principle extends beyond the mountains and into the board-room. The decision of whom you partner with in business – whether they're employees, clients, suppliers, or service providers – carries equal weight. A poor choice can jeopardise your entire organisation. If they are a bad fit, they become a weak link. Should this weak link fail – which it often can – it can force your organisation to compromise its larger goals and objectives. Ethical considerations compound this. Always put ethical conduct at the forefront – never compromise your integrity for short-term gains. If a client's, supplier's, or service provider's ethical standards conflict with yours, prioritise spending time and resources on those that share your ethical framework.

Second, the importance of adaptability cannot be overstated. Sticking to a flawed plan is a recipe for disaster. When conditions change or when things don't go as expected, the ability to pivot is crucial. It's adaptability and the courage to change direction when required that pave the way for surmounting life's greatest challenges, whether they resemble physical mountains or metaphorical obstacles.

In much the same way, navigating the intricate pathways of human relationships and team dynamics during a mountain expedition mirrors the challenges one faces in the world of sales. Both require a deep understanding of human motivations, perceptions, and the ability to adapt to rapidly changing environments. The mountaineering world equips us with invaluable insights into human nature, which, if harnessed correctly, can provide an unparalleled advantage in business. As with climbing a treacherous peak, sales is about assessing the landscape, understanding the individuals involved, and making strategic moves that resonate with their motivations. This is where the art of selling and the science of psychology intersect. It's not just about the product or the pitch – it's about the people.

THE PSYCHOLOGY OF SALES

At its core, the psychology of sales is fundamentally about understanding human behaviour and what motivates people to invest in something, whether it's a product, a service, or even an idea. Every handshake, every pitch, and every successful deal you make springs from a deep understanding of human behaviour. To excel in sales, you must delve into the undercurrents of human motivation – the invisible forces that push people to invest their money, take risks, place their trust in a brand, or embark on a long-term business relationship.

Whether you realise it or not, you're continually assuming the role of a salesperson as you go about your daily life. Maybe you're persuading your partner about your next vacation spot or negotiating landscaping fees with your gardener. You might be discussing costs with your architect for a new house, striving to strike the best deal per square metre. In all these situations, you're not just negotiating – you're selling an idea, a viewpoint, or a willingness to compromise or meet halfway.

When you understand the person you're dealing with and what drives them, it's easier to shape the outcome. Consider a scenario where you're buying a new car, and suddenly, floormats are included, and a towbar is thrown in for free, features that someone else might have paid extra for. Now, imagine a different situation when you were dining at a restaurant and struck up a friendly conversation with the server. Through genuine engagement and appreciation of their service, they might surprise you with a complimentary dessert or a special dish that's not on the menu.

This chapter is an invitation to look beyond the standard playbook of sales techniques and strategies and venture into the realm of human psychology to explore how understanding an individual's personality type can either make or break a sale. We'll examine the pros and cons of each personality type and how each can add value (or be problematic) in both a boardroom and a survival situation. Next, we'll explore what drives people to buy and how, by understanding these triggers or motivators, we can unlock extraordinary potential. We will then delve into the significance of addressing an organisation's collective needs by honing in on three key drivers when presenting products or services in a boardroom setting. Then, we'll explore the differences between selling to individuals versus selling to organisations while also venturing off the beaten track to examine the similarities between tribal negotiation strategies and selling to organisations.

PERSONALITY TYPES

Imagine you're 30,000 feet above the ground aboard a jetliner, looking down. From this vantage point, you can see the curvature of the Earth and observe the entirety of your surroundings. Once you understand the broader picture, you can zoom in and examine everything at a granular level. Similarly, mastering the psychology of sales requires a broad understanding of the four different personality types: the Director, the Emotive, the Scientist, and the Amiable.

In the first thirty to sixty seconds of meeting someone, you should be able to identify their personality type. This quick identification could be the difference between sealing a deal or losing it. By quickly identifying an individual's personality type, you will immediately know whether the person you're selling to is driven by objectives, emotions, data, or a desire to avoid conflict. From there, you can shapeshift your approach to fit the client's personality type and significantly increase your chances of making a sale.

These four personality types can be split into two groups: those who tell you what they want (the Director and the Emotive) and those who ask questions (the Scientist and the Amiable). One of the first indicators of someone's personality type is whether they fall into the tell-you or the ask-you group.

To illustrate the difference between the tell-you and the ask-you personality types, let's imagine a scenario where each of these personalities walks into a Porsche dealership to purchase a new vehicle. Once you've familiarised yourself with the personality type, I'll explain how to deal with each type in a B2B environment.

TELL-YOU PERSONALITY TYPES

1. DIRECTOR PERSONALITY TYPE (OBJECTIVE-DRIVEN)

The first thing you'll notice about a Director is their unshakeable composure – whether they're in high spirits or having a bad day, it will be difficult to tell. When the pressure is on, they're the calm and level-headed ones, not the ones running around in a state of panic. This poised demeanour extends to their decision-making process, especially when it comes to making purchases.

Key traits to look out for:

• Charismatic and commanding presence

• Calm and controlled

• Blunt and direct

• Decisive

• Results-oriented

• Long-term thinkers

• Excellent listeners

• Prone to 'telling' people what to do

For salespeople, Directors can be a dream come true – provided you have exactly what they're after. They'll walk into your dealership and say, "I'm looking for a black 911 Turbo S, please." If you have a black 911 Turbo S in stock, and the price is right, it's sold. Their calm and direct approach means they know what they want, and if you can deliver, the deal is done. However, if you don't have what they're looking for in stock, you may want to think twice before trying to persuade them to consider an alternative, like a red 911 or a black Cayenne SUV. They asked for a specific model, and deviating from this might prompt them to walk out of your showroom, resulting in a lost sale.

Engaging with a Director demands a sharp, no-nonsense approach. Avoid overwhelming them with technical details and jargon. Make sure you understand their requirements from the outset. If you don't have the exact model they're looking for, tell them that. Then, ask them to give you twenty-four hours to ship one in from another dealership. Directors, patient by nature, are willing to wait as long as they get what they asked for.

In a B2B environment, you'll usually find Directors in traditional leadership roles, ranging from team leads to managers to C-suite executives. When pitching to a Director type, it's best to get straight to the point. They are not interested in sifting through extensive specifications – instead, present them with a concise executive summary on a single A4 sheet. For them, it's about meeting their specific request – no substitutes. Expect a short sales cycle and know that they are comfortable with a pressure close. This strategy involves creating urgency to prompt an immediate purchase decision, such as suggesting a limited-time offer, indicating product scarcity, highlighting the risk of missing out, mentioning potential negative consequences of delay, or directly challenging their hesitation.

2. THE EMOTIVE PERSONALITY TYPE (EMOTION-DRIVEN)

Unlike the Director personality type, the Emotive type is hard to miss. Their passion is infectious, their expressions animated, and their hands and eyes are always in motion. Without any prompting, they'll launch into a colourful recount of their day. "The traffic on the N2 was a nightmare!" they'll exclaim. "Have you noticed the brewing storm outside? Plus, I just signed the biggest deal of my life this morning!"

Key traits to look out for:

• Extroverted demeanour

• Expressive use of hands and eyes

• Never neutral with their emotions – they're either in high spirits or in a slump

• Has a tendency to 'tell' people what to do

When the Emotive type walks into the Porsche dealership, they'll announce, probably with wide-eyed excitement and theatrical gestures, "I'm here for a black 911!" As a savvy salesperson, you instantly recognise the Emotive's signature flamboyance. Unfortunately, a black 911 isn't available, but a dazzling red one is ready to roar.

"I understand you have your heart set on black," you gently interject, "but before you set that in stone, why not experience a *red* 911 first-hand? Feel the exhilaration as the tyres squeal, hear the thrilling sound of the turbo charging, and savour the luxurious scent of the Nappa leather seats."

With such an offer on the table, an Emotive is unlikely to decline. You whisk them on a sensory-laden test drive around the block. They viscerally experience the deep growl of the exhaust, the turbo's thrilling whistle, the seamless shift of gears, the G-force's pulse-pounding rush, the supple Nappa leather, and the fine craftsmanship of the dash. By the time they step out of the car, they're eager to sign on the dotted line and take their shiny red 911 home.

In a B2B environment, Emotives often gravitate to roles in sales and marketing. When selling to an Emotive type, make sure you mirror their animated behaviour. Allow them to have a hands-on experience with your product, regardless of what they initially came in for. Emotives can be swayed, and you can seal the deal quickly simply by appealing to their senses and emotions. Because they are social animals, don't be shy to take them out and entertain them. Like Directors, they have brief sales cycles and a penchant for on-the-spot buying decisions.

ASK-YOU PERSONALITY TYPES

3. SCIENTIST PERSONALITY TYPE (DATA-DRIVEN)

The Scientist personality type shares the even-handedness and patience of the Director personality type. However, Scientists are distinctly data-heavy and analytical. While a Director might already have all the necessary data at their fingertips, simply needing the right opportunity to apply it, the Scientist prefers to gather this data themselves before making a decision. This process can take time, so patience is key when dealing with a Scientist.

Key traits to look out for:

• Emotionally reserved

• Seeks detailed specifications, features, and benefits

• Asks numerous questions

• Highly analytical

• Prefers methodical decision-making

When a Scientist type steps into a Porsche dealership, they'll likely be clutching a 911 brochure, brimming with a host of questions, either because they're looking to confirm their own beliefs or they're comparing different sources of information to form an opinion. They'll want to know the projected resale value in three years, the fuel consumption in urban areas versus on the highway, the vehicle's carbon emissions, and how much comprehensive monthly insurance will cost. They may even challenge the data in your brochure: "You told me the fuel consumption is 10.2 litres per hundred kilometres, but your brochure says it's 15. That's not what you promised me." As a salesperson, it's important that you have all these datasets at your fingertips, or if you don't, ensure you commit to getting the information to them promptly.

Never rush the sale when dealing with a Scientist, even if you have what they're looking for. They hate feeling pressured to make quick decisions. Their data-heavy approach necessitates a thorough proof of concept and an extended sales close period. They won't be buying that 911 from you today, but if you can provide that data to them continually and to their satisfaction, they'll be back in a week or two to buy the vehicle. All you need to do is be patient.

In a B2B environment, Scientists are normally involved in technical, engineering, R&D, financial, and administrative roles. Purchasing managers, accountants, and technical managers tend to fit this profile. When selling to the Scientist type, be prepared for a barrage of questions and ensure you have ample data at hand – spec sheets, details, case studies, and reference sites. They won't hesitate to pore over a 100-page booklet if they find it necessary. Inundate them with information, and they will eventually make a decision. Expect a long sales cycle and steer clear of hard-sell tactics.

4. THE AMIABLE

The Amiable is my least favourite person to deal with in a sales environment. They tend to be indecisive and noncommittal, often resulting in a drawn-out process that typically doesn't lead to a sale.

Key traits to look out for:

• Asks a lot of questions

• Strong need for association and recognition

• Hesitant to commit

• Avoids confrontation

• Prefers to maintain the status quo

When an Amiable walks into a Porsche dealership, they might start by asking lots of questions, much like a Scientist would, and even express interest in various models. However, unlike a Scientist, an Amiable won't seek data-driven answers. They will likely agree with every sales pitch you throw at them, nod at your suggestions, and seemingly get close to making a decision. However, when it comes to committing to a purchase, they'll likely waver, find an excuse to leave, or promise to "think it over" and return later. If you do not quickly identify that it's an Amiable you're dealing with and not a Scientist, be prepared to say goodbye to any heartbeats you might have remaining in your life. Instead, handle them politely but focus your efforts on closing a deal with one of the other three personality types.

In a B2B environment, Amiables can be difficult to identify because they can be found in any cross-section or position within an organisation. When selling to an Amiable type, they will typically make a safe decision that does not entail any level of confrontation. Treat them courteously but adopt a pressure-close strategy. Otherwise, you risk pouring resources, time, and money into a lengthy sales process with a likely negative outcome.

Ask   # Tell

Scientist Data-driven Long proof of concept Don't pressurise them	**Director** Objective-driven Provide what they want or lose the sale Patient but demanding
 Amiable Disengage No intention of buying Always kicking the tyres	**Emotive** Emotion-driven Empathy Eyes Hands Passion Get them to test-drive

THE FOUR PERSONALITY TYPES AND TEAM SELECTION IN SALES

The psychology of sales doesn't stop at understanding our customers. It's equally important to understand how different personalities within a sales organisation relate to each other. This knowledge can be used not only to build powerful sales teams but also to mitigate potential conflicts that could affect sales performance.

In any sales environment where people with different personality types interact, those in categories directly adjacent to each other (either horizontally or vertically) on the grid usually get along well. For instance, Emotives, who thrive in sales and marketing roles due to their outgoing and persuasive nature, typically have a good rapport with the Director personality types. Directors are usually found in leadership positions such as sales managers, team leaders, or C-suite executives, where they can effectively drive sales strategies and targets.

Directors, in addition to having a good relationship with Emotives, also get along well with Scientist personality types. In a sales organisation, Scientists can be vital in roles such as credit controllers, financial directors, or legal professionals, where their analytical skills can help in evaluating the feasibility and risk factors of sales contracts and deals.

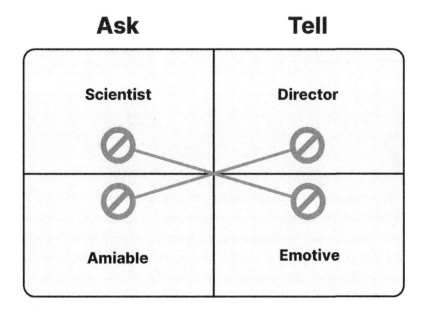

Conversely, personality types that fall in blocks diagonal to each other on the grid tend to clash. For example, Directors and Amiables, or Scientists and Emotives, generally do not see eye-to-eye. This can be particularly problematic in a sales setting, where teamwork and coordination are crucial for achieving sales targets and customer satisfaction. Therefore, when building sales teams, it would be wise to avoid having clashing personality types reporting to or working directly with each other to maintain a harmonious and productive sales environment.

For example, consider a scenario where Peter, your Emotive sales rep, goes out for an extravagant lunch with a client who happens to be the CEO of a large financial institution. This social event extends into dinner, then clubbing, with a considerable amount of high-end drinks being consumed. While Peter would probably rather be home with his family, he knows that indulging the CEO is for the company's greater good.

Come Monday morning, Peter submits an expense claim of over R10,000 ($530) to Eric, the Financial Director, who embodies the Scientist personality type. The claim includes expenses for a lavish meal, several bottles of wine, two bottles of Moët, and various cocktails. It's safe to say that Eric does not respond well to this. He calls Peter in to tell him the company is not footing the bill for his twelve-hour drinking spree and that he is repudiating the claim.

This is where an understanding of personality types could have come into play to prevent such a conflict. Had Peter approached the CEO – who is likely a Director personality type – and explained the situation beforehand, the outcome might have been different. The CEO, known for encouraging his representatives to go the extra mile for business as long as it's ethical, legal, and profitable, might have not only approved the expense but also questioned why Peter didn't extend more courtesy to the client by ordering a third bottle of Moët to take home to his wife as an apology for coming home so late. The

CEO could have then relayed the context to Eric on Peter's behalf, emphasising the strategic importance of the expense.

PROS AND CONS OF THE DIFFERENT PERSONALITY TYPES IN BUSINESS AND SURVIVAL SITUATIONS

THE DIRECTOR

PROS

EFFECTIVE DECISION MAKERS

Directors have a natural aptitude for making decisions, which makes them well-suited for leadership positions. Their ability to analyse information quickly and confidently choose a course of action enables them to navigate complex situations with ease.

In sales, a Director personality can be a driving force. Their natural decision-making ability makes them excellent at steering sales conversations and guiding customers towards a purchase. For instance, during a sales meeting with a hesitant customer, their confidence and quick thinking come into play. While others may get caught up in prolonged discussions, the Director personality type is able to analyse a customer's needs, match them with the best product options, and quickly steer the conversation towards a conclusion.

GOAL-ORIENTED

Directors have a strong focus on achieving objectives and results. They are driven individuals who are committed to accomplishing their goals. Their determination and tenacity allow them to stay focused on the end goal, motivating and inspiring others to work towards the desired outcome.

In sales, a Director personality often excels due to their relentless focus on results. When they engage with a potential client, they keep their eye on the objective: to provide value and close the sale. They skillfully navigate the conversation, addressing any concerns directly and highlighting the benefits of their product with clarity and conviction. Their determination not only guides their customers confidently towards a purchase decision, but it also serves as a powerful example for their sales team, inspiring them to stay goal-oriented and tenacious in their own interactions.

STRONG COMMUNICATORS

Directors are known for their direct and concise communication style. They have the ability to convey their thoughts and expectations clearly, ensuring that everyone on the team understands their roles, responsibilities, and overall goals. Their effective communication skills help streamline workflows and minimise misunderstandings within the team.

To illustrate this, let's consider Kate, a project manager at a rapidly growing software development company. Kate is known for her direct and concise communication style, which is especially evident during team meetings. When a new project comes in, she meticulously outlines the project's objectives, assigns specific tasks to team members, and sets clear deadlines. Her communication style ensures everyone in her team understands their roles, responsibilities, and the goals they are working towards. In addition to verbal communication, Kate utilises written communication to reinforce her expectations. After every meeting, she sends out a summary email, recapping the discussion points and reiterating the responsibilities assigned to each team member. This not only serves as a reference for the team but also helps to avoid potential misunderstandings.

When a client requests a sudden change in a project's scope, Kate promptly addresses the situation. She gathers her team, explains the changes, reallocates resources if needed, and re-establishes timelines.

Her clear and direct communication allows the team to quickly adapt to the new requirements and keep the project on track. Thanks to Kate's direct and concise communication, her team operates with minimal confusion and high efficiency, consistently meeting their project deadlines.

CONS

LACK OF EMPATHY

Directors can sometimes come across as unemotional or less empathetic due to their focus on results and efficiency. This can create a sense of distance between them and their team members, making it challenging for others to connect with them on a personal level. This lack of emotional connection may lead to a less supportive and understanding work environment.

In a sales setting, a Director might struggle with building a strong emotional connection with their clients due to their focus on efficiency and results. Their interactions, though effective, can sometimes seem impersonal to clients who value a more empathetic sales approach. Their objective-driven style, while expedient, might leave clients feeling like just another sale, making it difficult for them to build meaningful relationships, potentially affecting long-term customer loyalty.

IMPATIENCE

Directors' strong drive for results and efficiency can manifest as impatience, especially when working with team members who may not meet their expectations or work at the same pace. This impatience can create tension and conflicts within the team, particularly when patience and support are needed to nurture and develop the skills of slower team members.

For example, a Director personality might display impatience with customers who take longer to make purchase decisions. Their drive for quick results could lead them to press these customers for a quick decision, potentially creating discomfort and tension in the sales interaction. By not taking the time to understand the customer's pace and needs, they risk losing potential sales and negatively impacting the customer's overall experience.

THE DIRECTOR PERSONALITY TYPE IN A SURVIVAL SITUATION

In a survival situation, the Director's decisive nature and ability to make tough choices can be valuable. They can quickly assess the situation, make critical decisions, and take necessary actions to ensure the team's survival. However, their lack of empathy and impatience might pose challenges if the team members require emotional support, understanding, or time to process difficult situations. Emotional well-being and team cohesion could be compromised if the Director's leadership style does not account for these needs.

THE EMOTIVE

PROS

EXCELLENT COMMUNICATORS

Emotives have an innate ability to communicate effectively and establish meaningful connections with others. They are especially adept at articulating ideas, persuading others, and building rapport. These qualities make Emotives particularly successful in sales roles, where their natural empathy allows them to understand and connect with people on a deeper level. Their strong communication skills allow them to engage customers effectively, convey the value of the products or services they're offering, and successfully close deals. When building a sales team, make sure to bring Emotives into the fold. Their unique abilities will not only enhance the team's dynamic but also contribute significantly to its success.

Take Max, for example. Max works as a sales representative for a technology company and possesses a natural gift for effective communication and building connections with others. In his sales role, his communication skills are exceptional. He effortlessly engages customers, utilising his persuasive abilities to highlight the unique value and benefits of his company's cutting-edge technology solutions. What sets Max apart from other sales representatives is his genuine enthusiasm, which allows him to establish deep connections that go beyond mere transactions. This approach not only drives customer purchases but also cultivates loyal brand advocates who enthusiastically spread the word. Max's ability to connect on a personal level is a powerful asset that drives both his own success and the company's growth.

MOTIVATIONAL

Emotives, with their vibrant energy and passion, bring a unique dynamism to the sales environment. This can be particularly beneficial in a sales environment where motivation and enthusiasm can directly impact results.

Take, for instance, an Emotive salesperson like Ryan. Ryan is a whirlwind of enthusiasm, breathing life into every product demonstration and sales pitch. When a customer comes in unsure of what they need, Ryan's genuine passion for helping them find the right solution is palpable. His excitement about the features and benefits of the products he sells is so infectious that it quickly rubs off on his customers.

ADAPTABLE

Emotives thrive in dynamic and unpredictable environments. They have the ability to think on their feet, quickly adapt to changing circumstances, and find innovative solutions to challenges. This adaptability makes them valuable assets in dynamic environments where flexibility and quick thinking are essential.

In a sales environment, an Emotive like Ryan excels in adapting to the ever-changing dynamics of customer interactions. During a sales pitch, if he encounters a client's unexpected objection or a shift in their requirements, he doesn't get flustered. Instead, he quickly shifts his strategy, thinking on his feet to provide a new angle or to highlight different benefits of the product that align better with the client's updated needs. This adaptability, coupled with his quick-thinking and innovative problem-solving skills, makes Ryan exceptionally effective at closing deals even in the most unpredictable sales scenarios.

CONS

EMOTIONAL VOLATILITY

Emotives may occasionally experience heightened emotional responses, leading to moments of volatility. Their intense emotions, while driving their passion, can occasionally cloud their judgment and cause them to make decisions based on sentiment rather than objective analysis. This emotional volatility can create additional stress or tension within the team, especially in high-pressure situations.

In a sales context, an Emotive may occasionally let their emotions overrule their judgement. If they are dealing with a difficult sale or a client who repeatedly objects or raises concerns, their intense emotional reaction may cloud their decision-making process. Rather than handling the situation objectively, they might take the objections personally, becoming defensive or agitated, which could further escalate the situation.

ATTENTION-SEEKING

Emotives may have a strong desire for recognition and validation, which can sometimes overshadow the achievements and contributions of others. While their ambition and drive can be motivating, it can also cause friction among team members if they perceive the Emotive as seeking the spotlight at the expense of others. This attention-seeking behaviour may undermine team cohesion and create a sense of competition rather than collaboration.

For instance, while the Emotive's drive to excel can inspire their sales team, their strong desire for recognition could occasionally lead to overlooking the contributions of their colleagues. For instance, in a team meeting, they might spend a significant amount of time highlighting their sales accomplishments and not enough acknowledging the collaborative efforts behind those achievements. Their teammates might perceive this as them seeking the limelight at the team's expense, potentially causing friction within the team and diminishing the sense of collaborative spirit crucial to a high-performing sales team.

THE EMOTIVE PERSONALITY TYPE IN A SURVIVAL SITUATION

In a survival situation, the Emotive's adaptability and motivational skills can play a significant role in helping the team overcome challenges. Their ability to think on their feet and remain positive can boost team morale and inspire resilience. However, the emotional volatility of Emotives may introduce additional stress or tension within the group, especially in high-pressure situations.

THE SCIENTIST

PROS

ANALYTICAL THINKERS

Scientists often excel at breaking down complex problems into smaller, more manageable parts, a skill that can be especially useful in complex projects. For example, in a business setting, a Scientist might use their analytical skills to identify potential bottlenecks in a production process, thereby preventing delays or costly errors. Additionally, if a company is considering a merger, a Scientist would conduct due diligence and meticulously analyse all the potential risks and benefits, ensuring the business makes an informed decision. In a sales scenario, a Scientist might dissect a product into its fundamental components, carefully examining each one to understand its function and value. This understanding could be instrumental in persuading a client who appreciates a detailed breakdown of product features and benefits.

DETAIL-ORIENTED

The attention to detail that Scientists typically display ensures that nothing is overlooked. This trait is beneficial in roles that require a high degree of precision. For instance, a Scientist might notice a minor defect during a new product's testing phase that could potentially lead to product failure or customer dissatisfaction. By catching this detail early, the company can address the issue before the product goes to market, saving money and protecting the brand's reputation.

While interacting with a prospective customer, a Scientist's meticulous attention to detail might help them pick up on subtle cues about the customer's needs or pain points that others might easily miss. By noticing these details, the Scientist can tailor their sales pitch to directly address these needs and increase their chances of closing a deal.

RATIONAL DECISION-MAKERS

Scientists are generally driven by logic and factual evidence when making decisions. In a sales situation, a Scientist might rely on hard data and factual evidence to persuade potential customers about a product's worth. If a customer is sceptical about a product's performance, the Scientist could present them with data, reviews, and real-life case studies demonstrating the product's effectiveness, thereby addressing the customer's concerns with solid evidence.

CONS

SLOW DECISION-MAKERS

The careful, analytical nature of Scientists can also be a downside, particularly in situations where rapid decision-making is necessary. This can be a disadvantage in situations that require quick, decisive action. For example, in a fast-paced startup environment, there might not be enough time for the detailed analysis a Scientist prefers before making a decision. The requirement for quick pivots and instant decisions might leave them feeling overwhelmed and indecisive.

RESERVED

Scientists can sometimes come across as reserved or introverted, which may make it difficult for them to form strong bonds with colleagues. This characteristic can potentially affect team cohesion in collaborative work settings. For instance, if a Scientist is part of a cross-functional team, their reserved nature may make it difficult for them to actively engage in brainstorming sessions or social events, potentially leading to them feeling isolated or the team feeling a lack of full engagement. In a sales environment, a Scientist's reserved or introverted nature could potentially pose challenges as well. Sales often involves building strong relationships with clients, and an introverted disposition might affect these dynamics.

THE SCIENTIST PERSONALITY TYPE IN A SURVIVAL SITUATION

In a survival situation, the pros and cons of the scientific personality type become very clear. On the one hand, their analytical skills and detail-oriented nature can be extremely useful. For instance, they could determine the most efficient way to use limited resources or carefully plan an escape route that considers all possible dangers. On the other hand, their tendency to make slower decisions could be a liability if immediate action is required, such as when a predator is approaching. Similarly, their reserved nature might make it more challenging for them to build strong alliances or effectively communicate within a group, which are often vital for survival.

THE AMIABLE

PROS

TEAM PLAYERS

Amiable individuals are known for their exceptional ability to work collaboratively with others. Their cooperative and supportive nature can make them the glue that holds a team together. They are often the ones smoothing over conflicts, offering support to team members, and maintaining a positive and inclusive team culture.

STRONG NETWORKERS

Amiables have an innate ability to build and maintain strong personal connections. Their genuine desire for social connection and recognition fuels their motivation to actively engage with others. This skill extends to the business realm, where Amiables excel at cultivating and maintaining relationships with clients, suppliers, and partners. By investing effort in establishing and sustaining these connections, they play an important role in ensuring smooth business operations and opening doors to new opportunities.

EMPATHETIC

Amiables have high emotional intelligence and a deep capacity for empathy. Their ability to empathise allows them to relate to different perspectives and experiences, which is a valuable asset in roles that require significant human interaction. This makes them particularly well-suited for roles that require emotional intelligence, such as human resources, counselling, and customer service. For instance, in a human resources role, an Amiable person's ability to empathise can help effectively resolve workplace conflicts, promoting a harmonious and productive work environment.

CONS

INDECISIVE

Despite their many strengths, Amiables can sometimes struggle when it comes to decision-making, particularly when their choices might lead to confrontation or conflict. Their desire to maintain harmony can cause them to avoid making decisions that could upset others. In a team setting, this can lead to indecisiveness and delay in critical decisions that can potentially impact project outcomes.

In a leadership position, an Amiable might struggle to make crucial decisions, especially if they involve potential confrontation or conflict. For example, if a problematic employee is negatively affecting the team, an Amiable leader may hesitate to take the necessary corrective action due to their dislike of confrontation, which could lead to the problem persisting.

In a business context, Amiables can be equally challenging. If they're part of a decision-making process, they'll likely award the purchase order to the last representative who pitched an offer, merely to avoid upsetting anyone. It's not uncommon for them to allow every salesperson an extended pitch despite the resources this consumes.

PASSIVE

When working on a collaborative project, an Amiable's passiveness could prevent them from asserting their innovative ideas or valuable insights, especially if there's a more dominant personality in the team. Their tendency to avoid conflict can prevent them from pushing back against popular opinion or voicing their unique perspectives. This can be a disadvantage in team settings where their valuable ideas and input might be needed.

When it comes to forming a winning sales team, it's critical to reconsider the placement of Amiable personality types in sales roles, especially those that involve aggressive negotiation and conflict resolution. Amiables, while known for their agreeable and non-confrontational nature, tend to avoid high-pressure environments, making them less likely to push for a sale or assertively negotiate deals. This hesitance can translate into missed opportunities and, ultimately, an underperforming sales team, affecting the organisation's bottom line.

In your social circles, I'd suggest you keep a healthy distance from Amiables. They're fence-sitters who will rarely contribute to your personal growth. Unlike ambivalent individuals who have strong views for or against something, Amiables typically avoid taking a firm stance. Their strong desire to please and avoid conflict means they tend to agree with others, follow the crowd, and rarely voice a unique opinion, often to their own detriment.

THE AMIABLE PERSONALITY TYPE IN A SURVIVAL SITUATION

In a survival situation, the Amiable's empathetic nature and strong team-building skills can be greatly beneficial. Their ability to understand and respond to the emotional needs of their fellow travellers can help maintain morale and foster a cooperative spirit. In addition, their networking skills could help secure necessary resources or information from locals or other travellers. However, their tendency towards indecisiveness and passivity can be a challenge in situations that require quick, assertive decisions, like when faced with sudden dangers or unexpected obstacles.

SUMMARY

If a Director personality type is a guided missile, relentlessly zeroing in on objectives, and an Emotive personality type is a firework, bursting with colours and emotions, while a Scientist personality type is a supercomputer, meticulously processing data, then the Amiable personality type would be a friendly golden retriever – eager to please, avoiding conflict, and happily wagging their tail to whatever tune is being played. They're driven by a GPS that has

"Avoid Confrontation" set as its ultimate destination, with a bonus setting of "Agree with the Last Statement Heard". So, if you're looking for someone to enthusiastically nod along and avoid ruffling feathers, an Amiable is your go-to. But if you need decisive action, you might want to check if that golden retriever can fetch you a Director.

THE SIX PERSUASION BUTTONS

Human decisions are influenced by a myriad of powerful drivers. At the heart of these are what we can term the six drivers of persuasion: the thirst for power, the hunger for achievement, the longing for recognition, the desire for association, the yearning for safety, and the need for order. These drivers act much like receptors on a cell or elements within our DNA, each activated when the corresponding trigger, or 'button,' is pressed.

Power – Individuals driven by power are motivated by the ability to influence and control their surroundings.

Achievement – Achievement-oriented individuals are driven by the pursuit of personal accomplishments and the attainment of goals.

Recognition – The recognition trigger is tied to individuals who seek acknowledgement, praise, and appreciation for their contributions.

Association – Those who are driven by association place a high value on social connections and the sense of belonging within a group.

Safety – The safety trigger appeals to individuals who prioritise stability, security, and risk mitigation.

Order – The order trigger is activated in individuals who value structure, organisation, and predictability in their lives.

Influencing people's decisions requires understanding these key drivers that guide their behaviour. By identifying these drivers and

customising your approach to address them specifically, you significantly increase the odds of directing an outcome in your favour.

IDENTIFYING THE SIX PERSUASION BUTTONS

People's motivations and needs can be expressed subtly in their
behaviour, physical environment, and in the way they interact with
others. Visual cues are one of the most useful tools in terms of
providing valuable insights into what a person's persuasion buttons
might be.

To illustrate this, let's begin by considering the typical drivers of
BMW, Volvo, and Toyota vehicles. Which persuasion button (or
buttons) do you think might be most influential for each of them?

A BMW driver walks into a coffee shop meeting and casually places
their M5 keys on the table, the keyring bearing the vehicle's logo
prominently displayed. Which two persuasion buttons do you think
would most apply to this individual? It's likely that someone keen to
showcase their BMW keys for all to see is driven by a thirst for
power and a hunger for **achievement**.

A Volvo driver, on the other hand, is likely driven by a need for
safety. There may be other motivators, but safety is likely the
primary one. Volvo's reputation for safety and durability outweighs

its somewhat utilitarian aesthetic. Therefore, people choosing Volvo are often making a practical and safety-conscious decision.

Toyota drivers, on the contrary, might not be the first to show off their keys. This could be because Toyota, as a brand, focuses on reliability and functionality over flamboyance. We might assume that someone driving a Toyota values **association**, **order**, **safety**, or perhaps a combination of these drivers. In countries like Africa, where road conditions can be challenging, the ubiquitous availability of Toyota spare parts makes owning a Toyota a practical and reliable choice. For a Toyota driver, this would be an important factor driving their decision to purchase this particular brand.

Now, consider this logo:

To me, the difference between a Land Cruiser or a Hilux and a Land Rover is that one is a vehicle, and the other is an emotion. No matter how many tents you can mount on your Toyota bakkie, the vehicle remains just that – a practical but uninspiring Toyota bakkie. When venturing into Africa, I want photos of me posing next to my Land Rover, donning my wide-brimmed hat, a Masai warrior wielding his spear at my side, and a herd of elephants feeding off a baobab tree in the backdrop. Even if it takes a little digital magic from PhotoShop, Midjourney, or Stable Diffusion to perfect the scene, it's worth it. Replace the Land Rover with a Hilux bakkie, and the impact just isn't the same.

So, what motivates a Land Rover owner? In my view, none of the six persuasion buttons quite hit the mark. They're driven by something different: an undeniable thirst for adventure. And, more often than not, they tend to be dog lovers.

While these observations might seem generalised, it's important to take data cues from wherever we can find them.

Another visual cue could be what they have displayed on their desk or their wrist, or their office wall. Do they have their BCom or MBA certificate framed on the wall behind them? If so, why do you think it's there? The answer is simple: **recognition**. The reason their certificates are so prominently displayed is so that you can see them and comment on them. If you see their academic credentials, don't ignore them – engage in conversation about them. A remark like, "I see you attended my alma mater university?" or "So you got your MBA at Harvard?" can score you instant points. You'll be five steps ahead of anyone else who walks into their office to pitch their skills and fails to notice their wall of achievements.

Their car keys have been casually left on their desk, the M5 BMW or Mercedes AMG logo in plain view. What message are they sending? It's likely about **power**. They're signalling, and they want you to respond to that signal. If you want their business, press the persuasion button. If the thought of doing this makes you uncomfortable, reserve your discomfort for a private moment after you've secured the order.

See that flashy gold Rolex on their wrist? What kind of message is this? It's about **power**. It's about **achievement**. Comment on it. They're not wearing a Rolex to keep track of the time. They're wearing it because they want people to notice it. If you overlook it, you've missed the lesson.

Technicians and engineers are into **recognition**. If you're leading a team of such professionals, it's important that you recognise this driver and reward their efforts appropriately. If one of your engineers worked until midnight the previous night to fix a big network problem at a blue-chip client, don't hand them a large overtime cheque. Instead, publicly acknowledge their efforts. Send out an all-staff email lauding their dedication, saying, "Team, I want to share that Johnny went above and beyond last night. He worked until 12 o'clock without food or water, braving freezing conditions to get [insert company name]'s server up and running again. As your CEO, I couldn't be prouder of his commitment. His dedication sets a benchmark for us all." Acknowledgement costs nothing, and neither does an email. Yet, it will boost Johnny's morale, making him feel valued and appreciated. You didn't need to stroke his power or achievement drivers because, as a techie, you know recognition is his primary motivator – and you knew just the right button to press.

Now, if it were a sales rep who worked late, the story would be different. They aren't looking for a group email – they're after that commission check. Different professionals, different persuasion buttons.

Another powerful motivator for tech enthusiasts and engineers is a sense of **association.** They want to feel that they belong to a group – after all, they're part of a work family. Lean into this. For instance, you could provide them with a budget and encourage them to participate in a team-building activity like action cricket on a Friday afternoon. Take it a step further by gifting them branded company sports shirts bearing their names. Engaging with them in this way doesn't mean you're being insincere – it just means you have a better grasp of psychology than your competitors, who may overlook such opportunities to show their technical staff how much they are appreciated.

When interacting with finance managers, accountants, auditors, and financial directors, **safety and order** should be your focus. Weave words like *compliance, fiduciary duty, corporate governance,* and *risk management* into your narrative to assure them that you're not rushing –

you've done your background checks, you're accredited, and you pose no risk to the company or any individual. Only ask to proceed once every box on their checklist has been meticulously assessed.

Cue, cue, cue. Your job is to find those buttons and to press them.

By understanding an individual's personality type – whether they're a Director, an Emotive, a Scientist, or an Amiable – and then identifying what motivates them at a granular level, you'll know exactly which buttons to push. Get inside their heads, read the room, and play the tune that gets their feet tapping – that's the art and science of sealing the deal.

LEVERAGING THE SIX PERSUASION BUTTONS

Whether we are selling to organisations, working within a team, or exploring remote destinations, we are ultimately engaging with individuals. Each person is driven by their own ambitions, aspirations, and needs, influenced by a range of powerful motivators. To truly connect with people, we must uncover what activates these drivers, speaking directly to their inner motivations.

Let's now explore how leveraging these six persuasion buttons can enhance our approach and strategy in these diverse scenarios. This understanding can empower us to make deeper connections, whether in sales, within a team environment, or even when interacting with others while exploring remote destinations.

POWER

In a sales setting, appealing to the power trigger can involve showcasing how your product or service empowers the customer to make impactful decisions and gain a competitive edge. By demonstrating how your offering can elevate their position and influence, you tap into their desire for power, thereby increasing the likelihood of a successful sale.

In a team environment, this trigger can be engaged by involving these individuals in strategic discussions.

When exploring remote destinations, recognising the power trigger might involve assigning specific roles to team members, such as planning routes, making important decisions, or leading the team through challenging terrains.

ACHIEVEMENT

When pitching to a prospective customer, you can cater to the achievement trigger by emphasising how your product or team can help your customer achieve their desired outcomes or personal milestones. Highlighting specific achievements and success stories of previous customers can inspire confidence in potential buyers, reinforcing their drive to succeed. When pitching to a self-assured managing director, for example, they're not just buying a product – they're buying a ticket to success. Your pitch could emphasise how your product or service will supercharge productivity, bolster bottom-line results, and help them outmanoeuvre competitors.

In a team environment, recognising this trigger involves acknowledging and rewarding individual achievements. For instance, you could set challenging targets and publicly recognise team members who meet or exceed them.

When exploring remote locations, you can tap into the achievement trigger by setting challenging goals, such as reaching a particular landmark or conquering difficult terrain. By celebrating their accomplishments along the way, you will fuel their drive for achievement and boost their morale.

RECOGNITION

Incorporating this trigger into your sales pitch to potential customers can involve showcasing testimonials, awards, or positive feedback from other satisfied customers. By highlighting the recognition received by these customers, you create a sense of trust and reassurance that can motivate potential customers to choose your product or service.

In a team environment, you could showcase individual achievements during meetings or celebrate milestones achieved as a team. Recognising their efforts can foster a positive team culture and motivate others to strive for recognition as well.

When exploring remote destinations, recognising team members for their contributions and achievements works wonders for boosting morale. Acknowledging their efforts publicly, praising their problem-solving skills or innovative ideas, and expressing gratitude for their hard work will help fulfil their need for recognition.

ASSOCIATION

When pitching to a prospective customer, emphasising the social benefits of using your product or service can appeal to the association trigger. For example, if you are selling a collaboration tool for remote teams, you can highlight how the tool facilitates seamless communication, encourages teamwork, and strengthens the sense of camaraderie among team members. Emphasising the positive impact of your product on team dynamics and collaboration can resonate with customers who value association and the sense of belonging to a cohesive group.

In a team environment, recognising this trigger involves fostering a collaborative environment where teamwork and camaraderie are valued. Emphasising shared values, goals, and a supportive work environment can foster a sense of unity, encourage a positive team dynamic, and motivate team members to work harmoniously toward common goals. For example, you could encourage team-building activities or create opportunities for cross-functional collaboration.

While exploring remote destinations, the association trigger can be fostered by encouraging teamwork, shared responsibilities, and creating opportunities for bonding activities.

SAFETY

In professional settings, recognising this trigger means providing a sense of security and clear guidelines. In sales, addressing this trigger can involve highlighting the reliability, durability, and protective features of your product or service. For example, if you're selling camping gear for overlanding trips, emphasising the safety certifications, sturdy construction, and innovative safety features can reassure customers and increase their confidence in your offerings.

In a team environment, when assigning tasks or projects, considering the safety trigger means taking into account potential risks and implementing measures to minimise them. For instance, if a team member is responsible for handling sensitive customer data, providing secure data management systems, encryption methods, and training on data privacy can address their safety concerns and ensure the protection of confidential information.

When exploring remote destinations, acknowledging the safety trigger might involve conducting thorough safety briefings, ensuring the availability of emergency supplies, and having contingency plans in place for potential risks or challenges.

ORDER

In sales, recognising the order trigger means providing clear processes, guidelines, and well-defined roles and responsibilities by establishing efficient workflows, implementing project management tools, and maintaining transparent communication channels. For example, when pitching to a financial director, your pitch might emphasise the product's capacity to save company resources, bolster defence against cyber-attacks, and safeguard crucial company data. Explain how it's an economical choice that will ultimately save the company money. The goal is to present your product as a fortress — offering protection and ensuring the smooth operation of their system.

In a team environment, recognising the order trigger involves creating a structured, well-organised workspace with clearly defined roles and responsibilities. This helps reduce confusion and ensures everyone knows their part in achieving the team's goals. For example, implementing an effective project management system to provide a clear roadmap for a project, establishing deadlines, and assigning tasks in a way that everyone understands their contribution. This sense of order can increase productivity, create a harmonious team environment, and drive the team towards the successful completion of their objectives.

When exploring remote destinations, acknowledging the order trigger might involve creating detailed itineraries, establishing a clear chain of command, and ensuring that everyone understands their specific roles and responsibilities within the team.

ADAPTING YOUR SALES STRATEGY WHEN SELLING TO ORGANISATIONS

Pitching to a group of people sitting around a boardroom table is a fundamentally different process than pitching directly to an individual. When you're presenting your services or products to an organisation, you're stepping into a boardroom where you won't have the time or the opportunity to identify the personality type of each person present. As a result, it becomes impractical, if not impossible, to determine and target each individual's specific persuasion button. Therefore, instead of catering to personal interests, your focus must shift to addressing the collective needs and interests of the organisation as a whole.

When pitching to organisations, there are typically three key drivers or 'buttons' that you can leverage:

IMAGE

PERFORMACE

FINANCE

The key to successful pitching lies in understanding how your product or service aligns with the organisation's corporate image, how it can enhance the organisation's performance, and how it delivers value in a cost-effective manner. By moulding your sales strategy around these drivers, you can significantly increase your chances of clinching a deal.

Now, let's delve into each of these factors in more detail.

IMAGE

Organisations meticulously curate their image, knowing it speaks volumes to stakeholders both inside and outside their walls. When selling to an organisation, you're not just offering a product or service – you're proposing an enhancement to their corporate identity. Just as a logo or a tagline contributes to a company's public perception, so does the choice of products and services they utilise.

PERFORMANCE

Companies operate much like a production line, constantly seeking improvements and efficiencies. Your product or service is a proposed upgrade to their assembly process. Can it make their conveyor belt run faster (increase productivity), remove a production bottleneck (streamline operations), or deliver a superior final product (improve customer experiences)? Provide tangible evidence that your offering will make a measurable impact on their day-to-day operations and, ultimately, their bottom line.

FINANCE

Cost is a vital consideration in the strategic decision-making of any organisation. Be ready to lay out the financial case for your product or service. The focus is not just on the upfront cost but also on the long-term financial implications of their decisions. Can your product lead to cost savings, generate increased revenue, or promise a substantial return on investment? If the answer is yes, then that's the narrative you want to emphasise. Make it clear that your product is a financially sound investment and not merely an expense.

Let's examine how we can effectively leverage each of these three buttons in a real-world scenario. I want you to consider the following three logos. Now, imagine you're on the threshold of each of these organisations' boardrooms, about to pitch your range of PCs to their respective boards of directors. While the suite of products you're pitching remains constant, the audience – the board – changes with each organisation, thus necessitating a tailored narrative for each.

With this in mind, your task is to identify which of the three persuasion buttons (or perhaps a combination thereof) you would aim to press when pitching to each of these organisations.

INTEL

Intel, as you may already know, makes high-performance CPUs. For this organisation, performance is paramount. Therefore, the first checkbox you need to ensure you've ticked is demonstrating how your product or service will give them a competitive edge over competitors like AMD, Synopsis, NVIDIA, or any of the other chip manufacturers in the industry. The mantra here is 'performance, performance, performance.' Once you've convincingly addressed this aspect, then – and only then – move on to discussing the cost.

INVESTEC

For most banks, the number one persuasion button would be the finance one. In Investec's case, because it's an investment bank with a high-net-worth client base, it would likely be a close tie between image and finance. They may not place as much emphasis on perfor-mance, so it would be wise to steer clear of focusing on that. Instead, lean into what their purchase might do for their image. Sell them on the notion that Dell is the cutting-edge brand to opt for, while brands like IBM may seem a bit outdated, potentially appealing more to an older demographic. Highlight that Dell is the contemporary choice. And, since it's a bank and cost-efficiency is paramount, underscore the fact that investing in Dell represents an excellent return on investment.

BP

BP spent an astonishing $211,000,000 on its logo redesign, believed to be the most expensive in history. The chosen symbol, a stylised sunflower, is somewhat ironic given BP's reputation as one of the world's largest oil producers. The strategic use of green and yellow in the design is a clear attempt to 'greenwash' the company's public image.

So, what do you suppose is BP's top persuasion button? It isn't finance or performance – it's unequivocally image. The company is

171

well aware of its public perception and is willing to invest significantly to improve its image.

If you were to pitch the Dell solution to BP's board of directors, you'd focus on the machine's eco-friendly attributes. You would emphasise that the machines are completely recyclable after three years. However, instead of recycling them directly, your company would offer a unique value proposition. You'd propose to donate any still-functioning machines to a school, orphanage, or animal welfare society of BP's choice, providing a chance for the organisation to give back to the community. Furthermore, you'd make sure the donation event receives media coverage, thereby boosting BP's image as a socially responsible organisation. Concluding your pitch, you would reassure them that any remaining non-functioning machines would be recycled in an environmentally-friendly manner.

Let's now explore several general examples to further illustrate how best to press these persuasion buttons when pitching your products or services to an organisation.

In terms of image, suppose a green energy solution provider is pitching its products to a manufacturing company that has a strong corporate identity centred around environmental responsibility. In this scenario, the green energy solution provider can underscore how their solar power systems can enhance the manufacturing company's image as a sustainable and eco-conscious entity. They can highlight that switching to their solar power system not only decreases carbon footprint but also aligns seamlessly with the company's stated commitment to sustainability. They can point out that showcasing their use of solar energy for manufacturing would be a powerful message to their stakeholders, demonstrating a practical application of their environmental values. They can also emphasise that, by adopting their solution, the manufacturing company positions itself as a sector leader in environmental responsibility, thereby enhancing its corporate identity in the eyes of customers, partners, and the broader industry.

In terms of performance, let's imagine an analytics firm offering an AI-driven data analytics tool to an online retailer looking to optimise its operations. The analytics firm can highlight how its software increases productivity by providing real-time customer insights that will allow the retailer to focus marketing efforts where they're most effective. Next, they can demonstrate how the software will streamline the retailer's operations by identifying patterns in inventory turnover, thereby enabling the retailer to manage its stock more efficiently and reduce operational hitches. They can also point out that a better understanding of customer behaviour will allow the retailer to personalise the shopping experience, therefore boosting customer satisfaction. Finally, the analytics firm should provide evidence, such as case studies or data, to reinforce its claims. This might include metrics like increased sales, decreased operational costs, or improved customer satisfaction scores. In this way, they're not merely selling software but a strategic solution that can improve the retailer's performance and profitability.

Finally, in terms of cost, let's consider a company offering advanced cybersecurity software to a financial institution. The cybersecurity company can stress that while their software comes with an upfront cost, it can prevent expensive data breaches in the long term, saving the institution significant potential losses. Next, they could underline that their software could indirectly increase revenue by strengthening the institution's clients' trust in its ability to protect their sensitive financial information, which can help retain existing clients and attract new ones. Finally, the company could provide evidence of a substantial return on investment, such as examples of other financial institutions that were able to thwart costly cyber-attacks due to their software, highlighting that investing in their product is a financially prudent move, not just an expense.

NEGOTIATING WITH A TRIBE VS SELLING TO AN ORGANISATION

If you had to stop for the night in unfamiliar territory in the wild, what would be your number one concern? I would assume that your answer would be safety. Now, imagine there is tribal land close by, and you want to camp there for the night. If you were to negotiate with that tribe to enter their land for the night, what do you think would be the most important thing to an impoverished tribe living in the wilderness? Food? Clothing?

You can be certain that they're already growing their own crops and vegetables. They're hunting their own meat. They don't want your T-shirt or your braai packs. What they really want is currency – a negotiation tool that few will refuse. When travelling through Africa, therefore, you want to make sure you're carrying some good old USD.

Let me share a personal story that illustrates this.

When mapping out the route for our 1998-1999 overland journey through Africa, I made sure that it would allow me to celebrate my thirtieth birthday on the majestic Zambezi River in Zambia before setting off for the next leg of our adventure into Tanzania. One of the most beautiful sights in the world is the Zambezi at sunset, and I intended to immortalise it in my memory forever.

As the day began to wane, our group boarded a cruise along the serene waters of the Zambezi. The sinking sun cast a golden aura over pods of hippos bobbing in the water while their symphony of snorts and grumbles served as conversations that reverberated across the water. The sky transformed into a breathtaking canvas painted in hues of amber and crimson. With the vibrant colours reflecting off the gentle ripples of the river, I raised a toast to the closing day and the dawn of a new decade ahead.

A couple of days later, we embarked on our journey into Northern Zambia, where we would eventually cross over the border and into Tanzania. As we drew up to the border post that evening, the sun setting behind us, we noticed that the gates were padlocked shut. I glanced at my watch – it was 5:15 p.m. According to our map, the border post was supposed to close at 6 p.m., which would have given us enough time to pass through and get to our next camping spot before nightfall.

"The gate closes at five," the security guard on duty said, gesturing for us to turn around. "Come back at six tomorrow morning."

And then it dawned on us – we were stranded for the night.

One of the cardinal rules of overlanding through Africa is to be in camp at least an hour before the sun sets. The reasons are manifold. It could be a kudu crossing the road or a wandering lone elephant bull, an oncoming car without headlights, or even a trap – it's not uncommon for rocks to be placed in the road to slow a vehicle down before hijacking it. Besides the obvious dangers, pitching a tent after dark is no one's idea of fun – especially given how pitch black Africa gets at night. To avoid such predicaments, you always factor in at least an extra hour when planning your route for contingencies like refuelling, changing a tyre, or making a diversion.

We had just broken the one-hour rule.

From what we'd seen driving in, there were no camping spots or villages nearby – only the vast African wilderness with its silhouettes of acacia trees against the darkening sky. We were, quite literally, in the middle of nowhere. As the last rays of sunlight disappeared and darkness enveloped us, a sense of urgency permeated the air. We had no choice but to turn around and drive until we found somewhere safe to camp for the night, knowing that this night would be an unexpected test of our resourcefulness and resolve.

About half an hour from the border post, with the wilderness stretching endlessly around us, we noticed a vehicle coming up behind us. It seemed to appear almost out of nowhere, its headlights piercing through the night. They were edging closer and closer. My heartbeat quickened, and I felt a lump forming in my throat – I didn't have a good feeling about this. Why were they out on the road in the middle of nowhere at this time of the evening? I sped up to put about five hundred metres between us and then made a U-turn. As we passed the vehicle, I caught a glimpse of the shadowy figures inside. I counted at least four occupants. They were all peering out of the window at us, their faces masked in the darkness. And then, as if in a coordinated pursuit, they made a U-turn too. My mind raced – this wasn't going to end well. We had no form of radio communication and no safe haven. Our Johannesburg GP number plate was a dead giveaway that we were tourists. What's worse, we had no idea what their intentions were.

All of a sudden, the Landy's lights illuminated a white hand-painted sign on the side of the road. CAMPING, it read. A surge of relief washed over us. I slammed on the brakes, veered off the road, and navigated down a stretch lined with Marula trees. The road was rough and uneven – a normal car wouldn't have stood a chance handling these conditions. We had no idea where the road would lead or when it would end. We dared not stop, and our eyes darted back and forth, half-expecting to see the headlights of the pursuing vehicle emerge behind us. But for now, all that mattered was that we seemed to have lost them, and the dense trees around us felt like a protective cloak.

The path continued for about two kilometres (1.25 miles), winding through the dark African savanna until it eventually opened up into a clearing. Another painted white sign emblazoned with the word 'CAMPING' marked its entrance. Other than several bushes dotting the area, the only amenity was a red brick donkey boiler – a rudimentary water heating system – which would serve as our shower. A bit of steam wafted from it, revealing a rudimentary tap and showerhead.

A figure emerged from the shadows and strode towards us with an air of grace and majesty. As he drew near, he raised his spear in a gesture of greeting. Clad in a bright red Shuka and towering over us, it was obvious that he was a Maasai warrior. As he stepped into the light cast by our vehicle's headlights, his face caught my attention – it was adorned with intricate patterns of scarification. These fine, symmetrical lines – some small, some straight, and some slightly curved – were etched into the skin across his forehead and temples. They resembled ancient scripts, each telling its own story.

Remembering a bit about the Maasai culture that I had read before embarking on the journey, I decided to show my respect. Instead of extending my hand for a handshake, which could have been perceived as imposing my own cultural norm, I mimicked his spear-raising gesture as a way of greeting him in return. His eyes lit up for a moment, acknowledging the attempt at honouring his tradition.

"Do you want security for the night?" he asked.

When you're stranded in the wilderness, unsure of whether you're still being pursued, and a 6'6" Maasai warrior holding a spear asks if you need protection, there is only one answer.

"How much?" I asked.

"Two dollars," he replied, his voice calm and grounded. His modest request served as a reminder of the dignity and simple generosity that can still be found in the world.

At six o'clock the following morning, with the sun just coming up over the horizon and a thick blanket of mist hovering ominously above the ground, I zipped open our tent. There he stood in the same spot we'd left him the night before. For eleven hours, he hadn't moved. He gave his word that he would guard us, and that's what he did – right through the freezing cold night, with only his spear as protection.

The Maasai are some of the fiercest warriors on the continent, but they are also people of integrity; their word is their honour. I will be forever grateful to that Maasai warrior, on whom we had to depend to get us through the night so that we could get to the border crossing the following morning.

Reflecting on that night in the African wilderness, it's clear that our successful negotiation with the Maasai warrior was based on understanding needs, respecting cultural values, and building trust. Interestingly, these fundamental principles are not just confined to the plains of Africa – they apply to more conventional environments too. In the business world, particularly when selling to an organisation, a similar set of skills is indispensable. Let's consider how the art of negotiating with a tribe has surprising parallels with selling to an organisation.

SELLING TO AN ORGANISATION

Selling to an organisation is, in many ways, like negotiating with a tribe or a tribesperson. Both require a nuanced understanding of the collective needs of the group and the individual motivations of key decision-makers. Both require engaging with key decision-makers, respecting cultural differences, and aligning one's unique offerings with the organisation's unique 'tribal' identity.

Let's explore these factors in a little more detail.

IDENTIFY NEEDS AND PRIORITIES

Just as you would take the time to understand a tribe's key concerns, such as safety, resources, or preserving cultural traditions, it's important that you take the time to understand a prospective customer's specific pain points and goals, be it financial stability, market leadership, innovation, operational efficiency, customer satisfaction, or regulatory compliance. By aligning your product or service with these needs, you're not just selling a product or service – you're establishing yourself as a trusted partner by providing a solution that resonates with the company's strategic interests.

ENGAGE WITH KEY DECISION-MAKERS

Within every organisation – just like in a tribe – there are key decision-makers whose opinions carry significant weight. It's not enough to impress a single 'chief' or CEO. There are 'elders,' too, such as department heads or senior managers, whose unique needs and motivations should also be addressed. To win the tribe, you need to engage these influential members, understand their individual concerns, and demonstrate how your offering meets their requirements.

RESPECT CULTURAL DIFFERENCES

Showing respect for cultural differences is as important in a professional setting as it is in tribal negotiations. Every company, like every tribe, has its own culture, values, and way of doing things. In essence, whether negotiating for safety in the wild or selling a product to a multinational organisation, the key lies in recognising the underlying human elements. By identifying needs, engaging with decision-makers, and showing cultural respect, you can forge bonds that go beyond mere transactions.

In conclusion, whether negotiating for safety with a Maasai warrior or selling to a large organisation, the principles remain strikingly similar. Understanding needs, engaging with key decision-makers, and respecting cultural differences are the cornerstones of successful negotiation in any setting. As different as the plains of Africa and a corporate boardroom may seem, the human elements of trust, respect, and understanding are universal.

CHAPTER 6
IMPORTANCE VS URGENCY

I magine you're in the middle of a peaceful Saturday afternoon, finally taking the time to declutter and organise your digital photo library. This is important because you've been meaning to back up and preserve these precious memories for years. Suddenly, your phone pings with a notification. It's a message from a friend who just discovered that a local store is having a flash sale on T-shirts – 50% off for the next hour only! Your friend is ecstatic and urges you to rush over immediately.

Now, let's be clear: organising your photos is important – it's about safeguarding memories and ensuring your digital life is in order. But the T-shirt sale is *urgent* – it's happening right now and won't last long.

Your knee-jerk reaction is to drop everything, race to the store, and start frantically filling a shopping cart with T-shirts in an assortment of colours. The adrenaline is pumping as you grab the last T-shirt just before another shopper reaches for it. You feel victorious! But when you get home and see your collection of cotton shirts staring at you, you realise that you got swept up in the urgency of the moment, neglecting what was truly important. Your digital photo library remains a mess, and you're now the owner of 10 new T-shirts, wondering how things escalated so quickly.

This little T-shirt adventure is a perfect example of how the urgent can often distract us from the important. Just like the message from your friend about the sale was loud and demanding, people often make a lot of noise about things they consider urgent. When someone is trying to tell you that something is extremely urgent, and you don't get it, they'll increase the decibels and say it even louder.

In our everyday lives, when the world is screaming at us, it is human nature to pivot towards that which is urgent. This is particularly relevant when it relates to other people's emergencies. The louder a person shouts, the more difficult it is to focus on anything else. Usually, it's a false sense of emergency. It's safe to say that unless it's a personal emergency, such as a medical issue, a family member in distress, or an urgent situation like your website crashing during a peak sales period, it's not as pressing as it seems. A lot of these so-called "emergencies" are urgent simply because someone else did not plan properly or procrastinated.

It's incredibly difficult for humans to say no when there's a false sense of urgency being imposed. But you will never be truly successful if you can't say no to other people's self-imposed emergencies. The ability to lock out that noise and say no to the things that are urgent and yes to the things that are important will make you ten times more effective compared to someone who suffers a knee-jerk reaction every time somebody runs in saying that something needs to be done urgently.

Having understood the significance of distinguishing between urgency and importance through our T-shirt example, let's delve a little deeper. In this chapter, we will discuss the distinction between important and urgent decisions, explore the matrix for effective decision-making, and draw parallels between applying these concepts in the company boardroom and in overlanding or survival scenarios.

UNDERSTANDING THE DIFFERENCE BETWEEN IMPORTANT AND URGENT DECISIONS

Making decisions is an everyday part of business and life. When faced with a decision, it's crucial to recognise the difference between what's important, what's urgent, what is both important and urgent – and conversely, which is neither. Understanding the nature of each decision can help in prioritising them effectively.

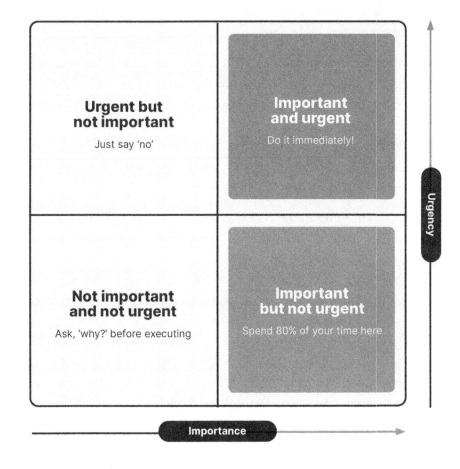

The matrix is divided into four quadrants, each representing a different combination of urgency and importance. The vertical axis of the matrix represents the degree of urgency, while the horizontal axis represents the level of importance:

1. Important and Urgent: These decisions usually relate to tasks with deadlines or consequences. They require immediate action and have a significant impact on one's long-term success or survival. From a business perspective, this might be when a client reports a significant issue with your product, causing substantial interruptions to their operations. This situation requires immediate action and resolution, as it impacts both your client's success and your company's reputation.

2. Important but not Urgent: Decisions here are crucial for long-term success or well-being but don't require immediate action. Ideally, most of your time should be spent in this quadrant. In a business context, this might include developing a long-term business strategy, planning for future expansion, or investing in employee training programs. These decisions are significant for the company's long-term success. We'll discuss this in more detail shortly.

3. Urgent but not Important: These decisions relate to distractions and unnecessary tasks that require immediate attention but do not contribute significantly to long-term success or survival. From a business perspective, this would include answering non-critical emails, attending meetings with no clear agenda, or handling minor administrative tasks. These activities demand immediate attention but do not significantly contribute to your success in the long term. The answer to these decisions should ideally be "No". Saying no does not necessarily mean ignoring these tasks – it just means that the issue can, for instance, be either delegated or delayed.

4. Not Important and not Urgent: These decisions relate to tasks that must be done but don't require your specific skill set. In the bigger picture, these decisions have minimal impact on long-term success or survival and can be avoided, delayed, or delegated. These could be tasks like organising the company's file system, updating the team's contact list, or other routine administrative duties. When faced with these decisions, always ask "Why?" before executing.

It's essential to recognise that not every urgent task deserves your immediate attention and that a normally urgent matter may, in fact, be given lesser priority while you focus on issues that are actually important.

Take, for example, when a colleague rushes into your office in a panic needing your help with a presentation they forgot to prepare, or when your teenager calls you urgently for something they need for a project due tomorrow. Their lack of planning has suddenly become your emergency. However, is it really critical for you to drop everything to help, or can it wait while you focus on your priorities?

By plotting decisions on this matrix and determining which quadrant a task falls into, you can better prioritise and allocate your time and resources.

DECISION-MAKING IN ORGANISATIONS AND SURVIVAL SITUATIONS

Effective decision-making is a critical skill in both the corporate world and life-or-death survival situations. In business, important decisions (as opposed to urgent decisions) are the building blocks of your organisation's future. Important tasks, though not always pressing, play a substantial role in shaping long-term growth and profitability. Urgent tasks, on the other hand, are like the alarm bells of your business and relate to time-sensitive issues that demand immediate attention. Perhaps it's a customer complaint that needs resolving, a looming deadline for a report, or a workplace conflict that requires mediation. While these tasks might not significantly affect your long-term goals, they can't be left on the back burner. Additionally, there are unimportant and non-urgent decisions that may not appear to have immediate consequences but still require consideration in the larger context. For example, in a business setting, these might include long-term plans for team-building activities, while in a survival scenario, they could relate to less critical resource gathering when basic needs are already met.

Similarly, in survival situations, where the stakes are immeasurably higher, and the consequences of poor decision-making can be life-threatening, decision-making also entails prioritising tasks. Important tasks include finding shelter, obtaining food, and securing water sources, while urgent tasks involve addressing medical emergencies or escaping immediate danger. Here, too, there are tasks that may be unimportant and non-urgent in the immediate context but still warrant consideration for long-term survival.

In essence, the corporate environment can be seen as a wilderness of its own, where the challenges and uncertainties demand strategic decision-making, much like in literal wilderness survival scenarios. In both cases, the ability to distinguish between important and urgent tasks and to maintain a balanced approach is crucial. This is true whether navigating a jungle with limited resources or steering a business through a competitive market.

Regardless of the apparent differences in these environments, certain skills and principles are essential for survival and success. These key aspects encompass prioritising decisions, demonstrating speed and adaptability, delegating, empowering others, and maintaining ethical considerations.

Let's explore each of these factors in more detail.

PRIORITISING DECISIONS

Let's start with a real-life survival example. Imagine you are stranded at sea on a life raft after your boat capsized in a storm. The open ocean is an unforgiving environment, and the decisions you make can be the difference between life and death. In this scenario, your immediate urgent decisions should be geared toward ensuring your safety – you need to check the raft for any punctures, secure yourself to avoid falling overboard and use any reflective materials to signal for help. You also need to protect yourself from the elements and ration any available food and water very carefully. The important decisions involve devising daily routines to maintain your mental well-being, regularly scanning the horizon for rescue, and figuring out a means to collect rainwater.

Now, translate this scenario to the business world. In the concrete jungle, you're dealing with competitors, deadlines, and customer demands. Just like deciding whether to signal for help or protect yourself from the elements, you need to determine whether to focus on addressing a major product design flaw or reevaluating your long-term marketing strategy. It's about identifying what's urgent and important, prioritising which is more important, and then strategically allocating resources and time to tackle those tasks in a way that ensures the overall survival and success of the business. Reevaluating your long-term marketing strategy will have to be put on the back burner temporarily while these urgent matters are attended to.

SPEED AND ADAPTABILITY

When you're out in the wilderness and need to prioritise what to focus on first, being quick and nimble is key. Again, let's consider a survival example. If you're lost in the wilderness, with limited supplies and no immediate means of communication, you have to decide whether to stay put and wait for help or try to find your way back to civilisation. In this situation, the urgent decision is to signal for help or determine the best route to increase your chances of being found or reaching safety. The important decision is to find shelter, water, and food to ensure your survival in the long term.

Similar principles apply to business decision-making, where you need to be able to think quickly and act decisively under pressure. This is where military strategies can provide valuable insights for both business and survival contexts. Legendary General George S. Patton once said, "A good plan executed today is better than a perfect plan executed at some indefinite point in the future." When Patton made this statement, he was emphasising the importance of action and decisiveness over prolonged indecision or continuous planning.

To illustrate this, imagine you're at the helm of a technology firm working on an innovative, industry-changing product. You've just put the finishing touches on an exciting new design that you believe will take the market by storm. Launch it quickly, and you capture the market before your rivals even know what hit them. However, if you linger too long in the pursuit of perfection, a competitor might outpace you. Don't get stuck in analysis paralysis. Waiting for the perfect plan can cause delays, missed opportunities, or even inaction. While you might not make the perfect decision, taking decisive action sets things in motion.

There's a hard truth in business and in life: you miss 100% of the shots you don't take. This adage highlights how the cost of a wasted opportunity through procrastination often far outweighs the potential cost of an incorrect judgment call. After all, an incorrect decision made in haste can usually be corrected or adjusted, but an inability to make a decision under pressure can have irrevocable consequences. In today's world, where business moves at breakneck speed and markets can change overnight, making an imperfect decision now is often better than a perfect decision made too late.

DELEGATING AND EMPOWERING

Just as adaptability is crucial in both the wilderness and the business world, so is the ability to delegate and empower those around you. This not only enhances the chances of survival but also contributes to thriving in challenging environments.

When faced with a life-threatening situation, consider a mountain climbing accident where a fellow climber has sustained a severe injury, and the weather is quickly deteriorating. The important decision is to ensure the injured climber's long-term well-being by providing proper first aid and stabilising their condition. The urgent decision is to determine whether to continue the ascent, wait for help, or attempt a risky descent to seek medical attention. In this situation, delegation is also essential. For example, someone with medical expertise could attend to the injured climber while others secure equipment or attempt to establish communication for a rescue. By delegating, you're making sure that everyone plays to their strengths. That way, things get done way more efficiently.

Now, let's bring it back to the boardroom. You're the head of a bustling start-up. Your in-tray is overflowing, your emails are backed up, and you have meetings stacked one after the other. This is where you take a leaf out of your survival handbook – start delegating! Let Jane, your tech wizard, handle the software updates. Let Mark, the marketing guru, take care of the ad campaign. By empowering your team members to make decisions and take ownership, you're not only freeing up your time but also creating a dynamic work environment where everyone's unique skills shine. The result? A thriving, agile company ready to take on the corporate wilderness.

An old business maxim says, 'Anybody can steer a ship in calm waters,' illustrating how easy it is to make decisions when everything is going smoothly. However, true leadership and skill are revealed when navigating through adversity or turbulent situations.

I firmly believe that the key distinction between good management and great management lies in the ability to execute decisions under pressure without succumbing to self-doubt or hesitation. As a business leader, this means empowering your line managers to make difficult business decisions independently, without the constant need for authorisation or escalation.

Now, let's return to the technology firm I mentioned earlier that was working on an innovative, industry-changing product, but this time, let's examine how delegating and empowering can play a significant role in a high-pressure situation.

The firm is up against a tight deadline due to a competitor planning a similar product launch. The market is turbulent, and there are many potential obstacles that could delay the product launch, including software glitches, supply chain disruptions, and team burnout. Samantha is a line manager in the company overseeing the product's final developmental stages. She has a reputation for being competent, innovative, and quick in her decisions. Under the pressure of the looming deadline and the threat from competitors, she identifies a critical software bug that could delay the product launch. Rather than waiting for approval from upper management, which could take precious time and further complicate the situation, she takes the initiative. Empowered to make crucial decisions, she reallocates resources to address the bug, collaborates with the tech team to devise a feasible solution, and simultaneously arranges for her team to work on enhancing other product features to compensate for any potential delays. All of this is accomplished under her authority without continually escalating to higher-ups.

In the end, thanks to Samantha's decisive action, the team fixes the bug just in time. The product is launched on schedule and even includes enhanced features. The technology firm not only meets the market demand but exceeds customer expectations, thereby asserting its dominance in the market.

This example illustrates the immense value of empowering individuals within an organisation to make decisions, particularly in high-pressure situations. By giving managers like Samantha the autonomy to act decisively, organisations can become more agile, respond more effectively to challenges, and capitalise on opportunities.

Whether you find yourself stranded in the wilderness or steering a business through the tumultuous seas of the corporate world, the principles of delegation and empowerment are fundamental for success. Just like in the wild, where quick thinking can mean the difference between life and death, in business, it can be the difference between failure and success. Surround yourself with a competent team and empower them to make decisions. By doing this, you'll not only survive but thrive in any environment you find yourself in.

ETHICAL CONSIDERATIONS

During a natural disaster, like an earthquake or a hurricane, ethical considerations come into play. The important decision might be to secure your home and gather essential supplies to ensure your family's safety during and after the disaster. The urgent decision is to evacuate or find immediate shelter to protect yourself and your loved ones from imminent danger. During this time, ethical considerations such as helping neighbours or ensuring that vulnerable members of the community are safe become significant.

Now, let's transport you from the scene of the natural disaster to the boardroom. You're not wrestling with survival anymore, but the essence of the dilemma remains. As a corporate leader, you're striving to maintain a balance. On one side, there's the relentless pursuit of profits – on the other, there's the pull of social responsibility and environmental consciousness. As a decision-maker in a corporation, your job isn't just about driving the bottom line – it's about making choices that respect the world around you. It's the ethical tightrope that every decision-maker, in the wilderness or the corporate jungle, must learn to walk.

In business, when making a decision in the heat of the moment, the key criteria to consider are:

1. Is the decision ethical and legal?

2. Does it make financial sense for the company?

Provided that the answers are a resounding "yes" to both and there is clarity in management's accountability, the company – and, by extension, its customers – will benefit.

In conclusion, effective decision-making is crucial both in business and survival scenarios. The key is to differentiate between important and urgent decisions, be adaptable, delegate responsibilities, and consider ethical and legal implications. By empowering individuals within an organisation to make informed decisions quickly and effectively, businesses can not only survive but thrive in a competitive market.

In business, we often find ourselves making split-second decisions, trying not to be swayed by distractions or allowing someone else's crisis to determine our course. It's a constant dance of prioritising and making the right call at the right time. This delicate balance of decision-making isn't confined to boardrooms and office corridors. Distractions, however minor, can cloud our judgement and lead us down unforeseen paths. Just as a lapse in attention in the boardroom can change a company's trajectory, a momentary distraction on a mountaineering expedition can be the difference between returning home and never being seen again. Kim and I learned this firsthand during a trek in the Himalayas.

FROM DISTRACTION TO DANGER IN THE FOOTHILLS OF THE HIMALAYAS

Every year, Nepal's majestic Himalayan Mountain range, home to eight of the world's fourteen 8,000-meter peaks, beckons thousands of trekkers eager to conquer its slopes and experience its renowned beauty. Yet, beneath this allure lurks a darker reality. On any major trekking route, lampposts tell a silent, disturbing tale. They're filled with flyers featuring the faces of the lost: "Missing Person, Last Seen..." Some are worn and faded, bearing testament to the passage of time, while others are disturbingly recent.

The reasons behind these disappearances vary widely from trekkers hiking treacherous remote routes alone and losing their bearings, succumbing to altitude sickness at higher altitudes, falling off a rock-face or a bridge or into a crevasse, getting stuck and freezing to death, to darker allegations of human trafficking. Many hike solo to save money or embrace the freedom of exploring lesser-trodden paths. However, the treacherous ground conditions, high altitudes, and unpredictable temperatures make it perilously easy to lose one's way.

By 2023, Nepal had banned solo hikes in all national parks in response to these concerns. But our experience dates back to 2010 when Kim and I decided to trek to Everest Base Camp. Back then, solo hiking was still permissible. The overarching recommendation, however, was never to trek alone.

Trekking offers a unique opportunity for peaceful solitude. Sometimes, you can walk for almost an entire day, wrapped in your own thoughts, with no need for conversation. Instead of measuring distance in kilometres or miles, you'll find rocks indicating the time it takes to the next village. For instance, a sign might read, "Next village: 4 hours." But whose four hours? Yours? Mine? It's a playful way of reminding us that time there is personal. It's your journey, at your pace. Yet, even amidst such beauty and solitude, the reality of the flyers bearing faces of the lost was never far from our minds.

After ten days of trekking to Everest Base Camp, our group of ten was en route to Lukla – meaning 'place with many goats and sheep' – the start and endpoint for most treks in the Everest region. From there, we'd fly out to Kathmandu. It would be another four days before we reached Lukla. Interestingly, Lukla has the reputation of being the most dangerous commercial airport in the world, notorious for its many fatal aircraft accidents.

The mountain pass is exclusively for foot traffic and narrows significantly in some sections, forcing trekkers to walk in single file. Despite setting off together at dawn, the rugged terrain, rocky steps, and each trekker's pace mean groups might splinter, with members arriving hours apart. Challenges are aplenty: from crossing swing bridges one by one to waiting for a yak – or sometimes even a herd of the shaggy beasts – to lumber past. Breaks at tea houses are common, where trekkers indulge in a warm apple tea or grab a quick meal or snack.

Though the trek might feel solitary, it's never lonely. The path often meanders through tiny villages, sometimes with only a handful of houses. Monks in their saffron or maroon robes or minimalist dhotis walk alongside children heading to school in the mornings. The friendly locals often join trekkers for parts of their journey before waving goodbye and disappearing into the next village. Regardless of these interactions, every trekker knows where they need to be by sunset.

However, the solitude can sometimes be deceptive.

Two days out from Lukla, a young boy, seemingly no older than six, approached Kim. I was slightly ahead, still keeping Kim within my sight. The boy, dressed in a neat school uniform, held a neatly tied bunch of paalungo ko saag (spinach). His broken English was filled with innocent curiosity, asking about her name, commenting on her "nice backpack", and asking where she was headed. After their brief interaction, the boy disappeared, only to pop up again later on the path, this time without his spinach.

"Where are the vegetables?" Kim asked.

He replied that he'd left them with someone and was on his way to his cousin's. It wasn't long before he waved goodbye to her, only to reappear sometime later, further along the path, when Kim was momentarily separated from the group. After disappearing and reappearing multiple times over a time span of about three hours, Kim began to grow uneasy. Was he innocently curious, or was there a hidden agenda? Kim battled internally, trying to listen to her intuition but not wanting to come off as overly suspicious.

As she neared another village, Kim decided to wait at a tea house, hoping to group with other trekkers. Oblivious to what was unfolding just behind me, I pressed on. When she resumed her walk, joined by three fellow trekkers, the boy was back, silently tailing them.

It wasn't long before Kim realised she was alone again. The group she'd joined had stopped to look at something, leaving her about twenty metres ahead of them. Despite the boy being out of sight, Kim had an uneasy feeling that he would reappear. Her instincts told her something wasn't right. By then, the path had veered sharply to the right, and a steep hill lay ahead of her. On edge and with her guard up, she quickly removed her metal water bottle from her backpack and secured its strap around her wrist. As if confirming her suspicions, the boy emerged from the foliage, suddenly blocking her path and grabbing her hand.

"You're coming with me," he said, his voice suddenly aggressive. With surprising force for his small stature, he yanked at her arm, almost pulling her off her feet. "My friends are waiting, and they will look after you."

In the ensuing struggle, Kim swung at him with her water bottle, hitting him on the side of his head, and then started running up the hill as fast as she could. The sound of his menacing laughter as she made her escape was chilling. When she finally reached the top of the hill, I was there, waiting for her, unaware of the trauma she had just endured.

After she recounted her ordeal, we sat in contemplative silence, absorbing the gravity of the situation. It was clear that the boy had been tracking her for a long time – perhaps he had been tracking the group as a whole. The missing-person flyers we had once naively glanced at now carried an ominous weight. It dawned on us that danger doesn't always announce itself loudly or from a distance – sometimes, it walks silently beside you, cloaked in innocence.

DECISION-MAKING IN YOUR PERSONAL LIFE

There are many things in life that are important but not urgent, and often, we tend to neglect them. Financial planning, taking care of your physical and spiritual health, your choice of life partner, the company you keep, and the location of your home all come to mind.

Prioritising the important aspects of your life over urgent matters doesn't mean urgent matters can always be avoided. There will be times when you have to drop everything to deal with something urgent. However, it's essential to recognise that constantly putting out fires and focusing solely on urgent matters is exhausting and unsustainable. This approach can divert attention and resources away from what truly matters in the long run, such as your health, which is foundational to your overall well-being and ability to manage other aspects of your life.

PHYSICAL HEALTH

Taking care of one's physical health is important. However, many people postpone taking care of their health because they are preoccupied with more immediate concerns, like work. The reality is that you're not going to be of much use to anyone – least of all yourself – when your health fails because you've been neglecting it.

To prioritise your health, you need to be proactive and incorporate healthy habits into your daily routine. This includes eating a balanced diet, taking necessary supplements, exercising regularly, and ensuring you get enough sleep. Keeping up with your annual health checks is equally important. Ask yourself: when last did you visit your oral hygienist? As a woman, when last did you go for a pap smear or have a mammogram? As a man, when last did you visit your doctor for a prostate screening? If you're over forty, when last did you do an

ECG? When last did you do a full liver and kidney functionality test? When last did you have a chest expansion check performed? Do you know what your current iron count is? The list goes on.

Neglecting your health might not show immediate consequences, but over time, it can lead to serious problems that could have been avoided with regular care and attention.

FINANCIAL HEALTH

Just as you would tend to your physical health, it's equally important to have a pulse on the state of your finances. When was the last time you took a comprehensive look at your cash flow? How does your income stack up against your expenses? Do you review your bank statements regularly, scrutinise each transaction, and ensure there are no discrepancies or questionable activities? Have you recently inquired with your bank about the possibility of reducing fees?

Investments are another crucial aspect of financial health. If you own shares, it's important to monitor their performance regularly. It's not just about establishing thresholds for gains and losses – it's about having a well-thought-out investment strategy. When shares depreciate, do you have a plan? Will you sell to avoid further losses, or are you comfortable holding them long-term despite temporary dips? Informed decisions are your best defence against financial uncertainty.

Let's not overlook the management of tangible assets, such as your car. As its value depreciates, it may be worthwhile to adjust your insurance premiums accordingly.

Now, let's talk about retirement planning. Do you have a retirement annuity? Being well-informed about its performance is non-negotiable. If you're in the dark about how it's doing, it's time to take action. Request regular performance analyses from your broker. Should your annuity be underperforming, don't hesitate to ask for an explanation and understand the investment strategy being employed.

If it doesn't align with your risk tolerance and retirement goals, discuss possible adjustments to better serve your objectives.

It may seem excessive, but maintaining your financial health requires constant attention. If you're prone to forgetting, schedule these checks in your calendar. Proactivity is key. Don't wait until retirement to realise that your capital is dwindling, putting you in a situation where you're ordering cat food when you don't even have a cat. By then, the situation is not just urgent but also critical, and unfortunately, you've run out of time.

Being vigilant and proactive in managing your finances is an investment in your future. Keep track of cash flow, manage your tangible assets wisely, monitor your investments, and monitor the performance of your retirement fund. Securing financial health is an ongoing process, and taking steps now can prevent unwelcome surprises down the road.

RELATIONSHIPS

Your personal relationships also require attention and nurturing. When was the last time you told your loved ones how much they mean to you? When did you last spend quality time with them? If you're fortunate to still have your parents around and you have a close relationship with them, how often do you visit them? And if you can't see them, how often do you call to check in on them?

Whenever faced with making a decision – whether it's about a new investment, taking a walk on the beach, or spending time with a loved one – ask yourself if the future you would be grateful for the decision. If the answer is yes, go for it. Do it because it's important.

THE WHEEL OF LIFE

To help put into practice what you've just learned, let's create a Wheel of Life as a visual representation of the various facets of your life. Begin by drawing a circle, which will serve as the wheel. Inside this circle, draw seven lines that radiate from the centre to the edge, forming the spokes of the wheel. Each spoke represents a different area of your life that contributes to your overall well-being. Now, label each spoke with the following categories:

• Physical Health and Sport

• Finances

• Career

• Social

• Skills/Qualifications

• Spiritual

• Family

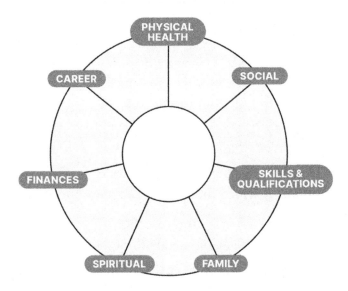

This Wheel of Life is a valuable tool for gaining insights into how balanced your life is and for recognising areas that may need more attention or development.

Next, I want you to rate yourself from 0 to 10 for each area of your life. The outer edge of the wheel represents a perfect 10, while the centre is zero. You might want to think of these numbers in terms of the temperature of a cup of coffee. An 8 is piping hot, 7 is just a step down from that perfect drinking temperature, and 6 is lukewarm. Anything below 6 is like a coffee that was abandoned halfway through a long, boring meeting – it's lost its heat (and its charm) and now languishes at room temperature.

Let's explore what these different ratings signify.

A rating of 8 suggests that you're doing well, but you need to stay attentive to maintain that level. Being at an 8 keeps you humble and aware that there's always room for improvement. It's a reminder not to become overconfident. A 9 is exceptional, indicating that you're excelling in that area. Avoid rating yourself as a 9 unless you're certain there's minimal room for improvement.

A 10, on the other hand, signals overconfidence, often referred to as hubris. Overconfidence can lead to complacency, and complacency can catch you off-guard when things don't go as planned. If you rate an area of your life as being a 10, implying perfection, you risk believing there's nothing more to learn or improve. In reality, there's always room for growth, and a perfect 10 is more of an ideal to strive for than an achievable state.

During this exercise, it's important that you're honest with yourself. There is no right or wrong answer – it's about understanding where you are now.

Consider your health, finances, social life, family relationships, career, skills, qualifications, and spiritual wellness. Reflecting on these areas will allow you to evaluate your current state, whether it's thriving, stagnating, or somewhere in between.

Consider your health: perhaps it isn't at the ideal level, sitting at a 6, or maybe it's a priority for you, and you're comfortable rating it an 8.

Reflect on your financial situation. Achieving financial wellness doesn't mean amassing wealth like a tycoon but rather working towards financial independence, where your passive investments support your lifestyle.

When thinking about your social life, remember that a higher rating doesn't necessarily mean having a large social circle. Rather, it's about whether you are spending enough quality time with the people you care about, even if it's only a handful of people. What about your family relationships? Are tensions or conflicts causing you to rate this aspect a 6, or is everything harmonious, warranting a 9? Evaluate your career; is it thriving at an 8 or stagnating at a 5, prompting thoughts of a new direction? Also, reflect on your skills and qualifications. Are you continually learning, or is it time to start upskilling?

Many people don't give much thought to their spiritual wellness, often using the terms 'religion' and 'spirituality' interchangeably. It's important to understand that while religion can be a form of spirituality for some, spirituality in itself is a broader concept. Attending a religious service can be a spiritual experience for some, but spirituality can also be found in nature, art, personal reflection, helping others, and various other aspects of life.

Now that you have a better understanding of what each rating means and the different areas of your life, it's time to assess and mark each area on the Wheel of Life. When you're ready, mark the spot on each spoke that correlates with your assessment for each aspect of your life. Connect the dots with a line. The shape created illustrates how balanced or imbalanced the different areas of your life are.

Do you see a near-perfect circle inside your wheel where everything is sitting at a 7 or an 8? This would represent a balanced wheel capable of rotating evenly. If your wheel appears somewhat off-balance, don't worry – it's normal for most of us to have areas in our lives that require work. By plotting where you are in your life right now, you will immediately be able to identify these areas. Each spoke of the wheel is important, and it's important to pay attention to any areas that are off balance. Off-balance areas of your life will need to be moved into the Important and Urgent quadrant with immediate effect. Once they have stabilised to a 7 or 8, you can move them into the Important but not Urgent quadrant.

If you can grab back the lost time and opportunities that the urgent stuff has imposed on you, you will have more time for the important stuff in your life.

CHAPTER 7

THE AGE OF ACCELERATION: HOW TO PREPARE FOR THE FOURTH INDUSTRIAL REVOLUTION

One Sunday afternoon in February 2019, while savouring a glass of Anura's exquisite 2018 Malbec Reserve, Kim and I found ourselves engrossed in a discussion about where our next thrilling adventure might unfold. It went something along the lines of – "What's the most foreign place you've ever heard of, how would we explore it, and how would we find a company that could provide us the resources to do the expedition?"

"What about dirt biking through Myanmar?" I suggested.

Situated in Southeast Asia, Myanmar (formerly Burma), known for its diverse landscapes, ranging from mountains and valleys to tropical forests and stunning coastlines, is bordered by Bangladesh, Laos, India, Thailand, and China, with the Andaman Sea and the Bay of Bengal forming the southern coastline. Under the rule of a strict military dictatorship, the country was off-limits to Western travellers for many decades. I had read in the news several days earlier that Myanmar had recently emerged from the grip of military junta rule following the victory of the National League for Democracy (NLD), led by the esteemed Aung San Suu Kyi. Reports indicated that Myanmar had officially opened its borders to tourists, but deep down, I knew it was only a matter of time before the fragile democracy would be threatened once again and the Tatmadaw would regain control. It is widely recognised that Myanmar, often referred to as the Golden Triangle in Asia, is entangled in a thriving cocaine trade – a trade from which the military junta reaps significant benefits. Unbeknownst to the military junta – and the world in general – when she first assumed power, Suu Kyi was about to embark on a campaign to crack down on corruption. I knew we only had a tiny window of time within which to visit Myanmar.

As that Sunday afternoon drew on, we poured ourselves another glass of wine and set about finding a reputable company that could offer us two dirt bikes along with an experienced guide. We eventually stumbled across a company that offered these resources, so I called them up. A man with a distinctive Russian accent answered, and I shared our plans.

"Trast me," he said. "Yust pay the money, and I'll have the bikes ready ven you arrive at the hotel."

He wanted his full payment upfront. I'd made a note of his name, so I googled him. He was nowhere to be found. He was also our only option. Kim and I looked at each other.

"Let's do it," we said.

I mean, what could possibly go wrong?

After an exhausting international flight via Thailand from Johannesburg, we arrived at our hotel in Mandalay. Shortly afterwards, two brand new Honda 250 CRF dirt bikes were dropped off at the hotel, each with 200 kilometres (125 miles) on the clock. They must have been driven there directly from the dealership. I asked the hotel porter whether they'd left us any insurance forms or needed copies of our driver's licenses, but he said the bikes were simply dropped off without any additional paperwork. I called the Russian guy just to make sure. I also wanted to check when our guide was scheduled to arrive the following morning.

"You vanted two bikes," he said. "Zere's your two bikes. Yust don't break my property."

Immediately, I understood why there was no point in having insurance. I asked about our guide.

"Sorry," he said. "My guy can't make it. But if you go vest and keep ze sun on your back all ze vay, you'll be fine."

Go west and keep the sun on your back, I thought. This was about to get very interesting. Our first stop was 800 kilometres (500 miles) away. In Myanmar, there are no proper national roads, no road signs, and everything is written in Sanskrit. If you think the Cyrillic alphabet is complex, you shouldn't go anywhere near Sanskrit. It's almost as if the Cyrillic alphabet walked into a field of burning ganja and took a deep breath in. Each letter is a mind-boggling collection of loops, curves, dots, and lines that make your average cursive handwriting look like a preschooler's doodles. It's almost impossible to tell where one word ends and another begins.

Despite not having the convenience of an English map at our disposal, we did have Google Maps. While Myanmar is predominantly rural and Third World, there is high-speed internet reception everywhere, thanks to Huawei installing 4G towers in even the remotest of areas where encountering a human being was considered unlikely. I asked the hotel porter to buy me a data SIM. I plugged it into my phone, strapped my phone onto my handlebar with cable (zip) ties, and opened Google Maps. I searched for the name of the village we planned to stop at for the night, and it said, "Follow this line".

Over the course of three weeks, we covered an impressive distance of 2,500 kilometres (1,563 miles), incident-free, relying solely on Google Maps and a Myanmar data SIM. With the benefit of hindsight, not having a guide added an extra layer of adventure, mystery and discovery to our journey.

During our journey through the western jungles of Mindat, we were deeply humbled by the hospitality extended to us by the mountain tribes we encountered. Despite the significant language barriers, the local people embraced us warmly and graciously shared their culture and food. Whenever we needed to purchase something, we would simply point at what we wanted, hand them a note, and they'd only take as much as they needed. Their whisky, known as Grand Royal Black, tasted remarkably similar to Johnny Walker Black, yet it was more affordable than a two-litre Coke – their Coke cost $2.50, whereas an entire bottle of whisky was only $2.

In some of the more remote regions, where encounters with outsiders were rare, the sight of a blonde, white woman like Kim attracted considerable attention. Each time Kim removed her full-face motorcycle helmet, the villagers would flock out of their bamboo huts, eager to reach out and touch her hair.

Because the roads were untarred and dusty, we needed to make sure that we checked our air filters regularly. However, the real challenge lay in keeping our chains well-lubricated – because if you lose a bike chain in Myanmar, it's game over. With our chains covered in mud and drying out faster than a sloth on a treadmill, we knew we were in trouble and needed to get our hands on a can of chain spray – and fast. While the locals all drive cheap Chinese scooters, we didn't realise that their parts were not interchangeable with those on our nice 250cc Honda scramblers. In Myanmar, there were no bike accessory shops, no spare Honda chains, no Honda chain repair tools, and no such luxury as chain lube in an aerosol can.

Eventually, out of desperation, we stopped in at a Chinese bike shop and asked about their chain lubrication methods. The attendant pointed towards a jar filled with a pungent, pitch-black, viscous liquid that could wake the dead. It was the unmistakable sight and smell of gearbox oil. He dipped an old toothbrush into the oil and generously applied it to our chains. While I had my doubts as to its efficacy, I also had the Russian guy's voice in my head telling me not to break his property. But we had no other option. From that point onward, we made it a daily ritual to locate a bike shop, acquire some of that foul-smelling gearbox oil, and meticulously apply it to our chains with a toothbrush. Two thousand five hundred kilometres later, we delivered our bikes back to the hotel in one piece, incident-free and fully lubed.

Interestingly, a couple of years later, an episode of a popular YouTube motorcycle channel called FortNine caught my attention. In this particular episode, the Canadian host embarked on a project to evaluate the world's best chain sprays. As any avid biker knows, chain spray does not come cheap. The big oil brands will easily charge you around R300 for a single can, and you'll be lucky if you can manage to squeeze out ten to twelve effective sprays before it's completely empty. What made this episode interesting is that the host didn't limit himself to conventional chain sprays. He also decided to test out some anecdotal alternatives that people often resort to when they don't have proper chain sprays, such as Q20 and WD-40 – the stuff you usually use on locks and the like. He even tested cooking oil. He conducted a series of scientific tests to determine which lubricant performed the best, examining factors like lubrication efficiency and non-fling properties.

Now, here comes the interesting part. Can you guess which lubricant outperformed all the others, surpassing everything else he tested on the planet? It was none other than gearbox oil, priced at R5 a pint.

Our journey to Myanmar remains etched in our memories as one of the most incredible trips we have ever experienced. Even though our meticulously crafted plan went completely awry within an hour of arriving at our hotel, instead of being discouraged, we decided to adapt. We abandoned our original strategy and adopted a new approach: to go west and keep the sun on our backs.

This experience served as a valuable reminder that no matter how meticulously you plan and prepare, sometimes things just don't go according to plan. However, if you're willing to approach the situation with a different mindset and embrace unconventional solutions, you may find yourself embarking on one of the most incredible adventures of your life.

RIDING THE WAVE OF THE FOURTH INDUSTRIAL REVOLUTION

Right now, the world is rapidly shifting beneath our feet. Technologically, we're advancing at a pace unlike any of us have ever witnessed. Technology is evolving at an unprecedented rate, while environmental challenges require urgent attention and innovative solutions. At the same time, globalisation is reshaping the way we think, act, and interact. However, if our Myanmar escapades taught us anything, it's that when we lean into change, not only do we survive – we truly come alive.

The world isn't asking us to become experts overnight – it's asking us to unlearn, learn, and then learn some more. This is no time for resistance. This is a time to roll up our sleeves, grease up our chains, and adapt to the changing terrain ahead.

As the dawn of a new technological era unfolds before our eyes, grasping the scale and depth of the changes taking place is something we can no longer ignore. The world has seen a series of industrial revolutions, each redefining the fabric of society and the contours of economies. The rumblings of the next colossal shift have already begun, and the astute minds of our generation have turned their focus towards this impending transformation. One such luminary is Klaus Schwab, the founder and executive chairman of the

World Economic Forum, who has not only acknowledged but also emphasised the significance of this rapid technological evolution. "We stand on the brink of a technological revolution that will fundamentally alter the way we live, work, and relate to one another," he said in an article published on the organisation's website on the 14th of January 2016. In this statement, he was describing the Fourth Industrial Revolution, where we find ourselves today. While it would be several years before generative AI or large language models entered the world stage, it is evident that Schwab was onto something and understood the direction in which the world was heading.

TECHNOLOGICAL ACCELERATION

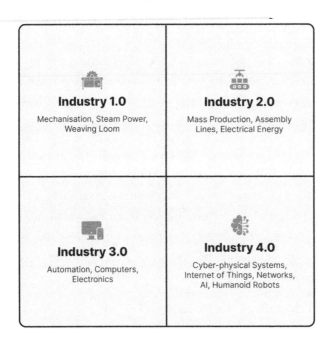

Each industrial revolution that preceded our current era was a transformative period, leading to massive shifts in manufacturing processes and having far-reaching impacts on society. To better understand these rapid transformations and their sociological implications, let's briefly revisit the three industrial revolutions that paved the way for the technological advancements we are experiencing today.

The First Industrial Revolution marked the transition from manual production methods to mechanisation, which was facilitated by the advent of steam power. The weaving loom played a significant role in this era as it revolutionised the textile industry, enabling the efficient production of fabrics. This period, which spanned from the late 18th to early 19th centuries, laid the foundation for modern industrial society.

The Second Industrial Revolution emerged in the late 19th and early 20th centuries and was characterised by mass production and the introduction of assembly lines, which greatly enhanced manufacturing efficiency. The widespread use of electrical energy during this period replaced steam as the primary power source, leading to significant advancements in manufacturing technologies and the rapid growth of industries.

The Third Industrial Revolution began in the 1960s and was marked by the integration of automation into manufacturing processes, facilitated by advancements in computers and electronics. This era saw a shift from mechanical and analogue electronic technology to digital electronics, paving the way for more efficient and sophisticated production processes and the introduction of robots into the manufacturing industry.

The Fourth Industrial Revolution (4IR), often considered to have gained momentum in the early 2010s, is the current phase in the evolution of the manufacturing sector, characterised by the integration of cyber-physical systems, the Internet of Things (IoT), and networks. Through the use of intelligent systems and networked machines, smart factories and industries have been created. Connectivity and data analytics are being leveraged to enhance manufacturing efficiency, customisation, and innovation, heralding a new era of technological and economic development. During this period, we have also seen the rise of 3D printing, augmented and virtual reality, nanotechnology, drones, Blockchain technology, NFTs (non-fungible tokens), and the Metaverse. Continuing into 2023, advancements in Artificial Intelligence inched closer to the goal of Artificial General Intelligence.

Highlighting this rapid progression, Tesla introduced Optimus, and Sanctuary AI launched Phoenix, prototype humanoid robots capable of walking, waving their arms, and picking things up with their fingers. Phoenix is genuine AI. Real-life, full understanding of its environment, conversational. And it can do over 110 tasks with full dexterity and manipulation. The robotic AI software that powers Phoenix is called Carbon, like a carbon life form. These robots are illustrative of how technology is advancing towards creating commercially available machines that can perform tasks autonomously and interact more seamlessly with the human world.

Where the rate of growth was once steady and linear, represented by a gradually inclining straight line, the rate of change in the modern world has shifted to an exponential curve. This means that the graph is steepening at an ever-increasing rate, and it's heading in one direction: upwards. This exponential growth is characteristic of the technological advancements that are defining our era. We've reached a point where our ability to adapt is being outpaced by the sheer explosion of new technologies. And I'm not just talking about chatbots and large language models like ChatGPT – the curve has become even steeper. We are now facing a nearly vertical ascent in technological advancements. The consequences of this rapid technological progression are far-reaching.

Eric Teller, in Thomas Friedman, *Thank You for Being Late*

The rate of change that our planet is currently experiencing is exceeding our ability to adapt. This rapid evolution has left many people scrambling to keep up. Before the advent of ChatGPT, blue-collar workers were already witnessing the effects of automation on their jobs. Many realised that their roles could be digitised within the next five years, rendering them obsolete. This same fear is now felt among programmers, database developers, spreadsheet experts, copywriters, graphic designers, and artists. With the rise of sophisticated AI like ChatGPT and MidJourney, they, too, are wondering when they will become irrelevant in their fields. It's no longer a matter of if but when.

The thought of commercialising humanoid robots like Optimus and Phoenix even unnerves me – and I'm immersed in the tech field. I find it hard to comprehend how those not familiar with technology or those outside the industry would react upon entering their work-place, only to be greeted by twenty robots. These machines have replaced the likes of Uncle Joe, Uncle Peter, and the rest of the crew, who now find themselves jobless. Unlike their human counterparts, these robots don't require lunch breaks or annual holidays. They never fall ill or take maternity leave. They don't partake in casual Friday afternoon drinks, they don't file lawsuits, and above all, they don't need salaries. Ever. The impact is sobering, even frightening, as we navigate this brave new world of technology and automation.

This looming threat of automation, coupled with job insecurity, has sparked widespread anxiety across societies. This anxiety, in turn, has led to a resurgence of nationalism and fascism, as feelings of uncer-tainty and fear become fertile ground for divisive ideologies. Dicta-tors and nepotistic world leaders have been capitalising on these fears, stoking subconscious anxieties to gain influence by tapping into the angst of their constituents and riling up the masses. From Trump's "Make America Great Again" slogan to Putin's nostalgia for the USSR to Bolsanaro's far-right views on social issues, these leaders scapegoat the 'others' (immigrants or foreign cultures and countries) for societal woes. This tactic fuels the fears of their supporters, securing votes and tightening their grip on power.

To further understand the accelerating pace of change and the forces behind it, one must turn to some of the thought leaders of our time. In his book *Thank You for Being Late: An Optimist's Guide to Thriving in the Age of Accelerations*, Thomas Friedman highlights the rapid pace of change in the modern world. He identifies three main forces driving this acceleration – what he calls the three M-s: Moore's Law (which says that the power of microchips will double every two years), the Market (digital globalisation), and Mother Nature (climate change).

Anyone wanting to understand these shifts and how they will impact businesses in the future should read this book.

To fully grasp the implications of these developments, let's delve into each of Friedman's three M-s in greater detail.

MOORE'S LAW

The rapid acceleration of technological progress is underpinned by the principle known as Moore's Law. Coined by Intel co-founder Gordon Moore, this principle suggests that the number of transistors that can be packed onto an integrated circuit effectively doubles roughly every two years, resulting in an exponential increase in computing power. This has fuelled remarkable advancements in fields like automation and the Internet of Things, all of which are fundamentally reshaping the way we work, live, and interact with each other. With the advent of artificial intelligence, which heavily relies on and further pushes the limits of computational power, this rate may even see further acceleration.

This escalation in technological innovation has had a domino effect, with each technological breakthrough serving as a springboard for the next, thereby creating a self-perpetuating cycle of continuous innovation. It may feel as though this progression is occurring at a dizzying pace, and indeed, it is.

Over the years, Moore's Law has undergone some recalibration. While the initial theory proposed that technological capacity would double every two years, the pace has quickened, with current estimates placing the rate of growth at every 18 months or less. This also implies that the cost of existing technology is likely to halve within the same timeframe. This constant evolution and obsolescence mean that a laptop or smartphone today can be reduced to nothing more than a 'doorstop' in less than two years, as newer software consumes ever-increasing amounts of processing power and storage.

To fully appreciate the dramatic reduction in the cost of technology, consider the price of acquiring one gigabyte of hard drive storage in 1965. At that time, obtaining just one gigabyte of storage would have cost a staggering one million dollars. Fast forward to today, and you can purchase that same amount of storage for less than two American cents. This striking reduction in cost demonstrates the power of Moore's Law.

Price of Local Storage $/GB

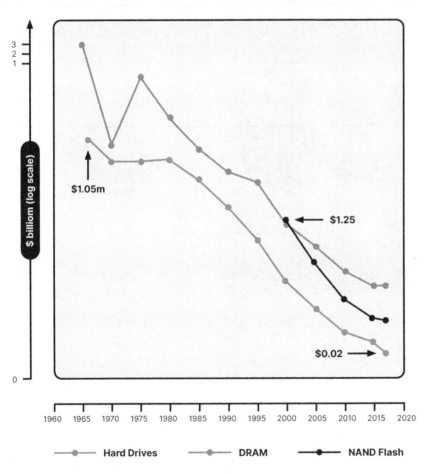

To provide some perspective, let's consider this image of a five-megabyte hard drive from the past being loaded onto a plane. This hard drive was nearly the size of a car. Contrast this with today's microSD cards, which can store 512 gigabytes of data and are no larger than a fingernail. This modern storage device has around a hundred thousand times the capacity of that five-megabyte hard drive at a fraction of the price – one one-hundred-thousandth to be precise.

The IBM Model 350 disk file with a storage space of 5 MB from 1956

Micro SD Card

This kind of exponential growth in technology is not confined to data storage – it also has far-reaching impacts on other fields like genomics. This graph illustrates the cost of decoding the human genome. In 2001, which is not too far in the past, it cost 100 million dollars to decode a single human genome. Now, thanks to the exponential increase in computing power that has significantly reduced costs, anyone can have their genome decoded for a mere $99.

Companies like 23andMe offer this service, allowing individuals to access their genetic information easily and affordably. The advancements in computing power have made it economically feasible to process extensive genomic data on an unprecedented scale.

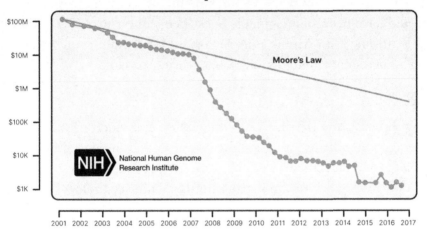

In 2006, Twttr (now known as Twitter/X) was founded, Google acquired YouTube, and Apple introduced the first Mac Pro. A pivotal moment took place in 2007 when a wave of innovations we now take for granted was launched. This was the year Facebook and Twitter went global, Kindle and Android were released, and Apple launched its first iPhone. The explosion of these technologies can be attributed to the convergence of three critical elements for the first time: storage, computing power (as predicted by Moore's Law), and big data.

STORAGE

Previously, storage was a significant barrier due to its high costs. However, by 2007, the costs of storage had plummeted. Today, it is essentially free, with services like Gmail, Facebook, iCloud, OneDrive, and Dropbox offering ample storage at no cost.

COMPUTING POWER

Computing power has also undergone a significant transformation. A few decades ago, storage devices were so large that they required forklifts to be moved. Now, an amount of computing power that would have been unimaginable back then can be contained on a tiny chip, in line with Moore's prediction that the number of transistors on a microchip would double about every two years.

BIG DATA

Big data was the missing piece that, when combined with affordable storage and advanced computing power, paved the way for the technological renaissance of 2007. Together, these factors catalysed a period of rapid innovation, altering both the technology landscape and our interaction with it.

To fully grasp big data's impact on this technological revolution, let's first understand the basics of data and databases.

Data can be broadly categorised into raw data and structured data. Imagine raw data as a cluttered box with mixed items – books, papers, photos, and notes – all jumbled together haphazardly. In data terms, raw data is information that hasn't been processed or organised into any structure. It can be anything from a bunch of text files, images, and logs to unsorted lists. It's usually messy and can come in various formats. Structured data, on the other hand, is like a well-organised library where all the books, papers, photos, and random notes are neatly arranged by categories and alphabetical order. In the context of data, structured data is information that is organised into a specific format or structure, such as tables with rows and columns.

Traditional databases, mainly using Structured Query Language (SQL), function like virtual filing cabinets on computers, where information is organised in tables. SQL is a powerful tool for storing, searching, and managing data efficiently. However, for enterprise companies, which handle massive volumes of data, SQL databases are not optimal. For instance, many large insurance companies track the real-time activities of their millions of members through various data streams, such as vehicle statuses, GPS locations, credit card transactions, and gym and health check-ins. The scale is staggering – data from multiple sources is collected for each member every second, resulting in billions of datasets daily.

The challenge is that this raw data, in its unprocessed form, is not very useful. Traditional SQL databases are ill-suited for handling it because they are designed for structured data, while this data is largely unstructured. Moreover, the data accumulates so quickly that processing it in real time is virtually impossible with conventional methods.

What is required is real-time decision-making. For example, if the data indicates that a member, Emma, accelerates too quickly while driving, the system should instantly adjust her driver status and, consequently, her premiums or reward points. Traditional SQL databases fall short in terms of enabling this kind of real-time analysis and decision-making for millions of individuals.

Before 2007, structured databases were predominantly used. However, the emergence of big data technologies has allowed companies to process and analyse large volumes of unstructured data efficiently. This transition has been instrumental in managing the enormous amount of data being generated and making instantaneous decisions that affect millions of individuals.

But what exactly is big data?

In 2005, Roger Mougalas coined the term 'Big Data' to describe the massive datasets that were almost impossible to manage and process with traditional business intelligence tools. These datasets were characterised by three main attributes: volume, velocity, and variety.

• Volume represents the massive amounts of data involved.

• Velocity refers to the speed at which this data is generated and needs to be processed.

• Variety indicates that the data comes in various formats, including text, images, videos, and more.

While traditional SQL databases can be part of the big data ecosystem, big data typically encompasses less structured information. Due to its sheer size and complexity, specialised tools and technologies are necessary to effectively store, process, and analyse big data.

BRINGING BIG DATA INTO THE MIX

In 2005, a groundbreaking development took place in the world of data when Doug Cutting and Mike Cafarella created Hadoop, an open-source framework designed to process massive amounts of unstructured data and extract valuable insights. Doug, who was part of the team at Yahoo! at the time, named the project after his two-year-old son's toy elephant, injecting a touch of whimsy into this revolutionary technology.

Hadoop's capacity to manage big data, along with its adaptable architecture, quickly gained traction not just at Yahoo! but in various industries. It became instrumental in the ascent of big data analytics, facilitating large-scale data processing and storage for organisations globally. This software, symbolised by a tiny yellow elephant, addressed the then-problematic issues of data storage, which became virtually cost-free, and computation time, in line with Moore's Law. Suddenly, databases could handle millions of data points per second and transform them into actionable information.

This breakthrough had a ripple effect. Before Hadoop, the market was dominated by feature phones like Blackberry and Nokia. With the technological leap facilitated by Hadoop, smartphones started gaining traction. The cloud-based storage solutions we rely on today became viable. Without Hadoop, the landscape of modern technology would not have evolved as rapidly as it did.

THE IMPACT OF TECHNOLOGICAL INNOVATION ON MODERN SOCIETY

Since 2007, humanity has witnessed an explosion of technological innovation that surpasses all the developments of the last 600 years combined. From the invention of the compass, gunpowder, papermaking and printing, and every other modern invention that followed, societies, cultures, and tribes have always found a way to adapt over time, usually over a span of a generation. Take, for instance, the transition from horses to the Model T Ford – there was initial confusion and uproar, especially regarding traffic rules. Questions like, "Who goes first? The horse or the car?" were common. But, in just about 20 years, the car became the norm.

Similarly, the transition from feature phones such as the Nokia 3210 to the now-ubiquitous smartphones happened over a decade. Of course, there were a few holdouts, like grandma and grandpa, who preferred the tactile buttons of the old phones. But, after about 20 years, feature phones like Nokia and Blackberry were almost completely phased out. This pattern of adaptation is evident across various technologies. For instance, the Wright brothers took their first flight, and in less than 20 years, commercial aviation was a reality.

Historically, with each technological advance, there was initial resistance, which gradually gave way to acceptance and, ultimately, full integration. However, something shifted in 2007 when Hadoop spurred a technological revolution. The pace of innovation accelerated so rapidly that few people could comprehend what was coming next and how they would adapt to it.

Let's explore the impact that this wave of technological innovation has had on different aspects of society in what is now known as the Fourth Industrial Revolution.

WORKFORCE AND JOB MARKET

The accelerated speed of technological innovation has disrupted traditional job markets. Automation has taken over many tasks, requiring workers to evolve and learn new skills. On the flip side, the advent of artificial intelligence and machine learning has opened up new avenues and job opportunities in data science, software development, robotics, and more.

COMMUNICATION

With the widespread use of smartphones, social media, and instant messaging apps, the way we communicate has been transformed. These tools have made global connectivity a breeze but have also raised concerns about privacy, security, and the spread of misinformation.

EDUCATION

Education has been democratised through online learning platforms and Massive Open Online Courses (MOOCs). Schools, colleges, and universities are harnessing technology to augment learning experiences and equip students with the skills required to succeed in an increasingly digital world.

HEALTH

Healthcare has benefited enormously from technological advancements. Innovations in artificial intelligence and machine learning have enhanced medical research, diagnosis, and treatments. Wearable tech and health apps now enable individuals to actively manage their health.

TRANSPORTATION

Autonomous vehicles, ride-sharing services, and electric cars have disrupted the transportation industry. These technologies have the potential to reduce traffic congestion, decrease greenhouse gas emissions, and improve road safety.

ENERGY

The energy sector is undergoing a transformation as renewable sources like solar and wind power become more efficient and affordable, challenging traditional fossil fuels. Smart grids and advanced energy storage solutions are transforming how energy is generated, distributed, and consumed.

HOW TECHNOLOGICAL ACCELERATION HAS BENEFITTED THE OVERLANDING COMMUNITY

It is undeniable that technology has played a pivotal role in reshaping numerous facets of our lives, and the sphere of overlanding is no exception. For avid adventurers, where the journey is as much a part of the experience as the destination, technology has revolutionised the way we explore by enhancing our vehicles, gear, and communication systems.

Here are some of the ways technology has been a boon to the overlanding community, transforming various aspects of the adventure into a safer, more efficient, and enjoyable experience in the great outdoors:

VEHICLE ENHANCEMENTS

SUSPENSION SYSTEMS AND SHOCK ABSORBERS

With the advent of modern suspension systems and shock absorbers, off-road travel has undergone a revolution. Adjustable air suspension systems allow drivers to easily modify vehicle height for different

223

terrains, and advanced shock absorbers improve comfort through optimised heat dissipation and damping control. Collectively, these innovations contribute to an unparalleled level of comfort and efficiency.

ROOFTOP TENTS

Rooftop tents have evolved with the introduction of improved materials, more comfortable sleeping quarters, and simplified setup and breakdown processes. With features like hard shells for added durability, expandable living spaces, and integrated awnings, rooftop tents now offer overlanders more convenience and comfort.

COMMUNICATION AND NAVIGATION SYSTEMS

RADIO COMMUNICATION AND SATELLITE TECHNOLOGIES

The evolution of communication technology has had a significant impact on the overlanding community. High-quality, long-range radio systems, including HAM radios, have significantly enhanced communication capabilities between overlanders and support teams. Furthermore, devices like satellite phones and two-way messengers facilitate communication in remote areas lacking cellular coverage, ensuring overlanders stay connected and can access emergency help when needed.

GPS TECHNOLOGY AND MAPPING TOOLS

The navigation aspect has seen substantial advancements with modern GPS devices and smartphone apps offering detailed maps, real-time tracking, offline map capabilities, point-of-interest databases, and route planning tools, enhancing the overall experience, and minimising the risk of getting lost.

TRIP PLANNING TOOLS

Digital platforms and apps dedicated to overlanding provide comprehensive resources for trip planning, including route suggestions,

224

points of interest, and user-generated content. These tools facilitate the discovery of new destinations, experience sharing, and communal learning.

GEAR ENHANCEMENTS

RECOVERY GEAR

Advances in recovery gear, including kinetic ropes and soft shackles, have made these tools lighter yet stronger, thereby making them easier to handle and more effective in vehicle recovery. The evolution of electric winches with synthetic (plasma) ropes has led to increased pulling capacity and reduced weight, improving safety and efficiency during recovery operations.

POWER SYSTEMS

Thanks to solar panels and advanced charging and inverter systems, overlanders can now maintain a steady power supply for their vehicles and devices. Portable, foldable solar panels offer lightweight and efficient power generation in remote locations, while integrated solar systems on vehicles provide a constant energy source for onboard electronics.

MODERN BATTERY TECHNOLOGY

The development of lithium-based batteries has been a game-changer for power storage. These batteries offer longer life cycles, faster charging times, and increased energy density than traditional lead-acid batteries, enabling overlanders to power their equipment more efficiently and sustainably.

MODULAR STORAGE SYSTEMS

Storage solutions for overlanding vehicles have evolved to be increasingly versatile. Modular drawer systems, cargo barriers, and roof racks ensure efficient organisation of gear and supplies. Customisable storage configurations tailored to specific vehicle models empower overlanders to maximise space while securing their gear during transit.

ADVANCED OFF-ROAD LIGHTING SYSTEMS

Thanks to advancements in LED technology, overlanders can now benefit from potent and energy-efficient off-road lighting systems. These lights enhance visibility during nighttime and adverse weather conditions. Light bars, spotlights, and floodlights are also popular for illuminating campsites and work areas.

TYRE PRESSURE MANAGEMENT SYSTEMS

Tyre pressure management systems have become indispensable for overlanders. Allowing drivers to continuously monitor and adjust tyre pressure according to the terrain, these systems optimise traction and minimise the risk of tyre damage. Portable air compressors and tyre deflators further simplify maintaining the right tyre pressure.

HOW BUSINESSES CAN ADAPT TO TECHNOLOGICAL ACCELERATION

According to Microsoft founder Bill Gates, "We always overestimate the change that will occur in the next two years and underestimate the change that will occur in the next ten." He cautions us not to allow ourselves to be "lulled into inaction".

This is particularly true when it comes to technological innovation. While predictions of flying cars being commonplace by 2025 are unrealistic – it is highly probable that most of us will experience taking off in one by 2035. This tendency to overlook transformative change is evident in several cases.

Within a span of ten years, advancements such as ChatGPT, the Internet, smartphones, electric vehicles, 3D printing, CRISPR for DNA editing, machine learning, and NFTs have significantly shifted paradigms, often within a ten-year timeframe, despite seeming too futuristic in the short term.

Klaus Schwab aptly captured the essence of today's rapidly evolving landscape when he said, "In the new world, it is not the big fish which eats the small fish; it's the fast fish which eats the slow fish". This quote encapsulates the importance of agility and adaptability, not just in business but also on a personal level. In striving to be a better version of ourselves or in running successful businesses, it's crucial to embrace the speed of change and adjust accordingly.

To succeed in the age of technological acceleration, businesses must embrace change and be willing to adapt. Here are some key strategies for business leaders:

LIFELONG LEARNING

With the rapid pace of technological change, business leaders and employees need to commit to continuous learning and skills development to stay relevant in the job market. Embracing a culture of learning within the organisation can help employees adapt to new technologies and drive innovation.

AGILITY AND FLEXIBILITY

Organisations must be agile and flexible to adapt to the changing technological landscape. This may involve restructuring business processes, embracing new business models, or investing in new technologies to stay competitive.

INNOVATION

Business leaders should create an environment that encourages creativity and innovation. This may involve investing in research and development, adopting a fail-fast mentality, or leveraging open innovation strategies to access external ideas and technologies.

DIGITAL TRANSFORMATION

Digital transformation is not just about adopting new technologies – it's about fundamentally changing the way organisations operate, engage with customers, and create value. Business leaders must develop a clear digital strategy and ensure that the entire organisation is aligned and committed to the transformation journey.

ETHICAL CONSIDERATIONS

As organisations leverage new technologies, they must also consider the ethical implications of their decisions. This may involve addressing issues related to privacy, data security, and the potential societal impact of their products and services. Business leaders should establish clear ethical guidelines and ensure that their organisation's actions align with these principles.

Businesses and individuals who can recognise the transformative power of technology and proactively adapt to these changes will be better positioned to succeed in the age of acceleration. By embracing lifelong learning, agility, collaboration, innovation, digital transformation, and ethical considerations, businesses can navigate the challenges and seize the opportunities presented by technological acceleration.

GLOBALISATION ACCELERATION

Globalisation refers to the increasing interconnectedness of economies, societies, and cultures. This process has been accelerated by advancements in transportation, communication, and technology, resulting in a world that is increasingly interconnected and interdependent.

From the free flow of goods and services to the cross-border movement of people, ideas, and cultures, globalisation has created a 'global village' where an event in one part of the world can have ripple effects across the globe. The rise of multinational corporations, the proliferation of global trade agreements, and the increase in international tourism are all manifestations of this trend. The digital revolution, particularly the spread of the Internet and social media, has further deepened these connections by allowing real-time communication between individuals and businesses across the world.

As a result, we are now witnessing a new phase of globalisation – digital globalisation, where data and information flow across borders more freely than ever before. This has brought about new opportunities but also challenges as nations and businesses navigate this increasingly complex global landscape.

Some of the key aspects of globalisation include:

INTERNATIONAL TRADE

The growth of international trade has led to the expansion of global supply chains, enabling companies to source raw materials, manufacture goods, and sell their products in different parts of the world. This has resulted in greater economic integration, increased competition, and the emergence of global brands.

With the advent of e-commerce, the landscape of international trade has been further transformed. Today, most trading is facilitated through digital platforms like eBay and Amazon. Consumers often order products online without knowing where they originate or understanding the complex logistics involved in shipping, manufacturing, and warehousing. This illustrates how digitisation has blurred geographic boundaries and how global supply chains have evolved to the point where products are no longer simply made locally for local consumption.

FINANCIAL MARKETS

The liberalisation of financial markets and the growth of multinational corporations have facilitated the movement of capital across borders. This has enabled businesses to access funding, invest in foreign markets, and participate in mergers and acquisitions on a global scale.

The proliferation of fintech and digital finance, which is a part of the Fourth Industrial Revolution, has further revolutionised the movement of capital across borders. The rise of crowdfunding platforms like Kickstarter, equity crowdfunding, peer-to-peer lending, and blockchain technology, particularly cryptocurrencies, has enabled an even more seamless flow of capital globally. For instance, blockchain technology has enabled businesses to raise capital through Initial Coin Offerings (ICOs) without the traditional confines and regulations of stock exchanges. Take, for example, Ethereum, a blockchain platform that raised funds through an ICO. It was able to attract global investments rapidly and has since become a foundational technology for various decentralised applications. This example highlights how the technological advancements of the Fourth Industrial Revolution are providing new avenues for capital investment, which is more democratised and accessible across borders.

MIGRATION AND DEMOGRAPHICS

The movement of people across borders for work, education, climate change, or other reasons has led to greater cultural exchange and diversity. This has also resulted in a more interconnected global labour market, with businesses increasingly relying on talent from different parts of the world.

This movement has been further amplified in recent times by the advent of remote working and telecommunication advancements. As the COVID-19 pandemic necessitated shifts in traditional work setups, many companies adopted remote work, discovering that they could tap into global talent without geographical constraints. For instance, a tech start-up based in the United States can now effortlessly hire software engineers from India or graphic designers from

Eastern Europe. This has not only expanded opportunities for individuals across the world but has also allowed businesses to benefit from diverse perspectives and skills. Moreover, this integration of global labour markets is gradually leading towards a more homogenised work culture where the exchange of ideas and practices is continually enriching and reshaping corporate norms and policies internationally.

INFORMATION AND IDEAS

The spread of information and ideas through digital platforms and media has made it easier for people to access knowledge, share their thoughts, and collaborate with others across geographical boundaries.

With this unprecedented ease of access to and sharing of information, a new era of innovation and creativity has emerged. As individuals from diverse backgrounds and cultures collaborate, they bring unique perspectives and insights, fostering innovation that might not have been possible within a more homogeneous group. Moreover, the cross-pollination of ideas through digital platforms has led to the global spread of social movements, such as environmental sustainability and social justice campaigns. For instance, social media played a pivotal role in propelling movements like the Global Climate Strikes and the Black Lives Matter movement, enabling people from around the world to unite, share information, and mobilise for causes that matter to them. This global connectedness through information sharing has not only democratised knowledge but has also enabled societies to collectively address shared challenges and advocate for positive change.

GLOBAL GOVERNANCE

The rise of international organisations and agreements has facilitated cooperation among countries to address global challenges, such as climate change, public health, and human rights. Global governance refers to the way international affairs are managed through these organisations and agreements.

As the complexities of global challenges evolve, the role of international organisations and agreements in global governance continues to adapt and expand. These entities serve as platforms where countries can engage in dialogue, build consensus, and develop collaborative strategies. For example, the Paris Agreement under the United Nations Framework Convention on Climate Change has been pivotal in setting targets for countries to reduce greenhouse gas emissions, which is critical in the fight against climate change. Another example is the role of the World Trade Organization (WTO) in regulating international trade. The WTO provides a platform for negotiating trade agreements and settling disputes among member countries, which helps in creating a fair and transparent trading system.

Such organisations and agreements not only provide the framework for collective action but also facilitate the pooling of resources and expertise, which is often essential in addressing challenges that transcend national borders. These collaborative efforts contribute towards the creation of a more stable and sustainable global community.

CHALLENGES, OPPORTUNITIES, AND STRATEGIES IN THE ACCELERATION OF GLOBALISATION FOR BUSINESSES

As globalisation accelerates, businesses are faced with both opportunities and challenges that can significantly impact their growth and success. To thrive in this rapidly changing environment, businesses must adopt strategies that enable them to leverage the opportunities while effectively navigating the challenges.

OPPORTUNITIES AND CHALLENGES

In an increasingly globalised world, businesses encounter a variety of opportunities and challenges that can shape their trajectory:

COMPETITION

The intensification of competition due to globalisation requires businesses to constantly innovate, maintain quality, and achieve cost efficiency to differentiate themselves in the global market. For instance, companies like Samsung and Apple are in a continuous race to innovate with new features in their smartphones to gain market share.

MARKET ACCESS

Globalisation provides businesses with access to new markets, providing opportunities for growth and expansion. However, it is crucial for companies to identify and adapt to the unique needs and preferences of customers in different regions. For example, McDonald's adjusts its menu in different countries to cater to local tastes, such as offering a McAloo Tikki burger in India.

TALENT MANAGEMENT

The globalisation of the labour market presents an opportunity for businesses to access talent from different countries. On the flip side, businesses must also develop effective strategies for attracting, retaining, and managing a diverse workforce. For example, Google employs people from all around the world, bringing diverse perspectives that help in creating global products.

SUPPLY CHAIN MANAGEMENT

With increasingly complex and interconnected supply chains, businesses must manage risks and ensure operational resilience. This may involve diversifying suppliers, investing in logistics infrastructure, or implementing advanced technologies for better visibility and control. For instance, after the Fukushima disaster in 2011, many companies learned the importance of diversifying their supply chain to mitigate risks associated with relying too heavily on one region.

CORPORATE SOCIAL RESPONSIBILITY (CSR)

Increased scrutiny on the impact of business practices on the environment, society, and local communities necessitates the integration of CSR into business strategies to enhance reputation and create long-term value. For example, Starbucks actively involves itself in the ethical sourcing of coffee and is committed to reducing its environmental impact.

ADAPTING TO THE RAPID PACE OF GLOBALISATION

Given these opportunities and challenges, businesses can proactively adopt strategies to adapt to the acceleration of globalisation by:

DEVELOPING A GLOBAL MINDSET

Understanding and appreciating cultural differences, being open to new ideas, and adapting to changing market dynamics is essential in cultivating a global mindset. For instance, Unilever, a global company with products sold in over 190 countries, attributes much of its success to the global mindset of its workforce. The company actively promotes diversity and inclusion, encourages employees to work in different geographies, and emphasises the importance of understanding local cultures and market needs. This global mindset helps Unilever to effectively tailor its products and strategies for different markets.

BUILDING STRATEGIC PARTNERSHIPS

Forming alliances with local and international businesses can offer companies new market access, shared resources, and valuable insights that can be particularly beneficial in an interconnected world. For example, automakers like Ford and Volkswagen have entered into strategic partnerships to share resources in developing electric vehicles.

EMBRACING INNOVATION

Continuous innovation is imperative for businesses to stay competitive, especially in a global marketplace where competition is intense. Innovation can also help in addressing supply chain challenges and in attracting a global customer base. Amazon, for example, continuously innovates through its Amazon Prime services and by exploring new technologies such as drones for delivery.

PRIORITISING SUSTAINABILITY

In line with CSR, businesses must incorporate sustainability into their operations, recognising the long-term benefits of resource efficiency, waste reduction, and positive social impact. This can also enhance the company's reputation and appeal to environmentally conscious consumers. Patagonia, an outdoor clothing company, is an example of a business that has built its brand around environmental sustainability and activism.

LEVERAGING TECHNOLOGY

Utilising technology, including embracing digital transformation to adopt new business models and enhance digital capabilities, can help businesses overcome geographical barriers, streamline operations, and enhance communication. This allows companies to better connect with customers, optimise supply chains, and efficiently manage a global workforce. Zoom, for instance, became indispensable for global communication during the COVID-19 pandemic, allowing companies and individuals to interact effectively regardless of location.

By effectively addressing these challenges and opportunities through adaptive strategies, businesses can position themselves to succeed in an increasingly globalised world.

CLIMATE CHANGE ACCELERATION

Everyone, unless they have been living under a rock and haven't budged since, is well acquainted with the terms global warming and climate change. Compelling evidence suggests that unless significant measures are taken, we will surpass the 1.5-degree Celsius global temperature increase target by 2028 – which aimed to limit global warming to well below 2 degrees Celsius above pre-industrial levels – rendering the COP21 Paris Agreement ineffective. As a result, we are likely to witness a surge in climate change-related issues.

Human activities since the First Industrial Revolution in the mid-1700s have drastically altered the Earth's atmosphere. The burning of fossil fuels, crucial for the production of materials such as cement, iron, steel, plastics, electronics, and clothing, has led to a continuous rise in carbon dioxide concentrations. The transportation industry's fuel emissions, widespread deforestation, industrialised animal agriculture, soil degradation, and ocean pollution have compounded this issue, plunging us into a planetary crisis where the survival of all living beings is at stake.

Climate change, driven by these human activities, encompasses long-term shifts in global temperature, precipitation, and weather patterns. The acceleration of climate change has profound implications not just for the environment but for society and businesses too. Increasing global temperatures are causing more frequent heatwaves, droughts, and wildfires, disrupting ecosystems and agricultural production, while the melting of polar ice caps and glaciers is causing sea levels to rise, threatening coastal communities and infrastructure.

From the mid-20th century onwards, industrialised nations, including Western countries and China, have been major contributors to pollution through excessive emissions of greenhouse gases like carbon monoxide, carbon dioxide, and methane. The cumulative impact of these emissions released by these industrialised nations is now causing the Earth's climate to change at an alarming rate.

Climate change is exacerbating the frequency and intensity of extreme weather events, such as hurricanes, floods, and storms, resulting in significant economic and human costs. Additionally, it is threatening the survival of many plant and animal species, leading to a loss of biodiversity and potentially disrupting ecosystems and their functions. The strain on resources due to climate change, particularly water and food, can intensify scarcity and lead to increased competition and conflicts over these resources. This strain and competition can stir up social instability, creating conditions conducive to the rise of radical organisations. In some instances, it may even indirectly facilitate recruitment into terrorist organisations, as the example below will illustrate.

The Sahel, a region that stretches across Africa, serves as a transitional zone between the arid Sahara Desert and the more fertile regions to the south. It hosts diverse ecosystems and provides habitat for numerous plant and animal species. Agriculture, particularly subsistence farming and livestock herding, forms the backbone of the region's economy. However, the Sahel is grappling with severe environmental challenges, including desertification, climate change, and food insecurity. To put this into perspective, if we were to travel back a hundred years, we would find a region that was considerably more fertile and hospitable than it is today. For millennia, nomadic tribes and Bedouin communities thrived in the Sahel, maintaining their livelihoods through farming and herding. Fast forward to the present, and one finds a land where little grows and water resources are scarce. The once-fertile soil has turned arid, making subsistence farming untenable.

The repercussions of climate change have left millions unable to continue farming, forcing them to migrate to cities in search of work. Unfortunately, employment opportunities are scarce. However, there is one organisation offering a lifeline of sorts by guaranteeing $300 a month to individuals willing to join them. This organisation is none other than the terrorist group ISIS. It is important to note that the allure for subsistence farmers in the Sahel to join ISIS is not driven by ideological or religious motives but by a desperate need to support their families. The ability to send $300 a month back home is a powerful incentive. Consequently, ISIS is experiencing a surge in recruitment.

This serves as a poignant example of the unintended consequences of climate change. The desertification and expansion of the Sahara Desert into the Sahel region are contributing to social and economic instability, creating conditions ripe for the recruitment of militants.

Climate change is not just an environmental issue but a complex crisis with far-reaching consequences for social systems, economies, and ecosystems. The situation in the Sahel is a stark reminder of how the effects of climate change can lead to unforeseen social and economic challenges. Addressing climate change is imperative not only for the health of our planet but for the stability and welfare of communities worldwide. It is important that nations work together to curb emissions, invest in renewable energies, and create sustainable policies that protect not only the environment but also the people most vulnerable to the effects of climate change.

CLIMATE CHANGE ACCELERATION AND ITS IMPACT ON BUSINESS

As the world witnesses an unprecedented acceleration in climate change, businesses are no longer mere bystanders – they are either victims of or contributors to the unfolding crisis. In addition to having moral obligations, businesses must account for many risks and opportunities brought on by climate change. It is essential that business leaders have a solid understanding of how the changing climate can reshape the business landscape. The main aspects to consider include physical risks, regulatory risks, reputation, and consumer expectations, as well as innovation and new markets.

PHYSICAL RISKS

One of the most tangible impacts of climate change on business comes in the form of physical risks. The increasing frequency of extreme weather events such as hurricanes, floods, and wildfires poses a threat to company infrastructure. For instance, a manufacturing plant situated in a flood-prone area might face operational disruptions, leading to significant financial losses. Supply chains, the lifelines of global business, can also be severely impacted. For companies with global suppliers, events like typhoons or droughts in different parts of the world can have ripple effects, hindering their ability to produce and deliver products. Similarly, agricultural businesses may suffer due to unpredictable weather patterns affecting crop yields. Additionally, businesses need to be vigilant regarding the safety of their employees, especially in regions that are highly susceptible to climate-related disasters.

REGULATORY RISKS

Governments around the globe are coming to terms with the seriousness of climate change and are enacting policies and regulations to curb greenhouse gas emissions. These regulations range from carbon taxes to mandatory disclosures of environmental impact. Businesses must keep abreast of the evolving regulatory environment to ensure compliance. Adhering to environmental regulations can enhance a company's reputation and make it more appealing to consumers and investors who value sustainability. Conversely, failing to anticipate and adapt to new laws can result in heavy fines, litigation, and loss of market share.

REPUTATION AND CONSUMER EXPECTATIONS

The court of public opinion is a powerful force. With the democratisation of information through social media, companies are under the spotlight for their environmental practices. Consumers are increasingly aligning their purchasing decisions with their values, and environmental sustainability ranks high among them. Investors are also scrutinising companies' environmental policies, as is evident in the surge of interest in Environment, Social, and Governance (ESG) investing – which refers to the three central factors in measuring the sustainability and societal impact of an investment in a company or business. Businesses that do not prioritise sustainability and demonstrate their commitment to addressing climate change risk tarnishing their brand image and losing both customers and investors to more environmentally conscious competitors.

INNOVATION AND NEW MARKETS

Despite the significant challenges posed by climate change, it also opens avenues for new opportunities. Necessity is the mother of invention, and the necessity to combat climate change has led to an explosion of innovation. Businesses can capitalise on this by investing in the development of renewable energy technologies, energy-efficient products, and sustainable agriculture practices. For instance, companies specialising in solar and wind energy technologies are experiencing significant growth. Other industries that are ripe for innovation beyond renewable energy include sustainable packaging, green construction materials, and electric vehicles. Sustainable packaging, for instance, reduces waste and the consumption of natural resources, green construction materials can significantly lower the carbon footprint of buildings, and electric vehicles are essential in reducing emissions from the transportation sector.

Consumer preferences are evolving, with growing awareness and concern over the impacts of climate change. Many are now more inclined to support products and services that are aligned with sustainable and environmentally friendly practices. This innovation leads to the creation of new markets and offers businesses a chance not only to contribute positively to combatting climate change but also to realise substantial financial gains.

By harnessing innovations that address the challenges of climate change, businesses not only play a critical role in stewarding environmental sustainability but also position themselves favourably in an increasingly eco-conscious market.

STRATEGIES FOR ADAPTING TO CLIMATE CHANGE ACCELERATION

Climate change is accelerating at an unprecedented rate, and this is not a phenomenon that businesses can afford to ignore. The combination of physical risks, regulatory changes, and shifting consumer expectations necessitate a rethinking of traditional business models. However, through proactive adaptation, innovation, and a genuine commitment to sustainability, businesses can turn the challenges of climate change into opportunities for growth and positive impact. Success in the age of climate change is contingent upon a company's adaptability and foresight.

With this in mind, let's delve into the key strategies that businesses must employ. These strategies will not only address the challenges but also enable companies to capitalise on the opportunities that climate change presents.

ASSESSING AND MANAGING RISKS

The first step for businesses is to identify and understand the climate-related risks they face. Regular assessments are crucial to stay informed of emerging threats. These risks can vary from physical damages due to extreme weather events to regulatory and reputational risks. Once identified, it's imperative to develop strategies for managing and mitigating these risks. For instance, diversifying supply chains can reduce dependence on a single geographic area vulnerable to climate-related disruptions.

241

REDUCING ENVIRONMENTAL IMPACT

Mitigating environmental impact is not only socially responsible but is increasingly a business imperative. This can be achieved by reducing greenhouse gas emissions, adopting energy-efficient technologies, minimising waste, and incorporating sustainable practices. Not only do these measures contribute to environmental preservation, but they can also yield long-term cost savings. Moreover, as consumers gravitate towards environmentally responsible brands, adopting sustainable practices can enhance a company's image and attract a broader market segment.

INVESTING IN RESILIENCE

Building resilience to the effects of climate change is an investment that pays dividends. This includes reinforcing infrastructure to withstand extreme weather, adopting water-saving measures, and ensuring that emergency preparedness plans are in place. Investing in resilience is about anticipating the challenges posed by climate change and making sure that the business is protected against them. This could extend to financial resilience, for example, by taking out insurance policies that provide coverage for climate-related damages.

DRIVING INNOVATION

Climate change, while posing challenges, also opens the door to new opportunities. Businesses that drive innovation and develop solutions to climate-related problems position themselves at the forefront of emerging markets. By investing in research and development to create products or services that mitigate environmental impacts or facilitate adaptation to changing conditions, companies can gain a significant competitive edge. The opportunities for innovation are vast, spanning from renewable energy technologies to sustainable agriculture.

COLLABORATING FOR CHANGE

No business is an island, and in the face of tackling a global issue like climate change, collaboration is key. Businesses should actively seek partnerships with governments, NGOs, and other stakeholders. Collective action magnifies the impact of efforts to combat climate change. Sharing knowledge, best practices, and resources and advocating for policy changes are critical components of collaborative efforts.

Businesses that recognise the gravity of climate change and align their strategies with collaborative approaches will be well-positioned to seize the opportunities that this global challenge inevitably brings.

HOW TO SURVIVE THE FOURTH INDUSTRIAL REVOLUTION

Our ability to survive and flourish rests largely on our ability to identify and manage risks. If you can pinpoint a risk within a given situation and strategically navigate around it, the potential for rewards often outweighs the inherent danger. However, recognising the risk is your first hurdle.

Let's simplify this concept by comparing it to a two-wheeled bicycle versus a three-wheeled bicycle. The latter represents static stability – it remains upright and perfectly balanced even when stationary. A two-wheeled bicycle, on the other hand, finds stability only in motion – if you stop moving, you topple over. This analogy plays a crucial role in our understanding of continuous self-improvement.

We've all grown up learning about the importance of the 3 Rs: reading, 'riting, and 'rithmetic. They're touted as the recipe for success: get an education, land a job, and you're set until retirement. This mindset, however, encourages static stability, similar to a three-wheeled bicycle. It's a comfortable ride, but it's static, immovable, and ill-suited to rapid changes.

As our world evolves, particularly with the onset of the Fourth Industrial Revolution, it's clear that traditional skills – the 3 Rs – while necessary, are no longer sufficient. They prepare us for a world that is stable and unchanging, not one that is in a state of constant flux. To navigate this new world, we must embody the properties of a two-wheeler in motion – just as it must keep moving to stay upright, we must also continually adapt and learn to thrive in the rapidly changing environment of the 4IR.

This necessity brings our focus to the four Cs – creativity, critical thinking, communication, and collaboration – which represent this necessary agility and adaptability. Creativity relates to the ability to think outside the box and come up with innovative solutions. Critical thinking involves logical reasoning and problem-solving skills. Communication underscores the importance of effective expression and understanding, while collaboration points to the need for team-work in a globally connected world. All four components working in tandem ensure that we remain balanced and moving, much like the two-wheeled bicycle, in this new era of perpetual change.

THE NEW PARADIGM: THE 4 C'S OF 21ST CENTURY SKILLS

It's a sad but true fact that people with a static mindset will be overtaken by robots, drones, and artificial intelligence. However, those who embrace the four Cs – will find themselves adaptable and ready for change. They will not only weather the storm of the Fourth Industrial Revolution, but they will use it as an opportunity to grow, innovate, and thrive.

Let's explore each of these 4 Cs in a little more detail.

CREATIVITY

Creativity – the ability to think outside the box and generate unique ideas and solutions – is essential in the era of the Fourth Industrial

Revolution. It's an era defined not only by artificial intelligence and automation but also by other breakthroughs such as big data, advanced robotics, the Internet of Things (IoT), biotechnology, 3D printing, blockchain, and quantum computing.

Understandably, individuals in creative fields, such as writers, artists, designers, and musicians, might feel threatened by the emergence of AI programs like ChatGPT, MidJourney, Amper Music, and myriad others. However, the reality is that tasks requiring creativity are less susceptible to automation, making this skill increasingly valuable.

Instead of viewing AI and other 4IR tools as competition, they should be seen as catalysts that can spark new ideas, potentially saving hours typically dedicated to brainstorming. Their purpose is to enhance, not replace, human creativity. At this stage, AI, fed by big data and connected via the Internet of Things, can only build upon existing information within its programmed system. In contrast, the human mind possesses the unique ability to conceptualise fresh ideas, each carrying nuances as unique as a fingerprint – an ability that current AI technology can't replicate.

Creativity isn't confined to artistic expression – it encompasses innovative thinking, problem-solving, and the capacity to envision what does not yet exist. Creative professionals who can harness AI and other 4IR tools to augment their work will not only stay relevant but also free up invaluable time to focus on the essence of creativity: the development and execution of ideas that can shape and colour our world in ways that machines alone cannot comprehend.

CRITICAL THINKING

Navigating our technologically advanced world demands solutions that stem from critical thinking – the ability to analyse information and form reasoned judgments. This process involves questioning assumptions, evaluating evidence, and integrating information from various sources. With the unprecedented proliferation of information we face today, these skills are vital for distinguishing truth from falsehood and making informed decisions.

Today, critical thinking extends beyond being a human-centric skill – it also needs to be adapted for interactions with machines. As we engage more frequently with AI systems, we must be equipped to question their outputs, understand the underlying logic and assumptions they're based on, and evaluate their conclusions.

The ability to critically analyse and interpret data is also particularly valuable. A thorough understanding of statistical and data analysis techniques, knowing when and how to apply them, and being able to interpret the results are essential elements of critical thinking in our data-driven world.

The speed and interconnectivity that characterise the digital age often require us to make quick decisions. Yet, effective critical thinking involves slowing down, reflecting on the information at hand, and considering its validity and applicability in specific contexts. Amid the urgency, finding the balance between speed and thoughtfulness can be a challenge. In a world where "deepfakes" and misinformation can spread quickly, critical thinking plays a key role in assessing the reliability of sources and the credibility of information. The ability to distinguish between high-quality information and misinformation or disinformation is increasingly important.

As AI systems continue to evolve, they may be able to assist in many aspects of critical thinking by organising vast amounts of information and identifying patterns. However, the human element of critical thinking – including intuition, judgment based on personal experience, and ethical considerations – is something that, at least for the foreseeable future, machines cannot replicate.

Individuals who can adapt their critical thinking skills to this interconnected world, who can balance human judgment with machine intelligence, and who can navigate the complexities of our data-rich environment will not only survive but thrive in this digital age. Their abilities will also be critical in guiding the ethical and responsible use of technology.

COMMUNICATION

Effective communication – the ability to convey and receive ideas clearly and compellingly – has become more important than ever in our rapidly evolving world. As technology continues to break down barriers and our global society becomes more interconnected, the capacity to communicate across various contexts, cultures, disciplines, and mediums has emerged as an invaluable skill.

But communication is more than just broadcasting messages. It also encompasses active listening and interpreting, as understanding others' perspectives is a crucial aspect of successful interactions. In a 4IR world, communication extends beyond human interactions and includes interfacing with machines and digital platforms. With the rise of AI and data analytics, our ability to decipher and effectively communicate complex information has become particularly valuable.

As the boundaries blur between humans and machines, new forms of communication are emerging. Interfacing with intelligent systems demands a new language – one that merges human creativity and empathy with the precision and efficiency of machine languages.

Equally important is the ability to translate complex technical information into language that non-specialists can understand, making ideas accessible and inclusive. Our messages, whether directed at humans or machines, need to be clear, concise, and relevant. This evolution in communication demands a new literacy: understanding how to command AI tools, interpret their outputs, and ethically use the data they generate.

Our digital world also requires an understanding of online communication etiquette and the ability to build and maintain relationships in virtual environments. As remote work and virtual collaboration become the norm, effective digital communication skills will be vital.

The Fourth Industrial Revolution, while driven by technology, also underscores the value of human skills. The ability to communicate empathy, emotion, and nuance – areas where machines currently lag – will keep us indispensable in an automated world. Individuals who adapt their communication skills to this multifaceted, interconnected world, balancing technical know-how with empathy and emotional intelligence, will not only thrive in this digital age but also help shape its evolution.

COLLABORATION

Collaboration – the act of working effectively with others to achieve a common goal – has taken on new dimensions in our globally connected, technology-driven world. It requires not just strong inter-personal skills but also respect for diversity, the ability to compromise and negotiate, and a high degree of adaptability and empathy.

In the context of the Fourth Industrial Revolution, collaboration has transcended traditional face-to-face interactions and expanded into digital spaces. As such, effective collaboration often happens across different cultures, time zones, and disciplines. This shift demands a refined understanding of digital tools and platforms that facilitate seamless communication and coordination among team members.

Collaboration is not just about working with other humans. With the rise of artificial intelligence and machine learning, we find ourselves increasingly collaborating with machines and AI systems. The ability to integrate these tools into our collaborative processes, understand their capabilities and limitations, and leverage them effectively to augment collective outcomes becomes critical.

Collaboration also requires a deep respect for diversity in all its forms – be it cultural, cognitive, or technical. As teams become more diverse and spread across the globe, appreciating different perspectives and ways of thinking – and integrating them to drive innovation – is an invaluable skill.

Collaboration also means being able to navigate conflicts and disagreements, which are inevitable when diverse minds converge. The ability to manage these differences, reach compromises, and negotiate effectively for collective success is fundamental.

Moreover, empathy – the ability to understand and share the feelings of others – plays a critical role in successful collaboration. This involves perceiving and respecting the feelings, thoughts, and experiences of others, even when they're communicated across digital platforms or through AI tools.

Lastly, adaptability – the ability to adjust to new conditions – is a key component of collaboration in a 4IR world. The pace of change demands that we remain flexible, open-minded, and ready to learn and unlearn as the situation requires.

Therefore, individuals who can effectively collaborate in this interconnected world, who can balance human interaction with AI interface, and who can navigate the complexities of global and diverse teamwork will not only thrive but also drive the evolution of this digital age.

CONSTANT LEARNING

My high school English teacher, Mrs Oosthuizen, consistently encouraged us – and me in particular – to "do your mind a favour: read a good book." This wasn't just a push towards literacy; it was an encouragement towards intellectual curiosity and continuous self-improvement. While I may not have realised it at the time, her insistence on reading was an early call to be prepared for the rapidly evolving future where information would be at our fingertips and where adaptability would be fuelled by our readiness and capacity to learn, unlearn and relearn.

Interestingly, after 35 years, I bumped into her at an old-age home in Stellenbosch while visiting my elderly mother. Even though it had been over three decades since our paths last crossed, I recognised Mrs Oosthuizen immediately.

Back in school, I was a bit of a rebel. Yet, Mrs Oosthuizen expertly channelled that rebellious energy by positioning me right at the front of the class. As a student in her First Language Higher Grade English class, I developed a deep appreciation for literature. From the raw genius of Shakespeare to the intricate beauty of contemporary works, a love for the written word was kindled in me – a passion that continues to fuel my curiosity and shape my worldview today.

Upon seeing her at the old-age home, I approached her and echoed those same words: "Do your mind a favour; read a good book." The smile that unfolded on her face was priceless. "Johan," she said, recognising me immediately. That phrase, which she uttered 35 years ago, changed my perspective completely. It transformed me from a bored, rebellious student to a lifelong reader with a passion for continuous learning.

Even though she was not explicitly teaching me the nuances of the Fourth Industrial Revolution, Mrs Oosthuizen inadvertently equipped me with the tools necessary to navigate its complex terrains. This foundational shift in my mindset towards embracing constant learning has been instrumental in my ability to stay relevant and effective in this digitally interconnected era. Now, as we delve into the importance of constant learning and its role in the 4IR world, I am reminded of how significantly one teacher's words can impact a lifetime.

Inspired by Mrs Oosthuizen's early teachings, I came to understand that the 4 C's are not standalone skills – they are interrelated and feed into each other. They also cultivate a mindset of constant learning. This constant learning isn't confined to formal educational settings – it also encompasses experiential learning, learning from others, and self-directed learning.

To illustrate this, imagine life as a bicycle ride. To keep your balance and avoid falling, you need to keep pedalling. In our modern world, this is akin to constant learning. We can express this idea as an equation where 'L' stands for Learning and 'C^2' stands for Change and Competition. It looks like this:

$$L > C2$$

This equation serves as a symbolic representation of the balance between learning, change, and competition. The variable "L" represents Learning, highlighting the ongoing necessity to acquire new skills, knowledge, and insights to stay relevant in our ever-changing world. The "L" is akin to the pedalling that keeps the bike going.

The variable "C^2" is divided into two components: Change and Competition. 'Change' resembles the hills and turns in a bike ride, representing the continuous shift in the global socio-economic landscape due to rapid technological advancements. Changes in technology, evolving business models, and even shifts in societal norms are all parts of the journey.

The second C stands for Competition. It's like the other cyclists we're racing against. This could be competitive pressure in any field, be it in terms of the job market, innovation, or business landscape. In a rapidly evolving 4IR world, competition intensifies as new players, strategies, and technologies continuously emerge. Succeeding in a 4IR world requires consistently outpacing, outmanoeuvring, and outlearning one's competition.

The equation $L > C^2$ suggests that to thrive in a 4IR world, we must prioritise learning at a pace faster than the rate of change, thus outperforming the competition. The importance of learning agility – the ability to quickly learn, unlearn, and relearn – underscores the need for continuous learning to maintain a competitive edge in a 4IR setting.

Once you embrace this understanding, investing a Sunday afternoon in an online course or spending a few hours watching YouTube videos to learn a new skill becomes a natural choice. Following Mrs Oosthuizen's wise counsel to "Read a good book" makes perfect sense. Just like a two-wheeled bike, we must keep moving, keep learning, and always remain open to change.

This principle of embracing change and constant learning is something that I've incorporated into my business practices. For instance, at First Technology, we place a high value on education and employee development. We've implemented a policy wherein we shoulder the cost for any degree, diploma or course that offers a tangential return on investment for the business. It's essential to note, though, that the courses should be aligned with our industry or business needs. Acquiring a helicopter license or becoming a certified diver, for instance, won't qualify under this policy.

Our approach is simple. Once the course is approved, the employee enters into a two-year training contract with us. If an employee opts to leave the company before the two-year mark, they will owe us a pro-rata amount. For instance, if an employee leaves after 12 months, they will need to refund 50% of the course, degree, or diploma cost. After 24 months, however, I believe that the company has already gleaned substantial value from the newly enhanced capabilities of the employee. Annually, this investment amounts to hundreds of thousands of Rand, but it's a strategic move. Our employees constantly evolve from when they joined, and I am confident that when they interface with a client, their elevated knowledge and skills will make a difference.

This policy puts our business at a competitive advantage. Unlike our competitors, who merely equip their staff with a price list or a catalogue and tell them to sell, we invest in our people. The result is not just an employee but a refined version who is more equipped and ready to face the challenges of the market. A client will undoubtedly prefer to interact with a constantly evolving version 3.0 rather than a stagnant version 1.0, who hasn't developed in five years.

This strategy is an embodiment of ensuring 'L' (Learning) remains larger than 'C^2' (Change and Competition), enabling us to continuously stay ahead in the fast-paced, competitive business landscape in which we find ourselves.

Kayaking, Nankoma Island, Lake Malawi

Diving at Mumbo Island, Lake Malawi

Acclimatisation climb in Georgia before our Mt Elbrus (Russia) summit attempt

Ex-military base camp: Mt Elbrus, Russia

Caught in a snowstorm on Mt Elbrus, Russia

An ingenious device for quickly drying out wet mountaineering shoes in Russia

Unstoppable snowcat on the slopes of Mt Elbrus, Russia

The summit of Mt Elbrus, Russia, minus 25°C, but with unspoiled panoramic views

A cheeky helicopter landing on a mountaintop outside Franschhoek, South Africa

Awaiting lift-off clearance for the R44 at a local airstrip in Cape Town, South Africa

Kim lighting the evening fire at a campsite deep inside the Okavango Delta, Botswana

Attempting to find signal on top of the Landy in the Kalahari, Eastern Namibia

Camping @ Maun, Botswana

Khwai River Bridge, Okavango Delta, Botswana

Rainy season, Chobe Game Reserve, Botswana

Lion country, Savuti Game Reserve, Botswana

Base camp for our summit attempt on Mt Aconcagua, Andes, Argentina

Morning coffee before an acclimatisation climb in the Andes, Argentina

At the summit of Mt Aconcagua with our proudly South African flag

Arriving back at advanced base camp after a 16-hour summit climb of Mt Aconcagua, Argentina

Ice cold and snowing at base camp, Mt Everest, Nepal

Outside the Khumbu Icefall, Mt Everest, Nepal

Khumbu Icefall, Mt Everest, Nepal

Buddhist monks outside Namche Bazaar, Nepal

Sadhu (Hindu) holy men outside Pashupatinath temple in Kathmandu, Nepal

Exploring the mountains in Chin State, Myanmar

Entrance to the Kakku Pagodas temple complex in Shaan State, Myanmar

Lake visit, Kakku Pagoda, Myanmar

Buddhist monk in the mountains of Chin State, Myanmar

Padaung woman with brass neck rings – Inle Lake in Shan State, Myanmar. The Padaung are also known as Kayan Lahwi

Mountain biking at Angkor Wat temple complex in Angkor, near Siem Riep, Cambodia

Kim in our motorised dugout on the Mekong River, Cambodia

Drinking thirst-quenching water from a jungle vine in the Cambodian rainforest on the border of Laos

Building our temporary shelter before the arrival of the daily monsoon rains, Cambodian rainforest

Constructing our survival raft from bamboo on the Mekong River in the Cambodian rainforest

Our ranger in the Cambodian rainforest (left) alongside the Kuy tribesman who shared his survival knowledge with us

Kim observing the finishing touches being made to our bamboo raft in the Cambodian rainforest

Dinner with Kuy family in their remote village in northern Cambodia

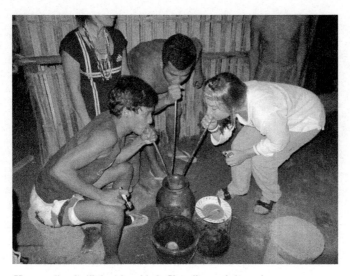

Kim sampling distilled spirits with the Kuy tribespeople in northern Cambodia

Arriving at Rumi on the island of Koh Rong Sanloem on the south coast of Cambodia

Early morning swim, Nosy Komba island, Madagascar

Visiting the lemur sanctuary on the east coast of Nosy Be, Madagascar

Diving off Sakatia Reef, Nosy Be Island, Madagascar

Scuba diving off Madagascar's north-west coast, Madagascar

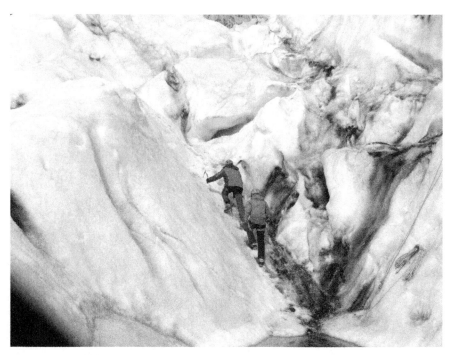

Ice climbing, Vatnajökull glacier, Iceland

At the summit of Langjökull glacier, Iceland

On the Artic Circle, Grimsey Island, north of Iceland

Amphibious vehicle in Iceland

Enroute to Grimsey Island, Artic Circle, north of Iceland

Abandoned DC3 plane (with bullet holes) on the black beach of Sólheimasandur on the south coast of Iceland

Silverback Mountain Gorilla, Volcano National Park, Rwanda (Photo credit @ Patrick Cruywagen)

Our beloved Monster Landy, Bloubergstrand, Cape Town, South Africa (Photo credit @ Peete Mocke)

CHAPTER 8
VOLUME VS VALUE IN BUSINESS

The Okavango Delta, a UNESCO heritage site and sanctuary for many of the world's most endangered mammals like the cheetah, the white and black rhino, and the African wild dog, defies common perceptions about wetlands. Although it is part of the arid Kalahari Desert, the delta stays lush year-round, not because of local rainfall but due to floodwaters originating 1,100 kilometres (688 miles) away in Angola's Planalto highlands. These waters journey through Namibia's Caprivi Strip and the Kalahari Desert before arriving in the delta around April or May. This influx sustains the wetland for the next 3 to 4 months, coinciding with Botswana's dry season. Unique among inland deltas, the Okavango never flows into the sea – instead, it eventually vanishes into the red sands of the Kalahari Desert.

In March 2018, Kim and I embarked on a three-week overlanding journey through Namibia, Botswana, Zambia, and Zimbabwe. By the time we reached Third Bridge in the Moremi Game Reserve in the Okavango Delta, we needed a day to recuperate.

The following day, refreshed and ready for our next adventure, and with Kim at the wheel, we activated our GPS, opened the Tracks4Africa app, and set out for the floodplains of the meandering Khwai River, one of Botswana's premier game-viewing locations, several hours away. Faced with the option of a longer route or a shortcut through a large jeep track-cut area filled with long pampas grass, we chose expediency. The Landy's extra clearance and our paper map confirming the track's existence convinced us we'd reach Khwai before nightfall.

It was the end of the rainy season – the roads were muddy and becoming increasingly muddier as we drove. Soon, the road disappeared entirely, and the mud gave way to marshland. Were we still on track? Both the road signs and Tracks4Africa confirmed it, so we carried on. It seemed only a matter of time before we left this soggy terrain for drier land. But the further we drove, the deeper the Landy sank, exacerbated by the pouring rain. As we continued, taking comfort in the fact that the road signs and maps were still in agreement that we were on track, we noticed a bow wave starting to form in front of us. It wasn't long before the water rose first to the level of the tyres and then to the doors. It felt as if we were driving into a shallow sea, the water rising quickly like an incoming tide. When we entered the marshland, the water was only 10 centimetres deep. Twenty minutes later, it was a metre-and-a-half deep and seeping in under our doors. Because we were pushing the bow wave away as we drove, we had no idea we'd sunk so deep, so quickly.

We were faced with five major challenges. First, we had no idea how high the tide would go. Second, this wasn't a tide that would recede in a few hours – it would take at least three months to go out. Third, there was no mobile reception, and it was unlikely anyone else would come this way for months. Fourth, swimming to safety was out of the question due to the crocodiles. Fifth, if not submerged, the Landy's roof was our only refuge, but we'd run out of food before the water level dropped.

Realising the gravity of our situation, we knew we had to leave, regardless of what the GPS was telling us. Turning back wasn't an option due to the risk of getting stuck in water-logged, two-metre-high pampas grass, with no trees nearby for a winch recovery. Our only way out was to try to reverse back along the submerged jeep track we'd come in on. But we had to do it quickly, and I knew we only had one chance to get it right.

"Let's swap seats," I said to Kim, quickly assessing our options.

With water pressing against the doors, neither of us could exit the vehicle. Kim, being smaller, would more easily move to the back seat and then to the front passenger seat. She did just that, clambering over our camping gear and fridge to land in the passenger seat while I shifted to the driver's seat and began our precarious retreat.

Because the Landy's elevated rear obstructed my view out the back, using the rear-view mirror to reverse wasn't an option. I had to depend on my side mirrors, maintaining a steady 25 km/hour (16.6 mph) while keeping to the submerged track for traction. Some 1,500 metres later, we reached semi-dry land. Sharing a glance, Kim and I knew we'd survived another day. Breathing a sigh of relief, we congratulated each other, executed a U-turn, and opted for the longer route to Khwai.

Once our nerves had settled, we assessed the situation. Why had Tracks4Africa misled us? We then realised that the crucial detail we'd overlooked was the early arrival of the floodwaters, something the app couldn't have warned us about. Being on those roads during early flooding nearly led to a catastrophic situation.

While diligently following the jeep track that our GPS had pointed us along, we soon found ourselves in trouble, forcing us to quickly re-evaluate our strategy. This serves as a cautionary tale for businesses as well. Understanding the dangers of the environment in which your business is operating is essential. You must decide whether to carry on, thinking it can't get much worse, or acknowledge that a tide is coming in and it's time to adapt.

UNDERSTANDING VOLUME AND VALUE

In the world of business, 'volume' and 'value' are two frequently used terms. Though they may initially seem intimidating, they're simply about the quantity of items sold and their worth.

'Volume' refers to the number of units of a product or service that a business sells. For instance, if a shoe company sells 1,000 pairs of sneakers in a month, that's their sales volume for that period. Volume indicates the quantity of a product or service sold. Typically, a higher volume translates to more profit, although selling a large volume at a low price may result in lower profitability if the production costs are high.

'Value' refers to the total worth of goods or services sold, calculated by multiplying volume (units sold) by the unit price. If the shoe company sells 1,000 sneakers at $50 each, the total sales value would be $50,000. Value measures the financial impact of sales on the business, and high value can result from either high prices, high volume, or a combination of both.

In simple terms, volume is about "how much" in quantity, while value is about "how much" in dollars (or whatever currency your business sells in). The next time someone mentions "volume" and "value" in business, remember: "How many did we sell?" and "How much money did we make?".

A successful business strategy might focus on increasing volume, value, or both. A budget retailer may focus on high volume with lower prices, whereas a luxury brand might concentrate on high value, selling fewer but pricier items.

In terms of a business model, both volume and value considerations are applicable to any business. Some businesses focus on a value-based, relationship-focused approach, while others concentrate on volume and competitive pricing.

To illustrate a business with a **value-based, relationship-focused** approach, consider a high-end gourmet restaurant. This restaurant sources premium ingredients and offers a luxury dining experience with a menu crafted by a renowned chef. Each dish is priced relatively high, reflecting the quality of ingredients and the culinary expertise involved. They may serve fewer customers each night compared to a fast-food chain (lower volume), but the value of each sale (the price of each meal) is high. Their success hinges on cultivating strong relationships with patrons who appreciate the fine dining experience and are willing to pay for it.

To illustrate a business with a **volume-based, competitive pricing** approach, consider a fast-food chain. This restaurant is designed for the mass-production of food items, keeping costs low and service quick. The prices are competitive, and the aim is to serve as many customers as possible throughout the day (high volume). Even though the profit margin on each meal is lower compared to the high-end gourmet restaurant, the volume of sales ensures profitability. Their success depends on efficient service and broad appeal to a large customer base.

In both examples, the restaurants are successful but employ different strategies based on their value and volume considerations.

THE BUSINESS PORTFOLIO MATRIX

To better understand the impact that volume and value can have on a business, take a look at the Business Portfolio Matrix below. The table is divided into four quadrants, each representing a different aspect of your business. The products or services that make up each aspect will fall into one of four categories:

• Core: These are the primary products or services that your business is built around, often representing the company's identity and main source of revenue.

• Commoditised: These are widely available products or services, often sold in large volumes at lower prices, where differentiation from competitors is minimal.

• Specialised: These are unique, high-value products or services that differentiate your business in the market, often appealing to niche customer segments.

• Augmented: These products or services enhance the value of your core and specialised offerings, often creating additional revenue streams by adding value or complementary features to the main product or service.

On the vertical axis (Y-axis), you have profitability. A product or service placed higher up on the axis signifies higher profit, while a lower position indicates less profit.

On the horizontal axis (X-axis), you have effort or cost. The further right a product or service falls on this axis, the more resources it consumes to bring it to market. These resources can include time, products, services, or the raw materials required for the end product. Whether it's time, resources, money, or skill, it all constitutes effort or cost to market.

The business portfolio matrix

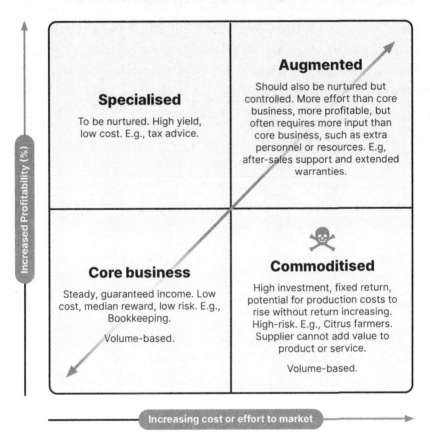

Let's now explore the four quadrants in a little more detail and understand the impact each quadrant has from a value and volume perspective. Once you understand this grid and its impact on your bottom line, you can use this information to devise strategies and differentiate your business in the market.

CORE BUSINESS QUADRANT

The core business quadrant represents your bread and butter, the products or services that your business is recognised for. It may not demand a large workforce or make you exceedingly wealthy, but it will ensure a steady, reliable income that covers your bills.

From a value perspective, your core business provides consistent and reliable value to your customer base. From a volume perspective, it usually comprises the majority of your transactions, given its core nature.

For example, for an academic bookstore, its core business would be selling textbooks. Despite the emergence of digital reading platforms, the physical sale of books provides a steady stream of income that allows the bookstore to operate and cover basic expenses. It might not make the bookstore owner exceptionally wealthy, but it keeps the business afloat and maintains its identity in the market.

Reading this, you should be able to immediately identify what constitutes your core business.

COMMODITISED QUADRANT

The commoditised quadrant represents your mass-market offerings, products, or services that are widely available from numerous providers and primarily compete based on price. Picture a super-market where identical products from different brands jostle for your attention, and the deciding factor is usually the impact on your wallet. From a value perspective, these products or services offer less differentiation and thus compete mainly on price. From a volume perspective, they often represent a large portion of the market but with narrow profit margins.

A classic example of a commoditised product is table salt. Regardless of the brand or packaging, table salt is essentially identical across all offerings, widely available, and primarily competes on price rather than unique features. When consumers purchase table salt, they often choose the cheapest option because they perceive no added value in paying more for another brand.

A product or service is categorised as 'commoditised' when no additional value can be added to it. Commodity contracts, such as those for wheat, oil, or gold, serve as good examples: their value remains fixed, and you can't increase the worth of a gold bar by sprinkling some extra gold dust on it.

A real-world example of this might be the fruit export market. In the Western Cape, for instance, citrus farmers may agree to sell A1 boxes of oranges to overseas supermarkets at a fixed price of £5 each. However, if labour costs unexpectedly surge due to union action, and fuel prices rise sharply, coupled with increased costs of chemicals due to reliance on Ukrainian suppliers amid the ongoing war there, the expenses keep spiralling. Environmental challenges like drought further exacerbate the situation. With extended periods of loadshedding, the farmer is forced to run generators to keep their packaging machines operational. The farmer's two most significant expenses, labour and fuel, rise between 20% and 40%, and their diesel usage skyrockets by 200%, thanks to load shedding (electricity blackouts). Just when it seems things can't get worse, the South African rand plummets. Yet, despite these escalating costs, the price per box of oranges remains contractually locked at £5. As a result, farmers often resort to dumping their fruit. The costs of transporting the fruit to port control outweigh the already dwindling margins.

Operating a business solely in the commoditised quadrant is risky. It demands significant effort, cost, resources, and skill but does not materially contribute to the bottom line. Businesses often fail due to poor cash flow management or inadequate working capital. However, another common pitfall is not realising when a significant part of their offering has shifted into the commoditised quadrant.

Businesses must be cautious when operating in this quadrant. If one of your offerings begins to consume too much effort, time, and resources without correspondingly increasing revenue and profitability, it might be time to rethink your strategy.

SPECIALISED QUADRANT

The specialised quadrant contains your unique, niche products or services that cater to a specific segment of customers. These offerings often have higher profit margins, and they are typically specialised in nature. From a value perspective, these offerings have a higher value due to their specialised nature and unique attributes. From a volume perspective, these offerings may not constitute a large portion of your transactions, but they contribute significantly to profitability due to higher margins.

The specialised quadrant is valuable, and nurturing it should be a key strategy for businesses. Even though the resources or time invested in this quadrant might be similar to those of other quadrants, the returns are generally higher due to the increased margins.

Consider an accounting firm as an example. If its primary business is bookkeeping, a service for which there are many providers, the firm might find itself in the commoditised quadrant, competing primarily on price.

However, the situation dramatically changes when we consider tax specialists. This is a niche service requiring advanced expertise and a higher degree of specialisation, placing it firmly in the specialised quadrant. Their services are not as readily available, nor are they easily substituted, which differentiates them from standard bookkeepers. Because of this, they can command higher prices. As such, the firm stands to make considerably more money employing a cadre of tax specialists than it would with a similar number of bookkeepers. Another service could include private wealth management. This might involve structuring retirement annuities, handling offshore investments, and setting up blind trust structures. Even though you'll need more people with specialised skills to offer this kind of service, you can charge significantly more for it. This is the power of the specialised quadrant.

Businesses should pay careful attention to the offerings in their specialised quadrant. By investing in and developing these services or products, they can increase their competitive advantage and, thus, their profitability.

AUGMENTED QUADRANT

The augmented quadrant includes products or services that enhance the value of your core offerings. These can occasionally also open up new income streams. This could be in the form of after-sales support, training sessions, extended warranties, maintenance and repair services, technology upgrades, or anything else that improves the customer's experience with your product or service.

From a value perspective, these offerings enhance the perceived value of your core business, improving customer satisfaction. From a volume perspective, they might not represent a large portion of your turnover, but they can open up new income streams and create customer loyalty.

Similar to the specialised quadrant, the augmented quadrant should also be nurtured, but it has a different set of management requirements. While the core business may demand extensive strategising and day-to-day hands-on operation, the augmented quadrant often calls for the inclusion of additional personnel or resources to deliver the value-added services effectively. Even though this might involve the coordination of additional resources, the effort can be offset by the potential profits and the enhanced customer satisfaction these services bring.

STRATEGICALLY MAPPING AND OPTIMISING YOUR BUSINESS OFFERINGS

In business, it's important to nurture and grow your value-based offerings. Yet, focusing on one quadrant shouldn't mean neglecting the others. A well-rounded, diversified business strategy should include a mix of offerings from all quadrants to accommodate various customer needs and manage risks effectively.

Having familiarised yourself with the core, specialised, augmented, and commoditised segments, you can now categorise your business offerings accordingly. Start by listing all your offerings and ask yourself:

1. Which of my offerings constitute my core business?

2. Which ones fall within my specialised quadrant?

3. Do I provide any augmented products or services?

4. Which of my products or services are commoditised?

For each of your offerings in each quadrant, determine whether it is volume-based or value-based. Remember, value-based offerings have higher margins and lower costs to bring to market, while volume-based offerings have narrower margins and higher costs related to time, effort, and resources required to bring them to market.

Now, create a grid with the quadrants: core, specialised, augmented, and commoditised. Draw a line from the bottom-left (core) quadrant to the top-right (augmented) quadrant. Everything below this line is volume-based, and everything above it is value-based. Ideally, your business should operate above this line.

Here's what to do next:

1. Place all aspects of your specialised offering into your specialised quadrant.

2. Examine your core quadrant offerings. Position offerings with higher margins and lower to-market costs in the top half of the line and those with narrow margins and high to-market costs below the line.

3. Repeat this process with your augmented quadrant.

4. Place all aspects of your commoditised offering into the commoditised quadrant.

Once completed, you'll have a visual representation that will help you optimise each quadrant to enhance your overall business performance.

Products or services in your specialised quadrant will always be profitable. While certain augmented offerings might be profitable, some might not justify the labour and resources required to bring them to market. Within your core segment, you might identify opportunities to increase profitability by cutting costs. The commoditised quadrant is always a high-risk, low-margin part of your business. It requires clever thinking if you want to continue selling commoditised products as part of your offering. I will explain how we managed this shortly.

Next, examine your commoditised quadrant. Each product or service in this quadrant requires one of three decisions:

1. Discontinue these products or services if the time, resources, or effort to bring them to market outweigh the benefits.

2. Increase the price by adding value (like adding a 'limited edition' sticker to the product) – although this may be difficult in a commoditised market.

3. Transfer the offering to your core business segment by reducing the cost and possibly outsourcing the offering.

The software development industry provides a perfect example of how to transition an offering from the commoditised to the core quadrant. Local software developers often demand high salaries due to their extensive qualifications and skillsets. However, you could offset this cost by outsourcing to developers in countries like India, where highly skilled developers work for significantly less.

Let me share a real-life example from my experience at First Technology to further illustrate this point. As a business, we need to tread carefully when it comes to supplying PCs and notebooks to our customers. These products are highly commoditised, so whether we supply a PC or a notebook or a retailer like Incredible Connection does, the product is identical – same brand, same box. The only difference is the price, which Incredible Connection may heavily discount due to their retail location, while we have higher overhead costs to consider.

At best, we could make a 5% gross margin on a notebook sale if we aimed to stay price-competitive with the big retailers. That's without accounting for costs like storage, invoicing, packaging, and delivery that eat into this margin. While the sale boosts our turnover, we are left with virtually no net profit after deducting all these costs.

Given that this product fell into our commoditised quadrant, we brainstormed and came up with three possible options:

1. We could increase our margin to, say, 15% by raising the price of the notebooks. However, customers won't pay a higher price for a commoditised product. They would simply opt for a cheaper vendor.

2. We could add value. This would allow us to charge more, but that doesn't work with notebooks due to their commoditised nature.

3. We could decide to stop selling notebooks and allow the customer to take their business for this particular product elsewhere.

Suppose we considered the third option. While considering the potential repercussions, we found ourselves imagining a scenario in which one of our major clients, who purchases a variety of specialised products from us, confronts us, saying, "I spend millions on Microsoft Enterprise with you. I buy all my data centres from you. You handle all my cybersecurity. But you won't supply me with notebooks? So much for offering a turnkey solution and being a one-stop shop. You'd better supply me with my notebooks, or I will reconsider our business relationship."

Obviously, none of the three options above was going to work. We couldn't raise the price or add value due to the commoditised nature of the product, and we couldn't just stop supplying it either. The only viable solution that emerged was to align the cost line with our core business by cutting costs. This could be done by eliminating logistical costs. For example, we could arrange for our distributors at HP, Dell, or Acer to deliver notebooks directly to the client, cutting out the need for us to physically handle the product. They could send us an electronic invoice, and we'd invoice the client the same way. The only thing we would receive is a Proof of Delivery. Now, the 5% margin we make on each notebook could cover the minimal administrative costs and still leave a profit. That way, we could supply thousands of notebooks without physically handling them. By pinpointing and eliminating costs within the supply chain, we were able to transition notebook supply into our core business and away from the commoditised grid.

SEGMENTING YOUR CLIENT BASE

Many of us display an astounding level of loyalty towards individuals in our social circles, including some who might have been better left in our past. I refer to these individuals as 'the crabs that keep you in the pot'.

Consider a person from your past, say Freddy, a former schoolmate. Just because you share a history doesn't mean there's an unbreakable bond you are obliged to maintain. This is particularly true if Freddy hasn't evolved over the years. The common ground you once shared at school gradually loses its relevance when juxtaposed with the personal, professional, intellectual and material growth you've undergone since then.

In such situations, you might find the relationship turning into a one-way street: you invest time, share skills, offer emotional support, and provide life advice but receive little to nothing in return.

So, how do you identify these 'crabs'? You consistently feel drained after spending time with them. If this feeling persists beyond your comfort level, it's time to reassess your relationship with them. Like crabs in a pot, the moment you attempt to climb out towards freedom, these individuals will try to pull you back. They would rather you remain in the pot with them – intellectually, culturally, financially, or even geographically.

This concept isn't limited to personal relationships – it's equally applicable in the business world. Clients who drain your time and resources could be seen as the crabs in your corporate pot. Identify them, and don't allow them to divert your focus from clients who truly deserve your attention and offer a tangible return on your investment.

Every business will have three types of clients. I call them A, B, and C clients.

'A' CLIENTS

Your 'A' clients are the crown jewels of your client portfolio. These high-value customers are your business's lifeblood, driving its success. They contribute significantly to your revenue stream through high-volume, high-value transactions.

'A' clients typically purchase premium products or services and are receptive to upselling and cross-selling opportunities. Their complex needs can also inspire diversified and innovative solutions, driving the evolution of your products or services. Their feedback is often insightful, helping you refine your offerings and processes, which can benefit your business overall.

Reliable and timely in their payments, 'A' clients respect your payment terms, maintaining a regular cash flow for your company. This financial reliability, coupled with their substantial contribution to your revenue, makes them a credit manager's dream.

Yet, the relationship with 'A' clients goes beyond just financial transactions. These are clients with whom you build strong, meaningful, and long-lasting relationships. You could even say you're "married" to them, in a business sense, of course. They're likely to stick around for your whole career or theirs. It's this deep connection that sets 'A' clients apart from the rest. They're not just clients – they're partners in your business's journey.

As such, a significant portion of your time, about 30 to 40%, should be spent on nurturing these relationships.

'B' CLIENTS

'B' clients are not inferior to 'A' clients. Instead, they are 'B' clients because they haven't yet matured into 'A' clients. Often, they are potential clients or prospects still in the process of being won over. Perhaps the purchase order hasn't come through yet, or you've only done minor work for them, but there's potential for larger projects if you handle this initial phase well.

While you're 'married' to your 'A' clients, you're 'dating' your 'B' clients. When you're married, you're unlikely to shower your partner with flowers and chocolates every day, firstly because it's not financially practical, and secondly, these gifts would eventually lose their charm. In contrast, when you're dating, most of your time is spent nurturing that relationship. If you don't, it's unlikely to evolve into a long-term bond or reach the equivalent of a business 'marriage'.

In business, your goal is to develop your 'B' clients into long-term partners – or 'A' clients. Aim to spend most of your time – ideally 60% – developing and nurturing your relationships with these clients.

299

'C' CLIENTS

When you consider your 'C' clients, think back to the crabs in the pot metaphor I referenced earlier. These clients tend to occupy a significant amount of your time without offering a substantial return on investment. As a rule of thumb, keep all communication with these clients electronic or telephonic, strictly avoiding face-to-face meetings.

While your account managers are investing time and resources in your 'B' clients – playing golf, entertaining, and giving presentations – they should refrain from extending similar efforts towards your 'C' clients. Investing time in face-to-face meetings with 'C' clients is not a profitable use of resources. 'C' clients are unlikely to help you meet your financial targets – they're the proverbial crabs in your business operations.

This doesn't mean you should close their accounts or ignore them completely. Instead, delegate the responsibility of handling their accounts to your sales assistants. Let them manage proposals and quotations for these clients. Remember, even crabs can fill a pot if there are enough of them. But ensure someone else oversees this process, maintaining communication and servicing these 'crabs'.

You likely already have an idea of who your 'C' clients are. Minimise the time you spend cultivating relationships with these clients. Remember, they should be maintained but not prioritised.

HEAT MAP YOUR BUSINESS

Maximising your business potential often involves uncovering hidden opportunities within your existing client base. A powerful way to do this is through a method known as heat mapping, a visual tool that uses colours to represent different stages of client engagement with your services. This technique allows you to identify which products or services your clients are currently using, those they've shown interest in but have yet to commit to, and those they'll likely never use. Importantly, it also highlights untapped opportunities – services or products your clients might benefit from, but you haven't yet proposed to them.

To heat map your business effectively, you might find it helpful to use Excel. Begin by segmenting your clients into 'A' clients, 'B' clients, and 'C' clients. Next, create a separate sheet for each client segment: one for 'A' clients and another for 'B' clients. For now, you needn't focus on your 'C' clients.

Start with your 'A' clients, listing each one by name down the left side of the spreadsheet. Across the top, list the products or services that your business offers. Then, repeat this process with your 'B' clients.

Next, assign a colour – red, green, or yellow, in the style of a traffic light – to each block on the spreadsheet, corresponding to a client and a product or service you offer, based on the following:

• Green: Services or products the client is currently using.

• Yellow: Services or products you've quoted on but are still awaiting approval.

• Red: Either you've lost this business opportunity to a competitor, or the client will never buy this service or product.

• White (open blocks): Services or products you can still pitch to that client.

For the purpose of this demonstration, let's assume you're running an accounting firm. We'll call your three 'A' clients Patrick, Gillian, and George. Your primary service offerings might include auditing, tax services, wealth management, estate planning, life insurance, and income protection advisory services.

In the example below, Patrick is utilising your firm for his auditing and tax advisory needs. Fill those cells with green. He has enquired about life insurance and income protection, and you have sent him a proposal, but he hasn't yet responded. Colour these cells yellow. He has told you previously that a close friend of his is handling his estate planning, so you're unlikely to secure that business. Fill that cell with the red. The remaining cell, wealth management, is a service you haven't yet discussed with him. Leave this cell white.

Repeat this process with all your 'A' clients, just as we have done with Gillian and George.

Client segment	Products and services					
'A' Clients	Auditing	Tax Advisory	Wealth Management	Estate Planning	Life Insurance	Income Protection
Patrick						
Gillian						
George						

Red   Green   Yellow

After completing the heat mapping:

• Follow up on the yellow cells. Give these clients a courtesy call and follow up on the proposals or quotes you sent them that they haven't yet responded to.

• Hone in on the white cells. These represent untapped opportunities and potential future revenue.

While it is important to acquire new customers for business growth, focusing on existing customers can be a more efficient way to increase sales and revenue. Many studies suggest that retaining existing clients and selling more services to them is often more efficient than acquiring new ones. The likelihood of selling to an existing customer is 60-70%, while the probability of selling to a new prospect is just 5-20%. This is due to a number of factors.

Firstly, existing customers, already familiar with your products or services and satisfied with their experience, are likely to trust your business and have established a relationship with you. This familiarity reduces resistance and opens them up to additional offerings.

Cost efficiency also plays a significant role. According to the Harvard Business Review, the cost of acquiring a new customer can be five times more than retaining an existing one, largely due to the higher costs associated with marketing and sales, such as advertising, staff time, and promotional offers required when attracting new customers.

Another element to consider is the higher receptiveness of existing customers to upselling and cross-selling opportunities, a result of their familiarity with your product or service quality. Finally, customer loyalty can't be overlooked. Loyal customers may become advocates for your business, offering valuable word-of-mouth referrals and positive online reviews that can help attract new customers.

With these considerations in mind and based on the identified white spaces in your client heat map, you could reach out to Patrick to arrange a meeting to discuss estate planning, since there is clearly a white space requirement there. Gillian may be interested in using your firm for her auditing requirements; within that conversation, you could also introduce personal aspects of tax and estate planning. A lunch with George could serve as an opportunity to update him on the wealth management and estate planning aspects of his portfolio and segue into a discussion on whether he has appropriate life insurance and income protection mechanisms in place for him and his loved ones.

WHY PERSONAL CONNECTIONS STILL MATTER IN MODERN MARKETING

In a similar vein, maintaining personal connections with clients plays a pivotal role in marketing, which is where below-the-line (BTL) marketing comes in. With today's digital overload, traditional advertising is losing its effectiveness. People are constantly bombarded with stimuli, leading to what I've termed "digital fatigue". This became especially evident during Covid when Zoom webinars and Teams meetings surged.

In my experience, BTL marketing methods, which include shared experiences like fishing weekends away, golf days, sailing trips, or even dinners together, are far more effective than advertising or direct mail campaigns. Rather than overwhelming clients with digital content and social media campaigns, which can contribute to digital fatigue, I believe it's far more valuable to focus on relationship-building through BTL marketing.

BTL marketing allows for a direct and personalised connection with your audience, making it easier to nurture long-term relationships. This type of marketing – which includes direct mail campaigns, search engine marketing, social media marketing, content marketing, email marketing, and other forms of direct communication with customers – is often more engaging and interactive, providing opportunities for real-time feedback and conversation. The result is higher engagement levels, improved customer loyalty, and stronger overall customer relationships. These 'one-to-one' marketing efforts often aim to create a more personal connection with the customer, making them feel valued and understood.

However, it's important to note that the effectiveness of these strategies largely depends on the nature of the business, the product or service being offered, and the target audience.

To illustrate the value of face-to-face interaction, during the Covid lockdowns, I attended a remote whiskey and wine-tasting event. While the concept was novel – attendees logging in on Teams to partake in a tasting experience – it was somewhat impersonal and often disrupted by home distractions, like pets making unexpected appearances or children seeking attention.

The lesson from this experience is clear: while remote connections have their place, they can't completely replace the depth and richness of face-to-face interactions. One-on-one meetings with clients, whether over a cup of coffee or a business lunch, offer a level of spontaneity and personal connection that digital platforms can't replicate. This direct interaction allows for a deeper understanding of the client's needs and a stronger, more authentic relationship.

Even in a digital age, a balanced, relationship-focused approach to marketing – one that values face-to-face interaction and personal connection with clients – can yield far better long-term results.

CHAPTER 9
THE ART OF WAR

The *Art of War* is an ancient Chinese military treatise attributed to Sun Tzu, a high-ranking military general, strategist, and tactician. Written more than two millennia ago, Sun Tzu's masterpiece is not merely a manual on warfare but a treatise on strategy, leadership, and human psychology. Historically, emperors and generals pored over its pages in search of insights that could tip the balance of power in their favour. Today, its teachings find relevance far beyond the battlefield, influencing decision-making in boardrooms, sports arenas, and even day-to-day life. Personally, it has served as an invaluable guide in both my adventures and business pursuits.

The treatise consists of 13 chapters, each addressing a unique aspect of warfare. Its key concepts include knowing when to fight and when not to fight, the art of deceiving the enemy, and the importance of understanding both oneself and one's adversary. These teachings serve as foundational principles for anyone seeking to navigate the complexities of competition, conflict, and leadership in the modern world.

In its initial chapters, Sun Tzu emphasises the foundational concepts for winning any battle. He discusses the need for careful planning and consideration of various factors that can affect the outcome of a conflict – be it tangible factors like terrain and weather or intangible ones, such as leadership quality and troop morale.

"The supreme art of war is to subdue the enemy without fighting."

The cost of warfare is a significant theme. Sun Tzu cautions against letting wars drag on, as they not only exhaust resources but also diminish the spirit and strength of the troops. While many view warfare as being predominantly about confrontation, Sun Tzu champions the idea that true mastery of war comes from winning without ever stepping onto the battlefield, where strategy takes precedence over brute force. For Sun Tzu, a master strategist doesn't just attack blindly but looks for the most effective point of contention – targeting the enemy's plans and alliances before considering direct conflict.

"When he utilises combined energy, his fighting men become as it were like unto rolling logs or stones. For it is the nature of a log or stone to remain motionless on level ground, and to move when on a slope; if four-cornered, to come to a standstill, but if round-shaped, to go rolling down."

In the chapter entitled *Use of Energy* (Chapter 5), Sun Tzu discusses the efficient deployment of resources and forces in warfare. He likens an army's strength to the flow of water, highlighting the importance of unifying one's troops into a single force and the need to adapt and direct one's energy where it's most effective, similar to how water naturally flows along the path of least resistance. The essence is to manage and channel one's resources wisely for maximum impact.

"All warfare is based on deception. Hence, when we are able to attack, we must seem unable; when using our forces, we must appear inactive; when we are near, we must make the enemy believe we are far away; when far away, we must make him believe we are near."

Sun Tzu teaches that a skilled strategist knows not only their own strengths and weaknesses but also those of the enemy. They know where and when to position themselves to maximise strength and minimise vulnerability. In Sun Tzu's view, deception, intelligence, and unpredictability are powerful tools, making it difficult for the enemy to decipher your next move. He highlights the importance of appearing weak when you are strong and strong when you are weak. If the enemy is strong in one area, avoid it. If they are weak, attack it. By manipulating an enemy's perceptions, one can control their actions and steer them into situations where they are vulnerable and exposed.

"When the enemy is relaxed, make them toil. When full, starve them. When settled, make them move."

Instead of sticking doggedly to rigid plans, Sun Tzu recommends adapting based on the enemy's actions. Whether it's manoeuvring through enemy territory, using the terrain to one's advantage, or recognising and responding to different combat situations, the emphasis is always on fluidity, adaptability, and the element of surprise.

> *"When you surround an army, leave an outlet free. Do not press a desperate foe too hard."*

In Chapter 7, *Maneuvering*, Sun Tzu speaks about surrounding the enemy but leaving an opening for them. When an enemy believes they have no route of escape, they might fight more fiercely, making the battle more difficult and costly. By "leaving a way of escape", the enemy will avoid fighting with the desperation of a cornered animal. Modern interpretations call this "building a golden bridge" for your enemy to retreat across.

> *"Treat your men as you would your own beloved sons. And they will follow you into the deepest valley."*

Sun Tzu emphasises the importance of maintaining the spirit and morale of one's soldiers to maximise their potential. He highlights the necessity of caring for their well-being and being attuned to their physical and emotional state, ensuring they are neither overburdened nor exhausted. For instance, he advises that soldiers should be given time to rest after a long march before being deployed into battle.

> *"If your enemy is superior, evade him. If angry, irritate him. If equally matched, fight, and if not split and reevaluate."*

Sun Tzu emphasises the importance of keen observation, adaptability, and a thorough understanding of both the environment and one's enemy. He offers guidance on interpreting signs from the enemy, such as the appearance and movements of their troops, to gain an understanding of their intentions and strength. For instance, he describes the different appearances of troops when they are in order, in disorder, intent on advancing, or intent on retreating.

> *"Be before the enemy in occupying the raised and sunny spots, and carefully guard your line of supplies. Then you will be able to fight with advantage."*

In Chapter 10, *Classification of Terrain,* Sun Tzu categorises and describes various types of terrains and the strategic implications associated with each. He breaks down terrain into six distinct types: accessible ground, entangling ground, temporising ground, narrow passes, precipitous heights, and positions at a great distance from the enemy. Each type of terrain presents unique challenges and opportunities, and Sun Tzu provides guidance on how to navigate and utilise them most effectively. For instance, he recommends establishing alliances and securing supply routes on accessible ground, while on entangling ground, he suggests pressing forward without hesitation.

> *"There are roads which must not be followed, armies which must not be attacked, towns which must not be besieged, positions which must not be contested, commands of the sovereign which must not be obeyed."*

He also highlights the need for leaders to be aware of their strategic position relative to the enemy, adapt to the situation at hand, and adjust their tactics accordingly. In Chapter 11, *The Nine Situations,* he outlines the different strategic positions or situations an army might find itself in and provides guidance on how to handle each. The nine situations are dispersive ground, facile ground, contentious ground, open ground, intersecting highways, serious ground, difficult ground, hemmed-in ground, and desperate ground. Each situation presents unique challenges and opportunities. For example, on dispersive ground, when an army is near its home territory, there's a risk of losing focus, and Sun Tzu advises against battling there. On desperate ground, where there's no retreat or way out, Sun Tzu recommends fighting with full force since there's no other option.

"Spies are a most important element in water, because on them depends an army's ability to move."

In the treatise's final chapter, Sun Tzu emphasises that leaders who master the art of intelligence gathering through the use of spies will hold a significant advantage on the battlefield. He categorises spies into several types, such as double agents and local spies, each serving a unique purpose and function. By leveraging this network of informants, a leader can make informed decisions, anticipate enemy moves, and deploy strategies that catch the enemy off-guard. The chapter reminds the reader that knowledge, acquired covertly and at times at great risk, is an invaluable weapon – often more potent than sheer military might.

In a rapidly evolving world where competition is fierce and the stakes are high, the wisdom contained within *The Art of War* remains remarkably relevant. Whether the 'enemy' is a business competitor, a rival team, or even personal obstacles we face, the treatise serves as a reminder that confrontations can be won without conflict and that true mastery lies in outthinking rather than overpowering one's opponent.

STRATEGY VS TACTICS

Had Sun Tzu been around today, he would have likely given modern-day consultants a run for their money. In *The Art of War*, he said, "Strategy without tactics is the slowest route to victory. Tactics without strategy is the noise before defeat". The terms 'strategy' and 'tactics' are often used interchangeably, but they serve different roles. A strategy is your roadmap for achieving long-term goals, while tactics are the steps you take to get there. Neglecting one is like trying to row a boat with one oar – you might eventually reach your destination, but it's going to be a cumbersome journey.

STRATEGY WITHOUT TACTICS

Having a strategy without tactics is like knowing you want to retire wealthy but not having a plan to get there. When you ask people about their ten-year plan, you sometimes get what I like to call the New Zealand sheep gaze. It's as if they're doing complex calculus in their heads, but really, they're just buffering. Aiming to retire wealthy is a commendable strategy, but without breaking it down into smaller, tactical steps – like a ten-year, a five-year, or even a one-year plan – your dream is going to remain just that.

TACTICS WITHOUT STRATEGY

Conversely, having a list of tactics without a clear strategy is like being a ship without a compass. Imagine meticulously managing your daily expenses to afford your Netflix subscription and Friday night pizzas, only to find out at retirement that you've neglected long-term financial planning. You might have been an excellent manager of your daily affairs, but the lack of a strategic plan sets you up for financial instability. This is what Sun Tzu would call "the noise before defeat".

A MORE BALANCED APPROACH

Switching gears, let's discuss a more relatable topic: weight management. The thing with weight is that it creeps up on you. On average, after the age of 18, most people gain an extra kilogram every ten years. That might not sound like much, but without a strategy, those kilos accumulate. Suddenly, you're 65 and realise that, well, things have expanded. If you have a strategy to maintain your weight, it guides your tactics – like portion control or trading Netflix binges for a brisk walk.

If you're planning to lose weight, your strategy might involve shedding four kilograms by the end of summer. This could mean saying goodbye to late-night snacks or that extra glass of wine and saying hello to regular exercise. A clear strategy helps guide your tactical decisions, making your path to victory – whatever that may be – more achievable.

THE ART OF WAR IN INVESTMENT STRATEGY

Applying Sun Tzu's *Art of War* principles to investment strategies seems especially poignant in a world that has drastically changed since 2020. Sun Tzu advocated for adaptability and situational awareness, both crucial in today's volatile economic environment. In terms of investments, a sinking market doesn't necessarily spell doom. Warren Buffett put it aptly when he said, "Buy when there's blood in the streets, even if the blood is your own". It's easier said than done, of course, as human nature tends to kick in, driving people to cash out when markets crash. However, if you align your thinking with the Art of War, you'll see a market crash as a temporary sale on blue-chip stocks. The goal is to overcome the emotional hurdle and seize the opportunity.

Global dynamics have also shifted. Interest rates are climbing, and global food security is in jeopardy due to production issues in

Ukraine. Additionally, we face unprecedented climate change. In May 2023, Shanghai recorded its highest-ever temperature of 36.7°C, while India now regularly sees temperatures around 45°C. These changes, along with political and economic instability, should be red flags that it's time to reassess your investment strategy.

Given the unstable landscape, my advice is to pivot to sectors showing incredible resilience and potential, such as tech companies specialising in generative AI. Converting investments from ZAR to USD can offer a hedge against local economic volatility. Tech giants like Meta, NVIDIA, Apple, and Amazon are not just promising in terms of capital appreciation and dividends. For South Africans, investing in USD also offers a hedge against a depreciating Rand, essentially making you wealthier every time poor policy decisions impact the local currency.

Taking these steps will require a drastic shift in mindset. It involves a willingness to execute – to actually make that call, sell those shares or property, and redirect your resources. Everyone talks a big game over dinner about their Allan Gray unit trusts or Naspers shares, but few actually take action.

Staying adaptable and maintaining keen situational awareness can turn challenges into opportunities. If you understand and embrace the risks, there are massive rewards. Instead of packing for Perth, which many South Africans are doing, the key is to seize these opportunities and act. As the old adage goes, fortune favours the brave.

INTO THE WILD: LESSONS IN HUMILITY FROM THE CAMBODIAN RAINFOREST

Speaking about bravery, in 2014, while exploring options for our next adventure, Kim and I stumbled upon an advertisement online. An adventure company in Cambodia was offering an authentic tribal experience in the Laos-Cambodian rainforest, one of the planet's last remaining indigenous rainforests. The package promised two weeks of trekking through the rainforest alongside local tribespeople, who would teach participants how to survive as native tribesmen. From the comfort of our Cape Town lounge, the idea sounded quite *lekker*. Without hesitation, we reserved our spots and booked our flights to Cambodia.

Before diving into our jungle experience, we decided to explore some of Cambodia's renowned tourist attractions. The Angkor Wat temple complex in the northern province of Siem Reap topped our list. This temple famously featured as a backdrop in the film *Tomb Raider*, starring Angelina Jolie. After taking a short flight from Phnom Penh, the country's capital, we landed in Siem Reap, the gateway to this vast temple landscape, cradled by the thick rainforest. Commissioned in the 12th Century by King Suryavarman II as a mausoleum, it is a testament to the grandeur of Khmer architecture and artistry. It boasts intricate sandstone sculptures and reliefs carefully chiselled to bring to life a pantheon of gods and mythical creatures.

Given the vastness of the temple grounds, we opted to hire mountain bikes to navigate the terrain – a journey that, on foot, would have taken us months. With over 72 temples and nearly 1000 buildings spread across roughly 400 acres, we encountered some of the most exquisite temples we had ever laid our eyes on. The sight of centuries-old trees weaving through temple ruins was truly surreal. Our visit solidified our belief that Cambodia deserves a prime spot on every traveller's bucket list.

With the touristy stuff done, we caught a taxi to the last missionary station in the Mekong Delta, also known as "the rice bowl of Vietnam". Once there, our mode of transport got decidedly more rustic. We found ourselves clambering into what can best be described as half a tree with a Yamaha motor strapped on the back – our motorised dugout. As the engine roared to life and we made our way upriver into the heart of the rainforest, the last vestiges of civilisation melted away into the distance.

Aboard the dugout, we met the game ranger who would be joining us for the two-week expedition. Fluent in Khmer and the local tribal dialect and, of course, English, he'd serve not only as our guide but also as our translator. He mentioned that only Kim and I had signed up for this particular adventure.

Our dugout eventually pulled up alongside the riverbank, where a group of diminutive Kuy tribespeople eagerly awaited us. Our initial excitement at making human contact quickly turned to alarm when several of the tribesmen smiled, revealing sharp, crocodile-like teeth. It felt like we were being stared down by a pack of snarling Rottweilers.

I nudged Kim. "Whose idea was this again?" I whispered.

After realising that we weren't on the menu for dinner, our guide announced that it was time to depart. Our party consisted of him, one of the tribesmen (with the pointy teeth), and us. We had no way of communicating with the outside world. All we had were our back-packs, a wok, and a large piece of folded blue plastic sheet each. The purpose of the sheets remained a mystery, but we knew that all would soon be revealed.

We followed the tribesman and our guide deep into the rainforest, grateful to have someone with us who spoke our language. Several hours later, we reached our first overnight spot. It was nothing more than a clearing in the jungle, devoid of anything man-made: no tents, no crockery, no cutlery.

"Where are we going to sleep?" Kim asked.

"You'll be building your own shelter every night," our guide responded, pointing to the towering bamboo that surrounded us and handing us each a hammock. This bamboo, ubiquitous throughout the rainforest, was unlike anything we'd ever seen before – so thick and so tall, it could easily be mistaken for trees.

Using a machete-like knife, the tribesman showed us how to harness bamboo's versatility. First, he demonstrated how to create cups using the sealed-off end of the base. Next, we fashioned knives and forks by splitting a piece of bamboo. Then came the table: we left about two feet of bamboo upright and spliced the remaining portion into eight sections, which we then splayed outwards and downwards, creating a table resembling a tarantula. We then set about building our individual shelters for the night. Using bamboo for the frame, we wove palm fronds together to make a rope to secure the frame. When we were confident that it could support our body weight with the hammock suspended above the ground, we covered it with the blue plastic sheet we'd been given earlier.

That sheet was our saving grace. At 6 p.m., a monsoon swept through the rainforest, drenching everything in its path for a solid twelve hours. While this would become a nightly occurrence, I'd never experienced a downpour like that in my life. The electrical storms only heightened the experience. Ten, sometimes twenty, flashes of lightning lit up the forest at once, turning the night into a firestorm. All I remember thinking as the lightning flashed was, 'Please don't hit me!' The last thing anyone would want is their meticulously built shelter collapsing, succumbing to the flooded ground beneath, especially with all the creepy crawlies – which included leeches, vipers, and tarantulas the size of lunch plates – lurking below.

The following morning, as we ventured deeper into the rainforest, bamboo emerged not just as a building material but also as a source of sustenance. Young bamboo shoots, often turned to for carbohydrates, taste remarkably similar to fresh asparagus. However, they require a good 90 minutes of boiling to become edible. Our primary protein came from small fish, freshly caught from the (often raging) river using a net. Their size meant there was no need for cleaning – we simply fried them in garlic and oil. Tarantulas also found their way to our plates. After boiling these hairy, eight-legged delicacies to soften them, we fried them up, much like the fish. Tarantula tastes like a combination of pork crackling and overcooked octopus tentacles – not the most appetising, but the garlic and oil subdued any lingering doubts. It became evident that with enough garlic and oil and perhaps a touch of chilli, almost anything could be made palatable.

The tribesman imparted invaluable forest wisdom, such as identifying water-bearing vines. Choosing the right one, we discovered, offered nearly a cup of fresh rainwater stored from the previous night. Before we knew it, the rainforest had made us self-sufficient in every way, from crafting cutlery and shelters to making tables and rope. There is nothing the forest doesn't provide.

One constant companion the forest generously provided was leeches. These blood-sucking creatures are truly in a league of their own, making vipers and tarantulas seem like mere annoyances. Spend more than two minutes stationary, and you'll hear the leaves rustling. Soon, you'll notice movement. On closer inspection, it was leeches advancing in their thousands. With infrared sensors attuned to your body heat, you've just been selected as their next meal. With a head on both ends of their body, they tumble head-over-head in your direction. No matter how vigilant you are, a few crafty ones always find their way up your trousers or into your socks.

Each of these uninvited diners varies in size – from thumb-sized to as long as your middle finger. Their saliva contains a natural anaesthetic, ensuring you remain oblivious to their bite. It also contains an anticoagulant, facilitating a free flow of your blood as they drink. Needless to say, we found ourselves constantly on leech-watch.

In the rainforest, there's a golden rule: never upset a leech. Understandably, their audacity in treating you like an impromptu blood buffet might get under your skin, but resist the urge to harm them. Squeezing or burning a leech will only make it regurgitate into your bloodstream, putting you at risk of blood poisoning. The safest removal method involves wedging a knife blade between its head (or one of them) and your skin and prying it off. Once removed, the bite site often turns into a mini geyser, oozing blood for up to half an hour. If a leech latches onto one of your feet and you stop to pull it off, your sock will eventually become so saturated with blood that you'll eventually have to stop alongside a stream to rinse off the mess.

Somebody had recommended that we slather our feet and legs in Tabard cream because the leeches don't have an appetite for the stuff. But here's the truth: African insects might *skrik [jump out of their skin]* for Tabard, but for a leech, it's as invigorating as a double espresso shot. Mosquitoes, too, seem equally unfazed. At one point, the sheer number of mosquito bites on my torso made it look like a measles breakout.

Bloodstains became a staple on our clothing. The initial shock on day one shifted to annoyance by day two. By day three? We simply accepted our blood-streaked fate. Welcome to Cambodia.

Towards the end of the expedition, we asked how we would be getting back to the missionary station.

"The only way to get out of the rainforest is to build your own raft and white-river raft 40 kilometres downstream," our guide replied.

And so we set about building our bamboo raft. The tribesman taught us how to make rope from thinly sliced bamboo, which we used to bind the thicker lengths of bamboo together. We were rather proud of our makeshift vessel, which even had its own special raised area to keep our backpacks and other belongings secure as we navigated the rapids.

We stopped off at the tribesman's village, where we would spend the night. Our raft was promptly disassembled for repurposing. The tribesman welcomed us into his home, introducing us to his family. Dinner was served on the slatted bamboo floor, making the lack of tables and chairs distinctly evident. Later in the evening, we were extended an invitation to sample what appeared to be their traditional version of witblits. After being distilled in wax-sealed pots for six weeks, we sipped the pungent liquid directly from the pot via elongated bamboo straws. It tasted like brake fluid, but we politely told them how delicious it was.

As I sat on the motorised dugout, leaving behind everything we had experienced in the rainforest, my mind started to piece together the experiences and lessons that had tested my mettle. There are few experiences that I do not want to relive, and this was one of them. The Cambodian rainforest challenged me on every conceivable level: communication barriers, unfamiliar terrains, language differences, cultural differences, and a reliance on someone else's expertise. Normally, I pride myself on navigating tricky situations alone, which is why solo overlanding appeals to me. But in the rainforest, I was out of my depth. It felt like a sharp descent from a privileged, first-world lifestyle.

To the tribes of the Laos-Cambodian rainforest, this is home. To us, it was daunting. There's no reality TV magic here, no surprise Nando's meal or a toolkit waiting for you. It's survival in its truest form. Accustomed to the conveniences of iPhones, laptops, DSTV, and Netflix, we often feel prepared to conquer the world with our education and technology. Yet, in the rainforest, these luxuries are non-existent. While we pop into a supermarket for food, the tribespeople hunt and forage. They live minimally and self-sufficiently, devoid of the comforts we Western Europeans are so used to. Surrounded by these comforts, we're ironically more vulnerable. A humble man with sharp teeth and ancient tribal knowledge showed us that we were ill-equipped for genuine survival.

I found myself recalling Sun Tzu's teachings in *The Art of War*, a book I had read but never fully appreciated until now. The ancient strategist's wisdom seemed to reverberate through the trials we had just faced.

"Know thyself, know thy enemy. A thousand battles, a thousand victories," Sun Tzu wrote. In the rainforest, the enemy wasn't just the elements or the wildlife – it was my own ignorance and overconfidence. I had underestimated what it meant to be a part of that ecosystem, and the tribesman had been the necessary bridge to understanding it. Our lives depended on his skillset and experience. Regardless of my educational background or monthly income, I would have been lost without him. Through him, we learned the way of the rainforest, understanding that to survive, you must first understand the intricacies of the terrain and its inhabitants.

"All warfare is based on deception," another one of Sun Tzu's principles, rang true in my thoughts. The forest was deceptive in its tranquillity. It appeared lush and beautiful but was filled with dangers that only became apparent when we had to confront them – from leeches and vipers to the strength and agility needed to build our own shelter and forage for food.

Sun Tzu often emphasised the importance of adaptability: "The general who wins a battle makes many calculations in his temple before the battle is fought." The tribesman made calculations based on years of lived experience. He adapted to the resources at hand, making tools and sustenance from the bamboo, the same bamboo that we had once viewed as just plants.

Sun Tzu said, "Opportunities multiply as they are seized." Each day in the rainforest presented new challenges but also new opportunities to learn and adapt. Whether it was finding out how to boil bamboo shoots to make them edible or how to build a raft that would carry us 40 kilometres downstream, each successful venture built our confidence and prepared us for the subsequent challenges.

The lessons we learned during this trip were manifold, but perhaps the most enduring of all was humility. It's a lesson that extends beyond the Cambodian rainforest and into the intricacies of our daily lives. In the business world, it's a reminder not to let success inflate one's ego. It's important to recognise our own limitations and value everyone equally. After all, that unassuming person might be the one who comes to your rescue someday.

THE ART OF WAR IN BUSINESS

The Art of War has been widely recognised for its relevance in business. The teachings provide insights that can help businesses face challenges and gain an edge over their competition.

PLANNING AND STRATEGY

Sun Tzu's teachings highlight the need for thorough planning to achieve objectives and minimise losses. In a business context, this directly correlates to the creation of comprehensive business plans, setting clear objectives, and formulating strategies to meet them.

While a clear strategy sets the stage for long-term success, remember, it's the tactical execution of that strategy that brings it to life. If your strategy is to dominate a particular market, your tactics should align with that goal. This could mean selecting the right pricing model, focusing your marketing on what sets you apart, and ensuring your distribution channels are optimised. When strategy and tactics are aligned, you're not just responding to the business environment – you're shaping it to achieve your long-term objectives.

EFFICIENCY AND RESOURCE MANAGEMENT

Sun Tzu emphasises achieving goals without wasting resources, and in business, this equates to effective resource management. Businesses have limited resources and must achieve their goals in the most efficient manner possible. This involves optimising operations, which could range from adopting automated systems to better resource allocation to reducing waste through lean manufacturing techniques. The aim is to do more with less, thereby conserving valuable resources.

GATHERING INTELLIGENCE

Sun Tzu highlights the value of intelligence and the use of deception in achieving victory on the battlefield. In business, intelligence equates to information – about competitors, market trends, customer needs, and more. At the same time, companies must protect their own sensitive information to maintain a competitive edge.

ADAPTABILITY

Sun Tzu speaks about the need for adaptability. In the ever-changing landscape of business, where consumer preferences evolve and markets fluctuate, businesses must be ready to modify their product lines, marketing strategies, or even business models in response to these changes to stay relevant.

STRENGTHS AND WEAKNESSES

Understanding one's strengths and weaknesses and those of the enemy is another principle Sun Tzu advocates, which can be directly applied in business through a Strengths, Weaknesses, Opportunities, and Threats (SWOT) analysis. By identifying the strengths, weaknesses, opportunities, and threats of both their own organisation and its competitors, businesses can formulate strategies that capitalise on their strengths, address their weaknesses, and exploit competitors' weaknesses.

THE GOLDEN BRIDGE

Another of Sun Tzu's lessons is to avoid cornering your enemy to the point of desperation. In business, a desperate competitor can become erratic and unpredictable, possibly engaging in actions that could destabilise the market and negatively impact your business. They could severely cut prices, start a negative public relations campaign, or even engage in unfair or illegal practices to stay afloat. Rather than eliminating the competition, it's strategic to weaken them to a manageable point and then provide an exit – a Golden Bridge. Allowing them a 'way out' can also have psychological benefits – a competitor who survives due to your 'mercy' may spread the word about your strength, prowess, and even your fairness. This can build your reputation not just among competitors but also among potential clients, suppliers, and other stakeholders. In essence, the Golden Bridge strategy emphasises the long-term gains of market stability and reputation management over the short-term satisfaction of defeating a competitor.

LEADERSHIP AND TEAMWORK

Sun Tzu emphasises the role of effective leadership and teamwork in achieving success in warfare. In a business setting, strong leadership sets the tone for an organisation, and cohesive teams are more likely to achieve their objectives. Leaders should set clear objectives, provide necessary resources, and foster an environment where open communication is encouraged. Teams should be well-coordinated and aligned with the company's objectives to execute strategies effectively.

TIMING

Sun Tzu often refers to the importance of timing in warfare. Knowing when to launch a new product or service, when to scale up operations or pull back, and when to enter or exit a market can be decisive factors in the success or failure of a business.

To better understand how these principles work in practice, let's take a look at some real-world examples. From L'Oreal's indirect attack strategy to Samsung's keen understanding of consumer behaviour, several companies have successfully applied Sun Tzu's teachings to gain a competitive edge.

• **L'Oreal:** Hindustan Unilever's challenge campaign for its skin-lightening Fair & Lovely cream caused a stir in the cosmetic industry. Instead of initiating direct competition, L'Oreal, demonstrating a strategy akin to Sun Tzu's principle of indirect attack, turned the situation to its advantage. They cleverly piggybacked on the massive attention the campaign was getting and channelled it towards their Garnier brand. By doing so, L'Oreal not only maintained its brand integrity but also managed to gain traction from a campaign they didn't even initiate.

• **Airtel and Vodafone:** In 2013, Airtel found itself in a price war when Vodafone drastically reduced its 2G data charges by 80%. Following Sun Tzu's advice on adaptability and quick response, Airtel strategically countered by cutting its own 2G prices by 90%. Not stopping there, Airtel also lowered its 3G data charges to secure a broader market share. This move showcases the principle of adaptability and quick response to changing circumstances, forcing the competitor to rethink their pricing strategy.

• **BMW:** BMW identified a market gap in high-end automobiles – cars were either luxurious or performance-oriented, but seldom both. Employing a strategy that mirrors Sun Tzu's teachings on knowing the battleground, BMW filled this gap by designing cars that offer both luxury and high performance. In doing so, they differentiated themselves from competitors like Mercedes Benz and Audi, appealing to a demographic that was, up until that point, untapped.

• **Bajaj Auto:** Bajaj Auto targeted Royal Enfield's strong presence in the Indian market by introducing the Avenger. While Royal Enfield motorcycles are popular, they are also relatively expensive and not as fuel-efficient. Bajaj Auto tapped into the sensibilities of the Indian middle class by offering a similar aesthetic at a lower price point and better fuel efficiency. This approach perfectly embodies Sun Tzu's principle of understanding both your own and your competitor's strengths and weaknesses, allowing Bajaj to carve out its own niche.

• **Johnson & Johnson and IBM:** Both these multinational giants took a somewhat unconventional route by decentralising decision-making. This strategy is in line with Sun Tzu's principle that effective leadership involves not just a centralised command but also the ability to delegate and empower. Such an inclusive approach ensures that innovation isn't confined to the top echelons but bubbles up from various quarters, leading to a richer pool of ideas and solutions.

• **Samsung:** Samsung India observed the local trend of people carrying multiple cell phones, often to separate personal and business communications. Anticipating the convenience a dual SIM phone could offer, Samsung introduced phones with dual SIM capabilities, allowing users to operate two numbers on a single device. This is a prime example of how understanding consumer behaviour and needs and then adapting product offerings to meet those needs can give a company a significant competitive advantage.

These examples serve as compelling illustrations of how principles from *The Art of War* can be seamlessly integrated into modern business strategy. From leveraging competitors' actions to addressing market gaps, from decentralised leadership to the significance of foresight and adaptability, Sun Tzu's age-old wisdom remains highly relevant in today's dynamic business landscape. By understanding and applying these timeless teachings, businesses can navigate challenges effectively, outmanoeuvre competitors, and consistently position themselves for success.

CHAPTER 10
AVOIDING DAY 2

n 1994, at age 34, Jeff Bezos resigned from his role as senior vice president at multinational investment management firm D.E. Shaw, fuelled by an ambitious dream: to launch an online bookstore. From his rented home in Bellevue, Washington, and with $250,000 in seed capital from his parents, he set about building the store, which would house the largest collection of books in the world, available to anyone with access to the Internet. At the time, the concept of online shopping was still gaining traction, but Bezos was steadfast in his mission to turn his online bookstore into an online superstore, or, as he called it, "an everything store".

On the 16th of July 1995, Amazon.com's website went live.

During those early days, every sale, which was usually from a friend or family member, was celebrated with a bell ring. Each time it rang, everyone would gather around, curious to see if they recognised the customer. Within a few weeks, the orders were flooding in from all over the country and at such a pace that the bell-ringing ritual became impractical. The rest, as the saying goes, is history. Today, Amazon is a global e-commerce giant, and Bezos is one of the richest people in the world. Love him or hate him, his vision and relentless drive transformed the way we shop and think about e-commerce, reshaping the retail landscape and setting new standards for customer convenience and service.

Central to Amazon's growth was Bezos's unique philosophical approach. Once a year, Bezos gives us a glimpse into his worldview and management philosophy. In his 1997 shareholder letter, he described the Internet and Amazon as being in perpetual "Day 1." For Bezos, Day 1 is more than a phase – it's a mindset. It's passion. It's urgency. It's about being willing to experiment, being adaptable, and embracing failure as an opportunity to learn. It's the same focus, energy, curiosity, and customer-centric approach a business has when it's just starting out. It was this mindset that became foundational to Amazon's ethos.

In his 2016 letter, Bezos introduced the concept of "Day 2," which represents the complacency that can follow success. Day 2 starts more subtly. It can take decades to get there, but now you're success-ful, you've gobbled up market share, and you've become one of the big dogs in town. Hubris sets in, telling you you're too big to fall. You're untouchable. You take your foot off the accelerator, compla-cency creeps in, and the business plateaus.

Bezos describes Day 2 as "stasis. Followed by irrelevance. Followed by excruciating, painful decline. Followed by death," adding, "And that is why [at Amazon] it is always Day 1." This decline begins when a company gets too comfortable in its success, becomes complacent, stops innovating, and loses its customer-centric focus. Eventually, that stasis leads to irrelevance.

A Day 2 mindset often starts with complacency in client relation-ships. You no longer entertain or even visit your clients, assuming they are committed to you, that the orders will always come through and that they will never leave. But be very careful. If you start ignoring your clients, they will eventually start ignoring you. When you stop investing in your relationships, you risk slipping into dangerous Day 2 territory. And when you do, you become irrelevant to your client base. Now, you're just *AN Other* supplier in their procurement system. While you were being complacent, somebody else was knocking on your clients' doors, making them feel special and doing all the things you used to do before hubris set in – and we all know what happens next.

A Day 2 mindset is the single biggest threat facing established companies that fail to maintain a Day 1 mindset. Less than 2% of the companies that were on the S&P 500 fifty years ago are still there today. The rest have disappeared, having fallen victim to a Day 2 mindset. The lesson is clear: If businesses want to remain relevant, they must avoid Day 2 thinking at all costs.

HOW TO RECOGNISE A DAY 2 COMPANY

Amazon stands as a beacon for what a Day 1 company embodies: agility, innovation, and a relentless focus on the customer. Day 2 companies, in contrast, often operate under traditional hierarchical structures.

Hierarchy is great for maintaining predictability and repeatability. It simplifies planning and makes it easier to control a large group of people from the top down, which is why military organisations rely so heavily on this type of organisational structure. As such, Day 2 businesses operate within tight structures. There's a clear line of command, and every person has a designated role. Such an environment prioritises stability and predictability, often at the expense of innovation. It operates by the book, with a clearly defined set of established rules, procedures, and policies that everyone follows. Employees know exactly what's expected of them, with the focus being on reproducing the same results.

There is an emphasis on tracking performance – everything is measured, documented, and reviewed, ensuring that everyone and everything is in line with predefined benchmarks. Leadership in such companies tends to be top-heavy, with senior management often calling the shots and leaving little room for lower-level inputs.

These companies are generally risk-averse. Rather than embracing new ideas and methods, they tend to stick to the familiar, preferring tried-and-trusted methods and approaches over new, untested ones. A telling sign of a Day 2 company is its treatment of customers as mere numbers on a balance sheet rather than invaluable stakeholders who can provide valuable feedback and drive growth.

In contrast, Day 1 companies are agile, have flat organisational structures, foster creativity and risk-taking, and are highly customer-centric. Day 1 companies value creativity and entrepreneurship. Employees are encouraged to think outside the box and innovate. There is a fluid and adaptive organisational structure with less emphasis on rigid rules and more on adapting to changes in the environment or market conditions. Risk-taking in pursuit of innovation and new solutions is encouraged. There is a more decentralised approach to decision-making, with individuals or teams being empowered to make decisions. Teams themselves are often cross-functional, combining members from different departments with the aim of facilitating innovation through collaboration among diverse skill sets. Finally, employees are usually empowered to make decisions and act on new ideas quickly without requiring approval from multiple layers of management.

Amazon's journey from its humble beginnings in a garage to a global e-commerce powerhouse serves as both a cautionary and inspirational tale. While structure and efficiency are important, it is flexibility, innovation, and an unwavering focus on customers that ensure long-term business success. Leaders must be vigilant, recognise when they are veering into Day 2 territory, and act decisively to steer their companies back towards a Day 1 mindset, ensuring enduring relevance in a dynamic market.

Day 2 Companies	Day 1 Companies
Operate under traditional hierarchical structures	Agile with flatter organisational structures
Prioritise stability over innovation	Emphasise innovation and responsiveness
Tend to be risk-averse and rely on tried-and-tested methods	Foster creativity, risk-taking, and value customer feedback
View customers as numbers on a balance sheet	Highly customer-centric

FENDING OFF DAY 2

To stave off Day 2 and preserve that venture capital, start-up, Silicon Valley sense of urgency, Bezos recommends businesses adopt four key principles: customer obsession, a sceptical view of proxies, the eager adoption of external trends, and high-velocity decision-making.

Let's explore these principles in a little more detail.

CUSTOMER OBSESSION

Customer obsession is not just about the product or service a business offers but rather about how effectively it meets – and even anticipates – its customers' needs. Jeff Bezos encapsulates this sentiment when, in his 2016 letter, he said, "Customers are always beautifully, wonderfully dissatisfied, even when they report being happy and business is great. Even when they don't yet know it, customers want something better, and your desire to delight customers will drive you to invent on their behalf. Staying in Day 1 requires you to experiment patiently, accept failures, plant seeds, protect saplings, and double down when you see customer delight. A customer-obsessed culture best creates the conditions where all of that can happen."

True customer obsession means placing the customer at the centre of all business strategies. Every company will tell you that "the customer is king", but does that statement carry weight? How much red tape stands between your people figuring out what your customers want and then giving it to them? In a Day 1 company, people are empowered to make decisions in the best interest of the customer without being hampered by stifling bureaucracy. This proactive approach prioritises customer satisfaction above all else, driving continuous innovation and preventing the complacency and stagnation of Day 2.

At First Technology, we're only interested in two things: our customers and our employees. We believe that if we can get the balance right with these two audiences, we'll always be on the right track. To ensure this customer-first approach, we implemented ERP systems, procurement processes, digital strategies, disaster recovery plans, and robust policies. These systems aren't just about efficiency – they're about ensuring our team can best serve our customers. We also implemented a flat organisational structure. We don't have ivory towers, and nobody 'reports to' anybody else in the traditional way. We encourage our people to steer toward opportunities and away from risks. We give them the power to make decisions as long as they are ethical, legal, and commercially profitable (in that order) for the company.

This commitment to customers and employees has shown its strength over the years. We were able to turn First Technology Western Cape from a R60-million turnover company with zero profit in 2010 into a R1.1-billion company a little over a decade later – with just twenty additional team members. That's what happens when you live and breathe a customer-first attitude.

RESIST PROXIES

In his 2016 letter, Bezos addressed the issue of proxies, highlighting the dangers of becoming "process-focused" instead of "results-focused". He noted: "As companies get larger and more complex, there's a tendency to manage to proxies. This comes in many shapes and sizes, and it's dangerous, subtle, and very Day 2 … The process becomes the proxy for the result you want. You stop looking at outcomes and just make sure you're doing the process right." By proxies, he means those process-driven behaviours that businesses tend to lean on as they grow. These proxies can often overshadow the core goals and values that underpin successful, innovative companies.

Bureaucratic entities, like governments and large organisations, tend to get hung up on the process. It's all about following a set plan: first A, then B, then C, and so on. But what happens when there's a problem at B? Perhaps you need to bypass some steps and go directly to H. However, rigid adherence to the process often prevents that.

Continuing in his letter, Bezos warns against an over-reliance on proxies as a measure of success, emphasising, "The process is not the thing. It's always worth asking, do we own the process, or does the process own us?" To illustrate this, let's consider a company whose goal is to deliver outstanding customer service. To accomplish this, it might track response times to customer inquiries as one metric of success. However, if the company becomes overly obsessed with reducing response times at the expense of actually resolving customer issues effectively, then the response time metric has become a proxy for the real goal, which is delivering excellent service.

Metrics and KPIs, while essential for tracking performance and making informed decisions, can also turn into proxies. A classic example is the click-through rate in online advertising. While a high click-through rate might seem good, if those clicks aren't converting into actual sales or the desired actions, then the metric is a poor indicator of true performance.

In his letter, Bezos discusses the pitfalls of customer surveys. A company might start by genuinely aiming to improve the customer experience. Over time, however, it may start focusing too much on improving its survey scores instead of genuinely enhancing the customer experience. In this scenario, the survey score becomes a proxy for customer satisfaction, and there's a risk that the company starts optimising for the proxy (the score) rather than the actual desired outcome (genuine customer satisfaction). For example, an online bookstore introduces a post-purchase survey to enhance the customer experience. Initially, feedback leads to improvements like a more user-friendly search function. However, because management ties bonuses to high survey scores, staff begin offering discounts for positive reviews. Over time, the bookstore boasts near-perfect scores but misses genuine feedback on its slow delivery times, leading to frustrated customers migrating to faster competitors.

Processes and metrics, in and of themselves, aren't the enemy. They offer structure and predictability and can greatly enhance efficiency. They only become problematic when they are followed blindly without questioning their relevance or effectiveness. Businesses should be in control of their processes, not the other way around. These processes should act as guidelines rather than strict rules. Employees at all levels should feel empowered to question and challenge existing processes if they feel there's a better way to achieve the organisation's goals. After all, ground-level employees often have firsthand experience of how processes play out in practice.

Shortly before Covid, I enrolled at London University to start an MBA. To my disappointment, the curriculum echoed the teachings of business schools from the 1960s, emphasising linear, top-down thinking and hierarchical command-and-control business structures. It felt reminiscent of 'Rithmetic, Reading, and wRiting – the classic Three Rs. Pursuing this degree would be like taking a step back. The material seemed disconnected from the demands of running a business in the Fourth Industrial Revolution. So, I withdrew. The time and money that I would have invested in an MBA, I instead used to attend various venture capital seminars around the world, including the famous Google for Start-ups Campus in London. The events provided innovative ideas and abundant networking opportunities, offering me exponentially greater returns.

This got me thinking: how many Day 2 organisations are staffed by MBA graduates? Consider the difference between NASA and SpaceX. After the Space Shuttle program concluded in 2011, the U.S. relied on Russian Soyuz rockets to transport astronauts to the International Space Station. Meanwhile, a trailblazer from Pretoria came along and proposed a novel solution: "Why don't you ride my Falcon rockets? I'll just bill you for the trip."

NASA, funded by billions of taxpayer dollars annually, invests heavily in exploration, research, and knowledge expansion. The tragedies from the Shuttle program made them exceedingly cautious. Fearful of what might go wrong, they become mired in an endless cycle of re-evaluation, redesign, and retesting. Years have since passed without any sign of notable progress.

In contrast, what's Elon Musk been up to? He's been relentlessly building and launching rockets. If one of his rockets meets an untimely end – or, in pilot vernacular, 'rapidly deconstructs' – he's back at it, building another. With all the detailed telemetry data at their disposal, they can pinpoint whether it was a seal, an oxide booster, or an aileron that was the issue. The game plan? Build a new rocket, rectify the problem – perhaps using a more robust oxide this time – and aim for the next launch. And he's not thinking years down the road. He's thinking next month.

While NASA has been metaphorically grounded for years, SpaceX has undertaken hundreds of launches. Out of hundreds of launches, they've had six failures. Yet the majority of subsequent launches have not only been flawless but have also demonstrated the capability to return to Earth. Now, Musk has his eyes set on Mars.

Both NASA and SpaceX have their fair share of MBAs, but their organisational philosophies are vastly different. NASA embodies the Day 2 mindset: conventional, process-driven, and risk-averse. SpaceX channels Day 1 energy: it's agile and Silicon Valley-esque. They believe in failing fast, burning through capital if needed, and constantly iterating. Musk's ethos suggests that with enough funds and ambition, you can correct course mid-flight, even if it means building a wing in freefall. These contrasting perspectives highlight two completely different organisational mindsets. NASA, with its over-reliance on perfecting processes, has lost its edge in the space race. As Bezos puts it, they're on the slow, agonising decline that precedes an organisation's decline.

When new people join the First Technology team and undergo their induction process, we tell them that if they can't get hold of a manager or a director for approval or authorisation on anything, they must ask themselves three pivotal questions:

1. Is what I'm about to do ethical?

2. Is it legal?

3. Is it commercially profitable?

If the answers are yes across the board, they have the green light to act. They can explain why they didn't follow due process *after* they've delivered the goods.

During a morning meeting in 2022, one of our salespeople discovered that a potential client had never experienced the thrill of a helicopter ride. Seizing the opportunity to create a lasting impression, he spontaneously arranged for a JetRanger helicopter to whisk them away for lunch at a scenic wine farm in Franschhoek that very afternoon. Although he hadn't secured prior approval to do this, when he submitted his expense claim the next day, attached was a sizeable purchase order from a prestigious corporate at an impressive margin. This initiative was completely above board. It was a memorable way to engage potential clients, proving that sometimes, thinking outside the box brings remarkable results.

Many large organisations might not consider such a unique approach, but we value initiative and creative thinking. Our colleague realised these potential clients wanted a unique experience, and he delivered. In return, they felt confident to provide a substantial commitment. Our emphasis on empowering our team and nurturing their agility and creativity is the competitive edge that sets us apart from other players in our industry.

EMBRACE EXTERNAL TRENDS

In today's rapidly evolving technological landscape, companies are faced with one of two choices: adapt and ride the wave of change or resist and risk obsolescence. Bezos highlighted this in his 2016 shareholder letter when he said, "The outside world can push you into Day 2 if you won't or can't embrace powerful trends quickly. If you fight them, you're probably fighting the future. Embrace them, and you have a tailwind."

Take, for instance, the disruption brought about by Artificial Intelligence (AI). AI is arguably the most significant technological disrupter since the introduction of smartphones in 2007. To shrug off or neglect AI's potential is to consciously step into Day 2 territory. As we see AI's integration into virtually every industry and aspect of life, it's clear that this is no longer a question of 'what if' but rather, 'how and where next'. Far from being a threat, AI offers businesses an unprecedented opportunity to optimise processes, better understand customers, and ultimately deliver more value.

The future of business is not just about predicting trends but actively participating in their evolution. By choosing to embrace change rather than resist it, businesses can ensure they remain relevant, innovative, and prepared for what's next.

HIGH-VELOCITY DECISION-MAKING

In his 2016 letter, Bezos draws a distinction between companies that make high-quality decisions and those that emphasise high-quality, high-velocity decisions: "Day 2 companies make high-quality decisions," he says, "but they make high-quality decisions slowly. To keep the energy and dynamism of Day 1, you have to somehow make high-quality, high-velocity decisions."

Most organisations, and indeed most individuals, fall into the trap of seeking near-complete data confirmation before pulling the trigger on a decision. They long for that 90 or 100% assurance, wanting the full story before taking the leap. However, Bezos underlines that in today's dynamic business landscape, waiting for 90% of the data could mean missed opportunities. "Most decisions should probably be made with somewhere around 70% of the information you wish you had," he advises. Put simply, 70% data confirmation is often enough to make an informed decision and gain a first-mover advantage against your competitors.

But what if, after following this strategy, your decision falls short? Bezos offers a comforting perspective: "Many decisions are reversible, two-way doors. So what if you're wrong?" If outcomes don't align with expectations, there's usually room to adjust or course-correct. Waiting for the 'perfect' moment, on the other hand, can cost you more than you think. Such hesitations might be more expensive than any adjustments needed down the line. A golden opportunity could slip through your fingers; a client might find another provider or a competitor could unveil a better product first.

Day 1 companies like DoorDash, Tesla, and SpaceX embody this philosophy of high-velocity, high-quality decision-making. Their strategy? Decide quickly, act, and then adjust if necessary. This agility allows them to stay ahead of the competition and capitalise on opportunities. In contrast, Day 2 organisations like NASA, for all their achievements, often find themselves bogged down by bureaucracy, which slows their decision-making. This delay can allow other, faster-moving competitors to step in and capture the market.

Bezos also champions the principle of 'disagree and commit'. When your team has an idea that you're not entirely sold on, but they've persuasively made their case, it's important to express your reservations. However, if their proposal aligns with 70% of your perspective, demonstrate trust by assuring them that they have your full backing in terms of resources, support, and time. Making such a gesture, especially in a senior leadership role where you're perceived as having the final say, can be tough. Yet, continually shooting down ideas can make your team hesitant to bring forward innovative solutions, thinking, "Why bother when the answer is always no?"

The principle of 'disagree and commit' isn't just about supporting a particular initiative – it's about fostering an environment where innovation thrives.

DAY 1 IN NOSY BE

I've travelled to over sixty different countries in my lifetime, but only three continually draw me back. One of them is Bali – not the bustling streets of Kuta, but the quieter, more soulful corners of the island. Here, volcanoes stand sentinel over black lava beaches, temples dot the landscape, and the captivating culture, coupled with the exquisite cuisine, envelops one in a sense of peace that's hard to put into words yet undeniably palpable. Next is the Okavango – Chobe, Moremi, Linyanti – each a gem in the Delta's crown, and each etched in my heart in a way that few other places can rival. Lastly, there's Nosy Be, the largest island in Madagascar's northwest archipelago. This relatively unknown oasis of beauty, with its dazzling white beaches and turquoise ocean, had already claimed my heart once.

I wanted Kim to experience Nosy Be too, so in 2017, we boarded a short SA Airlink flight from Johannesburg and landed just outside Hell-Ville (named after the oddly named French admiral Anne Chrétien Louis de Hell), the island's largest city.

Nosy Be, which translates to "Big Island" in Malagasy, carries a strong Italian and French influence from its colonial days. The island is adorned with Roman Catholic churches, and no matter where you are on the island, there is 5G reception, which extends right out into the ocean. The locals speak fluent French, and the schools all follow the French curriculum. The island is especially popular with Italian tourists and houses one commercial hotel which primarily caters to this demographic. This five-storey Italian enclave with a Day One business culture runs on Italian time, employs Italian-speaking staff, and serves Italian cuisine, allowing its guests to enjoy the beach, the natural beauty, the forests, and the ocean while feeling comfortably at home. The Italian government even donated a million-euro hyperbaric chamber to the island, a boon to the local dive schools. In this tiny place, where many live on just a dollar a day, the ability to treat decompression sickness on-site is almost revolutionary.

While on Nosy Be, Kim and I decided to visit Lokobe National Park, a tropical rainforest on the eastern side of the island, and home to two of the world's Critically Endangered lemurs – the Sportive Lemur and the Claire's Mouse Lemur – as well as the Endangered Black Lemur. The reserve offered guided walks through the forest, and we were told that by carrying small pieces of fruit in our hands, the lemurs would jump down from the dense foliage onto our shoulders to feed.

It took us about an hour to travel along the west side of the coastline to reach Zara Village in the east, where we would check in for the night. The following morning, we boarded a dugout canoe and began paddling into the rainforest. We were probably halfway there when my mobile phone rang. It was my business partner in Johannesburg. We both owned a significant number of shares in a listed company that had recently received some bad press. Being on holiday, I hadn't been following the news, but he had, and he was worried.

"I have a bad feeling," he said after quickly filling me in on the details. "I think this stock is going to crash. I'm cashing out now."

I shared that same unease. Based on the available information I had, I had to make a decision at 70% and pull the trigger. If I was wrong, I could reverse course, pay a small brokerage fee, and buy back those shares the following week.

We ended the call, and I immediately phoned my stockbrokers in Cape Town and instructed them to sell all my shares. A week later, the stock collapsed. If not for the excellent telecom infrastructure on this seemingly remote island, my business partner wouldn't have been able to reach me in time.

This incident is a textbook example of a Day 1 mindset, characterised by its emphasis on high-velocity, high-quality decision-making. Had I hesitated and adopted a Day 2 approach, opting to wait until I returned home to consult my wealth manager or wait for media confirmation, the stock would have tanked, and I would have lost a substantial amount of money.

Several days later, we set off for Sakatia Lodge on Nosy Sakatia, an island adjacent to Nosy Be. The island was a tranquil haven, with no cars and no roads. A short six-minute boat ride from Nosy Be transported us to this paradise, where a stunning stretch of beach, tropical gardens, and surrounding jungle awaited us. It was the perfect place to round off our holiday and indulge in some scuba diving before boarding our flight back to South Africa.

An underwater jungle teeming with sea life, Nosy Sakatia is renowned for its giant green turtles that inhabit the Ambohibe Turtle Reserve just off the beach. Whether we were scuba diving or snorkelling, dozens of these ancient beings, with their wise, gentle eyes and age-old, slightly battered shells, each telling tales of countless oceanic journeys, glided effortlessly past us. It was a paradise in every sense of the word.

Two days later, while boarding the boat for the mainland, Kim started crying. A hardened corporate litigation defence lawyer, Kim was not one to easily show her emotions. The last time I'd seen her cry was several years earlier when her father passed away.

"Are you okay?" I asked, concerned. "Did you hurt yourself?"

"I don't want to leave," she replied, brushing away the tears. "I'm not ready to go."

These magical islands had gotten under her skin, just as they had done all those years ago when I first visited. I was eager to get home to our dogs, but I understood her longing to stay. I was more than capable of taking care of the dogs and the house in her absence. Knowing there would be another flight out the following week, I called our travel agent and asked her to change Kim's flight. As I boarded the plane home, Kim waved me off at the airport and promptly returned to the lodge to ask if she could check back into our cabana.

Once this part of the world gets under your skin, it's impossible to shake it off. Being able to share transact from a dugout canoe in a rainforest and then witnessing my normally stoic wife shed tears because she couldn't bear to leave the island's giant green sea turtles transformed an already incredible trip into one I'll never forget.

CHAPTER 11
APPLYING STOICISM IN YOUR LIFE

After surviving those two weeks hiking through the Laos-Cambodian rainforest back in 2014, we returned to Phnom Penh for a few days of sightseeing before flying back to South Africa. Preferring to avoid commercial hotels, we opted for a charming boutique establishment in the heart of the city. The interior was an homage to Balinese architecture, featuring wood-panelled walls and dark teak furniture. Despite having only six rooms, the hotel felt spacious and private, complete with clean, beautiful rooms. Water features, the gentle waft of burning incense, and palm trees created an authentic oasis reminiscent of Bali amidst the urban sprawl of Phnom Penh.

While out sightseeing that first day, our taxi driver entertained us with tales of a mystical island off the south coast of Cambodia. He described it as an unspoiled tropical paradise, reminiscent of the setting in Leonardo DiCaprio's 'The Beach'. I remember leaving the cinema after watching the movie, believing such a paradise couldn't possibly exist, yet here was our driver, assuring us that it did. Intrigued, we pressed him for more details. The island, he said, was named Koh Rong Sanloem and was located in the Gulf of Thailand, just off the coast of Sihanoukville, Cambodia.

The only challenge was that Koh Rong Sanloem was a five to six-hour drive from Phnom Penh, and we only had three days before we were due to return home. Added to that, we weren't entirely convinced of the mythical island's existence. As we debated whether to embark on this adventure, we couldn't help but wonder if our taxi driver hadn't perhaps over-embellished his tale.

As we returned to our hotel after a leisurely breakfast the following morning, we spotted our taxi driver engrossed in conversation with an elderly gentleman who was leaning against a pristine white Toyota Camry. The taxi driver waved us over.

"He will take you to Koh Rong Sanloem," he announced.

Approaching the gentleman, I extended my hand. He grasped it and introduced himself as Mr Moon. His English was limited, so I jotted down the name of the island on a scrap of paper. Showing it to him, I used hand gestures to convey that we wanted to travel to the island and have him come back for us in three days. He responded by gesticulating that it was very far.

"But yes, I take you," he said.

"How much?" I asked.

"$50," he said.

"Per person?" I asked.

He shook his head. "For both."

"One-way?"

"No, no, no. Two-way."

Fifty bucks for a round trip covering hundreds of kilometres? It was an offer too good to refuse.

"JD," said Kim, shaking her head.

I know that when Kim calls me "JD", I need to pay attention. It's a bit like your parents calling you by your full name, including the one in the middle. It's generally when you've done something you shouldn't have, and you're about to face the music.

"JD, if we miss our flight home, remember our tickets are non-refundable," she cautioned.

She had a valid point. Missing our flight would mean shelling out thousands of dollars for new tickets. We'd also have to extend our hotel booking.

"But I trust this guy," I whispered, weighing the risks.

I paid him his $50. It was a gamble, but sometimes you have to roll the dice.

"We go now," he said.

Kim and I quickly threw some clothes and toiletries into a backpack, leaving our heavier luggage and survival equipment at the hotel for safekeeping. Almost six hours later, we reached the coast, where Mr Moon directed us to a little shack at the jetty. A small sign posted outside displayed photos of a ferry, a map, and a timetable. I knocked on the window and spoke to the person inside. She told us that the ferry was set to arrive within the hour but only ran every few days. Once on the island, it would circle back to retrieve us three days later. Perfect timing, I thought.

"JD," Kim cautioned.

I knew the schedule was tight, but we had no control over the ferry's timing. We'd have to chance it, trusting that Mr Moon would return for us, which he assured he would.

"Do you have accommodation booked?" the lady asked.

When I said no, she warned us that it was peak season on the island and that we'd struggle to find lodging. She didn't know that we'd recently roughed it in the jungles of Cambodia – we were prepared to sleep anywhere, even on the dunes.

"JD," Kim said again, her eyes narrowing as if questioning my judgement.

While waiting for the ferry, we came across a local vendor selling some rather potent vodka. By the time the ferry arrived, we were both ticking like time bombs – and Kim had stopped calling me JD.

Forty-five minutes later, we arrived at a picture-perfect tropical island. We spotted six chalets lining the beach, some vacant, and approached a Frenchman who seemed to be in charge.

"Sorry, all booked," he said, waving us off.

No problem, we thought, buoyed by the generous amount of vodka we'd consumed. We'd stroll down the beach and hope for the best. After covering some ground, we came upon what looked like a lodge. A signboard attached to a pole read "Rumi," with an arrow pointing right. Beyond that, everything seemed uninhabitable.

We followed a winding footpath and climbed a short flight of stairs to find another sign: Bar. Restaurant. Market. And the magic word: BUNGALOWS. Bingo! Continuing along the path, we came across several palm-fronted cottages. A young Ukrainian woman, probably in her late twenties and fluent in English, approached us. After introductions, she shared her incredible story. Daughter to a Ukrainian oil billionaire, she'd spent her life globetrotting on her father's dime. Falling in love with the island, she bought this lodge on a whim and renamed it 'Rumi', inspired by her love for the Persian poet's work.

"I wanted this, not a life in Monaco with a Lamborghini or a chalet in Europe," she explained, adding a poetic touch to her life story. "And yes, I have a bungalow open for you."

"How much per night?" I asked.

"$25," she said, "including breakfast and dinner."

Curious, I asked about the menu.

"Anything you want," she said. "We don't have menus. The staff will come to you in the morning; you tell them what you want – angel fish, butterfly fish, scallops, crayfish, crabs, parrot fish – and they'll dive for it on the reef.

The following morning, we placed our orders. Kim opted for angel fish, and I ordered an enormous South Asian pepper crab served in a traditional lip-smacking pepper sauce. That evening, as we feasted, it truly felt like a slice of heaven.

The island of Koh Rong Sanloem was the perfect tropical hideaway. White sand beaches, swaying palm trees, turquoise waters, reefs teeming with marine life, friendly locals, and the most gorgeous sunsets. And then there was the skinny stray cat who took an instant liking to me. I've always been an animal magnet, so naturally, I took the little furball under my wing.

After two idyllic days of paddling and snorkelling, we headed to the jetty, expecting to catch the 10 a.m. ferry. It wasn't there yet, so we strolled over to the local beach bar made of palm reeds for a cup of coffee. Kim had already made sure we had done our morning swim and paddle, so a good cup of Cambodian black coffee was a welcome thought. As we waited, the familiar Frenchman approached, puffing on a pungent Gauloises cigar.

"The ferry," he said nonchalantly, "it's already left."

"What do you mean?" I asked. It was only 9:30 a.m., and the ferry wasn't due to arrive for another half an hour. I thought that whatever he was smoking in that cigar had obviously impacted his ability to read the time.

"Zings aren't so precise 'ere on the island," he said. "9 a.m. or 10 a.m. – it's all ze same. It came earlier zis morning, and now it's gone back to the mainland. But it'll be back in tree days. You two want a drink?"

Kim shot me that all-too-familiar glance. "JD."

Panic was not an option. I had to think fast.

"Are there other boats on this island?" I asked him.

"Non!" he said, explaining that there were no other passenger boats.

I asked him how the locals got from the mainland to the island, remembering that there were only a handful of tourists on the little ferry that had brought us to the island a few days earlier. He told us there was a fishing village on the other side of the island where most of his lodge staff live. They must have had a way of getting across the bay.

"Ai, oui," he said and promptly explained that they used little fishing boats. However, the look he gave us made it clear that this was not an option we would want to stake our lives on. I asked him if he had any way of communicating with these people.

"Oui," he said again.

I asked him to arrange with them to get a fishing boat over to us.

"Zey are going to charge you," he warned me, rubbing his thumb and middle finger together. At that stage, we had no choice. We had to get back to the mainland to catch our flights, and swimming there was not an option.

He returned a few minutes later. "Good news," he said. "Zey 'ave a diesel fishing boat available. Zey will take you back to ze mainland for one 'undred dollars."

Forty minutes later, the rickety fishing boat arrived. A bit like a local *'snoekskuit'*, it was a weathered vessel with a long propellor shaft at the back. The skipper spoke no English, and we were unsure of the competence of his co-pilot. We quickly climbed on board and headed off, waving to the Frenchman, who was chuckling and shaking his head. He must have thought we were crazy.

As we sat in silence, it suddenly hit us: we were in the middle of the South China Sea, at the mercy of these fishermen.

"JD," Kim said about an hour into the journey. "Do you think Mr. Moon is still waiting for us on the mainland? We paid him in full already."

Her concern was valid.

"We're probably going to miss our flight," she added.

But I still had hope.

Spotting some fishing gear, Kim motioned to the skipper to ask if she could use it. He nodded, and Kim quickly baited a hook and cast a line into the water. Although it had more to do with passing the time than expecting to catch anything, to everyone's surprise, she reeled in a majestic king mackerel. She offered it to the fishermen, who gratefully accepted. Now, they had not only our $100 but also a sizable fish for dinner.

The snoekskuit, chugging along at 9 knots with its fishing net trailing behind it, took three hours to reach the mainland. And there, true to his word, was Mr Moon, waiting for us in his white Toyota Camry.

In Cambodian culture, your commitment is your word. Mr Moon promised us he'd drive six hours three days later to come and fetch us and then six hours back. And he honoured that promise.

We arrived in Phnom Penh at sunset, just in time to grab our luggage and make our way to the airport. Despite the odds and the potential for disaster, this part of our trip was an unexpected highlight. From Mr Moon's unwavering reliability to finding a paradise run by a young Ukrainian heiress to getting back to shore on a smelly old snoekskuit, it was an adventure we'll never forget. It was like something straight out of a Leonardo DiCaprio film, but real and undeniably poetic.

After reading about our adventure, you might think it was a series of risky gambles, chance encounters, and narrow escapes. And it was! But if we look a little deeper, we can also see it as a journey where decisions were made based on calculated trust, adaptability, and the wisdom to differentiate between what we could and couldn't control. We couldn't control whether the ferry would be there or whether we'd find lodging on a supposedly fully booked island, but we could control our reactions to these circumstances. We could decide to trust people and to make the most of whatever situation we found ourselves in. In that sense, our adventure was less about luck and more about mindset – a focus on actions and attitudes within our control and a willingness to adapt to those outside of it.

As exhilarating as our Cambodian adventure was, the lessons we learned weren't just about surviving in paradise. They were about thriving in life, which leads me to an ancient philosophy that has much to offer us in the modern world – Stoicism. While the term might be new to you, its principles are both timeless and universal. Stoicism teaches us to focus our energy on what we can control – our actions, our reactions, and our judgments. And for the things we can't control? The philosophy advises us to take them as they come without allowing them to disturb our peace of mind.

In this chapter, we'll delve into this transformative way of thinking that has guided wise men and women for centuries. Like us on that unforgettable journey in Cambodia, you might find that a stoic mindset turns life's gambles into opportunities for growth and its uncertainties into opportunities for gaining wisdom.

WHAT IS STOICISM?

Stoicism isn't just a topic relegated to dusty ancient philosophy courses – it's a philosophy aimed at helping us live a more resilient and meaningful life. Originating in Ancient Greece but gaining prominence under Roman philosophers like Seneca and Marcus Aurelius, Stoicism provides a practical framework for navigating the complexities of human existence.

Some of its principal teachings include:

• **Exercising Self-Control and Acceptance:** Some things are within our control – our thoughts, beliefs, and actions – and some things are not, such as external events and other people's actions. We should focus on what we can control and gracefully accept what we can't.

• **Building Emotional Resilience**: Suffering comes from our perception and interpretation of events, not the events themselves. By changing our perspectives and interpretations, we can manage our emotional responses.

• **Valuing Virtue**: Virtue, encompassing wisdom, courage (which includes being true to ourselves), justice, and temperance, is considered the ultimate good and the path to true happiness.

• **Recognising Universal Humanity**: All humans share a rational nature and, therefore, belong to a single, universal community. This encourages empathy, understanding, and a sense of responsibility towards others.

• **Appreciating the Impermanence of All Things**: Material wealth, physical comforts, and social status neither contribute to nor detract from one's moral worth.

• **Practising Mindfulness and Presence:** Live in the present moment, be mindful of current experiences and actions, and do not be overly concerned with past regrets or future anxieties.

• **Embracing Suffering**: Hardships and challenges are opportunities for growth and improvement.

• **Rational Thinking**: Analyse situations logically rather than emotionally to make informed decisions.

• **Living in Accordance with Nature:** Understand the natural order of the world and your place within it.

• **Managing Desires**: If what you desire aligns with your goals, formulate an action plan to pursue it. If it doesn't, let go of that particular desire. Practice gratitude for what you already have and focus only on desires that align with your core values.

In modern times, Stoicism has seen a resurgence, especially among people looking for practical ways to deal with the challenges of everyday life. Whether you're a business leader facing high-stakes decisions or someone juggling the myriad demands of life, it provides tools and practices that allow us to tackle life's uncertainties with grace and poise.

Since discovering these ancient Stoic principles, I have focused on weaving many of them into the fabric of my daily life. For the purposes of this chapter, I'd like to focus on the tenets of self-control, endurance, and authenticity, as well as offer guidance on what it takes to be a modern Stoic sage.

SELF-CONTROL

Tim Ferriss, the author of *The 4-Hour Work Week*, describes Stoicism as an "operating system for thriving in high-stress environments and making better decisions". In this analogy, he likens Stoicism to the software that powers our computers and smartphones, such as Windows, Android, or MacOS. Just as these operating systems manage the fundamental operations of our devices – running applications and allocating resources – Stoicism provides a foundational framework for managing our lives. It's especially useful for maintaining emotional stability and making rational decisions, particularly in high-stress situations.

One of the main teachings of Stoicism is the concept of focusing on what is within our control and letting go of what is not. Stoicism teaches us that while we can't control many of the events that happen to us, we can control how we respond to them. To do this, Stoicism advises us to separate issues into two categories: what we can control – our thoughts, beliefs, and actions – and what we can't, such as external events or other people's behaviour. By focusing our energy solely on the things within our control, Stoicism frees us from unnecessary stress and anxiety. Consider, for instance, being caught in a traffic jam – you can't control the congestion, but you can control your response to it. You might use the time to listen to an audiobook, practice deep breathing, or simply enjoy a moment of stillness amidst a busy day. The point is to shift your focus from the frustration of the traffic to the opportunity it presents for personal growth or relaxation.

With its emphasis on reason over emotion and long-term gain over short-term pleasure, Stoicism can serve as a guiding principle in many aspects of life, including the often overlooked but crucial area of social relationships. This stoic wisdom allows us to practice self-control not just in our emotional responses to those close to us but also in the choices we make about who to include in our social circle.

One of the reasons people often find themselves stuck in life is because their social circle holds them back. You may notice that some friends, perhaps unintentionally, act like crabs in a boiling pot. When one crab tries to escape, the others pull it back down. In the same way, people in our social lives can inhibit our progress, often without even realising it. This kind of inhibiting behaviour calls for a reassessment of your friendships. Think about those contacts in your phone whom you haven't reached out to in a year and who haven't reached out to you. Are they truly valuable connections?

To take this a step further, imagine a scenario where you find yourself in grave danger, reminiscent of a dramatic scene in a movie – a flipped car, a wheel slowly turning, steam billowing from the wreckage. If you had only enough battery for one call, who would you dial? Would they answer? Would they come to your aid? Would their assistance be of value? If you can't confidently say yes to these questions, then you might want to reconsider the time and energy you invest in such individuals. Although it may seem cold-hearted to evaluate friendships this way, doing so is an exercise in self-control, allowing you to deliberately shape an environment conducive to your personal growth and well-being.

ENDURANCE

Stoicism promotes qualities like endurance, the acceptance of discomfort, and a focus on self-control rather than self-pity or ego. I find that the activities I engage in – such as flying helicopters, climbing mountains, or off-road desert racing – align well with these Stoic principles. These activities require a high level of self-control and carry significant risks, which is why Stoicism's emphasis on self-control and endurance resonates with me.

While these activities are risky, I don't approach them recklessly. Instead, I exercise calculated caution. My planning and preparation is meticulous and goes beyond what most people would consider sufficient. Before I start the engine on my bike, rev up my Land Rover, or plunge my ice axe into a glacier, I make sure my preparedness is way better than the next guy. While I can't control external factors like the weather, I can control my own actions and level of preparation. In this way, Stoicism guides me in taking calculated risks and being fully prepared for the challenges I willingly face.

AUTHENTICITY

The Greek Stoic philosopher Epictetus once said, "Were I a nightingale, I would act the part of a nightingale; were I a swan, the part of a swan". Everything in the world, according to the Stoics, has its nature and purpose. For example, a nightingale is known for its song – it doesn't try to swim like a swan or hunt like an eagle. A swan, recognised for its grace in water, doesn't attempt to sing like a nightingale or run like a gazelle. They each have unique attributes and roles in the world, and they fulfil them to the best of their ability.

In a broader sense, Epictetus was emphasising the Stoic idea of living truthfully, without pretence, being true to one's nature and the idea that everyone has a specific role or purpose to fulfil. For humans, this means embracing our abilities and limitations rather than trying to be something we're not. In doing so, we align ourselves more closely with the Stoic ideal of living in accordance with nature – both our own and that of the larger natural world.

A classic example of someone who leverages his uniqueness is Tiger Woods. Now, I must confess, I'm not a golfer. Maybe when I hit the ripe age of 85 and have a Zimmer frame to steady my stance, I might entertain the notion of swinging a club. But I digress. While Tiger Woods has been criticised for his performance in tricky spots like the rough and bunkers, he has a unique strength that compensates for it: he's an incredible driver.

Given eight hours in a day, do you think Tiger Woods spends it trying to fix his rough game? No. He refines his driving. Being 99% accurate off the tee, he aims for perfection to ensure he doesn't find himself in the rough in the first place. His primary focus? Drive straight, drive accurately, and avoid the problematic rough altogether.

The takeaway here is simple: Tiger Woods knows where his strengths lie, and he hones them to such a level that his weaknesses become

357

almost irrelevant. Instead of worrying about poor play in the rough, he ensures he rarely finds himself there to begin with. And that's a lesson we can all learn from.

I apply a similar logic in my own life. While I might be known for using colourful language, when it comes to compassion for animals, I outshine many. I'd much rather be around people who might use strong language but show kindness to animals than someone who speaks eloquently but lacks moral character. So, do I make an effort to tone down my language? Not particularly. This is who I am. I'm being authentic. If you don't know me, my choice of words might initially seem off-putting. But if you take the time to get to know me, you'll quickly realise there's a lot more to appreciate. In that sense, I focus on my long-distance driving – my passions and values – rather than getting distracted by minor imperfections. I'm staying true to who I am.

Viewed through the lens of Stoicism, authenticity also warns against blindly emulating those we admire. While mentors can offer invaluable life lessons acquired over decades, the objective is not to become a carbon copy of them. I've learned valuable lessons from figures like Steve Jobs, Elon Musk, and Richard Branson, but I apply these lessons in a way that aligns with my principles and values. From Jeff Bezos, I learned the value of maintaining a Day 1 mentality; from Elon Musk, the importance of failing quickly to learn fast; and from Richard Branson, the courage to take calculated risks.

In the end, I strive to ensure that my actions and choices are reflective of who I authentically am rather than an imitation of someone else.

The journey towards authenticity is one we must all undertake. Whether you find inspiration in ancient philosophy, modern-day sports icons, or the lessons of business moguls, remember that these are merely guideposts on your own unique path. No one else can define your authentic self for you – only you can do that. Take the time to understand your strengths and passions, as well as your limitations, and embrace them all. The most authentic life you can live is one where you are true to yourself in alignment with your own nature and values. By doing so, not only do you fulfil your own purpose, but you also contribute to the world in a unique way that only you can.

As we've discovered, Stoicism offers invaluable guidance for managing our emotional responses, enduring life's challenges, and living authentically. But how do these principles converge to shape a well-rounded, modern individual equipped to navigate the complexities of today's world? Nassim Taleb provides a compelling answer in his book, *The Black Swan*, introducing us to the concept of the 'modern Stoic sage' – someone who "transforms fear into prudence, pain into information, mistakes into initiation, and desire into undertaking".

THE MODERN STOIC SAGE

So, who is this modern Stoic sage that Taleb speaks of, and how can we begin to incorporate such wisdom into the complexities of our own modern lives? Let's unpack what this means for us.

TRANSFORMING FEAR INTO PRUDENCE

Imagine standing at the edge of a precipice. Below, a chasm of unknown depth. Your heart races, a primal fear taking hold. Yet, the modern Stoic sage doesn't turn and flee. Instead, they take that raw emotion, assess the risks, and use it to inform their next step – be it forward, to the side, or even a step back. This is the essence of transforming fear into prudence.

Fear is an emotional response, often immediate and sometimes irrational, to a perceived danger or threat. While this emotion is natural and essential for human survival, it can lead to poor decision-making in complex modern societies. This is because decisions based on fear are often reactive, driven by immediate emotional responses rather than rational analysis. Prudence, in contrast, involves a more thoughtful approach to dealing with risk or uncertainty. It encourages proactive actions based on a careful consideration of potential outcomes, including worst-case scenarios.

In Taleb's framework, transforming fear into prudence means shifting from an emotionally charged, reactive stance to a more logical, proactive approach when confronting risks and uncertainties. This principle suggests that instead of allowing fear to drive decisions, one should control it through a heightened sense of caution.

This perspective is especially relevant when facing uncertainties, where the typical response might be to overreact. For example, after a major economic collapse, an individual might be too scared to invest in anything ever again. Prudence would involve understanding the risks, diversifying investments, and applying other risk management techniques rather than making blanket decisions based on fear.

This principle holds particular significance for business leaders, especially CEOs. For example, consider the rise of artificial intelligence (AI). Many CEOs fear its potential impact on their businesses. However, adopting a prudent approach would prompt them to think, "How can I utilise AI to improve productivity, efficiency, or cut costs?" CEOs failing to think along these lines will likely find themselves replaced.

In the eyes of an organisation's shareholders, every CEO has three primary responsibilities: First, they must deliver on financial goals such as budgets, targets, and shareholder return. Second, they need to continually scale the business, as achieving these financial goals requires growth. Finally, the CEO must innovate. If a CEO fails to integrate innovations like AI into the business's processes, platforms, products, or workforce, the shareholders will simply find someone else who will.

TRANSFORMING PAIN INTO INFORMATION

Stoicism teaches that emotional suffering stems from errors in judgment, suggesting that pain can serve as valuable feedback. Contrary to popular belief, Stoicism isn't about enduring pain quietly. It's also not that you can't express disappointment or frustration. Rather, it's about approaching pain, mistakes, or suffering holistically and seeing them as catalysts for change and growth, transforming pain into valuable information that guides future actions.

Similarly, Nassim Taleb argues that pain can be an avenue for growth and understanding. When Taleb talks about transforming pain into information, he recommends learning from life's setbacks. For instance, losing your job might be a catalyst for becoming an entrepreneur or pursuing your real passion. Ending a restrictive relationship could free you to enjoy activities that were previously off-limits. These experiences, though painful, can be catalysts for change.

To illustrate this point further, let's consider a business example: a company missed out on a significant contract they had been pursuing for months. They believed they had all the elements in place: a strong team, competitive pricing, excellent design, and quality materials. However, they neglected a crucial factor – their relationship with the decision-makers. Unlike their competitors, who took the time to personally connect with key individuals, the company relied solely on their product and pricing. As it turned out, the decision-maker was in search of a genuine business partner, not just a vendor. This oversight led to the loss of the contract but also became an invaluable lesson. Moving forward, the company plans to place greater emphasis on building meaningful relationships with its clients, effectively transforming its pain into actionable information for future growth.

TRANSFORM MISTAKES INTO INITIATION

"Just as nature takes every obstacle, every impediment, and works around it – turns it to its purposes, incorporates it into itself – so, too, a rational being can turn each setback into raw material and use it to achieve its goal."

– Marcus Aurelius

Stoicism teaches acceptance of mistakes and emphasises learning from them, seeing every challenge as an opportunity to practice virtue and grow in wisdom. In the same vein, when Nassim Taleb talks about transforming mistakes into initiation, he is building upon Stoic principles. He argues that mistakes should not be seen as failures but rather as starting points, new beginnings, or "initiations" into a deeper understanding or a new phase of personal or professional development.

In many cultures, the word 'initiation' is associated with rites of passage or entry into a new stage of life, understanding, or social position. They initiate us into a new phase of learning, skill development, or wisdom. Just like an initiation ritual or ceremony marks the beginning of new responsibilities and new roles, making a mistake can mark the beginning of a deeper inquiry into a subject, a change in strategy, or a shift in perspective.

By reframing mistakes as initiation events, Taleb suggests that we should embrace the lessons that come with them. Rather than calling it quits or retreating in shame or disappointment, we should allow these experiences to propel us into a new phase of growth or action.

362

TRANSFORM DESIRE INTO UNDERTAKING

When Nassim Taleb refers to transforming desire into undertaking, he is highlighting a fundamental Stoic concept: the idea of moving from a state of wanting something to actively engaging in the steps necessary to achieve or acquire it. In a Stoic context, desire is often seen as a potential source of unhappiness or frustration because it is rooted in wanting things that may be beyond our control. However, Taleb's modern interpretation suggests that desire can be channelled into constructive action. Rather than suppressing the energy of desire, we should redirect it toward proactive, purposeful action.

STEPS TO TURN DESIRES INTO UNDERTAKINGS

In the Stoic tradition, turning desires into actionable plans involves several key steps:

1. Clarification: Clearly understand what you desire and why you desire it.

2. Assessment: Assess whether the desire is rational, achievable, and aligns with your core values.

3. Plan: Create a clear, actionable plan to achieve your goal.

4. Execution: Consistently work towards achieving your plan while remaining emotionally unattached to the outcome.

5. Review and Adapt: Continually reassess your goals and make adjustments as needed, learning from mistakes or setbacks along the way.

THE POWER OF WRITTEN GOALS

A Stoic has a clear vision of what they want to achieve each day and sets specific goals to make it happen. Writing down your goals creates a psychological pre-commitment and self-expectation that increases the likelihood of you achieving what you set out to do. Writing down your goals establishes a contract with yourself to move from intention to action. This causes a cognitive shift: your desire evolves from a vague wish into a concrete plan. This is precisely the 'undertaking' Taleb refers to – it changes not just your actions but also refocuses your mental energies on achieving the goal.

FROM DREAM TO REALITY

Imagine you're with friends, and the topic of diving in the Maldives comes up. Everyone agrees it's a dream destination, but who will actually take steps to make it happen? Rather than leaving it at just talk, why not set up a savings plan? For instance, everyone could commit to saving R2,000 each month in an investment account expected to yield a 10% annual return. If all goes well, two years of disciplined saving will accumulate around R52,670 ($2,770) for each person, thanks to compound interest. That amount would be sufficient for the dream trip. The plan is simple: two years of saving a specific amount each month, and a target destination, the Maldives. That's how you turn a 'wish' into an actionable goal – and eventually, a vacation of a lifetime.

THE IMPORTANCE OF VISIBILITY IN PLANNING

Regardless of whether my goals are personal or professional, I plan and mind-map each one meticulously. Write down your goal – whether in MS Word, on a 3M notepad, or using mind-mapping software. Print it and make it visible, almost unavoidable, in your daily life. Then, take the necessary actionable steps to achieve it.

HONING YOUR STOICISM

At its core, cultivating stoic habits boils down to one thing: consistency. It's not just about making the right choices – it's about making them consistently. You can't just set your principles and guidelines for Monday and then rewrite the rulebook by Friday. That's like laying down tracks for a train and then suddenly shifting them – you'll end up derailed.

To put this principle of consistency into a relatable context, let's talk about those obligatory family gatherings. There's always someone insisting, "Oh, you have to go. The whole family is going to be there." But here's the thing: if it doesn't add value to my life and I'm just ticking a societal box, why should I? Let me paint a picture for you: Would I rather spend a day at Uncle Salie's 86th birthday bash in Worcester, nodding at relatives who can't even remember my name, or cherish a peaceful walk on the beach with my ageing dog? For me, it's a no-brainer. Uncle Salie will get a nice gift, and I'll continue living my life in the most authentic way I know how.

That way, when life's serious moments come knocking – like if my oncologist were to call and ask, "JD, how did you spend what could've been your last day?" – I'd have zero regrets about choosing quality time with my loyal companion over cake and small talk. That choice, made consistently and authentically, validates my own version of Stoicism. And that, my friends, is what I call an easy decision.

Just as the tracks guide a train's path, let your principles guide yours. Every decision you face, be it grand or seemingly inconsequential, is an opportunity to practice Stoicism. Think about what adds genuine value to your life and prioritise those choices. By doing so, you'll not only embrace Stoicism but also create a life of true purpose and meaning.

CHAPTER 12
RAY DALIO'S PRINCIPLES

I n 2017, I decided to surprise Kim with a trip through Botswana and the Okavango Delta in our Defender 110 Td5, affectionately named "The Monster". I timed the adventure to coincide with the April Easter long weekend.

For weeks, I meticulously planned our journey. Drawing from my flight school training, I compiled a comprehensive spreadsheet detailing our camping locations by date, the distances between them, and the nearest fuel stops. This ensured we could minimise the number of emergency jerry cans we needed to carry with us. The spreadsheet also included important notes like "river not crossable in rainy season" or "stop here to ask for directions".

Botswana's two major nature reserves, Moremi Game Reserve in the Okavango Delta and Chobe National Park, are home to several must-visit campsites. In Moremi, Third Bridge stands out, while in Chobe, travellers flock to Camp Savuti and the breathtaking Linyanti, situated just north of Savuti along the Linyanti River. Linyanti is especially renowned for its abundant lion and elephant populations.

I had it under good authority at the time that to secure a spot at any of Chobe's sought-after campsites, one should book in advance through SKL Camps in Maun (pronounced Ma-un). But hindsight has taught me that an advanced booking isn't always necessary. Nowadays, you can simply drive to SKL in Maun, check their live booking system, and adjust your itinerary based on available spots. Back in 2017, however, I pre-booked and prepaid for these exclusive spots in U.S. dollars, translating to roughly R1000 a night, non-refundable.

With every detail accounted for, we were finally ready to set off. The drive from Cape Town to Maun in The Monster is a test of endurance: a nine-hour journey to Upington in the Northern Cape, followed by another 12-hour drive to reach Maun. Considering it was Kim's second major overlanding adventure, I decided to split the trip. Our first overnight stop was at Tankwa Tented Camp, located about five hours from Cape Town. This camp lies along South Africa's longest continuous gravel road, the R355, midway between Ceres and Calvinia in the Tankwa Karoo. Tankwa itself is the site of the annual AfrikaBurn festival, South Africa's answer to Burning Man. As we drove, the remains of past sculptures served as silent testimonies to the many people who have left the festival having discovered new purpose and meaning in their lives.

After leaving Tankwa Tented Camp, an eternally long stretch of gravel road awaited us. It was day two of our three-week journey when disaster struck about 60 kilometres (38 miles) south of Calvinia, deep in the Tankwa desert. I was giving The Monster stick when her gearbox suddenly gave up the ghost. We went from cruising in fifth gear to having no gears at all. To make matters worse, it was a long weekend, and nobody takes this road to Calvinia on a long weekend – most sane people opt for the beautiful, tarred roads via Nieuwoudtville instead. As if on cue, we also found ourselves without cell phone reception.

Kim glanced at me. "JD," she began.

"I think I saw an old farmhouse about three kilometres back," I interrupted, hoping we'd find help there. Unsure if it was occupied, it was still our best shot.

We abandoned The Monster and started walking, and lo and behold, the planets lined up for us. The farmer was home, along with his two adult sons. Adding to the serendipity, his piece of land was used for the annual Tankwa Rally – the same event that First Technology sponsors every year – and he recognised me.

"Stay here," he said to Kim and me, directing his sons to accompany him. They climbed into his Pajero SUV, drove back down the gravel road and towed The Monster back to his workshop on the farm. Unfortunately, there was nothing they could do – the gearbox was beyond repair. We had no choice but to find a towing company with a flatbed truck to transport our 3-ton Land Rover back to Cape Town. Our three-week Okavango trip was officially in its *moer* [over].

Although there was no cell phone reception, the farmer had an old but working ADSL internet connection – a proper *boerelyn* [farmer's telephone line] – which meant we could make a Wi-Fi call from the farmhouse over the copper line. It was Easter, and the closest available towing service was six hours away in Laingsburg.

The next person I called was my then twenty-two-year-old son, Ryan.

"Ryan," I said, "Dad's three-week trip has come to an epic halt after twenty-four hours. I need you to come and fetch us."

"Dad," said Ryan, his voice somewhat muffled. "I'm on a date. If you've got Wi-Fi, surely it can't be an emergency?"

And then, just like that, he ended the call. I stared at my phone in disbelief, momentarily considering changes to my Will. Truth be told,

I think I would have done the same, and I'm glad he has his priorities right.

While waiting for the tow truck, the farmer and his sons, in the spirit of true boere (farmer) hospitality, set target practice boards up and down the river that flowed through their property and taught us how to use every hunting rifle with a scope that they had. They even served us a lavish lunch.

The flatbed arrived at 7 p.m. Our journey back to Cape Town was an unceremonious ride in the tow truck's cab. The next day, I was back in the office, surprising everyone with the shortest three-week holiday they'd ever seen me take.

The trip may have been a disaster, but there was a silver lining. During the 2015-2016 drought, the Tankwa Rally organisers told me that the farmers who allowed us to race on their land had run out of food for their Angora sheep. First Technology stepped up and contributed towards the Northern Cape Farmer's Association feeding scheme, shipping hay bales on 28-wheeler trucks to the region to help the farmers feed their sheep.

One farmer in particular had not forgotten that gesture, and it was his farmhouse we had stumbled upon that day. I'll never forget his words when Kim and I walked onto his farm: "First Technology, Johan de Villiers, dis jy. Dis jy [It's you]!"

Sometimes, what you give out in the universe comes back in unexpected ways.

As I reflected on the unexpected twists and turns of our trip, I couldn't help but think of one of the most important figures who has influenced how I approach life's challenges: Ray Dalio, the founder of Bridgewater Associates – the world's largest hedge fund – and author of the book *Principles: Life and Work*. His principles have not only guided me through the complexities of running a business but have also helped me navigate the unpredictable roads of life itself.

Just like our journey taught us about adaptability and the value of community, Dalio's life and work offer invaluable insights into turning challenges into stepping stones.

Allow me to share the story of Ray Dalio, a man whose principles have not just influenced but fundamentally shaped my approach to life and business.

RAY DALIO: A PIONEER IN SHAPING THE FUTURE OF FINANCE AND ORGANISATIONAL STRUCTURE

Ray Dalio grew up in a middle-class family on Long Island, New York, a far cry from the pinnacle of the financial world he would one day ascend to. As a child, he loved sports and spending time with his friends but found the structured academic environment, particularly the emphasis on rote learning, uninspiring. Nevertheless, Dalio was anything but lazy. Eager to earn his own spending money, he took on odd jobs ranging from mowing lawns to delivering newspapers and clearing snow from driveways.

At the age of 12, Dalio began caddying at the exclusive Links Golf Club, rubbing shoulders with Wall Street investors and notable figures like the Duke of Windsor (formerly King Edward VIII) and Richard Nixon, the future President of the United States. This early experience offered him a unique window into the world of power and finance, laying the foundation for his future career.

After graduating from Harvard Business School with an MBA, Dalio entered the world of finance, working at various brokerage firms. His tenure at one firm came to an abrupt end in a rather dramatic fashion – he punched his boss and was consequently fired. Despite this incident, Dalio's innate understanding of the markets made him an indispensable resource to brokers and clients alike, who continued to seek his insights. It was this unique magnetism and expertise that led Dalio to launch Bridgewater Associates from his modest two-bedroom apartment in New York City in 1975 at the age of 26.

Fast forward to today, and Bridgewater has become a financial powerhouse, generating more profits for its clients than any other hedge fund in history. Named by Fortune as the fifth most important private company in the U.S., and with Dalio himself gracing Time Magazine's list of the 100 Most Influential People, Bridgewater is no ordinary organisation. Dalio credits its unprecedented success to a distinctive company culture he describes as "an idea meritocracy" fueled by "radical transparency".

Dalio's groundbreaking principles extend beyond the corridors of Bridgewater Associates. In his inspiring book *Principles: Life and Work*, he distils the wisdom gained from his extraordinary career. He argues that life's complexities – whether in management, economics, or investing – can be broken down into rules and understood as one would understand the mechanisms of a machine. Let's explore some of Ray Dalio's principles in greater detail and examine how implementing them in your organisation can give you a similar competitive edge.

RADICAL TRUTH AND RADICAL TRANSPARENCY

In an age where misinformation can erode trust and hamper productivity, the principles of Radical Truth and Radical Transparency have never been more relevant. Introduced by Ray Dalio in his management philosophy at Bridgewater Associates, these principles have helped reshape decision-making and organisational culture in organisations across the world.

Radical Truth advocates for an organisational culture where employees are encouraged to speak their minds openly and confront issues directly without fear of retribution. The goal is to foster an atmosphere where problems are identified, and solutions are proactively sought.

Radical Transparency, on the other hand, emphasises sharing information freely across the organisation. This includes details about business decisions, performance metrics, and even where things have gone wrong or haven't worked out as planned. The idea is that by making all information transparent, everyone in the organisation is better equipped to make informed decisions. The aim of this transparency is two-fold: to root out inefficiencies and errors and to foster a culture of trust and mutual respect.

However, it's important to note that Radical Truth and Radical Transparency are not about unfiltered rudeness or indiscriminate sharing of sensitive information. Rather, they aim to create a culture that values truth and openness, welcomes constructive feedback, and shares relevant information for the benefit of all.

THE BENEFITS OF RADICAL TRUTH

• **Encourages Open Communication**: A culture of Radical Truth fosters an environment where everyone is free to share their ideas and feedback. This openness can stimulate innovation and break down the barriers of hierarchy and office politics.

• **Promotes Proactive Problem-Solving**: Practicing Radical Truth helps eliminate the risk of 'groupthink,' allowing the best ideas to rise to the top. This inclusiveness ensures that innovation and solutions can come from anywhere within the organisation.

• **Fosters Trust**: When both leadership and employees consistently speak the truth, a culture of trust is cultivated. This not only boosts job performance but also contributes to higher levels of employee satisfaction.

THE BENEFITS OF RADICAL TRANSPARENCY

• **Empowers Informed Decision-Making**: Having access to all necessary information empowers employees at all levels to make better decisions. This can dramatically increase efficiency and effectiveness throughout the organisation.

• **Fosters Shared Understanding**: Transparency helps everyone in the organisation understand its current state, goals, and challenges, fostering a more cohesive team.

• **Cultivates a Healthy Culture**: The act of being transparent helps discourage office politics and favouritism, leading to a healthier, more accountable work environment.

Both Radical Truth and Radical Transparency collectively contribute to informed decision-making and a healthy organisational culture. Netflix's "Keeper Test" serves as a compelling example of these principles in action. Managers are encouraged to continually assess their team members' performance and contribution, asking themselves which employees they would fight to keep. This transparent, no-nonsense approach to performance appraisal ensures that both managers and employees know where they stand, which in turn fosters an environment of accountability and high performance.

By combining these two concepts – Radical Truth and Radical Transparency – the goal is to empower everyone with the data they need for informed decision-making. Speaking the truth, especially when it's uncomfortable, forms the foundation of all discussions, while transparency ensures that everyone grasps the bigger picture. While the openness required by these principles can be challenging due to human tendencies to avoid confrontation or protect one's status, Dalio argues that the benefits outweigh the initial discomfort.

IDEA MERITOCRACY

In many organisations that operate with a top-down hierarchical structure, the weight of one's ideas often correlates with their position on the organisational ladder. This is typical of the traditional business model endorsed by MBA programs. At the apex of this structure sits the MD or CEO, whose word is often considered final. To challenge this norm, Ray Dalio proposes an alternative model called 'Idea Meritocracy,' where the best ideas win, irrespective of the individual's rank or seniority.

Dalio extends the core principle of Idea Meritocracy by introducing 'believability-weighted decision-making'. In this evolved model, the weight of each person's opinion is gauged by their track record and expertise in the subject matter. This nuanced approach has proved beneficial in my own business practice, particularly when making time-sensitive decisions. A junior engineer with a history of successful projects, for instance, would have their opinion carry more weight in engineering matters.

This principle aligns well with my practice of regularly consulting frontline staff, who are often the first to know about customer preferences or issues. In the realm of customer satisfaction, their opinions often carry more believability weight. It's important to note that the application of believability weighting should be done thoughtfully. It's not about disregarding the ideas of those with less experience or credibility but recognising where expertise truly lies.

Google serves as a model for organisations that aspire to build an Idea Meritocracy. Within this framework, team members at every level are encouraged to challenge decisions and contribute their perspectives. This cultivates a culture of innovation where the merit of an idea, rather than the rank of its proposer, determines its success. Eric Schmidt and Jonathan Rosenberg elaborate on this in their book How Google Works. They state: "When it comes to the quality of decision-making, pay level is intrinsically irrelevant and experience is valuable only if it is used to frame a winning argument. Unfortunately, in most companies, experience is the winning argument. We call these places 'tenurocracies' because power derives from tenure, not merit." They further add, "Meritocracies yield better decisions and create an environment where all employees feel valued and empowered. They demolish the culture of fear, the murky, muddy environment in which HiPPOs [an acronym for *Highest Paid Person's Opinion*] prefer to wallow."

It is, however, important that companies practising Idea Meritocracy have mechanisms in place to assess the merit of ideas objectively. This can be achieved through regular performance evaluations, peer reviews, and other mechanisms that assess an individual's competency and track record in different areas, as well as procedures for collective decision-making.

Dalio also emphasises the value of what he calls 'thoughtful disagreement'. In an Idea Meritocracy, disagreements are not only tolerated but are encouraged to facilitate a diversity of perspectives. This doesn't mean conflict for conflict's sake but rather an open and respectful exchange of diverse viewpoints aimed at finding the best possible solution. Creating this type of culture requires both a commitment to openness and the development of skills in constructive communication.

While human input is invaluable, Dalio also recognises the role of data-driven objectivity in enhancing decision-making. An Idea Meritocracy, therefore, leans heavily on data and algorithms to remove emotional bias and contribute to more objective decisions.

By integrating human expertise, data analytics, and a culture of thoughtful disagreement, an Idea Meritocracy creates a more nuanced and effective decision-making environment. It offers a compelling alternative to traditional hierarchical systems and is worth considering for any organisation that aims for high performance and inclusive decision-making.

HOW AN IDEA MERITOCRACY CAN BENEFIT AN ORGANISATION

• **Fosters a Culture of Innovation**: A free exchange of ideas, regardless of rank, leads to creative thinking and innovative solutions.

• **Enhances Decision-making**: Utilising collective intelligence leads to higher-quality, well-rounded decisions.

• **Reduces Errors and Risks**: When decisions are made by those who have shown consistent understanding and success in a specific domain, it naturally reduces the likelihood of errors and mitigates risks associated with decision-making.

• **Promotes Learning and Professional Growth**: An environment of open dialogue and thoughtful disagreement offers learning opportunities, which encourage employees to improve their skills, knowledge, and thus their 'believability.'

• **Cultivates a Harmonious Working Environment**: By valuing everyone's input, the organisation fosters an atmosphere of mutual respect and trust, which boosts employee engagement and satisfaction.

PRINCIPLES-DRIVEN DECISION MAKING

In *Principles*, Ray Dalio introduces the concept of principles-driven decision-making, which involves using established principles grounded in both practical experience and logical reasoning to make better decisions. Over time, Dalio recorded the reasons behind his decisions. This not only allowed him to learn from past experiences but also facilitated the development of guiding principles for handling similar situations in the future. By establishing a well-defined set of principles within your own organisation, you can ensure a consistent and effective decision-making process that aligns with your organisation's mission and values.

The principles that guide decision-making in an organisation can vary depending on the type of organisation, its mission, and its culture. However, here are five general principles that are often considered important:

• **Ethical Integrity**: Decisions should be made in a way that aligns with the organisation's ethical standards and values. This principle ensures that choices respect the rights and dignity of all stakeholders and avoid harm. For instance, a company might refuse to do business in regions known for human rights abuses, even if there are economic advantages to doing so.

• **Stakeholder Involvement**: This principle emphasises the importance of considering the interests and feedback of all relevant stakeholders in the decision-making process. For instance, before launching a new product, a company might consult with customers, employees, suppliers, and even the local community to understand potential impacts and concerns.

• **Data-Driven Decisions**: An organisation that abides by this principle values decisions backed by evidence and facts over those made on gut feelings or anecdotal evidence. With the rise of big data, many organisations emphasise the importance of using data analytics to guide their choices, ensuring that they are based on concrete information and can be justified.

• **Sustainability**: With growing awareness of environmental issues and social responsibilities, some organisations prioritise long-term sustainability over short-term profits. Decisions made under this principle would consider the environmental, economic, and social implications to ensure that they do not harm future generations or the planet.

• **Agility and Flexibility**: Especially pertinent in rapidly changing industries or uncertain environments, this principle prioritises the ability to adapt and pivot when necessary. Organisations embracing this principle will value decisions that leave room for adjustment in the future rather than locking themselves into a particular course of action.

To use principles-driven decision-making effectively, it is important that:

• You have clear, written-down principles to guide your actions.

• You consistently apply these principles across different scenarios, thereby creating a pattern of reliable decision-making.

• Your principles provide an objective framework that stands apart from emotional or impulsive decisions.

• Your principles are openly shared among team members to ensure that everyone understands the rationale behind decisions.

The key to this approach isn't just having principles but continually refining them based on experience and new insights. They should be flexible enough to adapt to changing circumstances yet robust enough to provide a stable framework for decision-making.

THE TWO YOU'S

In *Principles*, Ray Dalio refers to the idea of 'The Two Yous', which he describes as the tension between one's 'higher-level' self and one's 'lower-level' self.

1. The Higher-Level You: This is the self that sets goals and establishes the values and principles by which you want to live your life. It is the aspirational 'you', the one that has a vision for what you want to accomplish in the long term and what you believe is most important. The higher-level self is more thoughtful, reflective, and strategic, focused on achieving objectives that align with your deepest values and principles.

2. The Lower-Level You: This is the self, driven by emotions and short-term desires, that gets caught up in the day-to-day tasks, situations, and emotional states that can distract or pull you away from the path your higher-level self has set. The lower-level self might get stuck in immediate concerns, emotional reactions, or temporary setbacks that can make it harder to achieve your higher-level goals.

Dalio suggests that understanding the interplay between these two selves is crucial for making better decisions and for personal growth. The lower-level you can easily derail plans and decisions made by the higher-level you if not kept in check. By being aware of this dichotomy, you can recognise when your emotions and instincts are driving your behaviour and then attempt to make decisions from the higher-level perspective.

The concept of *The Two Yous* isn't merely a psychological framework for individual self-examination – it's also a powerful tool for organisational effectiveness and leadership. Businesses often fall into the trap of prioritising immediate gains over long-term sustainability or responding reactively to market changes rather than adhering to a well-laid-out strategy. By applying the understanding of *The Two Yous*, leaders and teams can operate with a more nuanced understanding of their actions, motivations, and decision-making processes and position their businesses for greater success, resilience, and growth.

Let's explore how this understanding can significantly influence different facets of business management and leadership.

Informed Decision-Making

Recognising the 'higher-level you' and the 'lower-level you' is essential for making well-informed decisions. When you're aware of the motivational forces at play, rather than reacting impulsively to immediate situations, you're better equipped to make thoughtful, strategic decisions that are in line with your business's long-term goals.

To illustrate this, consider a company facing a public relations crisis due to an unintended product malfunction. A 'lower-level' response might be a hasty decision to immediately pull all products off the shelf without proper investigation. However, the 'higher-level' self might opt for a more measured approach: acknowledging the issue publicly, conducting a thorough investigation, and taking appropriate rectification measures based on the findings.

Long-Term Planning and Strategy

Understanding The Two Yous creates a mental framework for more informed decision-making. It offers a checkpoint where leaders can stop and evaluate whether the decision at hand aligns with the long-term objectives and core values of the organisation or is merely a reactionary move to a short-term issue.

Take the scenario of a tech startup: driven by its 'higher-level' vision, it might prioritise developing a robust, user-friendly software platform over quick profit-making tactics like aggressive advertising. It understands that long-term user trust and satisfaction will lead to sustainable success.

Emotional Intelligence

Emotional intelligence is a key aspect of effective leadership. Recognising when the 'lower-level' you is taking charge can prevent hasty decisions driven by emotions like fear or anger that might not serve the best interests of the team or the organisation in favour of a more balanced, rational approach.

Imagine an employee makes a significant mistake: the 'lower-level' you might want to react with immediate disciplinary action fueled by disappointment or anger. The 'higher-level' you, however, would consider the employee's overall performance by reviewing past performance evaluations or discussing the issue in a one-on-one meeting to understand the root cause.

Resilience in the Face of Challenges

Every business goes through ups and downs. Understanding the interplay between your two selves can help you develop resilience by not allowing short-term setbacks to derail your organisation's long-term objectives.

Consider the aftermath of losing a major client: the 'lower-level' you might be fixated on the immediate revenue loss, spiralling into panic. The 'higher-level' you, however, sees it as an opportunity to refine your business model or to focus on diversifying your client base to reduce risk.

Improved Team Management

Understanding The Two Yous can help leaders guide their teams to think from a higher-level perspective, fostering a culture that values long-term growth and success. It can also assist in better understanding team dynamics, recognising when team members might be reacting from their 'lower-level' selves, and helping them realign with their 'higher-level' selves.

Consider a scenario where a project is falling behind schedule, the 'lower-level' you might urge the team to rush, potentially compromising quality. The 'higher-level' you would assess the situation comprehensively and may decide to negotiate a deadline extension to maintain the quality of work.

Personal Growth and Leadership Development

Mastering the understanding of your Two Yous is a journey of personal growth. As you get better at making decisions from your 'higher-level' self, you become a more effective and inspiring leader.

For instance, you might realise that your tendency to micromanage stems from your 'lower-level' anxieties. By addressing this, you cultivate a more trusting environment, delegate effectively, and allow your team to take more initiative, leading to increased overall productivity.

SHAPERS

In *Principles*, Ray Dalio introduces the concept of "shapers" – individuals who merge visionary thinking with practicality to bring groundbreaking ideas to fruition, often in the face of doubt or scepticism. Shapers exhibit a blend of characteristics: They possess intense curiosity, a compulsive need to make sense of things, and an almost rebellious approach to independent thinking. They excel at understanding both the big picture and granular details, valuing both equally. A defining trait of shapers is their cognitive flexibility: They can entertain conflicting ideas, deliberate them from various perspectives, and move seamlessly between overarching visions and intricate details. Shapers are also highly self-aware, making them effective leaders capable of assembling teams that complement their own strengths and weaknesses.

Dalio refers to legendary figures like Steve Jobs and Elon Musk, as well as historical personalities like Abraham Lincoln, as examples of shapers. Jobs, for example, not only envisioned a world transformed by personal computing but also had the acumen to bring this vision to reality, revolutionising multiple industries in the process. Similarly, Elon Musk has been a pioneering force in multiple sectors, including automotive with Tesla, aerospace with SpaceX, and even in ambitious ventures like the Hyperloop and Neuralink. His ability to envision a future shaped by sustainable energy and interplanetary life – and take pragmatic steps to achieve these goals – marks him as a quintessential shaper. Abraham Lincoln, despite the immense societal pressures of his time, displayed extraordinary leadership and vision in steering the United States through the tumultuous years of the American Civil War. Faced with the possible dissolution of the Union, he exercised a combination of strategic insight and emotional intelligence to navigate complex political terrain, ultimately succeeding in preserving the Union and abolishing slavery, marking him as another prime example of a shaper.

Shapers can be a huge asset to any organisation. Their results-oriented nature and eagerness to make an impact often make them key drivers of growth, propelling the organisation to achieve its goals. Their ability to challenge the status quo and push boundaries can provide organisations with a competitive edge in the marketplace. Because they can visualise the future and navigate toward it, they are instrumental in helping an organisation not only set a clear and compelling strategic direction but also guide its implementation. In times of crisis or significant change, their unique ability to view problems from multiple perspectives makes their contributions especially valuable. Beyond strategy and problem-solving, shapers also play a pivotal role in influencing an organisation's culture. Their drive, determination, and resilience inspire others, creating a high-performance culture.

While their impact is undeniable, working with shapers is not without its challenges. To fully leverage their potential, they need to be managed effectively. Their strong personalities and tendency to question norms can be disruptive and require an environment that is both supportive and strategically aligned with the company's overall goals and culture. By understanding and accommodating the unique qualities of shapers, organisations can better position themselves to harness their transformative power.

THE 5-STEP PROCESS

Ray Dalio developed a 5-step process designed to both achieve goals and navigate the obstacles encountered along the way. This framework consists of five interconnected steps:

1. Knowing what you want (your goals)

2. Understanding your current reality (the problems)

3. Identifying the root cause of your problems (the diagnosis)

4. Deciding on your course of action (the design)

5. Executing the plan (the doing)

These steps are part of a cyclical process designed to create a feed-back loop of continuous learning and improvement, allowing individuals and organisations to adapt, evolve, and achieve long-term success.

For businesses, implementing Dalio's 5-step process can be particularly impactful. By applying these steps, companies can expect to see tangible improvements in problem-solving, decision-making, and overall effectiveness. Here's how each step can be applied to create a more successful business:

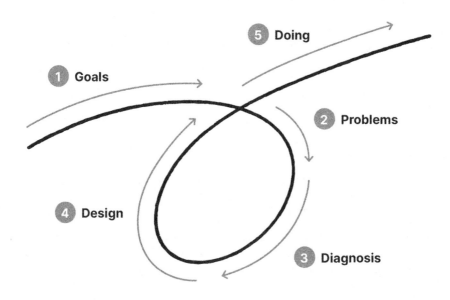

STEP 1: SET CLEAR GOALS

According to Dalio, "You have to have your audacious goals." In other words, define what you're aiming for and set ambitious and challenging goals that push the boundaries of what you believe is possible. The goals you set will determine the actions you take. In a business context, this could mean setting organisational objectives like revenue targets, market share goals, or product development milestones. Clear goals provide direction and purpose for a business and serve as the foundation for planning and strategy development.

To illustrate this, let's say you are the CEO of a manufacturing company. Your company has been doing reasonably well, but you aim for more than just reasonable performance. You decide to set a clear, audacious goal: reduce production costs by 20% within the next six months while maintaining product quality. This goal is specific, measurable, and audacious; it's not just a matter of incremental change but a significant leap forward. It also forces the entire organisation to align its efforts and think strategically to meet this objective.

STEP 2: IDENTIFY AND DON'T TOLERATE THE PROBLEMS THAT STAND IN THE WAY OF YOU ACHIEVING YOUR GOALS

While setting goals is the first step, the journey to achieving them is rarely straightforward or easy. In pursuing an ambitious goal, you're pushing the boundaries of what you or your organisation has done before. This often means venturing into unfamiliar territory, where making mistakes or running into unanticipated obstacles is likely.

Dalio emphasises that these "problems" should not be "tolerated". Instead of ignoring or accepting them, they must be acknowledged and addressed. According to Dalio's philosophy, encountering problems is not just normal but an essential part of the process. These 'roadblocks' are valuable cues for re-evaluation and adjustment. They highlight the gaps in understanding, skills, or resources that need to be filled to keep progressing toward your goal.

This is particularly true in a business context. Here, identifying these problems can mean recognising internal issues, such as skill gaps or inefficiencies in processes. It could also mean coming to terms with external challenges like market competition or regulatory changes. By understanding these obstacles, you can adapt and improve, thereby keeping your business on the path toward achieving its objectives.

Getting back to our manufacturing company, two months into your efforts, you start noticing frequent downtimes on the production line, which are clearly affecting your timeline and causing costs to rise instead of fall. According to Dalio's principle, this is a "problem" that should not be "tolerated." Instead of dismissing these downtimes as unavoidable or 'just part of the business,' you document each instance, noting the time, duration, and any observable issues such as machinery malfunctions or worker delays.

At this point, you haven't diagnosed the root cause or formulated a solution – that comes later. However, you've taken the crucial step of identifying the problem and refusing to accept it as an unchangeable reality. You acknowledge that these frequent downtimes are obstacles that need to be understood and eventually addressed if you're going to reach your ambitious goal of cutting production costs by 20%.

STEP 3: ACCURATELY DIAGNOSE THE PROBLEMS TO GET AT THEIR ROOT CAUSES

Once problems are identified, it's essential to dig deeper to understand their root causes rather than just treating the symptoms. As Ray Dalio advises, it's important to "distinguish the symptoms from the disease". Failing to do so can lead to temporary fixes that don't solve the underlying problem, causing it to re-emerge later. Detailed analysis or investigation may be required to accurately diagnose the issue at its core.

For instance, if a company is not meeting its sales targets, the symptoms might manifest as declining revenues or reduced market share. However, the root cause could be more nuanced – it could stem from poor sales strategies, product quality issues, or perhaps ineffective marketing. Understanding this underlying "disease" is crucial for developing effective, long-lasting solutions.

Let's return to the example of our manufacturing company. Having identified the frequent production line downtimes as a major problem affecting your goal, you decide to conduct a thorough analysis. This involves studying downtime logs, interviewing floor workers, examining machinery maintenance records, and even bringing in an external consultant to evaluate the production process.

Your investigation reveals multiple contributing factors: outdated machinery prone to breakdowns, a lack of preventive maintenance, and inadequate training of production line workers. You realise that these are the gaps that need to be addressed to continue progressing towards your ambitious goal of cutting production costs by 20%.

STEP 4: DESIGN PLANS THAT WILL HELP YOU GET AROUND THEM

With a clear understanding of the root causes, the next step is to develop strategies to get around these obstacles. This could mean implementing new processes, upskilling staff, redefining product offerings, or changing marketing strategies. The aim is to devise a targeted plan that directly addresses the root cause of the problem, thereby paving the way for the business to realign its efforts towards achieving its goal.

Building on our manufacturing company example, you've identified that frequent downtime is a problem, and you've accurately diagnosed its root causes. To eliminate these root causes, you propose to replace the most problematic machines with newer, more reliable models. Additionally, you consider leasing equipment as an option to minimise upfront costs. You also plan to implement a preventive maintenance schedule that includes regular checks and updates to avoid reactive fixes, thus reducing downtime. Finally, you design a training program to improve the skill set of your production line workers, focusing on areas that have led to the most mistakes and delays. You create a detailed action plan that includes timelines, responsible parties, and key performance indicators (KPIs) to measure the success of each initiative. You also allocate resources and budget to support the execution of the plan.

By designing a well-thought-out plan that aims to eliminate the identified root causes, you've set the stage for the final step: executing the plan to achieve the goal. Your plan becomes the roadmap that will guide your team toward rectifying the problems that have been standing in the way of achieving your ambitious 20% cost reduction goal.

STEP 5: DO WHAT'S NECESSARY TO PUSH THESE DESIGNS THROUGH TO RESULTS

The final step is where the rubber meets the road: execution. Plans and strategies are only as good as their implementation. Ray Dalio highlights the importance of this when he says, "You have to push through to results". This step involves taking the necessary actions to execute the plans, which could require changes at various levels of the organisation. It also involves monitoring progress and making necessary adjustments to the plan as required. By persistently pushing through challenges and adapting the plan where needed, you can turn a well-designed strategy into tangible results.

Let's get back to our manufacturing company. Having diagnosed the root causes of your downtime and designed a plan to address each one, you move on to the next phase: implementation. After getting budget approval, you proceed with purchasing the new machines. You also coordinate the installation to coincide with a low-production period to minimise disruptions. Next, you roll out the preventive maintenance schedule and assign specific tasks to team members. You also create a system for logging maintenance activities and reviewing them weekly to ensure compliance. Finally, you launch the training program, making it mandatory for all production line workers. You also set up periodic assessments to ensure that the training is effective and workers are up-to-date with the required skills.

As you implement these actions, you continually track the key performance indicators (KPIs) that were set during the planning phase. A month into the implementation, you notice a 10% reduction in downtimes and a corresponding decrease in costs. You continue to monitor and make minor adjustments. By the end of the six months, you successfully achieve a 20% reduction in production costs, meeting your ambitious goal.

By diligently following through on your action plan and making necessary adjustments along the way, you've effectively pushed your plans through to results. This completes one cycle of Ray Dalio's 5-step process, taking you from setting a goal to successfully achieving it through thoughtful identification, diagnosis, planning, and execution. The cyclical nature of the process means you can now set new goals and begin the cycle anew.

Whether it's improving manufacturing efficiency, growing a startup, or pursuing any other challenging objectives, consistently applying this 5-step process can serve as a comprehensive guide towards achieving even your most ambitious goals.

EMBRACING REALITY

Ray Dalio emphasises the importance of understanding how reality works (and learning how to deal with it) as a core principle to achieving success in life and work. For Dalio, confronting and accepting the truth of a situation, no matter how harsh or unpalatable, is essential to making informed decisions. Ignoring or denying reality leads to flawed reasoning and misguided actions, which can prevent individuals and organisations from achieving their goals.

Central to Dalio's philosophy is his formula: Dreams + Reality + Determination = A Successful Life. This equation underscores the balance required for achievement. 'Dreams' represent our aspirations and goals, the vision of what we desire to achieve. 'Reality' is the acceptance of our current circumstances – our strengths and weaknesses, what our resources are, and what obstacles we face – without sugarcoating or delusion. By recognising and understanding our reality, we can navigate obstacles more effectively, leveraging our strengths and collaborating with others to address our weaknesses. Lastly, 'Determination' is the willpower and resilience needed to persevere through challenges and setbacks. When these three elements align, according to Dalio, they pave the way to a successful life.

Dreams give you a destination, reality serves as your starting point, and determination is the fuel that helps you move from one to the other. Each component is essential: without dreams, you have no direction; without an accurate assessment of reality, your plans are built on shaky ground; and without determination, you won't have the stamina to overcome the inevitable challenges along the way.

In our personal lives, especially in the context of career development, recognising our strengths and weaknesses is crucial. It allows us to focus on improving areas of weakness and leveraging strengths to boost our performance and career progression. This understanding can also inform career planning. For example, if an individual realises they excel in creative thinking but struggle with detailed administrative tasks, they might pursue roles or careers where their creativity is a major asset and administrative tasks are minimal. In team settings, recognising one's own strengths and weaknesses can foster more effective collaboration. Individuals can take on roles that align with their strengths and seek help in areas where they are less capable.

Similarly, in a business context, embracing reality involves an objective assessment of a business's current situation. This could include the competitive landscape, the state of the market, financial health, customer sentiment, and more. It's about acknowledging the truth about where the company stands, including the challenges it might face. For example, a business that identifies customer service as a strength could focus its strategy around that while also taking steps to address weaknesses such as inefficiencies in its supply chain. This realistic assessment is critical for effective strategic planning.

In terms of using strengths as leverage, every business has unique strengths. By identifying them, a business can leverage them to gain a competitive edge. For instance, a business might excel in customer service, have a particularly efficient supply chain, or possess a highly skilled workforce. These strengths can be highlighted in marketing efforts, used to forge strategic partnerships or serve as the basis for business expansion. Equally important is recognising the business's weaknesses. Once identified, steps can be taken to mitigate or overcome them, whether it means investing in employee training, improving product offerings, or restructuring the organisation.

Leaders can apply Dalio's principle by assigning tasks in a way that allows team members to play to their strengths while encouraging collaboration to address weaknesses. This strategic approach fosters an environment where the collective skill set of the team is utilised most effectively.

Both individually and organisationally, facing and embracing reality requires a high level of self-awareness and honesty. When used effectively, this principle enhances strategic planning, boosts performance, and fosters successful collaboration. It's about leveraging your strengths and addressing your weaknesses to achieve the best possible outcomes.

PAIN + REFLECTION = PROGRESS

According to Ray Dalio, pain is inevitable, especially when pursuing ambitious goals. Yet, he believes that by facing and reflecting on this pain, we accelerate the speed at which we learn and evolve. His formula, Pain + Reflection = Progress, encapsulates his belief that genuine progress, whether in our professional or personal lives, often arises from confronting challenges, mistakes, or areas of ignorance.

Pain, in this context, doesn't necessarily refer to physical suffering but rather to the emotional or mental discomfort we face when things don't go as planned. It could be the sting of a failed project at work or the emotional toll of a strained relationship at home. It might also involve facing the realisation of a missed opportunity or the discomfort of acknowledging our weaknesses. Ever lost a job? Failed in an exam? Those are prime examples. Many people try to avoid or mitigate this pain by ignoring it, rationalising it, or shifting the blame elsewhere.

The second component of Dalio's formula – Reflection – is what transforms this pain into a powerful catalyst for growth. Reflecting deeply on our pain allows us to understand what went wrong, why it happened, and how to avoid similar mistakes in the future. This reflective process enables us to learn from our mistakes, adapt our strategies, and ultimately evolve in our thinking and behaviour. Without reflection, we run the risk of repeating our errors, perpetuating a cycle of stagnation in our personal and professional growth.

In essence, Dalio's formula suggests that pain is an inevitable part of life and growth. However, it's our response to that pain – our ability to reflect and learn – that determines our path forward. By embracing challenges, learning from our mistakes, and thoughtfully reflecting on our experiences, we can harness pain as a driver of continuous progress and development. This interplay between personal and professional growth is crucial; improvements in self-awareness and skill often translate into greater effectiveness and adaptability in the workplace.

On a personal level, recognising and reflecting on painful experiences can deepen our self-awareness and reveal areas in need of

improvement. The process gives us an opportunity to develop necessary skills or change unhelpful behaviours. This growth isn't limited
to personal development; it can also propel career advancement. By
showcasing our capacity to learn and adapt from past mistakes, we
demonstrate traits like resilience and adaptability – qualities highly
valued in any professional environment.

From a business perspective, setbacks or failures should not be
viewed negatively; instead, they should be seen as valuable learning
opportunities. Reflecting on the root causes of these setbacks allows
organisations to pinpoint what went wrong and make adjustments to
prevent similar mistakes in the future. This encourages employees to
take calculated risks and learn from their experiences, fueling both
innovation and growth. By identifying weaknesses in the business
model or inefficiencies in operations, companies can revise and
strengthen their strategies, resulting in a more robust and resilient
organisation.

Dalio's formula does have its limitations – not all pain leads to
progress, and reflection alone cannot solve every problem. However,
the principle offers a robust framework for turning challenges into
stepping stones to success for both individuals and organisations.

CHAPTER 13
THE POWER OF
ADAPTATION

I n 2015, motivated by an unquenchable thirst for adventure and a desire to push our physical and mental boundaries, Kim and I set off on a journey to Iceland. Our mission: to climb glaciers and face the dynamic challenges they presented. Our goal: to summit Hvannadalshnjúkur, the highest peak of the Öræfajökull volcano. Located in Vatnajökull National Park, this majestic, ice-capped mountain is the tallest in Iceland, reaching an impressive 2,110 meters.

The climb was gruelling, requiring us to rope in the entire climbing team on harnesses at all times due to the constant threat of hidden crevasses under the ice pack. Frequent exercises in arrested falling – a technique used to rapidly halt a slide by digging into the ice with our ice axes – became a staple routine of our daily climb. Nevertheless, the breathtaking views from the summit made every step worthwhile.

Known as the "Land of Fire and Ice," Iceland is a distinctive Nordic island nation, its stunning natural beauty characterised by volcanic landscapes, hot springs, geysers, and glaciers, all set against a back-drop of Northern Lights displays and near-endless summer daylight. However, despite its romantic imagery, its rugged environment is so inhospitable that it served as a training ground for the Apollo moon landing astronauts.

Yet, beneath its breathtaking beauty and inspiring challenges, we were acutely aware of the potential dangers Iceland could pose. The small nation sits atop one of the world's most volcanically active regions, where sleeping giants beneath the surface could awaken with devastating consequences. The Laki Eruption in 1783-1784 lasted eight months and released large amounts of basalt lava and toxic gases, resulting in a severe famine that killed about a quarter of Iceland's population. More recently, the 2010 Eyjafjallajökull eruption disrupted air travel across Europe for weeks due to massive ash clouds. Although no fatalities were reported, the ash presented significant health risks, necessitating the evacuation of hundreds of people. The following year, the Grímsvötn volcano erupted, causing the largest glacial outburst flood (jökulhlaup) in Icelandic history, leading to significant infrastructure damage.

Adding to the volcanic activity, Iceland's location on the Mid-Atlantic Ridge, where the Eurasian and North American tectonic plates pull apart, results in frequent seismic activity. Most earthquakes are relatively mild, but the larger ones can cause significant damage. For instance, a powerful magnitude 7.0 earthquake caused extensive damage in South Iceland in 1912. In June 2000, a series of earthquakes hit the Reykjanes Peninsula in Southwest Iceland, with the largest – having a magnitude of 6.6 – causing considerable infrastructural damage. More recently, in May 2008, two earthquakes with magnitudes of 6.1 and 6.3 struck South Iceland, causing structural damage and prompting the evacuation of thousands of residents.

Interestingly, thrill-seekers can experience this tectonic activity firsthand by snorkelling or scuba diving between these two plates in a location known as the Silfra Fissure – the only place on Earth where one can dive between two tectonic plates. Although the water temperature is extremely cold, underwater visibility is crystal clear. These tectonic plates are drifting apart at an exceptionally slow rate, making it safe to dive under normal conditions. However, if there's an earthquake, you might find yourself in hot water.

Something we had to prepare ourselves for was Iceland's unpredictable weather, which can give rise to strong winds and storms without warning. The conditions make driving treacherous, with the wind being strong enough to make objects – even animals – airborne. The phrase "pigs can fly" might find a surprising home in this context. Freezing storms are common during the winter, and the surrounding waters of Iceland, notorious for their strong currents and high waves, can be dangerous. Sudden weather changes can make conditions hazardous for inexperienced swimmers or boaters, and given the country's typically cold and wet climate, hypothermia is also a significant risk.

Iceland's winters can be particularly brutal. Houses have boundary walls built around them to shield their occupants from the punishing wind and snow, and in some areas, people and livestock often cohabit in the same space, relying on the animals' body heat as a vital source of warmth. While the warmth of a hundred animals can keep everyone alive, the stench, as one can imagine, can be quite overwhelming.

CLIMBING THE GLACIERS

Because hiking and exploring Iceland's glaciers is a high-risk activity, it's recommended to only undertake such journeys with experienced guides and proper safety equipment. Despite the recommended precautions, even the most prepared adventurers are not immune to risks. There have been numerous glacier rescue incidents in recent decades. In November 2004, a group of eight British mountaineers were stranded on the Vatnajökull glacier due to extreme weather conditions. ICE-SAR teams faced challenging conditions to reach the group, including hurricane-force winds, limited visibility, and the risk of avalanches. After a two-day rescue operation, all eight climbers were successfully evacuated and brought to safety.

In March 2017, a snowmobile accident on the Langjökull glacier left a man seriously injured. ICE-SAR teams were quickly dispatched to the scene, where they provided first aid and transported the injured person to a hospital in Reykjavik for further care. Continuing the series of incidents, in March 2019, a French tourist fell into a crevasse while hiking on the Mýrdalsjökull glacier. They were trapped in the crevasse for several hours before being rescued by ICE-SAR teams. The teams used specialised equipment to extract the tourist from the crevasse and transport him to a hospital for further treatment.

We set about climbing five of Iceland's most challenging glaciers: Vatnajökull, Langjökull, Hofsjökull, Mýrdalsjökull, and Dranga-jökull. Each glacier had its unique challenges and characteristics, yet all demanded the same rigorous levels of attention and preparation.

Our daily ritual involved strapping crampons – metal plates with sharp spikes – to our boots. This gear transformed us into what we dubbed 'human-goat hybrids', enabling us to navigate the slick, icy surfaces with surprising agility.

Glacial climbing is a high-stakes, adrenaline-fueled experience demanding unerring attention and trust. The dynamic nature of glaciers means there are no set routes to the summit, with their groans and cracks serving as a constant reminder of their relentless movement. To protect ourselves from the hidden crevices that might open up without warning, we were roped into our fellow climbers, each of us spaced six meters apart.

The ever-changing landscape of the glaciers added an element of nerve-wracking uncertainty to our adventure. A path that was solid one day could potentially open up into a precarious 300-meter drop the next, concealed beneath a deceptive blanket of fresh snow. Without any way to predict where the crevices were, every forward step became an act of faith. The thought that one of us could plummet into an unseen abyss at any moment kept our hearts in our mouths each time one of our crampon-clad feet pressed down on the icy surface. To counter this ever-present danger, we carried ice picks, ready at any moment to hit the deck and dig into the ice to secure ourselves or halt the unexpected descent of a team member.

Despite ground temperatures hovering around 4 degrees Celsius during the daytime, the wind chill could cause the temperature to plummet drastically. The severe weather was often so bad that even our cameras started to freeze up, and visibility became a challenge. The rapidly evolving conditions could transition from clear skies to disorienting whiteouts that blurred the line between Earth and sky within mere minutes. Despite these gruelling conditions, we were rewarded with some of the most breathtaking vistas that Iceland had to offer.

At times, our climbs led us up towering walls of ice that were potentially thousands of years old. Over centuries, pressure has squeezed the oxygen out of this ice, causing it to refract light differently and transform from what we typically perceive as white ice into a stunning shade of blue.

We were filled with a mixture of awe and sadness as we watched chunks of these ancient walls break free from the mountain, starting their inevitable journey downstream towards the Atlantic Ocean. At the same time, we faced the unsettling reality of the retreating glaciers. Just two decades ago, these areas were all firmly under the glacier's icy grip.

For anyone still on the fence about global warming, I'd strongly recommend they take a look at what's happening to the glaciers in Iceland. It's a real eye-opener.

EXPLORING ICELAND: A LESSON IN PREPAREDNESS AND AWARENESS

Having quenched our thirst for adventure, we used the rest of our time in Iceland to explore its unique landscape and immerse ourselves in its rich culture and history. One of the first things we noticed upon setting foot on Icelandic soil was the importance of planning and preparedness for any eventuality. This became immediately clear when we were advised to download the ICE-SAR app, a search and rescue tool developed by the Icelandic Association for Search and Rescue, which provides updates on weather conditions and flags road closures due to hazards such as avalanches or ice falls. The app even had an emergency button to relay our location to search and rescue teams if needed.

In Iceland, personal safety is largely your own responsibility. There are no guardrails on cliffs, and warning signs merely suggest caution. If you slip, it's on you. The country's roads mirror its landscape – rugged and challenging. Few roads cut across the interior, with most tracing the island's perimeter. These volcanic-rock-paved roads can be treacherously slick when snow and black ice cover the surface. In heavy snow, the only indication of a road's location may be the tops of yellow poles sticking out of the drifts. When a road becomes impassable or 'OFÆRT', warning signs are put up to caution drivers.

Fortunately, we had a reliable Suzuki 4x4 equipped with traction control and four-wheel drive to travel around in. Still, on certain high mountain passes, the margin for error was razor-thin. After travelling these roads, our vehicle became covered in a layer of black volcanic ash and ice, reducing visibility through the windows to zero. Only a hot shower from a specially equipped broom at a petrol station could remove the stubborn coating. Given these conditions, a principle that proved to be invaluable in navigating Iceland's rugged terrain was SIPDE (Scan, Identify, Predict, Decide, and Execute). This principle, taught in advanced driving courses, is a methodology for heightened awareness and quick decision-making in unpredictable conditions.

The SIPDE process begins with scanning your environment the moment you're behind the wheel. This is more than just passive observation – you're actively searching for potential threats. In suburbia, it might be a child chasing a ball, a dog running alongside the road, or a vehicle that looks like it might run a red light. In Iceland, the threats were different. The roads were often covered with black ice, so my eyes were continuously scanning for potential hazards.

While you're scanning and identifying these threats, the next step is to predict 'what-if' scenarios. If you're driving behind an overloaded truck, for example, ask yourself if you've left enough following distance should it suddenly slam on brakes. Ask yourself about the safest evasive manoeuvres: Can you swerve? Is the lane next to you free, or is it safer to move onto the shoulder? In Iceland, the 'what-if' scenarios were different but equally critical. Could that patch of snow be slippery? What if another car comes speeding around that blind curve? Having already decided what you'll do in each predicted scenario gives you an advantage, shaving crucial seconds off your reaction time. Because you've already predicted potential dangers and decided on your course of action, your response becomes almost instinctive. This SIPDE process has been a lifesaver for me, quite literally, on multiple occasions. By spotting potential threats early, predicting their actions, and adjusting my driving accordingly, I've avoided several serious accidents.

SIPDE isn't limited to driving – it applies to any situation requiring heightened awareness. Whether you're walking alone at night in a dangerous neighbourhood, driving on a highway, or even navigating a wildlife crossing, SIPDE helps you stay alert. It allows you to scan for and identify threats, predict their actions, and decide on your response in advance. In our case, SIPDE proved invaluable as we travelled through the rugged and unpredictable landscapes of Iceland, ensuring that we were always prepared for the unexpected.

While SIPDE became crucial for our own adaptability to Iceland's treacherous conditions, the Icelanders themselves show a remarkable aptitude for adapting to their challenging environment. During our travels, we noticed that most homes in the country have roofs overgrown with grass. This is not a sign of neglect but rather a deliberate choice, as the natural vegetation provides a significant amount of insulation. Iceland's electricity is among the cheapest in the world, mainly because it's generated from geothermal vents. Iceland is a pioneer in the use of geothermal energy, relying on it to heat homes and generate hot water. Currently, geothermal power facilities account for 25% of the country's total electricity production. This efficient and eco-friendly energy source is one of the few reprieves in a nation known for its extraordinarily high cost of living. Despite the affordable electricity, other aspects of everyday life bear a hefty price tag.

To maintain our lifestyle during the trip, we had to make some tough decisions. For instance, a bottle of Drostdy Hof – a cheap South African wine selling for around R52 back home – costs about R600 in Iceland. So, we chose to indulge in a bottle of wine each night while opting to share a single pizza, reducing our food intake but not compromising on our enjoyment of red wine.

When considering a visit to Iceland, one traditional tourist attraction you might want to bypass, especially if you want to avoid the crowds, is the well-known Golden Circle. This route, popularised by a multitude of tour packages, covers about 300 kilometres (188 miles) in a loop from the capital, Reykjavík, into the southern uplands and back again. The itinerary typically includes three main stops: Thingvellir National Park (Þingvellir), where you can see the rift valley that marks the crest of the Mid-Atlantic Ridge, the boundary between the North American and Eurasian tectonic plates; the Geysir

Geothermal Area, home to the frequently erupting Strokkur geyser which erupts every 6-10 minutes, shooting boiling water up to 30 metres into the air; and finally, Gullfoss Falls, one of Iceland's most iconic waterfalls.

However, if you're like Kim and me and prefer steering clear of popular tourist spots, you can find your own unique ways to experience Iceland. After a brief discussion in the car and inspired by the name, I decided to exit the car and create my own somewhat unconventional Golden Circle in the snow. This impromptu act of 'tourism' took less than 30 seconds to complete, starkly contrasting with the typical visitor's experience.

We also sought out lesser-known attractions, like the site of the 1973 US Navy C-117D crash in Sólheimasandur, located on the southern coast of Iceland. The old military Dakota made an emergency landing on the volcanic beach after running out of fuel. Miraculously, no lives were lost, and the aircraft was left right where it landed. This surreal sight, a plane resting on a black volcanic beach, has become a striking photograph and backdrop for many films. The patches resembling rust from afar are actually bullet holes – the aftermath of people using the plane for target practice. As a result, another unique Icelandic activity has emerged: shooting at a derelict plane. They are Vikings, after all.

As we navigated Iceland's rugged landscapes and embraced its unique culture, it became clear that the country and its people are masters of adaptation. From energy-efficient homes to innovative uses of natural resources, Iceland demonstrates that the key to surviving and thriving in any environment lies in the ability to adapt. This concept is not just relevant to Iceland or any single destination – it's a universal principle that applies across various aspects of life, both in the natural world and in our modern human society.

ADAPTATION AND ADAPTABILITY IN NATURE, BUSINESS, AND LIFE

According to the Cambridge English Dictionary, adaptation is "the process or act of changing to suit different conditions". In a biological context, the term is defined as "the process in which a living thing changes slightly over time to be able to continue to exist in a particular environment". These definitions emphasise that adaptation is not a one-time event but an ongoing process.

In this chapter, we will explore both 'adaptation' and 'adaptability'. While they are closely related, it's important to distinguish between the two. 'Adaptation' refers to the specific changes that occur in response to environmental pressures, be it in the natural or human-built world. 'Adaptability', on the other hand, is the capacity or potential to make such adaptations. Keep these definitions in mind as we delve into the ways both natural and human systems adjust to challenges.

In the natural world, *adaptation* is a long-term evolutionary process where an organism becomes better suited to its environment, guided by the principle of natural selection. Take the case of the Arctic fox with its dense fur coat, perfect for insulating them against the freezing Arctic temperatures. This coat is an adaptation to its freezing surroundings. Over multiple generations, attributes that provide survival advantages are passed down, while those that don't may eventually fade away. This is nature's trial-and-error mechanism at work, meticulously fine-tuning each species for optimal existence in its ecological niche. Failure to adapt can result in a species falling into the unforgiving pit of extinction, highlighting the relentless importance of adaptability in the natural world. On the other hand, the general *adaptability* of species is showcased in how different organisms might respond over generations to broad environmental changes, whether it's shifting climate patterns or alterations in their food sources.

In the human world, *adaptation* is multifaceted and tends to happen at a faster pace, thanks to a range of factors such as technology, social systems, communication, and collective learning. Here, adaptation involves a combination of cognitive decision-making, emotional resilience, and instinctual (unconscious) reactions to unforeseen challenges. While our mechanisms for adaptation are more complex due to higher reasoning and societal structures, the underlying principle aligns with that of nature: adapt or risk obsolescence. Within human societies, *adaptation* can take many forms, be it an individual learning new skills to stay relevant in their career, a community adopting sustainable practices in response to climate change, or a business evolving its product offerings based on customer feedback. *Adaptability*, on the other hand, represents a more general ability to anticipate and respond to change, operating at the level of individual resourcefulness, community resilience, or organisational flexibility. This broader trait equips us to navigate a range of unforeseen challenges and seize emerging opportunities.

In both the natural and human-built worlds, adaptation and adaptability are not just occasional necessities – they are constant demands, both requiring flexibility, ingenuity, and a willingness to change. Let's explore each of these worlds in a little more detail.

SURVIVAL OF THE FITTEST: HOW ADAPTATION SHAPES LIFE ON EARTH

In the natural world, adaptation is a compelling testament to the resilience of life in the face of changing environments and challenges. This evolution can manifest in multiple ways, each contributing to the survival and thriving of species in their respective habitats.

Physical or biological adaptations can involve changes in form or physical features. For example, animals living in colder environments might develop thicker fur coats, or a giraffe's long neck allows it to reach food that other animals can't. Physiological adaptations are also part of this category, like the ability of desert animals to regulate their body temperature or the metabolic adaptations found in organisms living in extreme environments, such as deep-sea creatures. Camels, for example, have a unique metabolism that allows them to withstand drastic temperature changes in the desert, and their bodies can tolerate levels of dehydration that would be fatal to most other animals. Similarly, deep-sea creatures like the anglerfish have developed specialised metabolisms that allow them to survive in environments with extremely high pressure and low oxygen levels.

Moving beyond physical traits, behavioural adaptations represent another layer of complexity. These are changes in an organism's behaviour that increase its chances of survival. For instance, some birds, such as the Arctic tern, undertake long migratory journeys to warmer climates during the winter to find food and escape harsh conditions. In contrast, animals like bears hibernate to conserve energy when food is scarce. Other creatures, such as the chameleon, display behavioural adaptations in the form of camouflage, changing their skin colour to blend in with their surroundings and avoid predators.

Adaptation extends further into the ecological context. Ecological adaptations involve changes in an organism's role or behaviour within its ecosystem that help it survive and thrive. For instance, some species have evolved to fill specific ecological niches or exploit resources that are not used by other organisms, thereby reducing competition for those resources. A classic example is the relationship between different species of finches on the Galápagos Islands. Each species has a uniquely shaped beak that allows it to feed on specific types of food, such as seeds, fruits, or insects. This specialisation allows multiple finch species to coexist in the same environment without directly competing for the same resources.

Another fascinating aspect of adaptation is the phenomenon of co-evolution. In many cases, the adaptation of one species can drive the evolutionary changes in another. This interconnectedness is particularly evident in predator-prey relationships, where shifts in one species' hunting or defensive strategies can lead to counter-adaptations in the other, creating a dynamic interplay that shapes both parties involved. In the African savannah, the cheetah and the springbok exemplify the concept of co-evolution in a predator-prey relationship. The cheetah, known for its remarkable speed, has evolved to become one of the fastest land animals, capable of reaching speeds up to 130 km/h (81 mph) in short bursts to catch prey. In response, the springbok has developed not only speed but also exceptional agility, including a unique leaping behaviour called pronking to evade predators. This high jump confuses and deters the cheetah by showcasing the springbok's fitness and making it a less appealing target. As a result, both the cheetah and the springbok keep evolving new ways to outsmart each other in a never-ending cycle of change.

Adaptation is a continuous process, as environmental pressures are constantly changing. Climate change, shifts in predator and prey populations, and changes in available resources can all drive the need for new adaptations. Species that can adapt rapidly to changing conditions tend to thrive, while those that cannot may face extinction.

FUTURE-PROOFING BUSINESS: THE ROLE OF ADAPTABILITY IN BUSINESS SUCCESS

The ability to adapt goes beyond merely responding to change – it's about proactively shaping the future. This principle is especially relevant in the fast-paced world of business. Here, companies face a multitude of shifting factors, from market trends and technological advances to legal regulations and changes in consumer behaviour. In much the same way that organisms in nature adapt to survive within their ecosystems, businesses that can effectively adapt to changes in the marketplace are better equipped to navigate uncertainty and seize opportunities for growth. Businesses that fail to adapt to these dynamic elements risk losing market share as customers shift their loyalties to more responsive competitors that meet their evolving needs.

To fully appreciate the complexities facing today's businesses, let's examine each of these factors more closely.

CHANGES IN THE MARKET

The business landscape can change rapidly due to new market trends, changes in consumer behaviour, or the emergence of new competitors, and businesses need to adapt their strategies, products, and services to remain competitive. This can include adjusting their pricing models, updating their product offerings, or exploring new markets.

To illustrate this, let's consider the streaming service industry and how Netflix, once primarily a DVD rental service, adapted to shifts in consumer behaviour towards digital consumption. As broadband internet became increasingly accessible and internet speeds improved, Netflix pivoted to offer streaming services, providing users with instant access to movies and TV shows, effectively capitalising on the new trend and positioning itself as a leader in the industry. When competitors like Hulu, Amazon Prime, and Disney+ entered the fray, each with unique offerings and pricing models, Netflix continued to adapt. It invested heavily in original content to differentiate itself and even adjusted its pricing strategy to offer multiple subscription tiers. This willingness to adapt has allowed Netflix to maintain a strong market share, even as the streaming landscape has grown more competitive and as consumer preferences have evolved towards wanting a diverse array of high-quality, on-demand content.

Another compelling example is Amazon, which has adapted not just to market trends but also diversified its offerings. Initially, Amazon started as an online bookseller. However, recognising the potential of the broader e-commerce market, Amazon quickly expanded into selling a wide variety of products. Amazon later branched out into cloud services with Amazon Web Services (AWS), digital streaming with Prime Video, and even physical stores with Amazon Go and Whole Foods Market. This relentless pursuit of adaptation has cemented Amazon's status as a multifaceted and resilient market leader, capable of anticipating and capitalising on a multitude of opportunities across various sectors.

TECHNOLOGICAL EVOLUTION

The advent of new technologies can dramatically transform the way businesses operate. To improve efficiency, meet customer expectations, and maintain a competitive edge, businesses must embrace and adapt to these technological shifts. For instance, digital transformation has become increasingly important in recent years, prompting many companies to integrate technologies such as artificial intelligence, machine learning, and cloud computing into their operations.

Take the finance sector, for example. Traditional banking has seen a profound change with the rise of fintech. Companies like Square and Stripe have leveraged technology to revolutionise payment processing, while robo-advisors use algorithms to offer financial advice, and mobile banking apps have made in-person visits to banks nearly obsolete for many consumers. These fintech solutions rely heavily on cloud computing for their infrastructure and often use machine learning to refine their services, highlighting the essential nature of technological adaptation in staying relevant.

Similarly, Microsoft has shown remarkable adaptability in the tech industry. Known initially for its Windows operating system and Office suite, the company found itself facing intense competition and rapid changes in technology, particularly with the rise of mobile computing and cloud-based services. Rather than sticking to its traditional business model, Microsoft adapted. They made a successful transition to cloud computing with Azure, transformed Office into a cloud-based subscription service (Office 365), and diversified their business into areas like gaming (Xbox) and professional networking (LinkedIn). Microsoft's adaptability has allowed it to remain a major player in the tech industry.

REGULATORY CHANGES

Laws and regulations are frequently updated, often requiring businesses to make significant adaptations to their operations. One sector where this is especially evident is the automobile industry. As governments worldwide impose tighter emissions standards, car manufacturers are pivoting towards electric vehicles (EVs). Tesla saw a gap in the market and took the opportunity to challenge the dominance of internal combustion engines.

Despite initial scepticism, Tesla continuously improved its battery technology, lowering costs and enhancing performance. They also developed home and grid-scale battery packs, such as the Tesla Powerwall and Powerpack, aiming for energy independence. To alleviate range anxiety, Tesla built a network of Supercharger stations, making long-distance travel and fast recharging possible. The company also integrated advanced features like autopilot into their cars. As a result, Tesla has become a leader in the EV market and has catalysed a broader industry shift towards sustainable transportation. While Tesla has thrived by focusing almost exclusively on EVs, traditional automakers like General Motors and Ford are now investing heavily in electric technologies to stay relevant in a rapidly changing regulatory environment.

CRISIS MANAGEMENT

Crises such as financial downturns, global pandemics, or natural disasters require businesses to adapt quickly to survive. This could involve developing new business models, shifting to remote work, reconfiguring supply chain strategies, redefining target audiences, or scaling infrastructure to meet new types of demand.

Take the example of Zoom Video Communications during the Covid-19 pandemic. Prior to the pandemic, Zoom was primarily a business-to-business service used for video conferencing. However, as the pandemic forced people to work, learn, and socialise from home, Zoom quickly adapted to meet the demands of a broader audience that included educational institutions, social interactions, and even virtual events like weddings or concerts. The company scaled its infrastructure, simplified its user interface, and addressed security issues, making it accessible and secure for a variety of users. As a result, Zoom not only managed to survive the crisis but also saw exponential growth, becoming a household name. This ability to adapt quickly to a crisis allowed Zoom to seize new opportunities and thrive in a challenging environment.

In a similar vein, Domino's Pizza serves as a practical example of a business that successfully adapted to changing circumstances. In the early 2010s, the company found itself in crisis due to declining sales and a deteriorating reputation. Recognising the urgent need for change, Domino's undertook a bold strategy to turn things around. It revamped its pizza recipe, a fundamental aspect of its product, and invested heavily in technology to streamline the customer experience. The company launched a robust online ordering system complete with a pizza tracker and multiple mobile apps, aiming to revolutionise the way people order and consume pizza. This commitment to adaptability not only reinvigorated its customer base but also transformed Domino's into one of the leading pizza delivery companies worldwide, showing that the capacity to adapt effectively can be a lifeline in times of crisis.

ORGANISATIONAL GROWTH

As a company grows, it needs to adapt its organisational structure, processes, and culture to manage increasing complexity and maintain efficient operations. The initial organisational structure that may have worked for a startup or a small team could become a bottleneck as the company scales, potentially stifling communication and decision-making processes. Implementing new processes that streamline workflows, enhance cross-departmental collaboration, and optimise resource allocation can help the organisation remain agile and responsive to market changes. Moreover, the company's culture must evolve to retain its core values while accommodating a diverse and growing workforce, ensuring that employees remain engaged, aligned with the company's mission, and capable of adapting to new challenges.

One notable example is Airbnb. In its early days, Airbnb had a relatively flat organisational structure typical of startups, with a small team managing everything from property listings to customer complaints. However, as the platform grew exponentially, the company faced challenges in terms of communication efficiency and the speed of decision-making. To address this, Airbnb restructured its organisation into various functional and regional teams, streamlining its processes to cater to the nuances of different markets and ensuring seamless coordination across departments. Additionally, they invested heavily in company culture, even hiring a Chief Employee Experience Officer. This allowed Airbnb to retain its foundational values of trust and community while also nurturing an environment where a global workforce could remain engaged and aligned with the company's overarching mission and goals.

INNOVATION

To maintain a competitive edge in today's fast-paced global marketplace, businesses must engage in a cycle of perpetual adaptation and evolution. This involves not only refining existing products and services but also proactively identifying new opportunities for growth and innovation. Beyond the product portfolio, companies need to reassess their business models to ensure they align with emerging market trends and consumer behaviours. Changes in technology, regulations, and consumer preferences can dramatically alter the landscape, making it critical for businesses to be agile and responsive. By investing in research and development, as well as fostering a culture of continuous improvement, companies can better anticipate market shifts and adapt accordingly, thereby securing a sustainable advantage over their competitors.

Adobe Systems, well-known for products like Adobe Photoshop, Illustrator, and the Portable Document Format (PDF), serves as a classic example of a business that has successfully adapted and evolved. In its early days, Adobe thrived by selling packaged software through a one-time licensing fee model. However, as the software industry began transitioning to cloud-based solutions and subscription models, Adobe realised that its traditional approach would soon become outdated.

Anticipating these industry changes, Adobe boldly shifted from selling packaged software to a cloud-based subscription model, launching Adobe Creative Cloud in 2012. This strategic move allowed Adobe to offer a more diverse range of services, deliver better and more frequent software updates, and establish a more predictable revenue stream. Customers could now access a suite of creative tools through a monthly or yearly subscription fee, reducing the upfront costs of software ownership while ensuring they always had access to the latest features. While the transition was risky and met with initial resistance, Adobe's foresight ultimately paid off. They successfully adapted to changing market conditions and consumer preferences. Their subscription model has since become standard practice in the software industry, and through constant adaptation and evolution, Adobe has maintained its leadership position in the world of digital creativity software.

WORKFORCE MANAGEMENT

As the demographics, expectations, and norms of the workforce evolve, businesses must proactively adapt to remain competitive in attracting and retaining top talent. Implementing flexible work policies can address a wide array of employee needs and lifestyles. Likewise, rethinking leadership and communication approaches can bridge generational and cultural gaps, contributing to a cohesive and forward-thinking organisational culture.

For instance, in 2020, Microsoft quickly shifted its work policies to align with new workforce expectations and societal norms, transitioning to a more flexible work model by allowing many of its employees to work from home permanently, depending on the nature of their roles. This change not only supported employees with various lifestyle needs, such as those balancing work and family, but also expanded the company's appeal to a larger talent pool. To enhance its organisational culture, Microsoft launched various internal initiatives that encouraged open dialogue and aimed to bridge generational and cultural divides.

MASTERING CHANGE: THE ROLE OF ADAPTABILITY IN PROFESSIONAL GROWTH

Adaptability is a sought-after trait in the professional world, mainly because the business landscape is constantly evolving. As markets shift, technologies advance, and global events reshape industry dynamics, adaptable employees often emerge as invaluable assets to an organisation. In contrast, those who panic or remain entrenched in the idea that "this is the way things have always been done" risk obsolescence.

Employers view adaptability as a sign of versatility, a willingness to change, and an ability to evolve alongside business needs and changes in the marketplace. Those who adapt easily are often the first to embrace new challenges, learn new skills, and provide solutions that others might not have considered. This proactive approach to change not only improves your professional resilience but also broadens your career horizons, opening doors to opportunities that might not have been accessible otherwise.

Being adaptable doesn't mean you have to compromise your core values or principles – rather, it allows you to approach challenges with an open mind and a flexible outlook, positioning you as a key player in any professional setting.

Adaptability is generally considered to be a combination of both hardwired attributes and acquired skills. Some people may naturally be more open to change and have a temperament that is more flexible and less risk-averse. These traits can make it easier for individuals to adapt to new situations without excessive stress or anxiety. However, adaptability can also be developed and refined by pushing your boundaries, exposing yourself to new ideas, or actively developing relevant skills.

Let's explore some practical ways to increase your adaptability in your career path.

LEARNING AND SKILLS DEVELOPMENT

Continuous learning and skill development are essential for enhancing one's adaptability. Take, for example, a programmer who takes the initiative to learn a new coding language in response to industry demand or a marketing professional who actively invests time in learning about emerging digital marketing tools and techniques. This proactive approach not only gives them a competitive edge but also helps them stay relevant in their respective fields. They are also better prepared to navigate changes in their professional environments.

By regularly updating and broadening your skill set through online courses, workshops, or self-study, you're not just keeping pace with change – you're staying ahead of it. This demonstrates your adaptability and prepares you for future shifts in your career.

NEW ROLES AND RESPONSIBILITIES

Throughout your career, you may find yourself taking on new roles or responsibilities that differ from what you're familiar with. This could involve managing a team, overseeing a project outside your area of expertise, or even starting a new job in a completely different industry. Adapting to new roles or responsibilities often requires stepping out of your comfort zone and acquiring a different skill set. For example, an engineer who transitions into a managerial role may initially face challenges in managing people – a skill set different from their technical background. This doesn't mean abandoning what they already know. Instead, it involves enhancing their existing skills with new competencies. By actively learning about leadership, team dynamics, and effective communication, they can successfully navigate this new role, potentially unlocking new avenues for career advancement.

Proactively acquiring new skills doesn't just prepare you for immediate challenges; it also sets the stage for future growth, additional responsibilities, and new opportunities.

NAVIGATING CHANGE AND UNCERTAINTY

Navigating change and uncertainty in the workplace requires a critical skill: the ability to remain flexible and open-minded. For example, an employee who is confronted with a sudden company restructuring may initially feel disoriented or anxious. However, by adopting a flexible mindset, they can adapt more readily to the new landscape. This could involve seeking clarity from supervisors, proactively upskilling, maintaining open communication, and embracing the new organisational structure. By taking these steps, the employee can more effectively align themselves with the company's new direction, easing the transition for both themselves and their colleagues.

By embracing a flexible and open-minded mindset in the face of change, we are better equipped to find our footing and continue to be effective contributors, regardless of the challenges we face.

RELATIONSHIP BUILDING

The skill of adapting to different people and situations plays a critical role in building and nurturing successful professional relationships. For instance, a sales executive who modifies their communication style to better resonate with different clients – be it technical language with engineers or layman's terms with non-specialists – enhances rapport and mutual understanding and fosters an environment of inclusivity and mutual respect. Similarly, learning to collaborate effectively within diverse teams, whether that diversity is in expertise, culture, or perspective, allows for a more cohesive and productive work environment.

This ability to adapt one's approach according to the situation or audience not only strengthens interpersonal relationships but also solidifies one's reputation as an adaptable and versatile professional, essential traits in any collaborative work environment.

OVERCOMING CHALLENGES

Being adaptable becomes especially evident when facing challenges and setbacks in one's career, all of which are inevitable at some point. For example, a sales executive who misses a quarterly target might initially feel discouraged. However, by adapting and developing new sales techniques or seeking guidance, they can turn the setback into a valuable learning experience.

Whether you're developing new strategies, seeking external guidance from a mentor or coach, or reassessing your career goals, the ability to adapt allows you to respond effectively in the face of adversity. This resilient approach not only aids in overcoming immediate challenges but also lays a foundation of adaptability invaluable for navigating future obstacles.

WORK-LIFE BALANCE

Adaptability is a critical skill in maintaining a healthy work-life balance because the challenges and demands we face are always changing. As technology advances and business models evolve, the nature of work itself is in a constant state of flux, often requiring us to juggle multiple roles or adapt to new schedules and responsibilities. Similarly, our personal lives are filled with unpredictable events – family needs, health issues, or social commitments – that require time and emotional investment. Being adaptable allows us to re-prioritise tasks and commitments as needed. Whether it's the ability to work from home when a family member is sick or adjust to a sudden project deadline, adaptability can be the difference between a life filled with unnecessary stress and one that is well-balanced.

Moreover, adaptability can enhance our resilience and overall well-being. Facing the pressure to excel both in our professional and personal lives, many people are prone to burnout. By being adaptable, people can recognise when they need to set boundaries, when to seek help, and when to prioritise self-care. For example, you might be more willing to delegate tasks at work to make time for a family event or to take a mental health day to recharge. Such choices contribute to a more balanced lifestyle, where neither work nor personal commitments are disproportionately neglected. Adaptability does not mean sacrificing one for the other – rather, it offers a way to optimise both.

MANAGING CAREER TRANSITIONS

Throughout your career, you may decide or need to make significant changes, such as switching industries, starting your own business, or even retiring. Moving into a new industry often requires you to quickly assimilate new skills, norms, and industry-specific knowledge, which can be daunting. Entrepreneurship, on the other hand, demands flexibility and a willingness to pivot when faced with new challenges or information. In both cases, adaptability enables you to keep pace with change, transform obstacles into opportunities, and continuously learn from experience.

When stepping into retirement, the shift from a structured work environment to a more flexible lifestyle often requires adjustments, both financial and emotional. Being adaptable helps you navigate this change, whether it involves exploring new hobbies or even embarking on post-retirement careers or projects.

THE POWER OF ADAPTABILITY IN NURTURING FULFILLING RELATIONSHIPS

Adaptability isn't just a valuable skill for career advancement or business success – it's also essential for building and maintaining healthy interpersonal relationships. Whether it's friendships, family ties, or romantic partnerships, relationships involve a complex set of interactions between individuals, each with their own unique set of personalities, backgrounds, and life experiences. As circumstances change and as people grow, the strength of a relationship often hinges on each person's ability to adapt. Adaptability equips you with the tools to navigate the complexities and uncertainties that come with any relationship, allowing you to cultivate relationships that are not just healthy but also deeply fulfilling.

Adaptation in relationships is about striking a balance between accommodating others and staying true to oneself, creating a dynamic that supports growth, understanding, and mutual respect. Let's take a look at some of the many ways that being adaptable can positively impact your interpersonal relationships.

UNDERSTANDING AND RESPECT

Every individual brings a unique set of perspectives, values, and beliefs into a relationship. Adaptability in this context means making an effort to understand and respect these differences, even when they don't align with your own views or lifestyle choices. This proactive approach to understanding and respect serves as a foundation for building stronger relationships and helps in averting misunderstandings or conflicts.

Imagine you have a close friend who follows a vegetarian diet for ethical reasons while you enjoy eating meat. Being adaptable could involve learning about the ethical or health motivations that drive your friend's dietary choices, even if you don't intend to adopt a similar diet. Instead of insisting on going to a steakhouse for dinner, you could opt for a restaurant that caters to both vegetarian and non-vegetarian preferences. This act of understanding and accommodation not only prevents potential tension but also strengthens and enriches your friendship.

COMMUNICATION

People have diverse communication styles and preferences. Some may prefer a direct, to-the-point approach, while others might appreciate a softer, more empathetic style. Adapting your communication style to suit the needs of those you're interacting with can lead to clearer, more meaningful exchanges.

Suppose you're coordinating a weekend outing with friends. One friend is outgoing and prefers quick text messages to get the basic details, while another is more introverted and appreciates a phone call to discuss plans in a more nuanced way. By recognising these preferences and communicating accordingly – sending a brief text to the first friend and taking time for a detailed phone call with the second – you not only make the planning process smoother but also show respect for each individual's communication style. This adaptability can help build stronger bonds in your social circle.

CONFLICT RESOLUTION

Conflicts and disagreements are inevitable in any interpersonal relationship. Being adaptable in these situations is crucial and can manifest in various ways – whether it's adjusting your perspective, seeking a middle ground, or recognising when old patterns of behaviour aren't working and opting for a new approach.

Consider a scenario where you and your partner frequently argue over household chores. At first, you both try to manage this through a set schedule. However, the schedule doesn't ease the tension. Being adaptable might mean agreeing to try a new strategy, like trading off tasks each week or hiring outside help for some of the chores. This willingness to compromise and explore new solutions serves to defuse the conflict and strengthen the relationship.

CHANGES IN LIFE CIRCUMSTANCES

Life is full of changes, whether it's relocating to a new city, embarking on a new career, welcoming a new family member, or grappling with health challenges or a personal loss. While these changes can put a strain on a relationship, successfully navigating these challenges together often serves to deepen the bond and strengthen the connection between individuals.

Consider a couple who've been living in a bustling city for years, thriving in the urban energy. One partner receives a career opportunity in a tranquil countryside town. While the move might mean leaving behind the city's vibrancy and adjusting to a slower pace of life, the couple decides to view it as a new adventure. They explore the countryside together, create new routines, and find joy in the serenity and simplicity their new home offers. Through adaptability and mutual support, what could have been a strain becomes a new chapter of shared experiences and deeper connection.

EMOTIONAL SUPPORT

The emotional needs of individuals can fluctuate depending on their current life circumstances. Being adaptable in providing emotional support – whether that's by lending an attentive ear, giving space when needed, or offering words of encouragement – can enhance the quality of your relationships.

Imagine your sibling is going through a challenging period at work. Initially, they may need to talk it out and appreciate your attentive listening. However, as the situation evolves, they might prefer some space to process things independently. Recognising this shift and adapting your support accordingly – first by listening and then by giving space – shows that you are attuned to their emotional needs. This adaptability strengthens the emotional bond between you, ensuring that your support is both effective and deeply appreciated.

PERSONAL GROWTH

As individuals, we're in a state of constant growth and transformation. Our ambitions, values, and interests can evolve over time, and it's important that our relationships keep pace with these shifts. This adaptability might manifest as accommodating a friend's new work schedule for get-togethers, supporting a family member through a life transition like retirement or a new baby, or joining a community group to share in a loved one's interests. In this way, relationships can flourish in tandem with individual growth.

Let's say when you and a close friend first met, you shared a passion for adventure travel. Over the years, however, your friend becomes increasingly interested in painting and art. Instead of allowing this shift to create distance, both of you adapt by occasionally swapping a weekend hike for an art gallery visit or a painting workshop. This willingness to adapt to each other's evolving interests allows your relationship to thrive and grow alongside your individual pursuits.

By harnessing the power of adaptability, we're better equipped to navigate the complexities of human relationships. By doing so, we can connect more deeply with others, navigate conflicts more effectively, and build relationships that are resilient in the face of change.

CHAPTER 14
DISRUPTIVE
INNOVATION

If there ever was a poster child for the saying 'adventure before dementia', I'd like to think it's me. If not, I'd like a recount. After my six-month solo trip through Africa in my Defender 110 300Tdi in 1999, I had a special place in my heart for Defenders, particularly the older models. As much as my brain was telling me, "Go for a Land Cruiser, sensible human", my heart was saying, "Are you kidding? Once you go Defender, you *never* surrender!" This is something only a Land Rover owner will understand – it's about loyalty until you die. It's a bit like having an old Golden Retriever that lies at your feet every night and does nothing but cost you a fortune in vet bills. The only difference is that the Defender doesn't require you to pick up its poop. Although, in fairness, I've had to clean up its leaks more times than I'd like to admit.

Over the years, a succession of Land Rovers found their way into my garage. First was a Defender 90 2.8i with a BMW M52 engine, then a Discovery 2 Td5, and finally a Freelander 2, which unfortunately ended up submerged in a river. Then, in 2015, destiny called: an ad on Gumtree showcased a white 2004 Defender 110 Td5 double cab with only 130,000 kilometres (81,250 miles) on the clock. I took it as a sign and flew to George to answer the call. At the dealership, it was automotive love at first sight. You know when you go to a dog shelter, and one dog gives you 'the eyes'? That's how I felt about this Defender. I bought her on the spot, skipping the test drive. I decided that the 450-kilometre (281-mile) journey back would be initiation enough.

I decided she wasn't going to be just another suburban poser. No, she was destined to become the ultimate overlanding war machine. Forget the standard Country Station Wagon oldies drive – I was going for Mad Max meets Bear Grylls. Given her formidable specifications and my ambitious vision, I affectionately named her "the Monster".

Working with Landy Guru and Alucab in Cape Town, we meticulously planned her transformation into a compact beast ready to dominate any trail. Every modification had a purpose, and we progressed as budget allowed. Energy autonomy was a priority, and one thing you should never be stingy about is solar power. I installed two solar panels on the roof to ensure that even while stationary, the Monster could generate power on her own. Watching campers scurry around a campsite, constantly repositioning their portable solar panels to chase the sun's rays every couple of hours, is a special kind of humour. It's almost a campsite spectator sport. But for us, that kind of choreography was unnecessary. Thanks to our roof-mounted panels, we could enjoy extended stays in remote locations without having to worry about draining the batteries. And that's important because, let's face it, cracking open a lukewarm beer midway through your journey – courtesy of an underpowered fridge – is about as enjoyable as a barefoot encounter with a rogue Lego brick.

Storage was another focus. I had load bars affixed to the wedge rooftop tent, allowing for the transportation of large, lightweight gear like a kayak or duffel bags. The rear seating area doubled as further storage and a home for the fridge. With multi-level rear load storage boxes, a drawer system, and additional rack space, the Monster was designed to be both functional and efficient. A total carrying capacity of 50 litres (13 gal) of water and 160 litres (42 gal) of diesel ensured we were well-prepared for long journeys.

Built with self-recovery in mind, the Monster was fitted with every-thing from a ten-ton Pro Warn winch on the front bulbar with a built-in industrial air compressor to a high lift jack with an extended base plate to an inflatable 5-ton jack to get us out of the mud. If the gadgets fail, I still have an old-fashioned spade as a backup – because you can't outsource survival to Siri. When it came to technology, I didn't hold back. Between an array of apps, switches, Bluetooth controllers, and a long-range VHF radio, it was as if the Millennium Falcon had a baby with an Apple Store. I also invested in a Garmin inReach Explorer (a handheld satellite communicator) so that I could bother my friends with location updates, update my mom from the middle of nowhere that I was still in one piece, or send out an SOS alert – all without needing a cell phone signal.

While functionality was key, I didn't ignore aesthetics. The Monster had to be a head-turner. And what better than a screaming orange wrap to match my KTM dirt bikes? If I ever rolled her down a mountain, at least the rescue helicopter would have no trouble spot-ting us. But aesthetic appeal isn't just about eye-popping colours – it's also in the details. I didn't want her to look like a hastily assembled farmer's job. Every vulnerable corner and surface was reinforced and protected. Silver aluminium inserts were added to the gauges and indicator stalk. Even the VHF radio in the roof console boasts brushed aluminium inserts. My aim was precision and elegance, even in the rugged world of overlanding.

Three years of dedication went into crafting the Monster. With more bells and whistles than a futuristic spaceship, she is arguably the best-equipped Land Rover in South Africa. And while the project might have made a noticeable dent in my finances, the experiences she's offered have been priceless. Together, we've traversed over 100,000 kilometres (160,000 miles) across 14 African countries. It's been a journey of a lifetime, and it's only just begun.

My experience with the Monster serves as a kind of personal innovation journey. It's about challenging the status quo, pushing boundaries, and redefining what a vehicle – or even an experience – can be. Much like businesses that stand at the crossroads of tradition and transformation, I had to decide whether to stick with what was familiar or to venture into the unknown. I chose to embrace a radical vision, transforming a standard vehicle into something revolutionary. This concept of redefining norms raises intriguing questions. Should we settle for what is comfortable and proven, or should we risk the unknown for the chance to redefine our boundaries and, perhaps, our very understanding of what is possible?

INNOVATION UNPACKED

In his groundbreaking 1997 book *The Innovator's Dilemma*, Harvard Business School professor and businessman Clayton Christensen explores the paradox that businesses face when they continue to focus solely on existing products and markets while overlooking new disruptive technologies. Christensen presents a dilemma: should businesses stick with proven, existing technologies that offer short-term returns, or should they invest in disruptive technologies that could redefine their industry over the long term?

According to Christensen, innovations can be broadly categorised into two types: Sustaining (or incremental) innovations and Disruptive innovations. Sustaining Innovations involve incremental improvements to existing products, aiming to meet the needs of a business's most demanding customers without creating new markets. Disruptive innovations, conversely, give rise to entirely new markets and value networks, often undermining established systems. While these innovations initially tend to underperform in mainstream markets, they improve over time and may eventually replace existing market leaders.

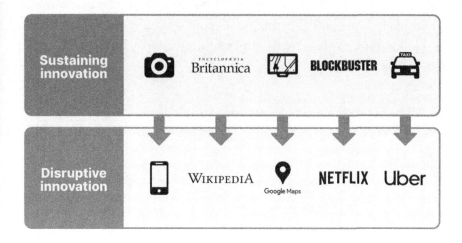

Since the publication of Christensen's book, the concept of innovation has evolved to include four distinct types: Incremental Innovation, Architectural Innovation, Radical Innovation, and Disruptive Innovation. The categorisation of each type is based on two key factors: the novelty of the technology (or innovation) in question and the degree to which the innovation disrupts or transforms the marketplace.

To better understand this, take a look at the diagram below. The X-axis gauges the novelty (or 'newness') of the technology in question. On the lower end, you might find familiar technologies like vinyl records. As you move towards the higher end of the axis, you'll encounter game-changers like Netflix. The 'newer' and more groundbreaking the technology, the more disruptive or even radical its impact on the market will be.

The Y-axis, on the other hand, measures the impact an innovation has on the marketplace. In this context, 'the marketplace' isn't limited to the everyday consumer – it can extend to sectors, industrics, or even specific companies. When we talk about 'impact,' we mean the ripple effect an innovation causes, changing how businesses operate or even giving birth to new industries altogether. For instance, the impact of the latest BMW model on the marketplace would likely be minimal – unless, of course, you've been pedalling a bicycle for the past four years. In that unique case, the impact would be revolutionary.

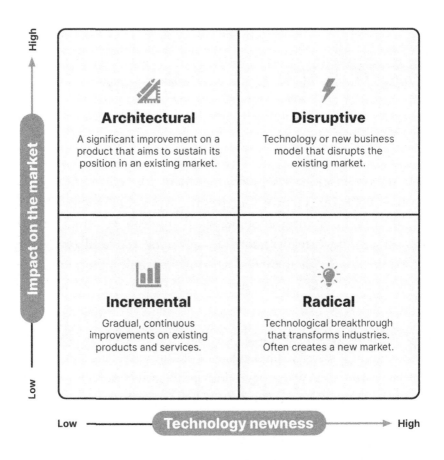

Now, let's explore these four types of innovations in more detail. While each form of innovation has its unique merits and drawbacks, our particular focus in this chapter will be on Disruptive Innovation, which stands out for its ability to completely redefine industries and consumer habits. Before we delve into the intricacies of Disruptive Innovation, however, it's important to understand the other three types – Incremental, Architectural, and Radical Innovation – to better appreciate what sets disruptive innovations apart.

INCREMENTAL INNOVATION

Incremental innovation involves making gradual, ongoing enhancements – improved performance or added features – to existing products or services rather than creating entirely new offerings. This form of innovation is prevalent across various industries, partly because it is less risky and often more budget-friendly than disruptive innovation. From automotive to technology, the focus here is on refinement and improvement rather than reinvention.

For example, in the automotive industry, companies like BMW frequently release new car models based on existing technology. Rather than introducing groundbreaking features, these new models often boast incremental improvements like increased speed or fuel efficiency. When BMW rolls out a new model of an existing vehicle, it's often only slightly more fuel-efficient, and yes, they've tweaked the shape of the kidney grill yet again. But in five years, it will still unmistakably be a BMW – evolutionary, not revolutionary. It's the same car, only slightly better.

Similarly, consider the technology sector and the latest iteration of the iPhone. When a new version is launched, the changes are usually refinements, like minor camera upgrades, rather than revolutionary shifts in technology.

Even everyday items like razor blades fall under this category. While earlier generations might have used single or double-bladed razors, today's versions feature five or six blades. Although the core functionality – shaving – remains the same, additional blades represent an incremental innovation designed to improve the user experience.

ARCHITECTURAL INNOVATION

Architectural Innovation tends to utilise existing technologies but reconfigures them in a way that opens up new possibilities for business and consumer use. Take smartwatches, for example. The manufacturers of these devices didn't invent new technology – rather, they repackaged existing cell phone technology into a wrist-wearable format. By doing so, they created a new product category while using tried-and-tested technologies.

Another noteworthy example is Peloton, the interactive exercise bike company. Particularly popular during the Covid-19 lockdowns, Peloton transformed the traditional home exercise bike by integrating it with internet technology. They combined stationary cycling with real-time online competitions and classes, allowing users to race against people from around the globe without ever leaving their homes.

Whether it's smartwatches leveraging existing mobile phone technology or Peloton reinvigorating home fitness with interactive, internet-based features, architectural innovation involves taking existing technology components and reassembling them in new, valuable ways.

RADICAL INNOVATION

Radical innovation refers to groundbreaking technologies or business models that not only disrupt existing markets but also create entirely new ones. Unlike incremental or architectural innovations, which improve upon or reconfigure existing products, radical innovation represents a seismic shift in how things are done or perceived.

Consider the advent of aeroplanes. This wasn't merely an improvement over horse-drawn carriages or automobiles; it was a revolution in human mobility. For the first time, travelling across countries and continents became not just feasible but commonplace, drastically expanding the horizons of what was previously conceivable.

Apple's AirPods serve as another example. By leveraging Bluetooth technology to eliminate the need for wired connections, AirPods not only replaced traditional earphones but also created new social norms. Now, it's common to see people in professional settings wearing AirPods without attracting attention, something that would have been socially awkward with bulky, wired headphones.

Similarly, Magnetic Resonance Imaging (MRI) has dramatically changed medical diagnostics. Unlike its predecessor, the X-ray, which provided limited, two-dimensional images, MRI offers detailed, three-dimensional imagery of the human body. This innovation opened up new avenues in medical diagnosis and treatment, effectively creating an entirely new market within healthcare.

In summary, radical innovation is transformative, altering the very fabric of existing markets or creating new ones altogether. Whether it's the dawn of aviation, the ubiquity of wireless earphones, or the advancements in medical imaging, radical innovations reshape our understanding of what's possible.

This now brings us to the most impactful of innovations – Disruptive Innovation.

DISRUPTIVE INNOVATION

Disruptive innovation is a process by which a product or service takes root at the bottom of a market and then relentlessly moves upmarket, displacing established competitors. These innovations, often introduced by startups or smaller companies, not only alter existing markets but can replace traditional approaches entirely. They offer new features, superior quality, or low-cost, more efficient alternatives. This disruption has the power to overturn industries, redefine consumer expectations, and render previously indispensable services or products obsolete.

In many cases, established companies, preoccupied with improving their products for their highest-profit customers, overlook the potential of these innovative solutions. This underestimation gives smaller players the opportunity to provide products or services that initially appeal only to niche markets but eventually resonate with a broader audience.

Typically, disruptive innovations may underperform existing products in mainstream markets at their inception. However, they often possess attributes such as simplicity, convenience, customisation, or affordability, which are valued by specific market segments. Over time, as these innovations refine and mature, they begin to match or even exceed the performance of existing products, drawing more of the mainstream market toward them.

There are generally two ways in which disruption unfolds. The first, referred to as Low-End Disruption, takes place when the innovation targets underserved market segments and then moves upmarket. Such products are usually cheaper, simpler, and more convenient. The second, New-Market Disruption, creates entirely new markets by catering to those who find existing products too complicated or pricey.

To illustrate, consider the tech industry. The launch of Apple's iPad in 2010 shifted consumer preference away from laptops towards more portable tablets. Similarly, Kindle devices offered a digital alternative to traditional books, drastically reducing the need for physical copies.

In the music industry, disruptive innovation has followed a clear evolutionary path. CDs initially ousted vinyl records due to their superior digital quality. However, the advent of MP3 players like the iPod and, later, streaming services like Spotify and Apple Music further changed how we consume music.

The decline of Kodak is a classic example of how an industry giant can be disrupted by new technology. Digital cameras eliminated the need for film development, offering instant gratification to users. The market was further disrupted when smartphones integrated high-quality cameras, diminishing the demand for standalone digital cameras.

In the computing world, personal computers disrupted mainframe systems. Now, cloud-based solutions are becoming the norm, replacing the need for powerful desktop computers as most data can be stored and accessed online. This narrative repeats across sectors. E-commerce platforms like Amazon have disrupted traditional brick-and-mortar retail stores, significantly changing the way consumers shop. Blockbuster Video was displaced by streaming services like Netflix and Amazon Prime, which offer vast libraries of content without the burden of late fees or physical rentals. Traditional taxi services – and even car ownership patterns – have been disrupted by ride-hailing apps like Uber and Lyft. Generative AI, like ChatGPT, is also poised to revolutionise various industries.

RISKS ASSOCIATED WITH DISRUPTIVE INNOVATION

It's important to note that while disruptive innovation offers substantial potential benefits, it also carries inherent risks. This form of innovation challenges existing business models and strategies and requires a corporate culture that embraces change, encourages experimentation, and accepts failure as part of the process. For these reasons, disruptive innovation may not be the right strategy for every business or in every situation.

Some of the key risks associated with disruptive innovation include:

MARKET ACCEPTANCE

A disruptive innovation may not always be accepted by its target market. It could be too ahead of its time, meaning the market isn't ready for it, or perhaps customers may not immediately recognise the value it offers. If the market doesn't accept the new product or service, the innovation could fail.

Sony's MiniDisc technology, introduced in the early 1990s, aimed to disrupt the portable music market. Although it offered better sound quality and rewritability compared to CDs and cassette tapes, it failed to gain widespread acceptance. Consumers were happy with their CDs and later shifted to MP3s and streaming, making Mini-Discs largely obsolete.

One of the factors that contributed to the MiniDisc's failure was its high cost – at $750, it was out of reach for many consumers, particularly teenagers. Additionally, there were only a limited number of pre-recorded albums available on MiniDisc, as relatively few record labels embraced the format.

FINANCIAL RISK

Disruptive innovation often requires significant upfront investment in areas such as research and development, marketing, and customer education. These investments are made with the expectation of substantial returns – however, if the innovation fails to gain market acceptance, these costs could translate into serious financial setbacks.

A case in point is the Segway Personal Transporter (PT), introduced in 2001. This product required substantial investment in research, development, and marketing, all geared toward the promise of revolutionising urban transportation. Despite these efforts, the Segway did not gain widespread adoption, falling far short of expectations. Segway Inc. ultimately discontinued the original Segway model in 2020, having incurred significant financial losses.

EXECUTION RISK

Disruptive innovations usually involve venturing into new territories where a business may not have the necessary expertise or understanding. Missteps in understanding customer needs, technical capabilities, or market dynamics could derail the innovation effort.

For instance, Google Glass, launched in 2013, represented Google's venture into wearable technology. Despite its innovative approach, the product failed to understand consumer privacy concerns and practical utility, leading to poor market reception and, ultimately, discontinuation of the consumer version.

BUSINESS MODEL DISRUPTION

By its very nature, disruptive innovation may require a company to alter its existing business model. This can be risky, particularly for established businesses with successful existing models. Shifting the business model could alienate existing customers or disrupt ongoing operations.

When Netflix transitioned from a DVD rental service to a streaming platform, it had to fundamentally change its business model. This was risky, as it could have alienated existing customers who were accustomed to the DVD service. However, the shift ultimately proved to be successful, propelling the company into a new era of growth. This serves as an important reminder that while changing a business model carries inherent risks, it can also open the door to unprecedented opportunities if executed correctly.

REGULATORY RISK

In highly regulated industries, disruptive innovations can often invite increased scrutiny from regulators. This heightened attention can lead to potential legal and compliance challenges.

Take ride-sharing companies like Uber as an example. When they first entered the market, their disruptive approach immediately caught the attention of transportation authorities and regulators. This not only led to various legal battles but also introduced compliance challenges across multiple jurisdictions, adding a complex layer of risk to their operations.

COMPETITION

Disruptive innovation can provoke a strong response from its competitors. This may include the rapid development of competitive products, initiation of price wars, or escalated marketing efforts.

When Apple introduced the iPhone, it upended BlackBerry's market dominance. In a bid to regain footing, BlackBerry tried to innovate rapidly. However, it also found itself embroiled in aggressive pricing and marketing wars with newer smartphone competitors.

ORGANISATIONAL RESISTANCE

Within organisations, disruptive innovation can meet resistance at various levels, from frontline employees to middle and senior management. Resistance often stems from a reluctance to change familiar processes, take risks, or possibly jeopardise career progression.

Take, for example, Kodak's attempt to pivot to digital photography. The company had actually been an early innovator in this field, developing one of the first digital cameras as far back as 1975. Despite this pioneering effort, Kodak was deeply invested in its highly profitable film business. The prospect of moving to a digital model raised concerns at all levels of the organisation. Employees and divisions that were closely tied to the film business resisted the shift, fearing that their skills and products would become obsolete. Meanwhile, management grappled with the 'innovator's dilemma': the conflict between the need for long-term innovation and the pressure to meet short-term profitability metrics.

This internal resistance significantly slowed down Kodak's adaptation to digital technology. While other factors also contributed, the reluctance from both employees and management to disrupt the existing film-based business proved to be detrimental. As a result, the company's transition to digital was slow and poorly executed, allowing competitors to dominate the emerging digital landscape.

While disruptive innovation carries inherent risks, its potential for high rewards often makes it a risk worth taking for many businesses. Managing these risks is important and can be achieved through a combination of careful market research, phased financial commitments, and effective change management. Equally important is fostering a culture of innovation and resilience within the organisation. By adopting these approaches, businesses can better position themselves to reap the substantial benefits of disruptive innovation while also preparing to navigate the challenges that inevitably come with it.

REWARDS ASSOCIATED WITH DISRUPTIVE INNOVATION

Just as there are risks associated with disruptive innovation, the rewards can be substantial for any business willing to embrace it.

MARKET LEADERSHIP

Businesses that consistently pursue disruptive innovation often become leaders in their industries. By redefining the market, they establish themselves as the go-to option for consumers and set the standards that competitors have to follow.

Take Netflix, for example. Today, the term "Netflix and chill" is part of the cultural lexicon, indicating how ingrained the service has become in our daily lives. Its disruptive innovation not only redefined the market but also established Netflix as the industry leader. Now, other companies like Amazon Prime Video, Hulu, and Disney+ are following suit, offering streaming services and original content, but they are essentially following the standard that Netflix has set.

COMPETITIVE ADVANTAGE

Disruptive innovation provides a significant competitive edge. By introducing a unique product or service that better meets customer needs, companies can distinguish themselves from competitors and secure a larger share of the market.

Apple's introduction of the iPhone in 2007 is a prime example. Before the iPhone, mobile phones primarily focused on calling and texting. Apple's iPhone combined a phone, an iPod, and an Internet communication device into one, introducing a touch interface and a thriving app ecosystem. This disruptive innovation met consumer needs in unprecedented ways. As a result, Apple gained a massive competitive advantage, distinguished itself from competitors like Nokia and BlackBerry, and secured a dominant share in the smartphone market. Within a few years, the iPhone became synonymous with smartphones, and competitors scrambled to create similar devices.

MARKET EXPANSION

The pursuit of disruptive innovation often leads to the discovery of new markets and customer segments, thereby offering long-term growth opportunities. By creating products or services tailored to these new audiences, a company can expand its customer base and revenues.

Airbnb is an example of this. Before Airbnb, the accommodation industry was dominated by hotels and traditional bed-and-breakfast establishments. In 2008, Airbnb launched a platform that allowed individuals to rent out their homes or rooms to travellers, effectively creating a new 'peer-to-peer' lodging market. This innovation didn't just compete with hotels – it uncovered a whole new market segment of people who preferred more home-like, authentic, and affordable travel experiences. By doing so, Airbnb expanded its customer base to include not just traditional travellers but also those who might have otherwise stayed home or chosen alternative forms of accommodation.

BUSINESS RESILIENCE

Disruptive innovation strengthens a company's resilience. By continually challenging the status quo and innovating, companies become more adaptable to shifts in technology, customer preferences, and the broader business environment.

Microsoft serves as a great example of business resilience through disruptive innovation. In the early 2000s, the tech giant was primarily known for its Windows operating system and Office software suite. As the tech landscape began to shift towards cloud computing and mobile technology, Microsoft embraced disruptive innovation by developing Azure, a leading cloud computing platform. It also focused more on mobile and cross-platform services by purchasing LinkedIn and transforming Office into a cloud-based subscription service with Office 365. This adaptability allowed Microsoft to stay relevant and competitive in a rapidly evolving technology sector.

SUSTAINABILITY

Many disruptive innovations focus on making products and services more efficient and less resource-intensive, benefiting both the environment and a company's bottom line.

IKEA has been increasingly focusing on sustainability as part of its business model. The Swedish furniture giant has set ambitious goals to become 100% climate-positive by 2030. This means designing products with a longer life span, using more renewable or recycled materials, and finding ways to reduce their overall carbon footprint. They've introduced various eco-friendly products, like solar-powered lighting and sustainably sourced wooden furniture. These moves not only benefit the environment but also appeal to a growing demographic of eco-conscious consumers, thereby potentially boosting IKEA's bottom line as well.

Disruptive innovation serves as a wake-up call, forcing industries and businesses to remain flexible and responsive to changes in market conditions and technology. Those that fail to adapt risk becoming obsolete or losing their market dominance.

SPACEX AND TESLA: REDEFINING INDUSTRIES THROUGH DISRUPTIVE INNOVATION

SpaceX and Tesla, led by visionary entrepreneur Elon Musk, are two organisations that have built their businesses around disruptive innovation. While SpaceX has made waves in the aerospace industry, Tesla has similarly disrupted the automotive sector.

Let's take a look at how they did it.

DISRUPTIVE INNOVATION AT SPACEX

SpaceX has employed disruptive innovation to dramatically alter the aerospace industry. Its most significant contribution is the development of reusable rockets. Before SpaceX, rockets were single-use items – a costly and unsustainable practice. With its Falcon and Starship rockets, which can return to Earth and land vertically after delivering payloads to space, SpaceX has drastically cut launch costs and increased launch frequency.

In addition to transforming rocket technology, SpaceX launched Starlink, aimed at delivering high-speed broadband internet worldwide, even in remote locations, via a satellite network. This project is another example of disruptive innovation with the potential to reshape the telecommunications industry.

In terms of launch costs, SpaceX operates at a fraction of the cost of traditional aerospace agencies like NASA. With its private funding model, SpaceX has greater freedom to take risks and innovate, unlike taxpayer-funded agencies like NASA, which often operate more conservatively. Through advanced manufacturing techniques, vertical integration, and iterative design, SpaceX has substantially lowered the cost of space travel. This cost reduction makes ambitious projects, such as Mars colonisation, more feasible – another potential disruptive innovation.

Rather than competing with NASA, SpaceX views its role as complementary. While NASA focuses on broader scientific and educational missions, SpaceX zeroes in on more specific commercial goals. NASA has, in fact, become one of SpaceX's major clients, commissioning cargo resupply missions to the International Space Station and manned spaceflights. In this way, SpaceX's innovations are helping NASA achieve its goals more cost-effectively, illustrating how disruptive technology can create beneficial new dynamics within an industry.

TESLA'S TRANSFORMATION OF THE AUTOMOBILE INDUSTRTY

Tesla has used disruptive innovation to significantly transform the automobile industry through the championing of electric vehicles (EVs). While electric cars were not a new concept, Tesla's approach certainly was. Starting with high-end, luxury EVs, the company demonstrated that electric cars could rival traditional ones in performance and desirability. In addition, Tesla disrupted the traditional dealership sales model by selling its cars directly to consumers, offering more control over the sales process, customer experience, and pricing. Further differentiating itself from traditional automakers, Tesla offers over-the-air software updates, much like updating a smartphone, thereby improving vehicle functionality, performance, and safety features without requiring a new model or service centre visit.

Against the landscape of traditional automakers, Tesla's approach to EVs has accelerated the industry-wide adoption of electric vehicles. Despite being a relative newcomer in the market, Tesla's market cap surpassing that of many traditional auto manufacturers speaks volumes about the market's belief in the value of disruptive innovation.

Both SpaceX and Tesla are prime examples of how disruptive innovation can shake up established industries. By challenging the status quo, these businesses are not just changing their respective sectors but are also charting the course for the future.

CREATING A CULTURE THAT EMBRACES DISRUPTIVE INNOVATION

Organisations like SpaceX and Tesla are prime examples of how disruptive innovation can shake up established industries. By challenging the status quo, these organisations, and others like them, are not just changing their respective sectors but are also charting the course for the future. Their success, however, isn't just about groundbreaking technologies or visionary leadership. At the heart of these achievements lies a deeply ingrained organisational culture that encourages, nurtures, and rewards innovation.

Creating a culture that embraces disruptive innovation can be challenging, especially if the current culture is resistant to change or risk-averse. Transformation begins at the top. Leaders must embody the innovative behaviour they wish to see in their teams. This goes beyond mere rhetoric – it's about action. If you're truly committed to building a culture that celebrates and drives change, it's important that you embrace taking calculated risks, encourage curiosity, be receptive to new ideas, and create an environment where challenging the status quo is not just allowed but encouraged.

Here are some key strategies to help establish a culture of innovation in your own business.

COMMUNICATE VISION AND PURPOSE

A strong vision creates a sense of purpose and aligns the team towards common goals. Clearly articulate why innovation is necessary and the role it will play in your business's future success. Ensure that everyone understands the vision and their part in achieving it. Regular communication, be it through company-wide meetings, internal platforms, or leadership updates, can reinforce this vision, keeping it alive and relevant as your organisation evolves.

EMPOWER EMPLOYEES

Employees are more likely to be innovative if they feel they have the power to make decisions and try new things. By removing bureaucratic hurdles that stifle innovation, you encourage autonomy and entrepreneurial thinking. This not only paves the way for faster decision-making and problem-solving but also boosts morale and job satisfaction. Training sessions, workshops, and open feedback channels can further help in equipping employees with the confidence and skills needed to take initiative and drive innovation.

ENCOURAGE COLLABORATION AND DIVERSITY

Innovative ideas often come from diverse perspectives. Encourage cross-functional collaboration and value the different perspectives that come from different backgrounds, experiences, and skill sets. Creating platforms for open dialogue, fostering inclusive team dynamics, and hosting brainstorming sessions with mixed teams can stimulate fresh thinking and novel approaches to problem-solving.

CREATE A SAFE SPACE FOR FAILURE

To innovate is to take risks, and with risks comes the possibility of failure. Instead of punishing failures, treat them as opportunities for learning and improving. This builds resilience and encourages your employees to take calculated risks, which can lead to significant innovations. Implementing a 'lessons learned' review after failed projects or setbacks can formalise the learning process, while positive recognition for risk-taking – even when it doesn't lead to success – can reinforce a culture that sees failure as a stepping stone to innovation.

REWARD AND RECOGNISE INNOVATION

Recognise and reward not only successful innovations but also the effort that goes into innovating. This could be through formal reward systems like bonuses or promotions or through more informal recognition like shout-outs in team meetings or company newsletters. The goal is to show that you value innovative thinking. Consistently rewarding and recognising efforts can contribute towards creating a cycle of innovation where the intrinsic motivation to innovate is as powerful as any external incentives.

PROVIDE RESOURCES AND TOOLS

Innovation requires time and resources. Provide teams with the tools they need to experiment, learn, and innovate. This may include allocating time for brainstorming sessions, offering access to continuing education or training programs, or making investments in innovation labs or research and development departments. By equipping teams with the right resources, you not only enable them to turn ideas into reality but also send a strong message that innovation is a valued and integral part of the organisation's strategy.

PROMOTE CONTINUOUS LEARNING

Encourage continuous learning and improvement as an ongoing commitment. Provide opportunities for employees to learn new skills, stay current with industry trends, and understand emerging technologies that could impact your business. Consider implementing a learning management system, offering regular workshops or seminars, or providing employees with 'learning days' focused on innovation. By equipping employees with the latest knowledge and skills in innovation and emerging technologies, you are giving them the tools not only to adapt to disruptive changes in the marketplace but also to become disruptors themselves.

Transforming a company's culture into one that embraces innovation is a long-term commitment that demands consistent effort. However, the rewards – such as increased creativity, greater adaptability, and sustained success – are well worth the investment.

LEVERAGING DISRUPTIVE INNOVATION IN YOUR CAREER

In today's rapidly evolving business landscape, leveraging disruptive innovation is not just an organisational strategy but also a critical career-building tactic. Embracing disruptive technologies or methodologies can offer a significant competitive edge, positioning you as a forward-thinking problem solver in your field. Rather than viewing innovation as a threat, incorporating it into your skill set can open doors to new opportunities, maximise your career growth, and solidify your role as a valuable asset in any professional setting.

There are many ways that you can utilise disruptive innovation in your career to differentiate yourself, advance your career, and potentially disrupt your industry. Let's explore these strategies in a little more detail.

SPOTTING OPPORTUNITIES

Identify pain points or unmet needs in your field that could benefit from innovative approaches or emerging technologies. For instance, if you're a software developer, perhaps there's a common task like data entry that consumes an inordinate amount of time and is prone to errors. By automating this task, you not only enhance productivity but also develop a unique solution that differentiates you from your peers and potentially changes the game in your field.

HARNESSING TECHNOLOGY

Emerging technologies often lay the groundwork for significant shifts in how industries operate. As a financial analyst, consider deploying machine learning algorithms for more accurate market predictions than traditional methods allow. Or, if supply chain management is your field, using blockchain could improve both transparency and security in product distribution. Keeping pace with technological advancements enables you to generate groundbreaking ideas that increase your efficiency, effectiveness, and overall value in your role.

CONTINUOUS LEARNING

In a rapidly evolving business landscape, maintaining a commitment to continuous learning is essential. This commitment could manifest in a variety of ways, such as enrolling in specialised courses, attending industry workshops, or independently mastering new areas of expertise. For instance, if you're a marketing professional with a background in print advertising, adapting to the industry's digital transformation by taking a digital marketing course would be wise. This proactive approach not only maintains your relevancy but also equips you with the resources to be truly innovative. In the end, your willingness to adapt and continually acquire new knowledge will position you to capitalise on opportunities for disruptive innovation.

CHALLENGING NORMS

Break free from the confines of conventional thinking, which often assumes that traditional methods are the only or best ways to achieve results. For instance, if you are a customer experience specialist and notice that common customer complaints are not being addressed efficiently, you might propose a chatbot solution to handle these queries 24/7. Look for opportunities to improve processes, introduce new ideas, or change old paradigms. This kind of thinking is at the heart of disruptive innovation.

EMBRACING RISK

Disruptive innovation involves taking calculated risks. This doesn't imply recklessness but rather a willingness to step outside your comfort zone to try new methods, even if they carry some risk of failure. This could involve pitching a new idea to your boss, switching industries, or even starting your own company. For example, if you're involved in the healthcare industry, you might propose incorporating telemedicine solutions in a hospital setting that has always relied on in-person appointments. This move entails risk but also holds the potential for transformative change within the healthcare system.

EXPANDING YOUR NETWORK

Connect with a diverse range of professionals, not just those in your immediate field. For instance, if you're a software developer with a passion for conservation, you might consider attending an environmental sustainability conference. By connecting with experts at the conference, you can gain insights into how technology can be used for conservation. These interactions can open new avenues for innovation and expose you to different ways of thinking.

CREATING GENUINE VALUE

The ultimate goal of disruptive innovation should be to create authentic value. If you're a product manager at a software company and notice a feature that users find challenging, consider focusing on usability rather than simply adding more options. Streamlining the user interface for increased intuitiveness can bring about significant improvements. Remember, innovation should not just represent change for its own sake but should result in enhanced solutions, processes, or products that truly benefit the end user.

DISRUPTIVE INNOVATION IN OVERLANDING

Disruptive innovation is reshaping the overlanding landscape in remarkable ways. From the advent of electric vehicles to high-tech camping gear and advanced digital technologies, including augmented and virtual reality, new forces are setting a revolutionary pace.

Electric vehicles, already a disruptive force in the broader automotive industry, are making significant inroads in the overlanding industry. Companies like Rivian and Tesla have produced electric SUVs and off-road vehicles, including the Cybertruck, setting a new standard for eco-friendly adventure. These vehicles offer immediate torque for handling difficult terrain, less noise pollution, and potentially lower environmental impact – features that are highly valued by outdoor enthusiasts. However, they also come with limitations, particularly when it comes to charging infrastructure in remote areas. This challenge is paving the way for next-generation solutions like fast-charging batteries and wireless energy transfer, offering promising alternatives for the future of overlanding.

Material and design innovations are doing more than just refining the camping gear we're familiar with – they're fundamentally reshaping what's possible in overlanding. The revolution starts with high-tech camping gear that leverages cutting-edge materials and designs to create products that are not only more lightweight and durable but also easier to set up. Smart tents, for instance, come equipped with integrated solar panels for renewable energy, LED lighting for enhanced visibility, and heat-regulating fabric for optimised comfort. But the disruption doesn't stop at mere comfort and convenience – it extends into the realm of sustainability. The advent of biodegradable waste solutions and advanced water purification systems are poised to rewrite the rulebook on waste management and environmental stewardship in overlanding. These aren't just minor upgrades – they're paradigm shifts that challenge traditional practices, making overlanding significantly more eco-friendly.

Digital technology is also revolutionising the overlanding space, fundamentally changing how adventurers navigate and experience their journeys. Gone are the days when overlanders relied solely on paper maps and instinct; today, mobile apps and devices equipped with advanced GPS tracking, route planning, and satellite communication are disrupting traditional navigation paradigms. These aren't just modern conveniences – they're tools that empower adventurers with real-time data and enhanced situational awareness, opening up new possibilities for exploration. Meanwhile, the advent of drone technology is another game-changer. No longer merely accessories for aerial photography, drones have become indispensable navigational aids capable of scouting paths and potential hazards ahead. They not only increase safety measures but also capture the grandeur of the journey from angles previously unimaginable.

While traditional overlanding emphasises a tangible, immersive connection with nature, augmented reality (AR) and virtual reality (VR) technologies are emerging as disruptive forces that could redefine the experience. Far from replacing the raw thrill of exploration, these technologies offer supplemental layers of interaction and learning. Imagine embarking on a challenging trail and utilising AR to overlay navigation hints on your real-world view or using VR to simulate various aspects of a route before you traverse it. Even stargazing could be enhanced, providing interactive constellations and astronomical facts as you look up at the night sky. The incorporation of AR and VR into overlanding could serve as a powerful tool for education, route planning, and safety, adding a new dimension to the adventure without diminishing the primal joy of a journey through the wilderness.

The integration of these disruptive technologies into overlanding is a delicate balancing act. They offer numerous benefits but must be thoughtfully incorporated to preserve the core values of exploration, adventure, and connection with nature. Poised for a new era of eco-friendly, data-enriched, and deeply engaging experiences, the future of overlanding looks brighter than ever.

APPENDIX

OVERLANDING TECHNIQUES – IN CASE YOU EVER NEED THEM

Surprisingly, most 4x4s never venture off-road despite being built for such adventures. If reading this book has inspired you to either purchase a 4x4 or take your current vehicle into the great outdoors, this chapter is for you. In it, I'll introduce you to the basics of off-road driving to ensure you get maximum enjoyment while minimising risk to you, your passengers, and your vehicle. I'll guide you through various 4x4 driving techniques, such as manoeuvring through mud and navigating water obstacles. Additionally, you'll learn how to use essential tools like snatch straps, Hi-Lift® Jacks, and winches to get your vehicle out of tough spots.

If you're new to the world of 4x4 ownership, I highly recommend enrolling in an off-road training course. Such programs will help you become better acquainted with your vehicle before you take it off-road.

SAND DRIVING

In South Africa, driving on beaches is strictly prohibited. In countries where it is permitted, drive between the high tide line and the sea to minimise your environmental impact. Before setting out on a sand adventure, make sure you are carrying essential equipment such as a good-quality air compressor and a tyre pressure gauge.

When driving on sand, especially if it's your first time, keep the following points in mind:

Tyre Lugs and Sand Driving

Lugs, the raised portions of tread on a tyre, play an important role in off-road situations. Their arrangement and spacing determine a tyre's performance on different terrains. When it comes to sand driving, tyres with closely spaced lugs offer significant advantages. Tight lug spacing distributes the vehicle's weight more evenly on the sand, enhancing its 'flotation' and reducing the likelihood of getting stuck. Additionally, closely spaced lugs minimise road noise, ensuring a quieter ride. For optimal tyre selection, consulting with a professional tyre fitting centre is recommended.

Optimising Tyre Pressure for Traction

To optimise traction on sand, your tyres should float atop the sand's surface. You can achieve this by reducing your tyre pressure to about 1.5 bar (22 psi) or lower – but never lower than 0.9 bar (13 psi) (unless you're seriously stuck) – to avoid the risk of the tyre detaching from the rim. Lowering tyre pressure increases the surface area in contact with the ground, which generates more friction and heat. This excessive heat can lead to wear and tear and, in extreme cases, dangerous situations like tread separation or blowouts. As a precaution, keep your speed under 50km/h (31 mph), depending on the chosen air pressure.

Maintaining Forward Momentum

Always maintain your 4x4's forward motion on sand. Braking on soft sand can create sand ridges in front of the tyres, making it more difficult to pick up speed again. When you need to stop, avoid using the brakes – rather, let the vehicle coast to a stop.

Starting, Stopping, and Handling Slopes

When starting your vehicle in sand, using the high-range gearbox in 1st gear generally works well. For those with more experience, the low-range gearbox in 3rd gear offers extra torque in challenging conditions. If you find yourself having to stop on a slope, direct the vehicle's nose downhill and ensure the front wheels are straight. This helps with restarting and prevents the front tyres from digging into the sand.

Dune Driving Techniques

Driving on dunes can be an exciting experience, but there are safety factors to remember. Never attempt a U-turn on the slope of a sand dune, and always approach dunes at a right angle with your vehicle, whether going up or down. Otherwise, the rear tyres might dig into the sand, and the vehicle could roll over. If you get stuck while ascending a dune, gently reverse back down. Descending a dune can be riskier, as the back of the vehicle tends to slide. Instead of braking, which can be dangerous, apply power gently to straighten the vehicle.

Tackling Wheel Spins

If your wheels start spinning while you're driving on sand, resist the urge to press the accelerator further, as doing so will only cause the tyres to dig deeper into the sand. Instead, stop the vehicle, put it in reverse, and backtrack slightly over your own tyre tracks, where the sand has already been compacted and should offer better traction. Then, try to tackle the sand obstacle again with a bit more speed. If your 4x4 is completely stuck, lower your tyre pressure to 0.2 bar (3 psi) to increase the surface area (and, therefore, traction), clear any sand ridges in front of the tyres, and attempt to reverse out. If you're alone and without any sand ladders, placing stones or branches beneath the tyres can provide additional traction. Alternatively, seek help from another vehicle.

Advanced Sand Driving Tips

It's advisable to avoid locking your differentials when driving on sand. This practice helps prevent an increase in the turning circle and reduces the risk of the vehicle overturning.

Follow Established Tracks

When driving on sand, it's generally a good idea to follow other vehicles' tracks. Doing so has a dual benefit: the sand is usually more compact, providing better traction, and it minimises environmental damage as well as unsightly tracks on the dunes.

Reinflating After Sand Driving

Once you're back on firmer ground, don't forget to inflate your tyres to the recommended pressure.

SNATCH STRAP RECOVERY

Snatch recovery straps are an essential part of any 4x4 owner's toolkit. Often known as 'tug-ems', these straps are the first item you should purchase as part of your recovery kit. Using another vehicle and a snatch strap, you can effortlessly free your 4x4 from deep sand or mud, eliminating the need for a high-lift jack or winch.

What to Buy

You can find good quality snatch straps at most off-road shops. Ensure the strap is at least 75mm (3") wide and about 9 metres (30 ft) long. Additionally, purchase a minimum of four D shackles with a breaking strain of at least 3,500 kgs (7,700 lb) to attach the snatch strap to your vehicle's mounting points. I also recommend adding at least two metres of heavy-duty chain and a quality tree trunk protector to your recovery kit.

How it Works

To an unseasoned off-roader, a snatch strap might look like a regular towing rope. However, it's more like a rubber band. This stretchable strap can expand up to a metre, storing kinetic energy from the recovery vehicle's forward momentum. The elastic property allows for a greater recovery force when it contracts, making it possible for even a smaller 4x4 to rescue a larger vehicle. This type of recovery, where the line isn't pre-tensioned, is known as a snatch recovery.

Usage Limitations

Snatch straps are not designed for indefinite use. After about 10 recoveries, they lose their elasticity, essentially becoming an expensive tow rope. Therefore, the standard 4x4 practice is to use the stuck vehicle's snatch strap for recoveries, not your own.

Safety Precautions

Snatch recoveries come with important safety considerations. Once a snatch strap is connected to the vehicles' mounting points, it's always 'live' and should be treated as such. No one should step over it – ever. Ensure both vehicles are aligned and that the strap is laid out flat on the ground without twists. Attach one end of the kinetic strap to the stuck vehicle's mounting point using a D shackle and do the same with the recovery vehicle. Keep all bystanders at a safe distance.

Common Mistakes

A frequent error among novice 4x4 off-roaders is attaching the snatch strap to the tow bar, a potentially fatal mistake if the tow ball breaks off. Instead, create a secure mounting point by wrapping a length of chain around a sturdy part of the chassis and then connecting the snatch strap to the chain using a D shackle.

The Recovery Procedure

Before initiating the snatch recovery, clear any obstacles from the recovery path and ensure there are at least two metres of slack in the snatch strap. Place a blanket, jacket, or towel over the middle of the strap as a safety precaution – this acts as a parachute, slowing down the strap or D shackle should they fail. Both drivers should select low range, 2nd gear before beginning the recovery. The recovery vehicle should accelerate at a moderate speed while the stuck vehicle's driver releases the clutch simultaneously.

Troubleshooting

If the first attempt fails, try again with at least 3 metres (10 ft) of slack in the snatch strap. Should the recovery vehicle be unable to reach the stuck vehicle at close range, you can extend the distance by linking two recovery straps. Avoid using a D shackle to connect the straps, as this can fail and become a hazard. Instead, hook the eye of one kinetic strap through the other and secure it by pulling a sturdy piece of wood through the protruding loop.

Maintenance

Regularly inspect your snatch strap for any small cuts or nicks. Even a 1cm tear can reduce its breaking strength by up to 50%. Store it away from direct sunlight to prolong its life.

MUD DRIVING

Mud driving presents its own unique set of challenges, some of which align with the general principles of 4x4 driving, while others defy them entirely. But more on that later.

Understanding Tyre Selection

Mud driving distinguishes itself from driving on other terrains in several ways, one of which is tyre selection. While sand driving calls for closely spaced lugs on your tyres to enhance flotation and minimise road noise, mud driving requires a different approach. Here, tyres with larger gaps between the lugs are preferable, as they offer better self-cleaning capabilities.

Navigating the Mud: Precautions and Procedures

While we haven't yet broached the subject of deep water crossings, some of the same guidelines apply when tackling a muddy obstacle. If there's an alternative route, take it to avoid the mud. If that's not possible, survey the terrain on foot first to spot hidden hazards like potholes or rocks. Start your wipers before entering the obstacle – dried mud can make it difficult to do so later if necessary. If another 4x4 vehicle is ahead of you, make sure they've cleared the obstacle before you make your move. Follow their exact tracks, maintain a steady speed, and avoid abrupt steering.

Trailers and Mud: A No-Go

Avoid attempting to tow a trailer through a mud obstacle whenever possible – the additional weight and drag can make it difficult to manoeuvre and increase the likelihood of getting stuck.

Different Types of Mud and Tyre Pressure

Mud varies in composition. One type is the thick, bottomless mire, where deflating your tyres can help your vehicle float. More commonly, you'll encounter mud with a slushy top layer over a firmer base. In this situation, keep your tyres inflated so they can cut through the soft top layer and find traction on the firmer ground underneath.

Engaging Gears and Locks

Before entering the mud, engage low range, third gear, and lock your differential. If the mud is particularly thick, you may need to shift to second gear, low range.

Techniques for Propelling Forward

If you find your vehicle slowing down or experiencing wheel spin, ease off the accelerator and gently turn the steering wheel from side to side. This '5th wheel' technique creates extra friction to help propel the vehicle forward. Contrary to general 4x4 rules, wheel spinning in mud can actually clean your tyre treads and improve traction.

If You Get Stuck

If you're stuck, try to reverse along your entry path. If that doesn't work, gently rock the vehicle forward and backwards in the appropriate gears. If you're stuck, first try reversing along your path of entry. If that fails, gently rock the vehicle forward and backward in the appropriate gears. Placing rocks, branches, or stones under the wheels can also provide extra traction. If all else fails, consider alternative recovery techniques, such as a Hi-Lift® Jack and space, snatch strap recovery, or winching, if another vehicle is available.

Winching Guidelines

When winching a vehicle out of mud, always do so in the direction the vehicle entered the obstacle. If you're equipped and trained to use a winch, attach the winch hook to the front bumper or bull bar before entering a muddy section. This way, if you need the winch cable, you won't have to go hunting for it in the mud.

Cleaning After Mudding

After a day of mudding, a thorough cleaning of your 4x4 is essential. Mud retains moisture against your vehicle's metal components, leading to rust and corrosion. Additionally, dried mud traps heat, which can lead to premature engine failure or overheating.

Make sure to:

• Remove all mud from under the wheel arches.

• Clean the rims and drive shafts thoroughly. Even a small amount of dried mud can unbalance your wheels or cause driveshaft vibration.

• Check the vehicle's door drain holes and clean as necessary.

• Clean the breather holes of the differential, axles, and gearbox.

• Clean the engine and radiator.

• Ensure the disc brakes are completely free of mud.

HI-LIFT JACKING

As you gain more experience with your 4x4 vehicle and prepare for increasingly challenging terrains, a high-quality jack becomes a must-have addition to your recovery kit. This versatile device can free a vehicle from nearly as many situations as a full-fledged winch but at a much lower cost. While many inexpensive replicas exist, opting for an original, American-made Hi-Lift ® Jack from a trusted 4x4 accessory store is advisable. Skimping on this tool may save money initially but could be costly should it malfunction during a difficult recovery.

Advantages Over Standard Jacks

A Hi-Lift Jack is not just a simple replacement for the standard bottle jack that comes with your vehicle. It offers superior articulation and can handle heavier loads. And, with the right accessories, your Hi-Lift Jack can even double as a manual winch by adding some chains and a pair of D-shackles.

Preparing for Unstable Ground Conditions

When you purchase your Hi-Lift Jack, also buy a jacking plate or have a 30 cm x 30 cm (12" x 12") steel platform with at least 4 mm (0.16") thickness welded. This platform ensures a stable base for the jack on soft or unstable ground.

Vehicle Preparation: Jacking Points

Unlike Land Rover Defenders or Toyota Land Cruisers, most modern 4x4s lack built-in jacking points. These reinforced areas on the vehicle body are designed to bear the full weight of the vehicle when lifted. If your 4x4 isn't one of the aforementioned models, consider having jacking points installed on your 4x4 to protect your existing plastic trim, bumpers, and running boards. Alternatively, Hi-Lift offers several accessories that can be attached to the underside of a curved bumper or even the bull bar of vehicles without jacking points.

When to Use Your Hi-Lift Jack

Your Hi-Lift Jack becomes particularly useful in scenarios where the break-over angle of your 4x4 is exceeded, and the vehicle gets stuck on a large rock or 'middelmannetjie'. Another time a Hi-Lift Jack comes in handy is when your vehicle is stuck in deep mud. The jack can break the suction holding your vehicle, allowing you to fill the gaps beneath the wheels with suitable traction materials like twigs, rocks, or leaves.

Safety Measures Before Jacking

Before operating your Hi-Lift Jack, make sure you've thoroughly read and understood the safety manual. Incorrect usage of a jack can lead to dangerous consequences for the user or bystanders. Before beginning the jacking process, ensure the gearbox is in neutral, the handbrake is engaged, and the wheels are properly chocked (using wheel chocks, wooden blocks, rocks, or bricks to prevent movement). Lift the vehicle and place support material under the wheels to clear the obstacle.

Using the Hi-Lift Jack as a Manual Winch

A Hi-Lift Jack can also be converted into a manual winch in an emergency. Attach the jack's top to a chain using a standard 3.5-ton

D-shackle and connect the other end of the chain to the vehicle using another 3.5-ton D-shackle. Link the movable leg of the Hi-Lift Jack to another chain using a D-shackle. Then, fasten it securely to a sturdy point, such as another vehicle or, if you're using a tree, ensure you have a tree trunk protector in place.

Ensure the jack's moving leg is at the lowest position, ensure both chains are under light load, and start to slowly jack the hi-lift horizontally. The recovered vehicle will move about 1 metre before the jack's moving leg reaches the top. Reset the moving leg to the lowest position and repeat the process until the vehicle is clear of the obstacle.

Practice this procedure at home before heading out on a trail, and remember to add extra lengths of chain (about 5 metres - 16ft - each) and properly rated D-shackles to your recovery kit.

Advanced Technique: Lifting and Pushing

If your vehicle gets stuck in soft mud or a rut, another handy technique involves lifting the entire front (or back) of the vehicle into the air and pushing the vehicle sideways to allow the front (or back) wheels to navigate the obstacle. This procedure requires observing several important safety rules due to the instability of your 4x4 with two wheels off the ground.

• Ensure the handbrake is engaged, the wheels are chocked, and the gearbox is in neutral.

• Engage manual diff-lock if available.

• Jack the vehicle no more than about 30 to 40 cm (12 to 16 inches) higher than the surrounding ground level.

• Position yourself between the vehicle and the jack and push the raised end of the vehicle until it falls off the jack.

• By repeating this process, the vehicle can 'walk' sideways out of the muddy rut or obstacle.

When the vehicle topples off the jack, ensure there's no physical contact between the jack and the vehicle body to avoid incurring repair costs once you return home.

Critical Safety Tips

Ensure that all bystanders are at a safe distance during the recovery operation. The jack could potentially spring out from under the vehicle with force, posing a fatal risk. Above all, never venture underneath a jacked vehicle.

DEEP WATER CROSSINGS

One of the more sophisticated procedures in off-roading involves crossing deep bodies of water like rivers or flooded areas. These water obstacles might be deeper than the average depth that most standard 4x4s can handle without modification. Many 4x4 owners encounter difficulties when making these crossings due to their limited experience with off-road driving, which often translates into apprehension about potential damage to the vehicle and the risk of getting stuck or submerged. However, with proper preparation and using the right techniques, deep water crossings can be quite gratifying.

If you're planning on tackling deep water obstacles while off-roading, I would suggest installing a high-quality snorkel on your vehicle's air intake and extending the differential breathers higher up the chassis using plastic tubing as a preliminary precaution. Most importantly, ensure that your recovery equipment is always readily accessible.

Assessing and Preparing for the Crossing

Always assess the depth of any water obstacle before attempting to make a crossing. An easy rule to remember is: if you can't walk through it, you can't drive through it. This rule is especially applicable for fast-moving rivers that are unsafe to cross on foot. Be sure to check for hidden rocks and potholes, as wheel spinning by other vehicles on submerged rocks can create these hazards. Mark these areas with sticks so that you can avoid them during your crossing.

Setup and Engine Precautions

If the water's depth exceeds your vehicle's bumper height, further preparations, like installing wading plugs to your clutch housing and/or differential axles, might be necessary before entering the water. You can also consider loosening or removing your fan belt to prevent water from splashing around in the engine compartment. Vehicles with a viscous coupling type of fan will automatically slow down upon water contact.

For vehicles running on petrol (gasoline), apply a water repellent such as WD40 or Q20 to the ignition system beforehand. Shield the front of the engine with a tarp to restrict water entry, which also helps prevent water from splashing over the ignition system and the fan from damaging the radiator.

If water enters your vehicle's engine, it can cause serious damage since water can't be compressed. Unlike air or fuel, which can be compressed within the engine's cylinders, water remains in its liquid state, creating excessive pressure. Petrol engines that have taken in water are likely to stall before any damage occurs. Should you stall your vehicle during a deep water crossing, do not attempt to restart it, as this can lead to the bending or breaking of engine components like the connecting rod, pistons, or valves. In such cases, it's best to seek external assistance for vehicle recovery.

Crossing Technique

Before you begin the crossing, unbuckle your seat belt and lower your window for safety reasons. Use low range, second gear, aiming for around 2,000 revs per minute. As you enter the water, accelerate gently to avoid wetting your vehicle's electrical systems. Once in the water, maintain a moderate speed to create a bow wave in front of the vehicle. This steady pace will also prevent stalling. If you start to wheel spin, ease off the accelerator to regain traction. It's crucial to avoid changing gears during the crossing as this could lead to a loss of momentum and risk water entering the clutch housing, which might result in clutch slip.

POST-CROSSING MAINTENANCE

Cooling and Differential Inspection

After completing the water crossing, allow your vehicle to cool down. A hot axle that cools rapidly upon contacting water can cause a pressure drop within the axle and differential housing. This drop might draw water into the housing through the axle seals if the differential breathers don't equalise the pressure quickly.

Once cooled, inspect the differential oil. Given that water is denser than oil, it will settle at the differential's lowest point. Drain approximately 20ml of the oil. If it appears milky, this indicates water contamination. In such a case, it's essential to flush the differential and replace the oil as soon as you reach camp or a service station. It's also wise to inspect the gearbox, transfer case, and engine oil for potential water contamination. This step is particularly important if you're planning regular water crossings.

Winch care

If your vehicle has an electric winch, it's good practice to disassemble it and lubricate it post-crossing. If the winch is not used for a prolonged period, it may seize up, rendering it ineffective when you need it the most.

Brake Consideration

Brakes, especially drum brakes, might retain moisture and perform sub-optimally until fully dried. This is especially important if you're planning a steep ascent or descent shortly after the water crossing, as they might not function as expected.

WINCHING

A winch, in the context of off-road vehicle recovery, is a mechanical device that is typically mounted on the front or rear of an off-road vehicle. Its primary function is to help extract a vehicle that's become stuck, whether in mud, sand, or any challenging terrain. The winch operates by winding a strong cable or synthetic rope (plasma) onto a drum, which is powered either electrically (most common in off-road scenarios) or hydraulically.

When a vehicle gets stuck, the winch cable is extended and attached to a fixed anchor point, such as another vehicle, a tree (using a tree protector strap), or a ground anchor. Once secured, the winch is activated to retract the cable or rope, pulling the stuck vehicle toward the anchor point and, consequently, out of its predicament.

Winches are invaluable tools in off-road adventures, ensuring that vehicles can be recovered from situations where they might otherwise remain immobilised. They offer a self-recovery option that can be especially important in remote locations where external help might not be readily available.

While a winch is arguably the most powerful tool in a 4x4 owner's recovery kit, it is also the most dangerous. It's essential that anyone using one adheres strictly to safety protocols and techniques. If you're inexperienced, I strongly recommend attending an advanced 4x4 Recovery course for some hands-on experience before attempting any winch recovery on your own.

Owing to the inherent risks involved, I've compiled a list of essential safety rules to keep you and your vehicle safe during a winch recovery operation. By following these guidelines, you'll be well-equipped with the basics of safe winching. This list is a handy resource – consider printing it, laminating it, and storing it in your 4x4 for easy access.

Essential Safety Rules

1. Every winching operation should have a single point of authority. This isn't a democratic process – the most experienced person takes charge.

2. Protective gloves are a must when handling a winch.

3. Spectators and passengers should maintain a safe distance from the operation. A strained cable can snap and inflict serious harm.

4. Never cross over a connected cable, regardless of whether it's taut or slack. Once connected, the cable should be considered 'live'.

5. If using a tree as an anchor, use a tree trunk protector strap. Directly wrapping a metal winch cable around a tree can damage the tree's bark, which can harm or even kill the tree over time.

6. Keep the cable low when connecting it to avoid pulling down the anchor (if using a tree).

7. Never loop a winching cable around any anchor and back onto itself. This can permanently damage the cable.

8. When the winch's remote control is plugged in, keep a safe distance from the drum, cable, and fairlead area.

9. Pay attention to the drum rotation decal. The cable must spool off the drum in this direction only – otherwise, the winch's automatic brake won't work in reverse.

10. Try to unspool as much of the cable as possible when winching. Leaving too many cable layers on the drum can cause the top layers to damage the bottom ones. If the distance to the anchor point (or between the stuck vehicle and the recovery vehicle) is too short, use a snatch block to halve the distance.

11. Snatch blocks can double the winch's effective pulling power. If necessary, connect a snatch block to a tree trunk protector with a D-shackle and loop the cable back to the vehicle.

12. The winch's pulling power decreases with each additional layer on the drum. Therefore, the first cable layer on the drum has the strongest pulling strength. However, never winch with fewer than five wraps of cable around the drum, as this may lead to cable failure.

13. Ensure the cable reels in as straight as possible. If needed, pause the operation, unwind some cable, and restart the winch to ensure the cable is winding around the drum evenly and tightly. Otherwise, the top cable layers could dig into the bottom layers and create a jam.

14. Place a blanket, jacket, or heavy sack on the middle of the cable to act as a "parachute" in case it snaps, which would slow down the recoiling cable. Some 4x4 drivers also raise the hood to protect the windshield in case of cable failure.

15. Know your winch's maximum load rating, and don't exceed it. If necessary, use a snatch block to reduce the load on the winch by almost 50%.

16. Never let the cable slide through your hands. Use the switch to intermittently take up cable slack, preventing shock loads on the drum and cable.

17. When using a recovery vehicle to extract a stuck one, ensure the handbrake is up, the wheels are blocked with stones or rocks, and the

gearbox is in neutral. The foot brake may be used to help anchor the vehicle.

18. During winching, the stuck vehicle can assist by selecting an appropriate gear (low range, 3rd) and spinning in place as the recovery starts. Make sure the stuck vehicle doesn't overtake the winch cable to prevent any slack cable from being wound onto the drum or having the recovered vehicle's wheels pass over the cable.

19. Stop the winch when the hook is within 1.5 metres (5 ft) of the drum/fairlead by releasing the remote-control switch. From this point, use small, intermittent uptakes to bring the hook all the way in. Don't over-tighten the cable, and always keep your hands clear.

20. Inspect the cable after use. If it's frayed or damaged, replace it immediately.

21. At times, you may need to re-spool the cable without load. The correct method is to hold the remote in one hand and the winch cable in the other, start the winch with the remote and walk the cable towards the drum for a metre or two. Stop the remote and repeat the process, remembering to stop when you're within 1.5 metres (5 ft) from the fairlead.

Important: Never use a winch as a towrope. The cable isn't designed for sudden jerks and could damage itself or the winch drum.

Alternative Anchors

When performing a winch recovery, you may not always have the luxury of a conveniently located tree or rock to use as an anchor. In these instances, a constructed anchor like a spare tyre, a log, or even a boat anchor might be necessary, as illustrated in the diagram below.

1. Bury the spare tyre or log at least 70 to 90 centimetres (28" to 35") below the ground.

2. Position it at least 20 metres (66 ft) away from the vehicle to serve as an anchor.
3. Once set up, proceed to winch as normal.

These steps will ensure that the anchor is secure and effective for the winch recovery.

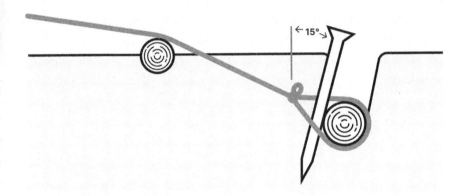

Winch Buying Guide

When purchasing a winch, sticking to reputable names like Ramsey or Warn is always a wise choice. It's important to ensure that the load rating is suitable for your vehicle and to familiarise yourself with the equipment before embarking on any off-roading adventure.

Environmental Considerations When Using a Winch

Winch recoveries, while crucial for vehicle safety, must be conducted with environmental sensitivity. The trails and terrains we enjoy with our vehicles are home to countless forms of wildlife and plant species. As enthusiasts, it's our responsibility to ensure that our off-road adventures do not negatively impact these ecosystems. Here are some specific guidelines related to winching that help ensure your recovery operations have minimal impact on nature.

1. Avoid Damaging Trees: As mentioned earlier, if using a tree as an anchor point, always use a tree trunk protector strap. Trees are vital to our environment and the ecosystems they are part of. Damaging a tree's bark not only harms the tree but can also affect the wildlife that depends on it. Beyond winching, be cautious about driving over tree roots, as compacting the soil around them can damage the tree as well.

2. Choose Anchor Points Wisely: If you're not using a tree, ensure your chosen anchor point doesn't disturb sensitive habitats. For instance, avoid anchoring to rocks that might be home to specific species or might result in soil erosion if moved.

3. Limit Ground Disturbance: Winching can sometimes disturb the ground, especially in softer terrains like mud or sand. Aim to minimise this disturbance by using mats or recovery boards when possible.

4. Monitor Noise: While this might not seem obvious, the noise from a winching operation can disturb local wildlife. Try to keep the operation as quiet as possible, especially in areas known for wildlife.

5. Leave No Trace: Winch recoveries can occasionally result in minor debris, whether from damaged equipment or disturbed soil. Always check the area after a recovery and remove any litter or debris you might have introduced.

It's our collective responsibility to ensure that our adventures don't come at the expense of the environment. By paying attention to these environmental considerations, not only do you ensure the longevity of your favourite off-roading spots, but you also play a part in preserving nature for future generations. With the right equipment, knowledge, and respect, every off-road adventure can be both thrilling and sustainable.

Here's to safe, successful, and environmentally conscious recoveries!

ACKNOWLEDGEMENTS

Patrick Cruywagen: Front Runner Outfitters and Land Rover Monthly Magazine

For all those bucket list adventures through the Serengeti, Ngorongoro Crater and Rwanda, as well as countless 4x4 competitions together.

Scott Brady and Graeme Bell: Overland Journal

For re-igniting the writing muses in me as OJ contributor and for providing excellent exposure for our Landy Monster.

Phillipa Mitchell: OTTB Book Editor

Guardian angel of prose and writing.

Cecil Penny: CPR Racing

For keeping our KTM off-road machines in tip-top shape.

Heidi Hamilton

We climbed the first of the Seven Summits together 20 years ago, igniting a mountaineering passion that will last forever.

Wayne van de Venter: Landy Guru

For modifying the Land Rover Monster and providing hours of patient expertise and maintenance.

Mariska Peens: First Technology WC, CFO

For being my trusted corporate right hand at all times.

Graham Duxbury

For including me on Giniel De Villiers' Dakar team in Argentina, marking the beginning of a whole new chapter.

Vladimir, Our Russian Mountain Guide

For safely guiding Kim and me off Mt Elbrus, Russia, when things took a turn for the worse.

ABOUT THE AUTHOR

Johan de Villiers is not your average CEO. As the visionary leader of
First Technology Western Cape, an award-winning IT provider in
South Africa, he's known for his unorthodox leadership style that
blends razor-sharp business acumen with a relentless thirst for adventure. Whether navigating through the dense African jungle, piloting
helicopters, scaling some of the world's highest mountains or leading
high-stakes boardroom meetings, Johan lives by his mantra: "Have
more fun, take more risks, and be more substantial in somebody's
life."

The formula for Johan's remarkable success lies in his balanced approach to life and leadership. He combines intellectual curiosity, critical thinking, and discipline with raw imagination and an adventurous spirit. He's a seasoned risk-taker, yet never dismisses the importance of meticulous planning and preparation. Committed to excellence, he consistently drives himself and those around him towards higher achievement through discipline, teamwork, and a relentless focus on personal growth.

Johan is not one to simply ride the wave of market trends – he anticipates them and then turns them to his advantage. He challenges the status quo and mainstream perspectives, questioning how facts are presented or interpreted, especially when driven by hidden agendas or outdated thinking. But he's not a contrarian for the sake of it. Instead, his approach is anchored in a firm belief that fresh perspectives can spark groundbreaking innovations.

A futurist at heart, Johan is deeply committed to harnessing technology for societal good. He's keenly attuned to the seismic shifts brought about by the Fourth Industrial Revolution – and its enormous implications for all of us – and believes that our collective future hinges on our ability to use technology responsibly.

Johan de Villiers is a rare breed – a visionary, a risk-taker, an adventurer, and a compassionate leader. He is a person who doesn't just see the glass as half-full but is constantly thinking of ways to refill it. Whether in the rugged terrains of untamed landscapes or the sleek corridors of corporate power, Johan remains a towering figure, leading with passion and living with a zest that beckons us all to aspire for more.

Printed in Great Britain
by Amazon

44436002R10274